DEMOCRACY IN BUSINESS

A Transdisciplinary Critique of Hierarchy

Volume 1: The Inception of Hierarchy

G. Michael Blahnik

IA&A Books
Cincinnati, OH
Copyright: 2014 by G. Michael Blahnik
All rights reserved.
ISBN: 1497530164
ISBN: 9781497530164

Library of Congress Control Number: 2014907718

Visit www.CreateSpace.com to order additional copies.

DEMOCRACY IN BUSINESS

A Transdisciplinary Critique of Hierarchy

Volume 1: The Inception of Hierarchy

CONTENTS

This book is an application of the philosophy of experientialism to the field of human organization as it applies to economic and political activities. The philosophy of experientialism has been developed in *Experience: An Exploration into the Structure and Dynamics of Human Consciousness, Sense, Sex and Sin: Foundations for an Experientialist Ethics, Experientialist Ethics: A Comparative Study*, and *Experientialism: Integrating Mind & Body, Spirit & Matter, the Many and the One*, and also applied to, and developed within, the field of psychology in *Emotional Investment: Transforming Psychotherapeutic Assumptions*. *Democracy in Business* is a transdisciplinary work. By this I mean that the work draws not only from multiple disciplines, as in an inter-disciplinary work, but it also utilizes ideas from various disciplines to transform the vary assumptions that underlie the disciplines themselves.

Experientialism is a philosophy that equates experience with reality, where "experience" is defined as a necessary combination of cognition, affect, behavior, sensation and the environment, as owned [by a person]. In equating experience with reality, the realistic and objective assumptions that underlie various sciences and religions become characteristics of experience rather than conditions for experience. When experience is understood as a reality from which no person can escape, then ultimate attention will be paid to it rather than to constructing traditional, objective theoretical systems of thought that some people tend to use to dominate other people. Traditional objective reality will be replaced by experiential objective reality, where the contents of experience will be what they are, regardless of any person's point of view. When attention moves from reality-outside-of-experience to experience as constituted by components of experience, then traditional objective reality and the construction of objective theories become a matter of prudence or pragmatism rather than an ontological endeavor. Science and religion become relative; their claims are subject to experiential analysis.

When the philosophy of experientialism is applied to human organization, it focuses on how and why we organize individual human beings into groups. According to most anthropologists, nine-tenths of human social history on earth (i.e. pre-history) is characterized by egalitarian social interactions, where people treated each other roughly as equals; one-tenth of human history (i.e. recorded history) is characterized by hierarchical social interactions. If this is so, then the question arises: why did we humans shift from predominantly egalitarian social systems to hierarchical social systems?

Anthropologists argue that population growth and the discovery of agriculture and husbandry (and the private property it spawns), is the cause of the transformation from egalitarian to hierarchical systems of organization. It is argued in this work that population growth etc. are the conditions rather than the cause of such a transformation. Why should population growth and more sedentary ways of providing for oneself cause people to alter their egalitarian ways so as to create hugely oppressive systems of human organization such as monarchies, autocracies, fascisms, totalitarian regimes, committee-run socialisms and, to a lesser degree, hierarchical business structures?

In order to answer this question, we need to transform the ways we think about reality. Recorded human history is replete with objective systems of thought; each vying for ascendancy; and often times this "vying" is characterized by deadly violence. Such thought systems reached their culmination in World War II, resulting in fifty million dead, many by annihilation.

When we shift our attention away from trying to understand nature and thinking of ways to impose that understanding upon others supposedly for their own good and toward trying to understand ourselves-in-nature, then we might be able to eliminate the grounds for social oppression and re-establish equality amongst individual human beings. This work, I hope, is a step in that direction.

PART 1: Establishing a Primary Social Unit in the Male-Female Bond

Proposition 1: People are social animals.

Though some people are able to live by themselves as adults, e.g. hermits living off the land, most people live in groups, whether in pairs, families, networks of friends, co-workers, social or religious groups, bands, tribes, states, countries, or nations. People over-whelmmingly need other people for at least some aspects of their survival and well-being. And all people, without exception, must be nurtured from birth if they are to live, even if that nurturance comes from wolves or other animals. If this is so, then society is the norm; independence is the exception; and it is only an exception when the person is capable of self-subsistence.

Theory criticism: A "State of Nature" is a Fiction.

Political and social philosophers have posited a "state of nature" from which we have emerged by forming rational contracts or agreements with each other, whether implicit or explicit, in order to protect ourselves as individuals and to help us thrive. This "state of nature" is populated by individual human beings who are free to do anything they please, who act upon their desires in any way they see fit, and are limited only by their own sense of survival and well-being, and sometimes not even by that.

Such a state has never existed. Once born, a child will act in accordance with how it thinks, feels, and senses its environment. If it feels pain (e.g. internally-generated pain, like hunger or disease or externally-generated pain, like heat, cold, spanking, etc.), it will tend to exhibit pained behavior (e.g. cry, fidget). If it feels pleasure (e.g. internally-generated pleasure like hunger satiation or health or externally-generated pleasure like comfort, warmth, and loving ex-pressions from others), it will tend to exhibit behaviors of satisfaction (e.g. smile, cooing, fixed attention, etc.)

To argue that this child is free to act as it sees fit in order to sustain its existence or improve its well-being is to grant it intentions that it doesn't seem to possess. Infants do not act, as far as we can tell, in order to achieve a desired response; rather, they act in accordance with the felt states that they are in. Not until they are able to realize that they are beings separate from other beings who can act in specific ways in order to prompt others to act so as to alleviate their pain and/or increase their pleasure can children be said to act freely. And even then, it seems, "freely" is heavily circumscribed. The range of responses for children, even those who have achieved self-reflection, is limited by their innate capacities and their environmental circumstances.

We might argue that the "state of nature" idea could apply to children who are self-reflective and are able to learn how to manipulate people around them so as to ensure their survival, decrease their pain, and increase their well-being. In other words, the "state of nature" idea might somewhat legitimately apply to children who act upon their environment in a strictly egoistic manner, and sometimes even to the detriment of their egoistic concerns.

Proposition 2: People propagate by male/female copulation.
The social aspect of humankind is very evident in humankind's method of propagation: males and females socialize sexually. Even if the sperm from a male is used to fertilize an egg from a female out of body or in the laboratory, some form of sexuality must take place, though possibly indirectly or *in absentia*. An exception could be propagation through cloning, if such could be achieved.

Male-female sexual bonding is the basic form of human society. The society of the family (e.g. parents and children) is dependent upon the sexual society of the parents, but only when viewed from the perspective of the parents.

Proposition 3: People need food (always), shelter (nearly always), and clothing (nearly always) in order to survive within their environment. They need to act in ways so as to provide these for themselves.

Proposition 4: Males and females will be naturally attracted to each other so as to form pair bonds, whether these pair bonds last but a minute or the rest of their lives.

Proposition 5: The male-female pair bond consists of sexual behavior and emotional investment in each member of the pair, no matter how short or long-lived, and this pair bond forms the basic unit of society.

Without the male-female pair bond there would be no society of any sort. Children would be impossible (note possible cloning exception today). Therefore, the male-female pair bond constitutes the original and most basic social unit.

Probing Question: If the male-female pair bond constitutes the original and most basic social unit, then what constitutes the natural way in which the "basic male" and the "basic female" interact with each other?

Proposition 6: Males and females tend to act in ways that further their survival and maintain or improve their well-being.
No human being seems innately to cause, will, or wish to cause their own death. Suicide seems to occur only after experience in the world is accrued. The survival motive does not seem to be a gender specific trait; it is a human trait.

No human being seems innately to cause, will, or wish to cause a decrease in their well-being. Infants respond to internally produced pain (e.g. biologically-induced pain like hunger, bowel discomfort, anatomical and physiological pain, etc.) with signs of discomfort, pain, and rejection. These signs signal caretakers to respond in ways so as to alleviate the discomfort. This supports the idea that pain is something to which people are naturally repelled. Infants also respond to internally produced pleasure (e.g. hunger satiation, bowel relief, anatomical and physiological pain reduction or elimination) with signs of satisfaction, pleasure and contentment. This supports the idea that pleasure is something to which people are naturally attracted.

Any human being who engages in behavior that decreases his or her well-being does so either because he or she does not know that the behavior will decrease his or her well-being (i.e. out of ignorance) or because of naturally distorted reasons (e.g. infants do not naturally cause their own pain or dissatisfaction though they might induce pain on themselves because of the psychological pain that has been imposed upon them from a source outside of themselves; for instance, a child might pull its own hair in response to sexual abuse).

Acts that might diminish one's well-being but are still chosen would tend to be chosen for reasons that are consistent with one's identity, perceived or real. For example, a moral principle might

3

guide a person to perform an act that will result in a reduction of his or her well-being, even to the point of death. Acts of this sort are considered to be consistent with the promotion of one's well-being if the act is consistent with one's true identity (e.g. Jesus chose to allow himself to be arrested though he knew that this would diminish his well-being). If it is not consistent with one's true identity, but only with one's perceived identity, then such acts would be the result of a distorted reality (e.g. Hitler committed suicide believing that he had done humanity a service by killing millions of Jews).

Synthesis and Extension: Since all human beings are naturally attracted to pleasure (and happiness) which maintains or increases their well-being and are naturally repelled by pain (and unhappiness) that decreases their well-being and might point toward their death, then it follows that both men and women are naturally attracted to pleasure, satisfaction or happiness and repelled by pain, dissatisfaction and unhappiness. Examples to the contrary tend to be distortions of reality.

Synthesis and Extension: Given that all people are naturally attracted to pleasure, satisfaction, and happiness and naturally repelled by pain, dissatisfaction, and unhappiness, then how do the "basic male" and the "basic female" determine who does what to provide them with the food, shelter and clothing they need to live and live as well as they can?

Theoretical Extension: Methods for the Division of Labor between a "Basic Man" and a "Basic Woman":
1. **Interests:** People in general tend toward doing work that interests them, as opposed to work that they find uninteresting.
2. **Talents:** People in general tend toward doing work for which they possess the appropriate talents.
3. **Skills:** People in general tend toward doing work for which they possess the appropriate skills.
4. **Intelligence:** People in general tend toward doing work that realizes their level of intelligence. Below that level, they might get bored; above that level, they might be overwhelmed.

4

5. **Physical Aptitude:** People in general tend toward doing work for which they possess a physical aptitude (e.g. men will do heavy labor requiring muscular strength; women will nurture their young by administering their breasts).
6. **Negotiation:** When the work is uninteresting for all people involved, yet must be done to maintain survival or well-being, then the people involved will conjointly determine a method by which that work will get done (e.g. take turns).
7. **Roles:** Men will do certain types of work because they are male; women will do certain types of work because they are female (e.g. the man will build the house and hunt game whereas the woman will tend to the home, cook, and clean, etc.) regardless of whether or not each possesses the necessary physical aptitude, skills, interests, talents and intelligence to do the other's work).
8. **Male-determined:** Men will determine who does what regardless of the other's interests, talents, skills, intelligence and physical aptitude.
9. **Female-determined:** Women will determine who does what regardless of the other's interests, talents, skills, intelligence and physical aptitude.

Proposition 7: People of all ages tend overwhelmingly to want to do work that is interesting to them.

Though people often do work that does not interest them or that only mildly interests them, they tend overwhelmingly to *want* to do work that interests them. They tend overwhelmingly not to want to do work that doesn't interest them. When they do work that doesn't interest them, they tend to do so for extrinsic rather than intrinsic reasons, e.g. money, power, etc. Interesting work tends to produce pleasure, satisfaction, and happiness. [In classroom polls over the past 15 years of roughly 3,500 students, nearly 100% said that "interest" was a good way to divide labor.]

Proposition 8: People tend to want to do work in which they are talented.

An expression of talents in work is usually experienced as gratifying to those doing the work. Sometimes this is not the case. Some people will possess talents that they have little interest in expressing in their work (e.g. a person talented in mathematics might find doing mathematics relatively unrewarding). But usually people tend to like expressing their talents in their work. Doing work that expresses one's talents tends to produce pleasure, satisfaction, and happiness. [In classroom polls over the past 15 years of roughly 3,500 students, nearly 100% said that "talent" was a good way to divide labor.]

Proposition 9: People tend to want to do work for which they possess the appropriate skills.

An expression of skills in work is usually experienced as gratifying to those doing the work. Sometimes this is not the case. Some people who possess the skills appropriate for a certain type of work will have little interest in expressing those skills in their work (e.g. a person skilled at carpentry might find doing carpentry to be relatively unrewarding). But usually people tend to like expressing their skills in their work. Doing work that expresses one's skills tends to produce pleasure, satisfaction and happiness. [In classroom polls over the past 15 years of roughly 3,500 students, nearly 100% said that "skills" was a good way to divide labor.]

Proposition 10: People tend to want to do work for which they possess the appropriate physical aptitude and tend not to want to do work for which they do not possess the appropriate physical aptitude.

An expression of physical aptitude in work is usually experienced as gratifying to those doing the work. Sometimes this is not the case. Some people will possess the physical aptitude for a certain type of work but will have little interest in expressing that aptitude in their work (e.g. a man who is physically strong might find physical labor relatively unrewarding). But usually people tend to like expressing their physical aptitude in their work. And they tend, overwhelmingly, not to like doing work that is inconsistent with their physical endowments (e.g. women might not like lifting weights that are too heavy for them). Doing work that expresses one's physical aptitude might or might not produce pleasure, satisfaction and happiness for the individual. Simply because a woman is endowed with the physical aptitude to nurture her child, such acts of nurturing might cause her more pain than pleasure (e.g. as in some disease or disorder

6

of the breast); also, such acts might produce more pain than pleasure if survival pressures (e.g. safety) make such acts difficult to accomplish. Also, a large-framed, well-muscled man might receive more pleasure or satisfaction from performing activities that do not require his particular body structure (e.g. a big man who prefers to write rather than construct buildings). But often time satisfaction does match with the expression of one's physical endowments, given that nothing else prevents, distorts, or usurps that physical endowment's expression. [In classroom polls over the past 15 years of roughly 3,500 students, nearly 100% said that "physical aptitude" was a good way to divide labor.]

Proposition 11: Some work necessary for survival and well-being requires people to do work that might not interest them and work for which they possess little talent, skill, or physical endowment. In these cases, people will tend to negotiate an equitable method for determining how the work will get done.

This proposition, I believe, given current theories and practices in regard to division of labor, might require an explanation more developed than those supporting the above propositions. It might require a more developed explanation not because the proposition itself escapes an intuitive rational appeal but because it does not seem to reflect current practices; it does not have much empirical support. In nearly all areas of human society (e.g. business, politics, medicine, education, religion, etc.), men dominate. The modern American family might be showing more signs of equal collaboration between partners in determining a division of labor for the partners and their family, but all other social institutions, aside from all-female or predominantly female groups, reflect male domination. In the majority of socialized cases (as opposed to familial cases) whereby a type of work must get done but relatively few people want to do it, men tend to decide who does what, and some type of force or coercion is used to get the job done. Much more will be said about this as this work unfolds. [In classroom polls over the past 15 years of roughly 3,500 students, nearly 100% said that "negotiation" was a good way to divide labor.]

Proposition 12: Gender roles are an illegitimate method of determining a division of labor.

7

Though gender roles have had a dominant role in the world as a method of determining a division of labor, in the United States and other advanced industrial countries, gender roles, when used to determine a division of labor, tend to be rejected as legitimate. In advanced industrial countries there tends to be laws protecting women from being discriminated against in regard to the hiring and firing policies and practices of businesses and organizations. Women are not to be kept from competing with men for jobs, and men are not to be kept from competing with women for jobs. These general statements are highly qualified: there are many cases of discrimination occurring despite the laws. Either the laws do not cover many situations, or the laws are sufficiently ambiguous so as to evade application to certain cases, or the laws are not enforced evenly or possibly at all in some cases. [In classroom polls over the past 15 years of roughly 3,500 students, approximately .04% said that "gender roles" was a good way to divide labor.]

Proposition 13: "Male-determined" is an illegitimate method of determining a division of labor.

Though men determining the division of labor had strong appeal in the past in modern industrialized countries and other forms of hierarchically structured societies and continues even to this day to be the norm in practice (even though people will give lip service to the method as being illegitimate), it is generally disparaged as a method of deciding who does what to provide for survival and well-being among males and females in advanced industrial countries.

Since there seems to be a huge disparity between the rhetoric of denouncing "male-determined" methods of the division of labor and the actual practice of male domination in not only advanced industrial countries but in all countries, the rest of this work will serve as an argument against the continued practice of male-determined methods of the division of labor and, therefore, support the proposition rejecting male-determination as a legitimate method. [In classroom polls over the past 15 years of roughly 3,500 students, approximately .04% said that "male-determined" was a good way to divide labor.]

Proposition 14: "Female-determined" is an illegitimate method of determining a division of labor.

Aside from divisions of labor being determined around the home involving children, or in relatively rare instances of female domination in business and politics in the past, or in less rare but still unequal instances of female domination in the present in business and politics, women have not determined divisions of labor.

Since there seems to be no great disparity between the rhetoric of denouncing female-determined methods of determining the division of labor (since there is so little rhetoric; it is just assumed to be bad), and since one of the theses of this work is that hierarchies in general need to be transformed into more egalitarian forms of organization, this proposition will not require more support. But the rest of this work can serve as an argument against any feminist rhetoric that supports the retention of hierarchies where males and females are equally represented in positions of power. Rather, it supports those feminists who argue for the transformation of hierarchies into more egalitarian or democratic forms of organization. [In classroom polls over the past 15 years of roughly 3,500 students, approximately .01% said that "female-determined" was a good way to divide labor.]

Proposition 15:   Interests, talents, skills, intelligence, physical aptitude and negotiation are legitimate ways for people to divide their labor.

Proposition 16:   Gender roles, male-determined, and female-determined methods are illegitimate or distorted ways of dividing labor.
It will become clear as this work develops what "illegitimate" and "distorted" means when applied to division of labor or anything else.

Probing Question: If interests, talents, skills, intelligence, physical aptitude and negotiation are natural ways for people to divide their labor, then how have we created a predominantly male-dominated world? How is it that males, overwhelmingly, determine the methods by which labor is divided?

Theoretical Response: Three Types of Theories for Hierarchies
There are several general theoretical answers to this question offered: 1) evolutionary theories, 2) learning theories, and 3) pragmatic theories. Evolutionary theories argue that when men gather into

groups they will, because of their genetic endowments, form hierarchies. Learning theories argue that at some point in human history men have seized power and forced others (women and men alike) into submission. Pragmatic theories argue that even if hierarchies are not natural (i.e. biologically determined), they serve the practical end of ordering human behavior and forcing human cooperation in order to achieve human goals.

Theoretical Extension: Leaders vs. Rulers

There is a fundamental difference between leadership and rulership. Rulership entails the unilateral use of power or the ability to impose one's will upon another without the other's free consent. Leadership entails the ability to influence the will of another so that the other will freely align him or herself with the will of the leader.

Hierarchical structures require rulership, though leadership traits are valued in most hierarchies. Democratic structures require leadership, and rulership traits are generally devalued, only to be used in times of emergency, and only as a temporary fix.

Hierarchy, in this work, refers only to structures admitting of unilateral power, not to status, where some people can more easily and successfully influence others because of their intelligence, skills and acumen. Status hierarchies are not hierarchies (in this sense); rather, they refer to levels of leadership and are applied differentially, i.e. one person could have high status in one area of human endeavor and not in others. Levels of status are considered in this work to be normal, natural, and imbedded in all human interaction. They serve humanity by extending survival and improving well-being. But when status levels become hierarchical, leadership converts to rulership; leaders become dominant and followers become submissive.

Business structures around the world are overwhelmingly hierarchical. Anywhere we hear dichotomous terms such as "boss" and "underling", "employer" and "employee", "master" and "slave", we are involved in hierarchy. The phenomenon is the same within all of these dichotomous pairs, only differing in degree. Anywhere the few make rules for the many to live by, even when the rules include the rule makers, and even when those ruled give permission, either explicitly or implicitly, to the rule makers to make rules, we are involved in hierarchy.

But when *all* of the people in a given group actively create, sustain, and alter the rules under which they freely subject themselves, we are involved in democracy. When the distinction between ruler and subject, dominant and submissive, and master and slave is eliminated and replaced by holistic terms such as populations, citizens, and workers, wherein there are leaders and followers that are differentially applied, we are involved in democracies.

The world admits of both structures: hierarchies and democracies. But there seems to be a contradiction between the two. One structure is supported by ideologies that maintain that when people associate with one another, they will naturally form hierarchies; in other words, it is human nature to form hierarchies, implying that any attempts to change this natural disposition will prove fruitless. Such ideologies include the various forms of non-democratic governments such as monarchy, oligarchy, aristocracy, dictatorship, fascism, committee-run socialism, communism, etc. as well traditional managerial capitalism, scientific evolution as applied to society, and including theistic religions such as Christianity, Judaism, and Islam.

The other structure is supported by ideologies that maintain that when people associate with one other, they will naturally form cooperative structures based on equality and leader-follower dichotomies. Such ideologies include democracy, one form of democratic socialism, worker-controlled capitalism, and other forms of egalitarianism.

If this is a legitimate contradiction, then which type of being are we: hierarchical or democratic, dominating and submissive or equal; competitive and forceful or cooperative? If we are the former, then how is it that we so value democracy and seek to convert the world to democratic ways of being? If we are the latter, then how is it that we have so overwhelmingly developed hierarchical structures throughout many aspects of human life, particularly in business? Or are we both? Perhaps under some conditions (e.g. when survival is threatened) we are naturally disposed toward hierarchies and under other conditions (e.g. when we are healthy and safe) we are naturally disposed toward democracy.

It is the general thesis of this work that hierarchies are natural forms of organization only inasmuch as nature can become distorted through the physical, sexual, and emotional abuse of human beings; that human beings are fundamentally egoistic, social and cooperative, and that democracy is, if run properly, a much healthier form of human organization than are any forms of hierarchy.

Proposition 17: The "basic male" and the "basic female" need each other's cooperation in order to form a sexual pair bond.

A pair bond usually refers not only to a sexual union between a male and a female but also to a relationship between the two people that will provide for the nurturing of offspring. At this point, "pair bond" is used specifically to refer to a sexual union.

Though it is conceivable that one member of a pair bond, let's say the male, who tends to be physically stronger than the female, can force himself sexually on the female against her will and therefore not need her cooperation, it seems improbable that such force stems from a genetic disposition to do so. There exists overwhelming evidence that argues against such a conclusion. Most men do not force themselves on women for sex. Rather, they tend to seek out cooperation from women, though that cooperation might involve some degree of manipulation.

Proposition 18: The "basic male" and the "basic female" require each other's cooperation in order to form a relationship pair bond.

When the basic male stays with the basic female, having produced children or not, the pair will require each other's cooperation in order to promote their survival and improve their well-being. They will naturally tend toward Division of Labor reasons 1-6 in order to accomplish this task.

There seems to be no genetic or biological disposition to require one of the pair to force the other to do what the one wants. In reference to our human situation, there seems to be no genetic or biological disposition to require a basic male to force a basic female to do what the male wants. If there were such a genetic disposition, then we would witness its occurrence as we would the occurrence of blue eyes or long, straight hair. In some patriarchal societies such 'evidence' might be found where male domination is quite obvious and prevalent. But in the more economically prosperous, democratic societies, the 'evidence' is considerably less. It seems to be considerably less at the family level of society and at the political level, where politics is purely or (at least to some degree) represent-

12

tatively democratic. In business the 'evidence' seems to support the idea that males are genetically disposed to force their wills upon females (and upon other males), though this force has shifted from physical means to emotional or psychological means.

Theoretical Response: The Physical Evolutionary Theory
The theory of evolution as presented by Darwin is a biological theory of the origins of human beings, and when combined with genetics it argues that human bodies are formed based upon the blueprint of each individual's genetic structure. Human behavior is understood to promote one's genes into the next generation. Those genetic structures that produce people who, for whatever reason, are biologically unable to promote their genes into the next generation will tend to die out, and those who are successful will tend to proliferate, given that the environment is conducive to proliferation.

The theory of evolution hinges on the theory of natural selection. Natural selection maintains that the environment is either conducive to some degree to the proliferation of one's genes or it is not. If genes produce organisms that cannot reproduce or that die out before they reach the age of reproduction, environment doesn't matter; the organisms will die out. If genes produce organisms that can reproduce but cannot sustain themselves within the environment (e.g. get killed by predators, die in the cold climates, etc.), then they will tend not to proliferate. If genes produce organisms that can reproduce and can sustain themselves within the environment, then those genes will tend to proliferate.

The passage of genes from one generation to the next is not only circumscribed by the environment but also by the ways in which genetic structures form. Chromosomes from the male will combine with those from the female to form a genetic structure that serves as the blueprint for some of the organism's qualities and characteristics, ranging from hair and eye color to behavioral tendencies.   Combining chromosomes is subject to alteration. Chromosomes do not combine the same way each time. Some combinations admit of alterations referred to as mutations. Mutations produce qualities and characteristics that are different from the norm. These qualities and characteristics either fit into the environment or they do not. If they do, they proliferate. If they don't, they die out. Those qualities and characteristics that serve to perpetuate the organism's life, promote its reproduction into the next generation, and protect it from early death will tend to thrive.

Most (all?) evolutionists admit that no genes have been found that might account for a minority of people becoming rulers and a majority of people becoming the ruled, but this does not mean that there are no such genes. Likewise, most (all?) evolutionists would not claim that there are specific genes or gene clusters that directly account for some men (or all men) forcing women to do what they want them to do. But, again, this does not mean that there are no such genes. The hunt goes on.

Theoretical Response: The Socio-Biological Evolutionary Theory

Even if there are no such genes to be found which might support a biological determination of males forcing females to do their will or males forming the hierarchies that we witness today, socio-biologists argue that genetic structures in males and females differ sufficiently to account for the creation of hierarchies that place men at the top. The argument goes like this: men tend to possess more testosterone than women; testosterone causes men to be more aggressive than women; hence, it is natural (biological) for men to form hierarchies.

The problems with this argument are significant. At best it only addresses why men might be at the top of most hierarchies and not why hierarchies are formed in the first place. In effect, it says that men are more aggressive than women and because of this, they will take it upon themselves to force women under their rule, but it says nothing as to why some men (a minority) would force other men (a majority) to be under their rule. Unless it can be shown that most men possess low testosterone and that those men happen to be the same men who are the ruled, and that a few men possess high testosterone and that those men happen to be the same men who rule, then this theory is probably more reflective of the theorists' hopes or wishes (i.e. biases) than anything based on empirical reality.

Also if we grant the validity of the first premise, i.e. that men tend to possess more testosterone than women (which is easily empirically verified) and even the second premise i.e. that testosterone disposes men to be more aggressive than women, then there is still no reason to conclude that men will naturally aggress against women to the extent of forming social hierarchies with them at the top, or that some men will aggress against all others and thus form social hierarchies with them at the top. Simply because one is more easily disposed than others toward aggression does not mean that others will submit to the aggressors. Rather, there is good reason to assume that it is more natural for the many to rise up collectively against any individual who aggresses against them. Unless one somehow forfeits his or her freedom to act "by one's own lights" rather than by "the lights of others," one seems bound to defending oneself in regard to survival and well-being by warding off others' attempts to determine one's behavior and who one is.

And even if we agree with this argument and maintain that men will tend to aggress against women, and some men will aggress against all the other men (majority), we have no reason to believe that the majority's submission to the minority is natural or somehow biologically determined. Even if we use fear, which is ultimately based upon survival, as the motive for the majority submitting to the minority, we have to ask why fear of the few would serve to force the many to submit to the will of the few. If there are no genetic structures to determine this, and if there is no correlation between the testosterone levels of those who dominate and those who submit, then why, in the construction of hierarchies, does the majority submit to the minority?

Theoretical Extension: The Beginnings of Human Beings According to Anthropology

Philosophers, evolutionists, anthropologists, historians, and others have speculated as to the origins of human organization, i.e. how we as a species organized ourselves into groups at the beginning of human existence on earth. Anthropologists tend to align themselves with the idea that at the evolutionary beginnings of the genus, homo sapiens, human beings organized themselves into small, egalitarian bands of hunters and gatherers, where no one in particular ruled anyone else and where anyone who tried to dominate another was chastised or punished in some way. They base their theories in part upon archeological findings from which they infer certain social structures but mostly upon their research into modern-day examples of hunter-gatherer bands, and argue that since there are some hunter-gatherer bands that exist in modern times that are egalitarian in structure, that egalitarian organizations dominated "pre-civilized" or pre-historical human organizations.

15

When scientific anthropology emerged in the nineteenth century, anthropologists assumed the task of researching and explaining groups of people that populated a wide variety of locations in the world who didn't seem to have any leaders with any real authority (e.g. some African tribes including the Kalahari foragers and groups of "bushmen"). People in the groups seemed to come and go as they pleased (Boehm, 1999). Leaders tended to be 'weak' and would act more like facilitators when decisions had to be made (Knauft, 1991). Upstarts who tried to impose their wills upon others were rebuffed, sometimes banned, shunned or even killed.

British social anthropologists, Fortes and Evens-Prichard (1940), identified three types of political society in Africa: politically centralized chiefdoms, stateless societies that fell into the category of "tribes," and some hunter-gatherer bands who had no discernible leader, who behaved much like a large family but without a "head."

Service (1975) pointed out the "self-effacing" behavior of a headman in a band or egalitarian tribe who acted more like a facilitator than a ruler, who might possess skills in hunting and warfare but who was also kind, generous and even-tempered. Such a headman would share his ideas with others and offer suggestions but would not impose his will upon them.

Interestingly, some anthropologists believe that the bands, though egalitarian as a group, were constituted by various nuclear families whose structure tended to be hierarchical, where parents controlled their children, men controlled women, and elders controlled youngsters (Service 1962).

Many anthropologists propose four stages of human organizational development: 1) hunter-gatherer bands, 2) tribes, 3) chiefdoms and 4) the modern state.

These anthropological theories are difficult to support for at least two reasons: 1) there is no direct evidence (e.g. historical documents) or indirect evidence (e.g. archeological finds) that support the conclusion that bands of hunters and gatherers, in fact, conducted themselves in an egalitarian fashion, and 2) there is no necessary connection between modern-day egalitarian bands and pre-hierarchical human organizations. In regard to the first point, that period in human history precedes literacy and physical archeological evidence does not convey any social information that would indicate any specific organizational conclusions. In regard to the second point, even though there is strong reason to think that modern-day egalitarian tribes indicate that egalitarian organization among humans is possible, and that such groups seem to modern "civilized" humans as throw backs to more primitive times, there is no reason necessarily to conclude that human pre-history is universally characterized by egalitarian systems of organization. Maintaining so is, at best, an education guess, i.e. a speculation that might carry with it some prima facie justification but no degree of certainty.

Equally, there seems to be no degree of certainty surrounding the proposition that human pre-history is characterized by primitive forms of hierarchy. Though there is considerable evidence that hierarchy existed within human 'civilized' society in the form of chiefdoms and, later, various forms of autocracy (e.g. monarchy, totalitarian regimes, etc.), there is no reason to assume that such hierarchies characterized all forms of pre-historical organization. Just because hierarchies dominated human organizations at some point in human history does not mean that they have always dominated human history.

The upshot from this discussion is that an argument for "natural" forms of human organization cannot be made from the speculations about human pre-history. We cannot conclude that because human beings might have organized themselves in an egalitarian fashion prior to the "invention" of human civilization that we, as a species, are egalitarian by nature. Nor can we conclude that we are hier-archical by nature simply because there are many hierarchies at any point in human history, including the present time.

Theoretical Extension: A Modern-Day Argument
It might be more fruitful for us to argue that there is modern-day evidence supporting the idea that humans are capable of creating both hierarchical structures as well as egalitarian (e.g. democratic) structures. The growing number of democratic political structures around the world attests to the egalitarian tendency in us, whereas the overwhelming number of hierarchical structures in business and a strong history of hierarchical political structures attest to the tendency in us to form hierarchies. Are we to conclude from this evidence that humans are both egalitarian and hierarchical by nature?

One problem with this conclusion is that it is contradictory, unless the grounds for adopting each method of organization can be

17

shown to be mutually exclusive. That is, perhaps under certain circumstances, we will form hierarchies, and under other circumstances, we will form democracies.

For instance, there is evidence to support the idea that autocracies, especially totalitarian regimes, might flourish in relatively poor economies, whereas democracies might flourish in relatively prosperous economies. This argument has some support if we consider that many of the current democracies in the world (e.g. USA, England, France, Germany, etc.) are relatively wealthy countries, whereas many current autocracies in the world (e.g. Cambodia, Cuba, Mongolia, Pakistan, etc.) are relatively poor countries.

But many autocracies in the past, in the form of monarchies, have achieved great wealth relative to other countries (e.g. Spain, England, France, etc.), thus supporting the argument that autocracies are associated with wealth as well as poverty. Also, all democratic countries are not financially wealthy (e.g. Tuvalu, Nicaragua, Benin, Georgia, etc.) In addition to this, some contemporary autocracies possess relatively wealthy economies (e.g. China, Iran, Venezuela, and Egypt).

With these exceptions indicated, there is still reason to support the idea that democratic countries do, overall, tend to be associated with prosperous economies. Of the top 30 countries in the world, measured in terms of GDP as determined by the International Monetary Fund (2010), 27 possess some form of democratic government, the exceptions being China, Saudi Arabia, and Iran.

If democratic countries do, in general, tend to possess relatively wealthy economies, and autocracies do, in general, tend to possess relatively poor economies, then might we hypothesize that there are economic advantages to democratic political structures? Or that democratic political structures tend to allow the freedom necessary for citizens to create businesses on their own, without having to get approval and/or funding from government?

This might be so, but there is still ample evidence that human beings are capable of simultaneously forming democratic political structures and autocratic (sole proprietors) or oligarchic (corporations) hierarchical economic structures. We seem very able to live in political democracies and autocratic and oligarchic economies at the same time. This lends more support to the idea that human beings are both egalitarian and hierarchical by nature, which puts us back into the land of contradiction.

Perhaps the hypothesis should be that though the empirical evidence seems to indicate that we are both egalitarian and hierarchical by nature, we are actually one or the other and that the opposite is natural only in that we are capable of manifesting it and not in that it is an expression of who we actually are.

Theoretical Extension: Egoism as a Natural Limitation to Forming Hierarchies

Psychological egoism, as an ethical, psychological and social theory, states that all human beings are naturally hard-wired or genetically constituted to be concerned about their own survival and well-being. The theory holds that we, as individuals, seek to maximize our happiness and minimize our pain. We tend to seek happiness and satisfaction and to avoid pain and dissatisfaction. But often times in seeking satisfaction we come up against others trying to do the same. Our self-seeking behavior often challenges the self-seeking behavior of others. When a conflict of self-interests occurs, we are at a crossroads. Do we impose our self-interests upon others, allow others to impose their self-interests upon us, or seek ways to balance our opposing self-interests?

Another way to understand egoism is that we, as individuals, seek to express ourselves as we are, and at least tacitly expect that that expression will be accepted by others. For example, a child might want to be released from mother's arms in order to investigate his surroundings. He might struggle to be released. If mother doesn't wish to release the child, and hence, restrains his movements, then the child might become irritated and more aggressive in his movements.

From the point of view of egoism, the child is trying to maximize his own self-interest or to increase his well-being because the well-being that was connected to mother's holding him has decreased and has given way to his attraction to investigate the room around him. Mother attempts to decrease her pain, which is caused by child's squirming to get out of her grasp, by restraining him more aggressively. Again, the question arises: do we impose our self-interests upon others, allow others to impose their self-interests upon us, or seek ways to balance our opposing self-interests?

19

The need to maximize survival and well-being seems to exist in all humans, child as well as adult. All humans seem to act in ways consistent with their own survival and well-being. No humans seem to decrease their well-being purposefully, unless they figure that such a decrease is temporary and will be helpful to them in the future, or that acts of self-sacrifice are consistent with their overall survival.

If this is so, then humans are survivors and maximizers of their own well-being, and they will press for self-expression and for that self-expression to be accepted by others. Any rejection of expressions of self will tend to decrease their well-being.

The child's expression of himself and, hence, his attempts to maximize his well-being by struggling to release himself from mother's grasp and to investigate his surroundings is a natural expression of his egoistic tendencies. If mother's attempts to restrict the child's attempts to express himself are not, or cannot, be experienced by the child as being for his own good, then the child will continue to press mother to accept the legitimacy of his self-expression (i.e. to let him do what he wants to do). If such attempts are met with stronger, more forceful restriction, (e.g. physical coercion, punishment, etc.), then the child is in position to capitulate to the stronger force. Such capitulation might be a matter of socialization (e.g. "you don't act that way in these situations"), or a matter of will (e.g. "I want to get my business done and you need to behave while I do it"), or a matter of rejection (e.g. "stop squirming you bad child"). If the force is exerted for one of the first two reasons, then the chances of altering the child's self is much less than the chances determined by the third alternative. The third alternative admits of a rejection of the child himself and is not simply a limitation placed upon the child's behavior. It is this alternative that usually admits of force, coercion, imposition of will, aggressive manipulation and abuse.

When a parent exerts force upon a child for the child's benefit, the child will tend to realize that force's legitimacy, but only if the parent is consistent with his or her forceful behavior and generally consistent with his or her support for the child in other areas of its life. Periodic force will be accepted by the child because the child realizes in some way that the force is exerted for its own good (i.e. survival and well-being). Force can legitimately be exerted upon a child if that force is experienced as being consistent with whom the child is, though, perhaps, inconsistent with the child's immediate wants. But when the force is experienced as inconsistent with whom the child is, i.e. with its' natural expression of self, then it becomes a means of altering the child's identity. It is an act of unilateral power, a type of coercion, aggressive manipulation, or abuse.

In many cases of socialization the battle of wills results in the parent winning out over the child, where the immediate gratification of the child is nullified and the child learns to suspend gratification and to behave in a more social manner (relative to the social demands of that society). In suspending gratification the child actually increases its well-being in the long run. Often times, when immediate gratification is submitted to by the parents, the child will not learn how to suspend that gratification in the family, only to run into a lot of problems in the larger society when the larger society will not tolerate the child's self-centered behavior.

In situations of socialization children's egoistic tendencies are realized but only in the wake of behavioral limitations placed upon them by parents. Long-term gratification outweighs short-term, immediate gratification. But this only works when parental force is used for the recognized benefit of the child. If the force is not for the benefit of the child, but for the parent, or if it is not recognized by the child as being for its own benefit, then the force is either unilateral and imposed upon the child (i.e. the force of a ruler) or the child, for whatever reason, is not understanding the force as it is. It might take repeated parental efforts before the child can recognize the force as being for its own good.

When parental force is for the benefit of the parent rather than the child, then the child will tend not to recognize it to be for its own good, and it might tend to seek self-expression in a more aggressive manner. If the parent does not recognize the self-seeking motives behind his or her behavior, and persists in forcing the child to conform to his or her will, then the child is in position to reject its own self-seeking behavior and conform to the will of the parent. Such a dynamic constitutes the essence of abuse. It involves the alteration of a self by force. When a self is altered by force, then the ground rules of egoism or self-gratification behavior are undermined and egoism is distorted. What initially constituted natural egoistic limitations of others' behavior becomes distorted oppression.

If the parent is able to ascertain the self-seeking motives behind his or her limit-setting behavior and realize that he or she is curbing the child's natural behavior for his or her own good, whatever that is, then the parent will be disposed to allow the child to act as it sees fit and the child's self will be affirmed. The child will realize its self-fulfillment, and the parent will adjust to the child's behavior and realize his or her own self-fulfillment.

Theoretical Extension: Aggression and Response
Aggression can come in many forms: irritation, anger, rage, intimidation (physical, psychological, and social), abuse (physical, psychological or emotional, and sexual), lying, manipulation, deceit, fraud, and various other forms of control, etc. All of these forms of aggression do not necessitate the use of force or the formation of hierarchies.

A husband might get irritated by his wife's behavior and show his irritation behaviorally, but this does not mean that wife will respond to his behavior in a manner consistent with husband's wish for her to stop her behavior unless we can posit that wife will naturally know that husband wants her to stop. If she knows that husband's behavior is aimed at her behavior, and if she knows that such behavior is a warning that more aggressive behavior is forthcoming if she doesn't stop, i.e. she naturally feels fear in relation to husband's behavior, then we might legitimately conclude that wife knows that husband wants her to stop acting the way she is acting. But even if we grant all this, why should we think that wife will stop her behavior because her testosterone level is lower than that of husband? After all, wives are capable of exhibiting similar irritations over husbands' behaviors and are capable of aggressing against them to some degree, even if their testosterone levels are lower than their husband's. But whether it is husband or wife aggressing against the other, it doesn't mean that the other will automatically submit to the aggression.

Perhaps husband is irritated about some behavior that is natural to wife. It is not a behavior motivated by any intention to irritate husband; it is, rather, an expression of who she is, and that expression happens to irritate him. In such a situation wife, if she possesses the ability to do so, might not lend any credence or justification to husband's irritation. Rather, she might believe that his behavior is irrational, unfair, or the result of being in a bad mood. If she believes

22

it unfair and she has the ability to reject the validity of his behavior and its implicit rejection of her, then she can confront husband by asserting herself in relation to him. If the assertive confrontation prompts husband to recognize the illegitimacy of his behavior, then he will back off, perhaps apologize, and allow wife to consider his apology. If the assertive confrontation prompts husband to be more aggressive, then the situation can spiral easily into more obvious forms of manipulation, aggression and control.

Simply because husband wants wife to stop behaving the way she is behaving does not automatically mean that wife should stop behaving that way. If her behavior is natural to her, and she sees no problem with it herself and would have no problem with it if her husband weren't there to become irritated over it, then there is no reason for her to change it. The fact that husband is irritated over it doesn't mean that it is wrong or bad in any way. It just means that *he* is having difficulty with it.

But if husband forces wife to stop her behavior by executing some form of aggressive manipulation, like intimidation or shows of anger, or coercion, like physical abuse, then wife, if unable to withstand the force, will, by virtual necessity, have to halt the natural development of her self and conform that self to the demands of husband. At this point husband becomes ruler and wife becomes the ruled. Natural human development is replaced by learned domination and submission.

Proposition 19: The basic male is not genetically disposed to force the basic female to do his will and, hence, is not biologically disposed to dominate her.

Proposition 20: The basic male is naturally disposed to maintain or improve his well-being and will act to satisfy this disposition by force if force appears to improve his well-being.

Proposition 21: The basic female is naturally disposed to maintain or improve her well-being and will act to satisfy this disposition by force if force appears to improve her well-being.

Proposition 22: The basic male is physically stronger than the basic female.

Proposition 23: The basic male will tend to be more successful in forcing the basic female to do his will, rather than the reverse, because he possesses the physical capacity to intimidate, aggress, or abuse the basic female into submission.

Proposition 24: Hierarchies are formed in pair bonds in part because basic males have learned that physical intimidation, aggression and abuse work to prompt basic females to do their will.

Theoretical Synthesis and Extension: Though the basic male is biologically disposed to preserve his life and maintain and improve his well-being, and though he tends to be physically stronger than the basic female, and though he is capable of imposing his will upon the basic female if he so wanted, there is no biological necessity for him to impose that will. Thus the basic male's imposition of will upon the basic female is the result of learning. He learns that when he does impose his will upon her that she, at least in some cases, will submit. Her submission prompts him to believe that such an imposition is good and right because the effects of the imposition are in accord with his perceived egoistic concerns.

For example: a man might realize that a certain task must be done if the pair is to survive or improve their well-being, but he also knows that he doesn't want to perform the task, for whatever reason. He therefore imposes his will upon the woman either through physical force or intimidation, and the woman submits and does the task; his survival is maintained or his well-being is improved and he never has to decrease his well-being at all by having to perform the unwanted task. The man, in effect, avoids the pain of having to perform the unwanted task, imposes his will or forces the woman to perform the task (for which he is biologically capable), and reaps the happiness rewards from such an imposition. He learns that force works not only *not* to decrease his happiness but to maintain his survival and increase his happiness.

Probing Question: Why does the basic male force the basic female to submit to his will if the basic male is naturally disposed to act cooperatively with the basic female in order to survive or improve his well-being?

Probing Question: Why does the basic female submit to the basic male in situations of force if the basic female is naturally disposed to cooperate with, rather than submit to, the basic male?

Probing Question: If the basic male and the basic female are disposed to act cooperatively with each other rather than engage in a dominant:submissive relationship, then how is it that the evidence of dominant:submissive relationships abounds through-out human history and persists to this day, especially in business organizations?

Theoretical Extension: Egoism as a Limitation on Unilateral Force

One response to the above questions is to argue that it serves the basic male's long-term best interest to gain the unforced or freely chosen cooperation of the basic female in the performance of the unwanted task, even if that cooperation requires that the basic male experience some degree of unhappiness through his performance of the task. On balance, the unhappiness-experience in the performance of the task is outweighed by the happiness-experience in the long-term.

Whereas if the basic male were to gain power over the basic female by utilizing some form of force, aggression or intimidation, that power would tend to be temporary because the utilization of it decreases the happiness of the basic female, which is counter to her egoistic nature. She would tend either to reject the force exhibited by the basic male or to circumvent its execution, thus eliminating or mitigating the effects of that use of force.

But in order for the basic female to reject or repel the basic male's use of force, she must employ methods that are equal or superior to those used by the basic male. Since the basic female tends to be physically weaker than the basic male, equal physical force seems to be unlikely. In fact, such expressions of force might only prompt the basic male to increase the strength of his physical force against her, though it might, in some cases, impress upon the basic male the need for him to stop using physical force against her; he might realize that his use of physical force is harming her, and his ability to empathize is a source of pain. If so, he would tend to apologize for his use of physical force.

If the unilateral use of physical force by the basic male upon the basic female is effective in gaining her submission, then the basic female is in position to gain whatever happiness she can within the delimited parameters of her actions. She is forced to perform the unwanted task, thus reducing her happiness, but she still benefits from the association with the basic male, enough so to maintain the 'cooperative' relationship.

But in submitting to the basic male's force, the basic female tends to feel resentment, which is an added pain, thus further decreasing her well-being. At least in regard to the unwanted tasks, her relationship with the basic male becomes antagonistic. She might mitigate some of the overall pain she experiences by acts of passive-aggression, circumvention, and sabotage, but these acts are distortions of who she is, of her natural way of being. Her natural way of being involves experiences of direct satisfaction in regard to cooperation, even when that cooperation involves some degree of reduction in well-being (e.g. performing unwanted tasks); it is more consistent for her to sacrifice some happiness (or experience some pain) in the performance of unwanted tasks when the methods by which she comes to agree to perform those tasks are acceptable to her. Physically forcing her to perform the tasks and maintaining that physical force through intimidation or threats of punishment is not an acceptable method for a division of labor; it is inconsistent with her natural way of being; it distorts her happiness by forcing her to resort to methods of gaining happiness that involve passive-aggression, circumvention, forms of retaliation, and sabotage.

Persistent Probing Question: Even though the theory of egoism might supply us with some explanation of why the basic male might impose his will upon the basic female, and why the basic female might submit to that will, it doesn't seem to answer the question of why we witness the signs of such ubiquitous dominant: submissive relationships in the world, even today, especially in business.

Yes, women might submit to men because such submission, and the pain it causes, might be outweighed by the happiness gained in maintaining the relationship, but why should such submission be accepted over time? How have women come to accept male domination throughout the world and throughout history when it is against their own nature to do so? And how have men come to promote their

26

domination over women when it is against their own nature to do so? The egoistic argument that on balance it serves women's best interests to accept the pain involved in submission is a distortion not only of human nature but of the theory of egoism itself. For the theory of egoism maintains that the happiness sought by all of us is, by definition, the best form of happiness possible. It would make the basic female happier to cooperate with the basic male in regard to divisions of labor if the methods of reaching that cooperation are agreed upon by the basic female. If the methods involve force, then the basic female's happiness is either eliminated (which is unacceptable) or forced underground or distorted; it is gained by means of passive-aggression, etc.

If this is so, then how have women come to 'accept' this distorted form of happiness, and how have men come to fail to recognize the distortedness of their own happiness gained through forcing women to do their will?

Theoretical Extension: The Experiential Theory
In order to answer the above questions adequately, we must turn to a philosophical theory called experientialism. I beg the reader's indulgence because an exposition of this theory will be quite lengthy. More information on this theory is available in *Experience: An Exploration into the Structure and Dynamics of Human Consciousness* (1997); *Sense, Sex, and Sin: Foundations for an Experientialist Ethics* (1998); *Experientialist Ethics: A Comparative Study* (2001); and *Experientialism: Integrating Mind & Body, Spirit & Matter, the Many & the One* (2011).

Experientialism maintains that reality is equal to experience, where experience is defined as a necessary combination of components: cognition, affect, behavior, sensation, environment, and the "I" or ownership:

Cognition: thoughts, ideas, images, understandings, cogitations, etc.
Affect: feelings, emotions, moods
Behavior: body in motion: internal (physiology); external (comportment)
Sensation: five senses (sight, sound, taste, touch, smell)
Environ: the physical environment, including our own body
"I":   ownership

The first five components (cognition, affect, behavior, sensation and environment) constitute consciousness; add to that the "I" and we have experience. The components support each other, are consistent

27

with each other, and help maintain each other's existence through time.

Each component can be 'filled in' with the appropriate content. For example:

Cognition: red ball
Affect: pleasure
Behavior: looking (at ball)
Sensation: ball
Environ: backyard
"I":   ownership

Here one is looking at a red ball in his backyard, knowing that the object is a ball and that it is red, and feeling pleasure in relation to it.

The entire structure or "frame" of experience consists of focal and peripheral components: Each focal component has a corresponding peripheral component aligning with it:

FOCUS	PERIPHERY
Cognition: red ball	orientation, things in yard, own body, etc.
Affect: pleasure	comfortable, familiar, etc.
Behavior: looking	standing, blinking, heart beating, etc
Sensation: red ball	things in yard, sounds, smells, own body, etc.
Environ: backyard (focused)	backyard (unfocused)
"I": ownership	

The content of any focal component of experience is that which we are focused upon. The content of any peripheral component of experience is that which we are not focused upon but exists within consciousness nevertheless and can be focalized or made focal. Each content of each component, focal or peripheral, inasmuch as it is discernible, is clearly supported by other components. For example, if I have a slight pain in my foot as I am looking at the red ball and feeling pleasure, the slight pain might be associated with a slight irritation. When the pain increases, thus pushing itself into focal consciousness, the irritation will come along with it, as will all the other corresponding components of consciousness. Thus the peripheral "pain in foot" will replace the original "red ball" as the sensation component of consciousness, and the peripheral "irritation" will replace the original "pleasure" as the affect component.

Experientialism contends that we do not remove ourselves or transcend the experiential structures within which we participate in order to understand reality-as-it-is. Every attempt to do so lands us back in the experiential structure. Problems arise when we do not recognize this and, instead, assume that what we experience to be so is so not only for us but for everyone, and we are prepared to impose the content, especially the cognitive content (e.g. statement, proposition, belief, etc.) upon others.

For example, the creationist might contend that God created us and the universe. This is a traditional objective claim, meaning that the claim, as a cluster of words, refers to an actual something (person, thing, power, event, process, etc.) that exists independently of the claim, and that this thing creates, influences or determines the existence of the experiential structure itself. In this case, "God" as a word refers to an actual supernatural being that exists independently of the experiential structure within which the word exists, and that this being has created, or at least made possible the instantiation of the experiential structure itself.

Traditional objective claims tend not to be owned. That is, "God created us and the universe," as a claim, is supposed to be, in effect, the cognitive capturing of an ontological or actual thing, event, process, etc., and not simply a belief that is owned by the individual expressing the claim.

For traditional objective thinkers, owning a claim relativizes reality, and the relativization of reality is contradictory, because traditional objectivism is defined as one reality, not many. If all beliefs are of the same importance, and these beliefs are not the same in content, then all beliefs cannot lay equal claim to capturing reality.

Therefore, when the creationist claims that "God created us and the universe" and the evolutionist claims that 'The universe was created by billions of years of evolving matter," they are making contradictory claims. Both claims, unless they are somehow shown to be the same claim, cannot be true, i.e. capturing reality, because there is only one reality; at least one of the claims must be false.

Experientialism argues that reality claims are contents of cognitive components of experience, and that is all they are. Whether or not the claims "capture reality" is of no consequence. We cannot remove ourselves or transcend the experiential structures within which we participate, so any traditional claim we make will automatically be *in* the experiential structure. And that claim will be made, necessarily, within an environment specific to the claim.

"Reality," as the term is traditionally used, refers to that which is outside of one's own mind and has a nature of its own. Whether our mind matches reality is subject to argument and verification, but that reality exists as such is not up for debate. Experientialism argues that

29

all reality claims are made within an experiential structure and that these structures are not transcendable. Therefore, any claim we might make concerning reality is owned. It is *our* claim. Whether or not our claim matches 'reality-as-it-is' is an inappropriate question. There is no way to remove ourselves from the structure in order to determine what 'reality-as-it-is' is or in order to substantiate our traditional objective claim.

For instance, the creationist might argue that her claim is accurate, i.e. that it captures actual reality, whereas the evolutionist's claim is false. She might support her claim by citing the Bible, presenting a philosophical argument for the existence of God, giving personal testimony, etc. All of these arguments lie within an experiential structure:

C: God created universe	Bible quote	phil argument	testimony
A: confidence	confidence	confidence	awe
B: talking	reading	talking	talking
S: person (evolutionist)	Bible	person	person
E: room	room	room	room
"I": ownership			

Each of these arguments exists as a cognitive content of a cognitive component of an experiential structure. Likewise, each of the arguments for the objective existence of the evolutionary theory exists as a cognitive content of a cognitive component of an experiential structure:

C: We are evolved matter	archeological data	anthropological data	comp. anatomy
A: confidence	confidence	confidence	confidence
B: talking	reading	showing	talking
S: person (creationist)	book	objects	person
E: room	room	room	room
"I": ownership			

Both the creationist and the evolutionist make traditional objective claims, while neither of them can remove themselves from the experiential structures within which they participate. At best they can *believe* that they have so removed themselves, and have thus *discovered* (e.g. science) or *deduced* or *intuited* (e.g. theology) objective reality. But when they do make these claims, and believe that they have transcended the experiential structures within which they participate and have somehow grasped objective reality, without realizing that they must own their own claim, they are open to creating a meta-experiential construct.

A meta-experiential construct is a claim (idea, concept, construct, or proposition) that refers to some idea, being, process, event, or cause that creates, determines, controls, or somehow influences the very experiential structure within which one participates, without owning the claim.

All traditional objective claims, inasmuch as they are not owned, are meta-experiential constructs.

For instance, I am looking at a cup. I believe that the cup is something that will not go out of existence when I'm not looking at it. I verify this by closing my eyes, then opening them only to see that that cup has not gone out of existence. So I make the claim:

C: This cup does not go out of existence when I'm not looking at it
A: confidence
B: looking at cup
S: cup
E: room
"I": ownership

Simply because I experience the cup to be something that does not go out of existence when I'm not looking at it does not mean that it does not go out of existence when I'm not looking at it. For all I know, it might. I can't tell what happens when my eyes are closed.

Perhaps I can hold the cup, then close my eyes, then open my eyes, and I coordinate my sense of touch with my sense of sight to realize that I felt it while my eyes were closed, and it felt just like it felt before I closed my eyes. This gives me more reason to make such a claim.

But this would just support the idea that my sense of sight is not determinative of the existence of the cup. What if I lost all sense contact with the cup? If I'm looking at the cup at a distance (i.e. not touching it), then close my eyes, then open them, and the cup is still there, there seems to be no way I can tell via sensual contact that the cup, in fact, did not disappear when I was not in some way sensually connected to it.

The point here is that it doesn't matter if the cup exists while I'm in sensual contact with it or not. Even if it did go out of existence when I'm not in sensual contact with it, then suddenly came back into existence when I re-gained sensual contact with it, and it appears to be the same cup as before, and this happens every time I re-gain sensual contact with it, I will tend to believe that the cup never went out of existence. So what matters is not whether or not the cup exists objectively, independent of my experience of it, but rather my experience of it as existing objectively. The objectivity of the cup exists as an aspect of the experiential structure within which I participate, and since I cannot remove myself from the experience within

31

which I participate, I must own that objectivity. When I don't own that objectivity, that is, when I believe that I have somehow transcended the structure within which I participate and have "reached objective-land," then I am open to creating a meta-experiential construct. In this case, I am open to claiming that the cup does not go out of existence when I'm not looking at it, and if you disagree with me, no matter what reasons you might give for your disagreement, you are wrong, because there is only one objective world and I happen to have grasped it: cups do not go out of existence when one is not sensually connected to them.

When reality is understood to be equal to experience, and "experience" is defined as a necessary combination of cognition, affect, behavior, sensation, environment and the "I", and all traditional claims of objective reality are owned, then the ontological focus shifts from the world outside of one's own mind (e.g. the nature of science) to the necessary connection between one's mind and nature, i.e. the integration between the individual and the environment. Once the environment is understood to be a necessary component of experience, and experience is understood to be non-transcendable, then we can better understand just how the basic female might come to submit her will to that of the basic male, and how females of today continue to submit their wills to males, and how the majority of males today continue to submit their wills to the minority of males, especially in business.

In order to understand the depth of this explanation for how men have managed to gain power over women, and how some men have gained power over other men in regard to the division of labor, we can expand the experiential theory to include an ontological division not between real and unreal but between real and distorted.

Theoretical Opposition: Empiricism

Empiricism argues for the existence of two realities: 1) mental reality and 2) physical reality. The mental exists in the mind; it is represented by thoughts, ideas, feelings, some aspects of sensations, etc. The physical exists outside of the mind; it is represented by objects in the world including other people, parts of our own bodies, and interactions between these elements.

For the empiricist the mental world is separate from the physical world, and the mental world, for the most part, is dependent upon the physical world. The mental world need not match the physical world, and the physical world can exist on its own. The physical world is assumed to have a nature of its own, and the mental world's job, so to speak, is to align itself with the physical world. Hence, what exists in the mental world need not be real in the sense that the physical world is real. For instance, when looking at a stick in water, the mental world is represented by the image of crooked stick, but 'in reality' the stick is straight; it just appears to be crooked. Hence, what exists in the physical world need not exist in the mental world as its match. The mental world is thought to be unreal inasmuch as it does not refer to the physical world.

Theoretical Extension: Critique of Empiricism
Experientialism rejects the dualism of empiricism as well as its realistic underpinnings but only as an ontological system; it accepts it as a mode of experience within an experiential world. In experientialism there is no real:unreal dichotomy. Simply because a thought in our mind does not match with an object outside of our mind does not mean that the reality of the thought is in any way diminished. In fact, the experientialist would argue that the thought in our mind is inextricably connected to an environment, though that environment need not be the same environment to which the thought refers.

For instance, I can think that a stick in the water is crooked at one time and later that the same stick is straight. This does not mean that while I am looking at the stick in the water, it, in fact, is straight and it only gives the appearance of being crooked. Rather, it means that I believe that the stick in the water is crooked. If I never see it as straight, then the stick, for me, is crooked. If everyone all the time saw the stick in the water as crooked, then the stick in the water would be crooked for everyone. But if someone came along and pulled the stick out of the water and saw that it was straight, then we might very well believe that the stick is straight but only appears to be crooked while in the water, that perhaps there is something about water and light that makes sticks appear crooked. But for us to say that the stick is in reality straight and in unreality (appearance) crooked is to deny the full existence of the appearance.

Here experientialism aligns better with phenomenology than with empiricism, where the appearance (crooked) is a phenomenon and so is the actual (straight). Opting to accept one phenomenon over another, or to act upon one phenomenon instead of another, is a matter of prudence, not ontology. Ontologically, the experience within which the person is participating might look like this:

Cognition: That stick is crooked
Affect: confidence (some level)
Behavior: looking at stick in water
Sensation: stick as crooked
Environ: stick in water
"I":   ownership

What are real in the above experience are the contents of all components of experience, including their peripheries (not shown). The individual cannot remove himself from the experiential structure within which he participates, and if his experience never changes every time he sees the stick, then the stick as crooked will be real for him. It only becomes real in a 'realistic' manner when an experience occurs that conflicts with the one in which he is participating. Hence, realism is understood as a form of experience in which one experiential structure understood as real conflicts with another experiential structure also understood as real. When the real of the crooked stick conflicts with the real of the straight stick, and the real of the straight stick is accepted as the more real of the two, whereas the real of the crooked stick is relegated to a category of unreal or appearance, then we are ordering experiential structures into types: one type is that of appearance-experience and the other of actual-experience. We might test our ordering by lowering the straight stick into the water to see if it appears crooked, then pulling out the stick again to see if it's straight. After satisfying ourselves with our ordering, we proceed to understand and act upon the stick in the water, regardless of its appearance, as a straight stick.

But simply because we act upon the stick in the water as a straight stick does not mean that it as a straight stick is real and it as a crooked stick is unreal; it only means that we experience the stick in the water to be a straight stick that appears to be crooked. Had we not, nor anyone else, ever experienced the stick in the water as a straight stick in some way (either by sight, touch, etc.), then it would be understood and acted upon as a crooked stick.

In this manner, the real-experience of the stick as objectively crooked is as real as the real-experience of the stick as objectively straight. When the latter exists in conflict with the former, and the latter is experienced to be the actual, independent reality and the former to be an appearance or a dependent reality (dependent upon the stick's environment being water), then the latter will be accepted as actual and the former will be accepted as appearance. But the actual is an aspect of the experiential structure within which the person participates and not an object in any 'actual world'. No one is able to remove him or her self from experience to determine just what exists in this 'actual world'.

An experiential analysis of this example might look like this:

Focal	Peripheral
C: That stick is crooked	oriented, stick as solid, other things in environ, etc.
A: confidence (some level)	familiarity, comfort, etc.
B: looking at stick in water	standing, blinking, moving parts of body, etc.
S: stick as crooked	things in sensual field, own body, etc.
E: stick in water	surrounding environment
"I": ownership	

In this experiential structure the stick is experienced to be solid (as opposed to an illusion or hallucination), and it is experienced to be crooked (as opposed to straight). These components of experience exist in the periphery of the structure. They are experientially object-tive components (as opposed to traditionally objective).

When the stick is pulled out of the water, the structure might look like this:

Focal	Peripheral
C: This stick is straight!	oriented, stick as solid, stick as same, other things in environ, etc.
A: surprise/confidence	familiarity, comfort, etc.
B: looking at stick in hand	standing, blinking, moving parts of body, etc.
S: stick as straight	things in sensual field, own body, etc.
E: stick in hand	surrounding environment
"I": ownership	

In this experiential structure the stick is experienced as straight, and the crookedness of the stick experienced before is in conflict with the straightness of it now. Because the stick experienced in the first experience is believed to be the same stick experienced in the second experience (as indicated in the periphery of the cognitive component), and because the person has no reason to believe that pulling on the stick did not straighten the stick out (we will say), then the person is in position to order the two realities and thus integrate his experience. He does so by understanding one experience (stick as crooked) to be appearance and the other experience (stick as straight) to be actual. His actual-experience is the one he believes to be the actual reality, and the appearance-experience is the one he believes to be an appearance reality. Both are realities. He even tests the legitimacy of his ordering by re-submerging the stick and confirming that it looks crooked, even though he believes it to be straight. Experientially, the appearance-reality is just as real as the actual-reality and the ordering of actual over appearance is accepted as prudent.

Theoretical Objection: Persistence of Realism

An objection might arise at this point. It might be argued that the experience of the straight stick consists not simply of a prudent choice between two opposing realities but of an imposition of one reality upon another, a complete displacing of one reality (crooked stick) with another (straight stick). The experience of the stick being straight so overpowers the experience of the stick being crooked that there is really no choice of reality going on here; reality is imposing itself upon the person.

Experientially, this argument, as put, offers no serious problem. The experience of realism does tend to be imposing in nature. We tend to believe that what we experience to be real *is* real not only for us but for everybody. It is only when we run into people who don't experience the world as we experience it that we question the validity of our own experience and/or the validity of their experience.

For instance, a color-seeing person might experience an object to be red, but a color-blind person might experience the same object to be a shade of gray. Both are aware that they are looking at the same object. Both will experience their color as the real objective color. Neither person can remove herself from the structure within which she is participating. Each might tend to disbelieve the other and/or discredit the other's experience. Such is the strength of realistic experience. This is also why people will be momentarily, or even over a long period of time, disoriented when they realize that what they once held to be objectively real is actually something else.

The real-experience of the crooked stick in water is replaced by the real-experience of the straight stick that appears crooked in water but only after a moment of disorientation. But simply because one real-experience replaces another does not mean that the first real-experience was any less real at the time it existed. It becomes 'less real' only in the sense that it is rejected as being something that one will base his understanding on and direct his actions toward. His orientation toward the second real-experience becomes a practical concern rather than an ontological concern. In this sense, experientialism is closer to pragmatism than empiricism or realism.

In regard to the color-seeing and color-blind experiences, since neither the color-seeing person nor the color-blind person can remove herself from the experiences within which she participates, and neither can alter the circumstances by which her perceptions will change (e.g. tamper with the cones in her eyes), each experience is to be accepted as real or objective, but that reality or objectivity must go inside experience; it must become that which it always was, i.e. an aspect of the experience within which each participates. For the color-seeing person, the object is red, and for the color-blind person the object is a shade of gray. Each must respect the reality of the other. The contradiction does not exist within the experiential structures within which one person participates (e.g. the crooked stick/straight stick example); rather, it exists between experiential structures within which different people participate.

When two opposing experiential structures collide, and one replaces the other in order of reality, then accepting the one (straight stick) even when contradictory evidence exists for the other (crooked stick in water), no matter how strong the experience of the one is, is a choice, a practical decision, a matter of prudence. It can be rendered thus: "I know the stick is straight even though it looks crooked right now; if I pull it out of the water it will look straight." The stick in the water is now experienced to be one of a type, i.e. a type in which the object seen is one way in "actuality" and another way in "appearance," and the environmental content within the appearance-experience is recognized as an appearance and not an actuality. This experience might look like this:

C: that stick looks crooked, but it's actually straight
A: confidence
B: looking at stick
S: stick as crooked
E: stick in water
"I": ownership

This type of experience includes the negation of what appears to be actual and an assertion of the existence of the appearance at the same time. The actual is, at this moment, imagined or cognized conceptually while the appearance is perceived. The person accepts that though the object appears crooked, it is actually straight, and the crookedness, though real, is appearance. It so behooves the individual to align her understanding and future actions with the imagined or conceptually cognized aspect of her experience rather than the appearance perception aspect of it; it is prudent and practical for her to do so.

Theoretical Extension: Realism vs. Experientialism
The realist assumes that there is only one world within which everyone lives, that that world has a nature of its own, and that that nature is able to be understood or grasped by some or all individuals as it is. Therefore, for the realist the crookedness of the stick in water is an illusion and, hence, unreal. The stick as crooked does not exist. Appearances might or might not match reality. When they do, then appearances are real or, more accurately, they are neutral but they reflect reality. When they don't, they are either non-existent, neutral and reflect something non-existent, or they exist as appearances but reflect something non-existent. The realist might accept the existence of an appearance, as appearance, but not as something real. The appearance exists as appearance but not as reality. The question arises: How can something exist and not be real?

The experientialist understands such a paradoxical, contradictory situation to be untenable. What the realist is doing, argues the experientialist, is not simply denying that the appearance matches reality but that the appearance isn't real; he also assumes that reality is understandable apart from experience.

In the realist's world the stick in water is straight; it only appears to be crooked. But if the stick's straightness is never experienced by anyone, ever, then why should anyone believe or assert that the stick is straight? It wouldn't occur to anyone that the stick is straight unless they had reason to doubt their perception. If, for instance, people never saw sticks in water, that they only saw them in air, and experienced them to be both straight and crooked, and then someone sees a stick in water, and it appears to be crooked, then it might quite naturally be understood to be crooked: a crooked stick is in the water.

But the experience of a crooked stick in water is not the same as an experience of a crooked stick in air. The stick in water-experience consists, in part, of reflections: slight differences in line and color, etc. The artist can experience this reality better than the regular person. The artist can see the appearance as real, as a category of experience on its own; he will pay attention to the details of reflection, e.g. line, color, etc., whereas the regular person will tend not to notice those details. The regular person might deemphasize these reflection details and categorize the object existing in water as it exists in air. This would be an experiential category mistake, and not an ontological error. The experiential category of "crooked stick in air" would be conflated with the experiential category of "crooked stick in water," and the person would believe that the stick in water is crooked.

The regular person would understand the crookedness of the stick to be a characteristic of the stick as he experiences sticks in air. He experiences sticks in air to be both crooked and straight. When he experiences a stick in water for the first time, he might very well disregard how the aspects of the sensory component of experience in relation to that part of the stick that is out of the water or in the air (e.g. its' clear lines, colors, etc.) conflict with the aspects of the sensory component of experience in relation to that part of the stick that is in the water (e.g. its blurry, wavy lines, colors, etc.) Because he is used to experiencing sticks in air, he, in Hume's terms, becomes accustomed to seeing crooked sticks. When he sees a stick in water that appears to be crooked, he naturally experiences the stick in water as crooked. But this is only because he doesn't yet possess a category of experience of "stick in water." So instead of creating a category of "stick in water appears crooked but is actually straight," he experiences the stick as crooked.

From the experientialist's point of view, the realist makes the mistake of raising the person's experience of stick in air above that of stick in water in relation to their shape. The realist will claim that the stick in water is actually straight (in a traditional objective way) simply because he experiences the stick in air to be equivalent to 'actuality' or 'objectivity' and that thoughts, ideas, perceptions, etc. are dependent upon that 'actuality'.

The experientialist will argue that the experience of the stick in air is just that, an experience. It could be rendered thus:

Focal	Peripheral
C: this stick is straight	oriented, stick as solid, clear lines, clear colors, etc.

A: confidence
B: looking at stick
S: stick in air
E: backyard
"I": ownership

In this experience the line and color of the stick and its solidity are clearly perceived; they are contents of the periphery of experience. Whereas in the experience of the stick in water, if we grant that the differences in line and color of the stick outside of the water and those inside the water are cognized, we will have something like:

Focal	Peripheral
C: that stick looks crooked	oriented, stick as solid, line and color of stick above water as clear and well-defined; line and color of stick underwater as blurred
A: curious	some degree of importance
B: looking at stick	
S: stick as possibly crooked	
E: stick in water	
"I": ownership	

Here the artist, or one who is used to experiencing how things appear, is experiencing the stick in water as possibly crooked. He is aware that how the stick appears in water is different from how it appears in air: he notices the blurred line and color of the stick under water, as opposed to its clear line and color above water. This difference prompts him to question what he is perceiving; he experiences some doubt. This doubt registers in experience and has some staying-power. He then might investigate his doubt if he is so disposed. Whereas the regular person's experience, granting some amount of recognition of difference, might look like this:

C: that stick looks crooked	oriented, stick as solid, line and color of stick above water as clear and well-defined; line and color underwater as blurred
A: curious	
B: looking at stick	
S: stick as possibly crooked	
E: stick in water	
"I": ownership	

which suddenly changes to:

C: that stick is crooked	oriented, stick as solid, line and color of stick above water as clear and well-defined; blurred line and color underwater as unimportant
A: confidence (some degree)	some degree of indifference
B: looking at stick	
S: stick in water as crooked	
E: stick in water	
"I": ownership	

In the experience of the regular person, relatively no significance is attached to the difference in appearance of the stick above the water and its appearance below the water. The difference is cognized, but little significance is attached to it, and therefore the stick is understood to be crooked.

Such an understanding reflects a category mistake, not an ontological one. The individual has placed the stick in water-experience on par with the stick in air experiences by ignoring the reflection details or by not attributing significance to them. This lack of significance exists in the periphery of experience as disinterest or indifference. Because the person is disinterested in the reflection details of the stick in water, the initial experience of the stick in water *looking* crooked is replaced by the experience of the stick in water *being* crooked.

But when the stick is pulled out of the water, and experienced to be straight, the stick as crooked in water-experience is contradicted by the stick as straight in air-experience, and the stick looking crooked-experience is confirmed in its doubtful aspect as the stick as appearing crooked but is actually straight-experience.

In none of these experiences does there exist anything that doesn't exist. Everything that exists does so in its fullest aspect, though it might well be that it is changing by the second. We cannot speak of anything that is coming to exist until it exists in experience; and once it exists in experience, any cognitive reference to anything that might or might not exist outside of experience is irrelevant.

The realist would have us believe that that which is outside of experience is more real than experience, but once we include the environment within experience, then that which is "outside of experience" is actually a component of experience. Once this is done, traditional objective reality comes inside experience and is owned.

So in our example, the realist would argue that the initial stick looking crooked is wrong or not real, as if he could somehow remove himself from experience, land himself in the objective world, find the straight stick, put it back into experience, and rejoin experience. But this is impossible. The experientialist, on the other hand, would argue that the stick as crooked-experience is actually an experiential category mistake, that it is just as real as any other experience, including the stick in air-experience. The mistake lies in attributing characteristics of one category (crooked stick in air) to another category (crooked stick in water). The person disregards the experiential distinctions and conflates the two categories.

But this does not mean that the crooked stick in air-experience is more real than the crooked stick in water-experience. Each experience is real; they can be represented thus:

Focal	Peripheral
C: this stick is straight	oriented, stick as solid, clear lines, clear colors, etc.
A: confidence	
B: looking at stick	
S: stick in air	
E: backyard	
"I": ownership	
C: that stick is crooked	oriented, stick as solid, line and color of stick above water as clear and well-defined; blurred line and color underwater as unimportant
A: confidence (some degree)	some degree of indifference
B: looking at stick	
S: stick in water as crooked	
E: stick in water	
"I": ownership	

In the stick in air-experience there exists no indifference in the peripheral aspect of the affective component, and the confidence in the focal aspect of the experience is full, i.e. not compromised by doubt. There is nothing in experience indicating that there are any significant differences between one part of the stick and another; it is understood as a whole, solid in all aspects, clear line and color throughout.

In the stick in water-experience there exists some degree of indifference in relation to the cognized distinction between the above water aspect of the stick and the underwater aspect of the stick, but that distinction is disregarded: some degree of indifference exists in the peripheral aspect of the affective component of experience.

The two experiences are ontologically different. But that difference is not recognized by the individual. Rather, the two experiences are conflated. When this happens, experiencing the stick in water to be straight when pulled out of the water will tend to be slightly disorienting to the individual. But once a new category of experience is created, i.e. "stick in water appears to be crooked but is actually straight," then future experiences of crooked sticks in water will register as "stick in water appears to be crooked but is actually straight."

Experientially, reality is equal to experience but the contents of experience are changeable, mutable, and alterable. One experiential structure (stick as straight) can trump another (stick as crooked), but this trumping is a practical matter, a matter of prudence. It makes practical sense for us to understand the stick in water to be straight and only appearing to be crooked. So if we were to want a straight stick to use for a task we would not be disappointed when we pull out a seemingly crooked stick out of the water.

Of course, it could work out that the stick in water as crooked actually is crooked (crooked stick in air) but it is crooked differently from how is appears in water. But then we will have to create a new experiential category to account for the slight disorientation we will experience in relation to our previously established categories.

Since no one can remove himself from the experiential structures within which he participates, objective reality comes inside experience, experienced as an aspect of experience, is owned, and is changeable, mutable or alterable. When one objective experience replaces another, it does so not because the experiential structure has somehow been transcended but because the new objective experience makes more sense to us, is more important to us, satisfies us more, is more beneficial to us, and has more value for us, practical or otherwise.

Theoretical Extension: Realism and Empiricism as Types of Experience

The stick in water/air example shows how experiential structures conflict with each other and thus produce a new structure, where the new structure is added to the other and at times replaces the other in practice, value, and orientation. But the color-blind/color-seeing example is different. These two experiences occur in relation to two different people. Two different people participate in two different experiential structures, each possessing the same environmental component content. The color-seeing person sees an object as red; the color-blind person sees the same object as a shade of gray, and nothing seems to change in their experience each time they look at the object.

If the world is one, exists independently of experience, and is graspable by some or all individuals (realism), then which person is correct? Is the object red or a shade of gray? Simply counting up those who see it as red and those who see it as gray will not do the job because the majority could be wrong. In fact, both could be wrong. But both could not be correct. In the realist's world, a battle for

43

accuracy is inevitable. What method is the best method by which we can determine what is real and what is illusion?

Religion tends to be realistic in its orientation: religionists determine what is real from what is not. But they tend to posit supernatural phenomena as real and determinative of natural, physical realities.

Science has replaced religion in many venues in modern Western society in determining questions of objective reality: according to many scientists the scientific method is better than all other methods of distinguishing what is real from what is illusion. Hence, empiricism has challenged supernatural realism and has, in many circles, replaced it as an ontological method of choice. But empiricism is realistic at its roots; it just eliminates the supernatural from reality and concentrates on the natural, i.e. the sensible. It still adheres to the basic realistic assumption that there is only one reality, and that that reality is separate from experience, and that some or all people are able to grasp or understand it as it is.

In the experientialist's world experience *is* reality. All of the contents that exist within an experiential structure exist as they are, and not as we or anyone else might see or understand them to be. Anything that might exist beyond the structure is irrelevant, since we can never remove ourselves from those structures to determine what might exist beyond them. Therefore, realism and empiricism are subsumed under experientialism; they are types or categories of experience, i.e. those experiential structures that pertain to sensory connections to the environment (empiricism) and those experiential structures that pertain to all traditional objective claims, whether supernatural or natural (realism).

Proposition 25: Reality is equal to experience, when experience is defined as a necessary combination of cognition, affect, behavior, sensation, and environment, as owned.

Traditional notions of "reality" and "experience" tend to separate reality from experience. Reality is something that we experience; experience is the medium through which we contact or grasp reality. But since there is no way for us to remove ourselves from experience, as defined above, to reach that reality, any reality we come into contact with is that which constitutes a part of experience, including the environmental component of experience. Hence, in 'experiencing reality', we are automatically thrown back into experience.

Proposition 26: Traditional objective reality claims are cognitive contents of experiential structures.

Any traditional objective claim, usually in the form of some sort of declarative sentence or proposition, is a content of a cognitive component of experience. These claims tend to refer to things, phenomena, events, processes, etc. that are not a part of the immediate claim-experience. For instance, "God created the world and us" is a traditional objective claim. It refers to an event (creation) that supposedly occurred at some time in history. The claim itself, though, will tend to occur in an environment that differs from the environment referred to in the claim (e.g. in a room); (no one was there when God created the world and us). The same is true for "We evolved from primordial matter." This proposition refers to a process (evolution) and, possibly, an event (i.e. big bang) that supposedly occurred at some time in history (big bang) and throughout time (evolution); (no one was there when the event occurred (big bang) or when the process occurred (primordial history), though we believe that the process is happening right now. As cognitive contents, traditional objective claims exist. What they refer to (i.e. events, processes that supposedly exist beyond the immediate structure within which the claim exists) is ontologically inconsequential. It doesn't matter if God created the world and us or if we evolved from primordial matter through a big bang and evolution; what matters is what we believe to have happened; and since we cannot remove ourselves from experience, that belief is vital to us.

Proposition 27: Traditional objective reality claims that refer to things, events, processes, phenomena, etc. that are supposed to exist beyond, outside of, or transcendent to the experiential structures within which they exist and are held to influence, control, create and/or sustain the existence of the experiential structure itself are necessarily distorted because no one can remove his or her self from any experiential structure to determine what might exist beyond the structure.

Traditional objective claims, transformed into experiential objective claims, refer to things, events, processes, phenomena, etc. that are considered to exist outside of immediate experiential structures exist within some other human being's experiential

45

structure at some time in history. Any reality that might exist outside of all experiential structures is ontologically inconsequential. Traditional objective claims, when owned, are ontologically relevant. When not owned, traditional objective claims tend to form meta-experiential constructs or distortions of reality.

Proposition 28: Traditional objective claims must be owned in order to have any ontological merit.
Once the locus of objectivity is transferred from a quasi-environment (i.e. reality outside of experience) to experience (including the environment), objectivity is owned. A rejection of that ownership constitutes an ontological infraction. It results in a distortion of reality.

Theoretical Extension: Experiential Objectivity and Simple, Strong and Right (SSR) Structures
When traditional objectivity is moved inside experiential structures, and is owned by the individual who is participating in the experience, then traditional objectivity is transformed into experiential objectivity. Experientially objective claims might appear to be the same as traditional objective claims, but the difference is that they tend to be owned, whereas traditional objective claims tend not to be owned. Rather, traditional objective claims tend to be asserted as true-beyond-experience. When objective claims are owned, then traditional reality becomes relativized. It no longer matters what one holds to be objectively true; it only matters how one holds what one holds to be objectively true.

If the structure within which one is participating is simple, strong and right, then the objective claim that constitutes the cognitive component of the experience is real. Whereas if the structure within which one is participating is complex, then the objective claim that constitutes the cognitive component of the experience is a distortion of reality.

Simple, defined negatively, means not complex. The extent to which a structure is simple is the extent to which it is not complex; the extent to which a structure is complex is the extent to which it is not simple. *Strong* refers to the capacity of the structure to prompt confirmation experiences, where confirmation experiences are simple, strong and right experiences that confirm the rightness of any given target (analyzed) experience. Strengthening SSR (simple, strong and right) structures through confirmation experiences constitutes the fundamental way beliefs are formed. *Right* refers to the intra-experiential consistency between all components of experience, both focal and peripheral, and is indicative of an identity. It does *not* refer to an accurate connection between experience and reality (this is traditional objective thinking).

When an experiential structure is simple, strong and right (SSR), one's identity consists of all the components that constitute the structure within which one is participating. One's identity, or who one is, cannot be ontologically detached from the environment within which one exists; it can only be intellectually detached or separated.

The realist intellectually detaches himself from his environment and allows that environment, whether it be natural, supernatural or a combination of both, to supersede him in importance. His environment is reality, and he understands himself to fit into that environment in some way.

The experientialist integrates himself with his environment and owns that integration. He is inextricably connected to his environment: this is represented by the inclusion of the environmental component in all experiential structures. Conceiving himself as separate from his environment is an aspect of experience, not an ontological condition for determining reality.

For instance, I experience this cup to be real (i.e. solid, constant). The reality of the cup is an aspect of the experience within which I am participating. The experience could be represented thus:

Focal	Peripheral
C: a cup	oriented, object as solid, object as capable of being experienced by others as I experience it, object as existing even when I'm not looking at it, object as red, object as shaped a particular way, etc.

A: indifference
B: looking at cup
S: cup
E: room
"I": ownership

In this experience traditional reality comes inside experience and is represented by "object as solid", "object as capable of being experienced by others as I experience it," and "object as existing even when I'm not looking at it." I need not experience the object as I do; I might experience it as appearing solid but is not (e.g. hallucination,

47

electrically-induced phenomenon, etc.), and the object need not be how I experience it to be (but this is irrelevant or inconsequential). The fact is, my experience is constituted by these components, and I am limited to that experience.

If a later experience were to contradict this experience, then I would experience a type of disorientation. Who I am (what I believe to be true and own) is shaken. How severe the disorientation is depends upon, at least in part, how strong and how many experiences there are within the totality of experiences that constitute me and my reality that serve to determine my identity at the time. Some disorientations are slight (e.g. the crooked stick in water example), but some could be very severe (e.g. realizing spouse has been cheating for years, losing religious faith, coming to believe that the earth is round and not flat, realizing that chicken soup does not cure cancer, etc.)

Contradictory experiences do not mean that experience has been transcended; it only means that what we once believed to be so is not what we now believe to be so. Our new belief will often time contain a negation of our old belief, but the negation will be a part of the experiential structure. It does not remove us from experience; it only negates previous content and replaces that content with new content.

Probing Question: Does being consigned to the confines of the structure of experience force us to accept some form of relativism?

Theoretical Extension: The Relativity Problem
Relativism only makes sense when pitted against traditional objectivism. If we assume that there's only one world and that someone can actually understand that world as it is whereas others either cannot or will not, then what one claims to be so either is so or is not so. Once the dualistic assumption of being:not being or existing:not existing is held to be the ontological status of all reality, then arguments for relativism have some merit. People's experience tends to be objective from their own point of view. When they come into contact with people who believe differently from them, then they tend to defend their beliefs. Their beliefs are based on their own experience, and it's difficult to reject the validity of that experience. Experientially, such a rejection is tantamount to an abdication of oneself. Therefore, when traditional objective claims conflict, we

tend to defend our own experience and reject that of others, or we will assert the validity of each of our claims and agree to disagree, i.e. we will take a relative stand in relation to the issue.

But if experience is equal to reality, then what we claim to be so (e.g. the cognitive content of experience) is not reflective of reality as it is, no matter how many times we can repeat that experience. It is simply what we believe to be so. We might alter those beliefs in the wake of contradictory experience, but such contradictions do not remove us from experience and place us into a reality that is beyond experience.

If this is so, then traditional objectivism is erased and so too is traditional relativism. When the dualistic assumption is replaced by the "monistic" assumption of experience equaling reality (i.e. components of consciousness as owned), then relativism moves from outside experience to inside experience just as objectivism does. Cognitive contents as contents are objective (real, independent of the person's self-assessments and others' assessments of the person), but as beliefs that refer to supposed realities that exist beyond immediate experience, they are relative. People's beliefs can conflict and each person's belief could be correct, but now "correct" refers to consistency within the experiential structure and between structures and not to a mental matching with a traditional objective state of affairs. Correct beliefs are now those that are simple, strong and right. Incorrect (or better, distorted) beliefs are those that admit of complexity.

When we assume that experience is non-transcendable, then we transfer our ontological investigations to experiential structures rather than to traditional objective reality. What are real are the contents and processes of experience. Realities become alterable by virtue of changing experiences in relation to the environment and when people who participate in their own experiential structures come into contact with each other.

Theoretical Extension: Compound Structures

A compound structure consists of at least two conflicting SSR experiential structures. When one belief comes into contact with a conflicting belief, whether generated from within the individual or between individuals, then a compound structure might occur.

When we learn something new, and that which we learn is not in conflict with what we already know and believe, then the learning might be considered to be SSR. (But this will be dependent upon the nature of the experience being taught.) For instance, if we learn that eating a particular type of mushroom might make us sick, and this information is imparted to us within an SSR structure, then our learning is SSR. We can experience this ourselves or we can trust those who are communicating this information to us; we trust ourselves in our appraisal of the nature of the experiential structures within which those who communicated the information participated, as well as we can know this.

But when a belief opposes our own, then we are in position to assess the validity of the opposing belief and to assess the validity of our own belief. We might find ourselves in conflict. The history of science if full of examples whereby one belief came in contact with an opposing belief, and a period on conflict ensued, until one belief replaced the other, or one belief sustained its adherents in the face of a challenge, or one belief got modified due to contact with the opposing belief, or both beliefs were maintained and kept in tension with each other, etc.

For example, a young woman might believe that abortion is wrong in all instances. She understands it as a type of violence perpetrated upon an innocent being. She sees it from the baby's point of view and overlooks it from the mother's point of view. She is able to empathize with the baby but not the mother, or she never even considers empathizing with the mother. And let's say that the experience within which she participates is SSR (consistent). If the belief is a part of an SSR structure, then the belief is real and needs to be accepted as real by others, even if they disagree with it.

Let's say that the young woman gets raped and becomes pregnant because of it. She undergoes a number of experiences whereby she feels unjustly victimized, undeserving of her situation, and resentful, and she entertains the idea that an abortion might be the right thing for her to do in this situation. She believes her resentment will be transferred to the unwanted baby if birthed and that it is already being transferred to the unborn baby. She is pained by the trauma of the rape on a daily basis and wants to rid herself of the pain. But these experiences conflict with her experiences of believing that abortion is wrong in all instances. She still can empathize with the baby and

50

experience anguish in relation to the idea of aborting an innocent being. At this point she is in conflict. Her experiential structure is compound; it consists of two SSR structures. One structure indicates that abortion is wrong in all cases, the other that abortion might be right in rape situations. These structures might look like this:

C: abortion is wrong in all instances	abortion might be right when raped
A: confidence	confidence, doubt
B: -	-
S: -	-
E: -	-
"I": ownership	
SSR	SSR

In these two experiential structures, the contents of the cognitive components are in conflict. Underlying the conflict is the traditional objective notion or the realistic assumption that there is but one reality and to hold two conflicting points of view in relation to that one reality creates a tension that ranges from slight and tolerable to great and intolerable. This traditional objective notion exists within and between experiential structures. It is a part of the cognitive periphery of consciousness. It can be represented thus:

Focal	Peripheral
C: Abortion is wrong in all instances	orientated, etc., belief as objective
A: confidence	
B: -	
S: -	
E: -	
"I": ownership	

In this experience, the belief as objective exists within the peripheral aspect of the cognitive component of experience. After all, it need not be the case that she experiences her belief to be objective; she might very well experience it to be relative, e.g. "It's just my belief; you can believe what you want." In that case, belief as relative would constitute a part of the peripheral aspect of the cognitive component of the experience.

But after she is raped, a new experiential structure comes into being:

Focal	Peripheral
C: Abortion might be right when raped	orientation, etc., I might be wrong about abortion being wrong in all cases
A: confidence/doubt	
B: -	
S: -	
E: -	
"I": ownership	
SSR	

In this experiential structure the cognitive content opposes the cognitive content of the original structure. It is conceivable that simply because two cognitive contents contradict each other it doesn't mean that there must be a felt conflict, but such a lack of felt conflict would be indicative more of a machine than a human being. Machines can simulate "cognitive contents" without attaching a feeling to them, but human beings seem to be incapable of doing so. An affective component always accompanies a cognitive one, even if the affective component gets buried under supposed cognitive control.

The second experience consists of a focal affective component content of "confidence/doubt." This means that the young woman possesses some degree of confidence in relation to her belief, as represented by "abortion....be right when raped" and some degree of doubt represented by "...might...." Also, peripherally, she is entertaining the possibility that her previous belief might be wrong, or partially wrong.

The new burgeoning belief carries with it its own strength. Its strength is opposed to the strength of her original belief as being experienced currently. In other words, the strength of her original belief experienced prior to the rape has probably been diminished after the rape. She is less likely to be attracted to people and situations that might support her original belief and more attracted to people and situations that might support her new, burgeoning belief. Whether she is more attracted one way or the other is an ontological question: strength is an objective aspect of experiential structures, i.e. it exists as it does whether or not one or anyone else realizes and confirms it. Strength is defined as prompting confirmation experiences. If the original experiential structure is stronger than the new experiential structure, then she will tend to be attracted to those people and situations that will further strengthen the original structure and diminish the strength of the new structure. But if the new structure is stronger than the original structure, then she will tend to be attracted to those people and situations that confirm the rightness of the new structure.

Let's say in this case, the young woman is more attracted to those people and situations that confirm the rightness of her new structure. She seeks out friends who might agree with her new belief; she seeks out literature on abortion; she seeks out people to talk to at abortion clinics, etc. All of these people and situations pose challenges to her original belief as well as confirmation of her new belief. The two sets of conflicting experiences constitute compound experiential structures. None of the structures can be transcended; the young woman is in the midst of an ontological, moral, and identity alteration. How the situation will resolve itself depends upon the ontological components that constitute the experiential structures within which she participates and her ability to realize those components into the future. In other words, it depends on how well she knows herself, is herself, and is prepared to deal with the consequences of being herself.

For instance, if our young woman is attracted to those people and situations that will serve to confirm the rightness of her new experiential structure, then she will come to affirm that abortion is right when raped and wrong in all other instances. Her reality will have changed; her beliefs will have changed; she will have changed.

But change might not occur only in this way. Change occurs in many different ways.

Theoretical Extension: Complex Structures

Using our example above, let's say that the young woman, though consistently believing that abortion might be right when raped, informs her parents of her decision. She knows that her parents are against abortion, but she doesn't know how strongly they'd react to her growing new belief. Her parents "hit the ceiling," rejecting the idea that she get an abortion, even under these circumstances, and communicating to her in some fashion that she is bad, wrong, or evil for even considering it. They might even threaten to disown her. This rejection is not simply a disagreement in regard to her impending behavior but a rejection of her, i.e. of who she is inasmuch as who she is coincides with her new belief.

Sometimes, if the rejection is intimidating enough, it need only register once in a person to create the circumstances for complex-ification. More often it will take repeated rejections in order for the rejected person to create a false self that will align with the values and beliefs of the person or people rejecting her. Depending upon the psycho-emotional needs of the person being rejected, such rejections could result in the creation of a false self.

If the young woman is not psycho-emotionally dependent upon her parents for her own identity, she might well assertively confront her parents after they reject her by affirming the legitimacy of her new belief and being prepared to suffer the consequences of such an assertion. She might even be prepared to be disowned by them. Such an assertive confrontation would reflect consistency within and between the experiential structures within which she participates. Her new identity, as indicated by her new belief, will persist and, probably, become stronger, even without her parents' support.

But often times such assertive confrontations, if engaged in at all, will pale next to the rejection suffered at the hands of significant others. Repeated rejection by significant others tends to prompt remedial efforts on the part of the rejected person to stem the tide of rejection and secure acceptance. But this is done at a price. The person being rejected will deny some aspect of herself and create a new self that is more acceptable to those doing the rejecting. In these situations the real self of the individual will be replaced by a false self. The process might be represented thus:

C: I think I want to get an abortion	I'm bad?	I'm bad	I'll keep the baby
A: confidence/doubt	confusion	self-rejection	false confidence
B: talking	reflecting	looking down	false talking
S: parents	parents	environ	parents
E: room	room	room	room
"I": ownership	ownership		

In this series of experiences, though simplified, the young woman initially tells her parents that she wants to get an abortion. She probably will say this with some confidence but also with some doubt; she's not firm on this course of action. At this point (not represented but alluded to), her parents reject her ("hit the ceiling"). She is confused or disoriented in response to her parents' rejection. As far as she's concerned, her growing belief is good, right and real for her (SSR). She is surprised by her parents' response. She will then probably reconsider the legitimacy of her new belief. She is, in effect, thrown back on herself and must either confirm in some manner or disconfirm in some manner this new belief. If she is psycho-emotionally dependent upon her parents, then she will tend toward a disconfirmation of her new belief. But in order to accomplish a disconfirmation of an SSR structure, she will have somehow to replace that structure (i.e. cover it over) with another structure. The new structure will tend to align with the wishes, values, and demands of the parents. The young woman will, in effect, reject the legitimacy of her real self (indicated by her new belief) and create a false self that will align with her parents' values (indicated by her having the baby).

The false self that is created could range in coverage from shallow to deep. The shallow false self is represented by the conscious lie, the willful misrepresentation, or the known hypocrisy. This individual will do what others want her to do even though she knows she doesn't want to do it. She will tend to act so as to gain extrinsic rewards, e.g. emotional acceptance, money, power, approval, success, cooperation, etc., but this is done at the expense of self-acceptance and self-affirmation. One "puts on a face" to those from whom one seeks approval, acceptance, cooperation, and affirmation. But each act of misrepresentation or hypocrisy requires an extrinsic confirmation in order for the individual to feel 'good about herself.' In our example, the young woman gains these confir- mations from her parents when her parents stop condemning her and instead supply her with 'acceptance'. When she is acting in their good graces, she feels accepted and affirmed. But it is the false self that is accepted and affirmed. When this affirmation is repeated, she becomes more comfortable with her self-rejection and her false self is strengthened and honed. She is on track to replacing her real self with her false self through denying the legitimacy of her real self and affirming the 'legitimacy' of her false self. She is engaged in a complex structure, and this complex structure is, as are all complex structures, distortions of reality.

Complex structures are usually the result of someone's beliefs, wishes, wills and/or values being imposed upon an individual intentionally or unintentionally through the rejection of the rightness of the individual's experiential structure, the eventual rejection of the rightness of that structure by the individual himself, and the replacement (covering over) of the real self structure (SSR exper- ience) by a false self structure (complex experience). This imposition can occur in at least three ways: 1) through some form of emotional or psychological abuse, 2) through some form of physical abuse or physical intimidation, and 3) through some form of sexual abuse.

In our example above, the parents use a form of emotional or psychological abuse to prompt the young woman to change her mind in relation to her intended abortion, her thinking, and her feelings, i.e. to change her self.

Such intentions might be fully conscious but they usually are not. Usually they are experienced to be simple reflections of how the person feels about a given situation. The young woman's parents might have no conscious (focal) wish to change her mind, just as they might have no conscious (focal) wish to relieve the pain they feel in relation to her new, burgeoning belief and impending action. These intentions are relegated to the periphery of consciousness. They might be instantiated when challenges to identity occur, especially challenges to identities constituted by false self constructions. But they do tend consciously (focally) to reject, through thought, feeling and action, the very idea of her considering an abortion and the very rightness of the experience within which she participates. So whether the parents realize it or not, they are rejecting *her* and not simply her behavior.

Theoretical Extension: Dominant:Submissive Relationships

The essence of dominant:submissive relationships, argued from the experiential point of view, is the formation of complex structures. When the parents in the example above reject the rightness (experiential legitimacy or identity) of their daughter through their repeated condemnations of her and her considered future behavior, they provide the circumstances for the creation of a complex structure. The condemnation is experienced as a type of force, emotional in this instance, exerted upon the young woman either intentionally or unintentionally. Its conscious or unconscious goal is to cause the young woman to align her beliefs, values, and behavior with those of her parents. When successful, the parents establish domination over their daughter. Their daughter rejects the rightness of the very structure she participates in and, hence, denies a real aspect of herself. She comes to accept a view of herself that is alien to her own experience, but because of her dependence upon her parents (i.e. her need to be accepted by them), she allows herself to reject that aspect of herself and replaces it (covers it over) with an experiential construction that is acceptable to her parents.

This experiential construction, or false self, will likely align with her personality and dispositions enough so as to be sustainable over time. For instance, if the young woman's personality is passive and leans toward introversion, she might forgo the abortion, have and raise the baby, and cover up her resentment, only to experience

56

physical problems (e.g. colitis, ulcers, and other bowel-related diseases), whereas if more active and extroverted, she might resort to drinking excessively and engaging in rebellious types of behavior in order to deal with her internal conflict.

However the young woman deals with her internal conflict will constitute her false self. The rejection of her real self creates a hole in her identity. This hole is filled by a constructed self. Self-abdication has occurred in this area of her identity, and this self-abdication disposes her to submissiveness toward her parents. It allows her parents to dominate her and establishes a distorted tendency for her to submit to that domination. It creates the fundamental basis for a dominant:submissive relationship.

Proposition 29: The basic male can force the basic female to do his will when he is able to create complex structures within which the basic female participates.

Proposition 30: The basic female will tend to submit to the will of the basic male when the basic male is able to create complex structures within which the basic female participates.

Proposition 31: The basic female will create complex structures within which she participates when she rejects the validity of the SSR structures within which she participates and forms a false self that aligns with the wishes, will, and values of the basic male.

Proposition 32: The basic male will create a dominant:submissive relationship with the basic female through the use of force; this force will tend to be exerted in the forms of physical, emotional and sexual abuse.

Probing Question: Why does the basic male engage in force when his natural disposition toward the basic female is one of cooperation?

Probing Question: Why doesn't the basic female engage in force in relation to the basic male?

Theoretical Extension: An Egoistic Response

In addressing the second probing question first, we will argue that the basic male is biologically stronger than the basic female and this biological strength might lend itself to force when wills collide. It is easier for males to dominate females than the reverse because males tend to be physically stronger than females and can therefore abuse and intimidate them into submission.

The basic female can, though, force males into submission when those males are young and relatively weak. Such force can create complex structures with long-lasting distortive repercussions.

In addressing the first probing question, an egoist might argue that the male is not primarily disposed toward cooperation but rather toward self-satisfaction. The male will tend to force a female into submission if it serves his interests to do so. If, for instance, basic male does not want to perform a certain survival task and yet knows that the task needs to be performed, then he might be disposed toward forcing the female to do it. Since he tends to be physically more powerful than the female, he could use physical force or the threat of it to accomplish his goal.

But this form of self-satisfaction is gained at the price of the self-satisfaction of basic female. The female must sublimate her own satisfaction to that of the male. The long-term ramifications could work against the expected consequences on the part of the male. The male might expect cooperation from the female, even when the female is forced to do the will of the male, but when the female retaliates in order to restore her own satisfaction level, she will circumvent the male's expectations and he will learn that such force is counter-productive to him. He will learn that it is better for him to cooperate with her than to force her to do his will.

This argument seems to have some merit if the basic female and the basic male are equally capable of warding off an attempted imposition of will by the other. But if we accept that the male is physically more powerful than the female, then the female is not as capable of warding off physical force as is the male. She is vulnerable to the physical force that the male is capable of employing.

When the male learns that he can attain satisfaction in the form of forced 'cooperation' from the female, he does so only by distorting his own identity and the identity of the female. Since the female has not freely consented to the method of determining jobs employed by the male (i.e. male-determined or male-dominated), which would only minimally reduce her satisfaction level by agreeing to do her share of the unwanted task, she distorts her satisfaction by 'agreeing' to do the will of the male. Her satisfaction becomes disowned and she is virtually at the disposal of the male; it depends upon the male's acceptance.

Likewise, when the male learns that he can attain satisfaction in the form of forced 'cooperation' from the female, he distorts his own natural satisfaction (i.e. that obtained through cooperation and free agreement) by replacing it with a satisfaction dependent upon forced 'cooperation'. When satisfaction in the egoistic theory is able to be divided into types (e.g. real and distorted), where one form of satisfaction (i.e. real) is preferable to another (i.e. distorted), then egoism is consistent with experientialism. Real satisfaction will be preferred over distorted satisfaction, and the male will prefer freely agreed upon cooperation over forced 'cooperation'.

Theoretical Extension: An Experiential Notion of Human Identity (excerpted from *Emotional Investment: Transforming Psychotherapeutic Assumptions***)**

Experientialism will argue that the basic male will tend toward cooperation with the basic female when his identity is interdependent with hers. The evolutionary theory's basic family unit is the pair bond formed between the male and the female, but evolutionary theory has tended to disregard love and to overemphasize lust in its concept of "pair bond." For the evolutionist, a pair bond is simply a male and a female that have sex with each other. The pair might stay together for varying lengths of time, but this staying together is more the result of genetic determination than anything that might be called love. So in order to address why the male will tend toward cooperation with the female, we must develop a notion of human identity that can shed new light on this issue.

When Descartes moved the locus for determining reality from God's heaven, the Bible, and the clergy to the human mind, he set the stage for Kant and the naturalization of the self. In Descartes' system, the self lay between the physical world of objects and the spiritual world of God, as it did for Augustine and Aquinas. But in Kant's hermetically sealed rationalism, he argued away the objective existence of nature and forced a division of the rationalist world into the transcendental ego (self) and everything else mental. The physical world as-it-is was unreachable; only our version of the physical world was attainable. But Kant was not primarily a relativist. He objectified the reality of reason, the categories of mind (e.g. space, time, causation, etc.), and other things mental. For Kant, the structure of mind was objective reality.

So within Kant's rationalism, when we look at a physical object in the environment, we see a particular object, as opposed to other objects, and/or as opposed to the background or environment within which the object is located, but this object is an object not because it possesses qualities of object-ness outside of our mind, but rather because our mind disposes us to experience the object as an object. For instance, if we look at an object (e.g. a cup) on another object (e.g. a desk) in a room, we know that the object is an object, separate from other objects like the desk, because object-ness exists in the mind. We could have looked at the cup and understood it as just a part of the desk which projected out and had a different color and texture, etc. In other words, the cup would not be an object in itself but part of an object. The same could be said about the desk and the floor it rests upon.

The fact that human beings can see objects as objects is, for Kant, the result of innate categories of mind. So in Kant's rationalistic system, if we are to study reality, we need to study the structure of our own minds and see how our minds condition all that we come into contact with, even our own bodies. But how do we study the structure of our own minds? What constitutes the "we" in that question?

In order to study the structure of the mind and its effects upon the world around us, Kant had to utilize the notion of a transcendental ego. The transcendental ego is that which studies the structure of the mind and its effect on the environment. The transcendental ego is at once in the mind and apart from it. It is at once similar to and dissimilar from the rest of the mind. And since the categories of mind were, for Kant, objective realities, then it was natural for him to think that the transcendental ego was also an objective reality (Kant, 1956).

Kant and the medieval thinkers had one thing in common: their idea of the self was primarily a static one. Though the Catholic Church established the age of reason to be about seven years, and hence, allotted some thought to developmental ideas, the self or soul was something given to us whole by God. We could put stains on our souls when we sinned, but that was the only way the soul was subject to change. Kant eliminated the changeability of the soul or self (transcendental ego) altogether. For Kant, it was like we human beings were born adults. He was not very concerned about development.

It was Hegel who introduced the notion of change into onto-logical constructions. This change in philosophy paralleled a growing recognition in the young sciences of the importance of the scientific method. Science recognized that the physical world outside of the human mind, which included the human body, needed to be understood as well as possible on its own terms, i.e. as it really is and not just as we understand it to be. But at the same time, science realized that scientists were people, subject to human limitations, and, hence, had to understand this world through the mind. Since the mind can distort the physical world, it was important to keep grounding statements, theories, and laws about physical reality *in* physical reality. In order to keep our biases and distortions to a minimum, scientists had to support their claims with empirical evidence. The more evidence there was, the stronger the claim.

But this method of determining reality admitted of a continuous process of grounding and re-grounding understanding in the empirical world. Not only were people set up by Descartes and Kant to be the ultimate determiners of reality, but now with Hegel the history of people was introduced into ontological determinations. What people determine to be real at one time might not align with what they determine to be real at a later time. Change is inherent within the scientific method. And change is inherent within Hegel's dialectical ontological system (Hegel, 1977).

Hegel accepted Kant's rationalism, admitting that the mind con-ditions everything it comes into contact with, but he rejected Kant's hermetically sealed version of rationalism. Hegel accepted science's empirical leanings, along with its underlying realism, but he rejected its hermetically sealed version of it, i.e. materialism. For Hegel (at least one aspect of Hegel), reality was determined by the interaction between the human mind and the physical world. The mind acted upon the environment as it understood it to be, and the environment acted upon the human mind as it did. If human understanding of the environment did not match the environment's action upon the mind, then the mind either had to re-organize itself in relation to the environment or find a way to alter the environment to fit its understanding of it. When the mind re-organized itself, it changed. When it changed, so too did our understanding of the environment.

Where Hegel parted with science was in his contention that this dynamic interplay between mind and physical world was transpiring within a grander objective idealism. Hegel invited a type of super-naturalism back into his naturalistic accounting of reality by arguing that the dialectic between mind and body, the mental and the physical, the many and the one, took place within an objective ideality of Spirit. Spirit was the all-embracing reality that was evolving through the dialectic between mind and body. So even though Hegel rejected Kant's hermetically sealed version of rationalism by allowing a real mind to interact with a real physical world, thus producing reality, he affirmed the mind or the mental as objective. The physical world was subject to or dependent upon the evolution of the mind.

Balancing Hegel's dialectical idealism was Marx's dialectical materialism. Marx accepted the dialectic between the mind and the body (matter), but he rejected the all-embracing ideality of Spirit. Instead, he located the objective, all-embracing aspect of reality in economic organization. It is how we organize ourselves econom-ically that gives rise to, and conditions, other ontology-producing activities, i.e. religion, science, government, etc. In grounding ultimate reality in economic organization, Marx aligned himself with the material realism that underlay the methods of science. In grounding ultimate reality in Spirit, Hegel aligned himself with the idealism that underlay religion. The battle between mind and body, the mental and the physical, the many and the one, continued.

For Hegel, the self is an active agent that interacts with and alters its environment, and that environment, in turn, interacts with and alters the self. The dialogue between self and environment takes place in time, and the self is continually changing itself into something new. The self is dynamic. For Marx, the self is the result of economic forces. The proletariat's self differs from the bourgeoisie's self in that the proletariat finds meaning for being within the determinations of the bourgeoisie. One class of people creates a self for another class of people by exploiting them economically. Marx agreed with Rousseau when he said that a master is as much a slave as the slave, because in order to retain his position of power the master must be ever vigilant in his control of the slave, thus giving the slave power over him. But ultimately, when push comes to shove, it is better to be a master than a slave. The freedom and the spoils are to the master's advantage (Marx, 2011).

Hegel's sense of self aligns quite well with traditional religion and Kantian rationalism, and Marx's sense of self aligns quite well with materialist empiricism. Again, we see the mind:matter or mind:body problem at work.

Husserl picks up where Hegel leaves off, and he goes Hegel one better by positing his theory of intentionality. When Husserl said that whenever we are conscious, we are necessarily conscious of something (i.e. his theory of intentionality), he linked consciousness with an object of consciousness (Husserl, 1931). The idea that consciousness is something totally separate from those things of which we are conscious was rejected. The empirical conception of reality that preceded Husserl's phenomenological conception argued that the world outside of the mind (and consciousness) existed on its own and that the world inside the mind (consciousness) likewise existed on its own. That is, the empiricist accepted both the rationalistic idea that we cannot get outside of our minds so as to understand the world around us as it is and, hence, are subject continuously to conditioning that outside world, and the realistic idea that there is, in fact, a world outside of our minds that has a nature of its own, whether we are in contact with it or not. But Husserl argued that the conception of two worlds (mind and matter, mental and physical, etc.) was faulty because we can never be simply conscious. Whenever we are conscious, we must be conscious of something, whether that something is mental (e.g. thoughts, feelings) or physical (e.g. tables, behavior). The theory of intentionality forces a necessary link between mind (consciousness) and mind (thoughts, feelings) or between mind (consciousness) and body or matter (physical environment, including our own body). If we understand Husserl's theory of intentionality to be the first step in integrating the mind with the environment (or the world outside of the mind), and the first step in defining consciousness as something more than a medium or state of being through which we know the world, then we might be in a better position to understand and appreciate the fundamental shift in thinking that an experientialist conception of reality and ethics might afford.

63

Let's take Husserl's lead and transform it. If we understand the mind's connection to the world outside of the mind to be represented linearly as: "I"–consciousness–object, then Husserl's theory of intentionality alters this fundamental representation to look like this: "I"–[consciousness–object]. Consciousness cannot be understood without an object of consciousness. If we flesh out the objects of consciousness imbedded within the theory of intentionality and identify all of the possible objects of consciousness, it seems that we will find:

Cognition: which include all thoughts, ideas, understandings,
images, memories, etc. that are in our minds
Affect: which include all emotions, feelings, and moods
Behavior: which include internal behaviors or physiology and
external behaviors or comportment
Sensation: which include sensations and sense data from all
senses
Environ: which includes all aspects of the physical world
outside of our minds, (including our own bodies)
with which we are in contact

When we are conscious, we are necessarily conscious of something. That something, I am arguing, consists of all of the components listed above. This contention can be verified experientially by answering the following question: When you are conscious, what are you conscious of? Possible answers are: objects in the environment (in motion or standing still), light, sounds, thoughts, feelings, ideas, relationships, moods, own body, looking, moving, people (in motion or standing still), odors, crying, etc. These objects can be categorized in this fashion:

Cognition:	Affect:	Behavior:	Sensation:	Environment:
thoughts	feelings	moving	light	objects
ideas	moods	looking	sounds	own body
relationships		crying	odors	people

When you reflect upon yourself, what exactly constitutes your reflection, or what is it that you are reflecting upon? Possible answers: face, body, blemishes, clothes, odors, aspirations, wanting, traits, aches, pains, happiness, irritable, rocking, blinking, being angry, bleeding, burping, tickles, possessions, slumping posture, hunger, crying, tapping fingers, scratching head, memories, goals, pressure in stomach, things to do, being conscious, boredom, clothes, itches, proximity to others, relation to room, interest, memories, etc. These objects of self-reflection can be categorized in this fashion:

Cognition:	Affect:	Behavior:	Sensation:	Environment:
aspirations	wanting	rocking	aches	face
traits	happiness	blinking	butterflies	body
memories	irritable	tapping	itches	blemishes
goals	boredom	scratching	hunger	proximity to

				others
things to do	hating	bleeding	hearing	relation to room
being conscious	interest	crying	pleasure in stomach	clothes

When Husserl's theory of intentionality is fleshed out, we can see that when we are conscious, we are conscious of components of consciousness, and when we are conscious of ourselves (self-reflection), we are also conscious of components of consciousness. The difference between consciousness and experience is the owning of components of consciousness. In experience, these are *my* thoughts, *my* feelings, *my* behaviors, *my* sensations, and *my* environment. The "I", or ownership, is inextricably intertwined in the structure of experience. And experience is ontological. The traditional triad: "I" – consciousness – object and Husserl's significant alteration of it into the dualistic "I" – [consciousness – object] is altered yet again into the "monistic" experiential structure. Experientially, not only does the object of consciousness collapse into consciousness itself, but so too does the "I". We cannot detach the ownership of components of experience from those components without destroying experience altogether.

In a non-reflective experience, we are not focally aware of ourselves, but we are peripherally aware of ourselves. For instance, when we are listening to a piece of music, we might be caught up in the music and not be aware of ourselves listening to it. The experience might look like this:

Cognition: solo violin
Affect: longing
Behavior: listening
Sensation: violin sound
Environ: violin sound in room
"I":   ownership

In this experience we own our knowledge of what instrument is making the sound we are listening to; we own the longing we feel in relation to the sound; we own the listening behavior in which we are engaged; we own the sound of the violin; and we own our location; yet we are not focally aware of ourselves owning any of these components. But we *can* become focally aware of ourselves in relation to all of them if experience shifts from non-reflective to self-reflective. For instance, an ache in the periphery of the sensation component of experience might become focal as it increases in intensity. Our focus during the non-reflective experience is on the violin sound in the room (i.e. the environmental component). When the ache in our foot (let's say) becomes focal, experience immediately shifts to:

C: my foot hurts
A: slight irritation
B: inclining head toward foot
S: pain in foot
E: foot in room
"I": ownership

In this self-reflective experience, the sensation component becomes the self-indicating component. It is that component that draws us to ourselves in relation to components of experience. Without a self-indicating component, we would not be aware of ourselves in relation to components of consciousness. A pain in our foot would not be experienced as a pain in *our* foot. We might be aware of the pain in our foot, but we would not be clearly aware of the pain or, possibly, even the foot being ours. This type of experience would look like this:

C: pain in foot
A: slight irritation
B: inclining head toward foot
S: pain in foot
E: foot in room
"I": ownership

In this experience, we recognize that there is a sensation that one might call pain and that the pain is in a foot, but we wouldn't be clearly aware that the foot and the pain are ours. It would be as if we were referring to our own foot and pain from a third person point of view. These types of experiences characterize forms of dissociative experiences and experiences of brain damaged people. In this instance, the sensation component is either not a self-indicating component of consciousness, though it is owned [by us] (if the ownership can be focalized), or it is a self-indicating component that is deficient in strength. For instance, if someone were to ask us if our foot hurts, we would be able to affirm that it does even though we wouldn't feel the pain as clearly, intimately and inextricably attached to us. We might display behavior that doesn't seem to match what we are saying, but it would match the way we are saying it. We might appear somewhat dazed and confused.

If experience shifts from non-reflective to self-reflective with a (strong) self-indicating component, then the ownership which existed in peripheral consciousness shifts to focal consciousness and becomes cognitivized, while also remaining in peripheral consciousness, and we are clearly and intimately aware of the pain as ours. The cognitive component of consciousness would consist of the self-indicating component, which is the sensation of pain in foot and a cognitivized "I" (i.e. my). We would simultaneously own this component of consciousness. The ownership is the "I", which is never removed from peripheral consciousness but "split" into peripheral ownership and the cognitivized "I". So when we are self-reflective, we also own the self-reflection. Or, to put it another way, the cognitive component consists of a cognitivized "I" and a self-reflective component, and that cognitive component is owned. A self-reflective experience minus a cognitivized "I" would be similar to the dissociative experience above. That is, without the cognitivized "I", the self-indicating component, though focal, possesses little strength. We can connect it to ourselves, but not very clearly or intimately. We are to some degree dissociated from it.

When the self-indicating component possesses a much greater strength then the cognitivized "I", then we are either hallucinating or engaged in a similar experience whereby the self-indicating component seems to take on environmental status.

For instance, a man who hears voices that aren't actually in the environment is engaged in an experience that would look like this:

	Real Self		False Self
C:	["stay away from me"]		"stay away from her"
A:	[defensiveness]		ambivalence
B:	[speaking forcefully]		unusual stare
S:	[her]		voice of person
E:	[her in room]		voice of person in room
"I":	[ownership]		

In this experience the real self consists of what the person would think, feel, do, and sense in that environment if he were not hallucinating. The real self experience is simple, strong and right, but because of a history of rejection and distortion of the real self, the person hallucinating will protect the real self from more rejection and distortion with the false self. The cognition "stay away from me" is the self-indicating component, but the "me" aspect of it (i.e. the cognitivized "I") is virtually gone. Instead of telling his mother (let's say) to stay away from him (because she is attacking the validity of his real self), he objectifies his own thought within the hallucination. He detaches or dissociates himself from his own thought and substitutes "her" for "me", which serves virtually to remove the cognitivized "I" from experience, leaving him with an over-powerful self-indicating component. The thought becomes 'real', out there, in the environment. The hallucination, in effect, protects his real self from annihilation by over-strengthening the self-indicating component (the thought itself) while virtually eliminating the cognitivized "I".

Proposition 33: The self is ontologically attached to traditional objective reality, transforming traditional objectivity into experiential objectivity.

Most of the time we experience traditional objective reality to be something independent of us and having a nature of its own. For instance, we look at a tree and experience it as something apart from us, solid, and constant (i.e. exists without our sensing it). But simply because we experience it to be so does not mean that it is so. What it might be beyond our experience is irrelevant because we cannot get beyond our experience to determine this. Therefore, the objectivity of the tree is an aspect of experience and not a characteristic of the object independent of the experience within which we participate. No matter how many times we verify the qualities of the tree, and strengthen our belief that the tree is, in fact, the way we sense it to be, we cannot remove ourselves from the experiences within which these verifications exist.

Empirical verifications are types of experiences and not independent means of verifying a reality that is independent of us. We might all experience a tree as possessing certain qualities and agree with each other that the tree does, in fact, possess those qualities, but there is always a chance of someone coming along who experiences it differently.

Using our color-blind/color-seeing example, a color-seeing person might experience the leaves of the tree to be green, whereas a color-blind person might experience them to be a shade of gray. Both experiences are constituted by traditional objective qualities, but one of those qualities is in conflict, i.e. color. How is the conflict to be resolved?

Science offers a resolution or explanation, stating that the color-blind person's anatomy is differently constituted from the color-seeing person's. The color-blind person doesn't possess the cones in the eye necessary to see certain colors, or the cones they do possess don't function properly.

Experientially, if this accounting were merely a description of what cones in the eye are and how they function as determined by experience, then there is no problem with the accounting, as long as the accounting is owned. But when the accounting takes on a value by asserting or assuming that the anatomical situation of the color-blind person is in some sense wrong, deficient, or inaccurate, then science moves beyond describing and into valuing. The assumption here is that the color-seeing person's anatomical situation (i.e. more cones, accurately functioning cones, etc.) is superior to that of the color-blind person's.

But if most people's anatomical situations were that of the color-blind person's, then the reverse might well occur: color-blind people would assume that their anatomical situation is more accurate than that of color-seeing people, and then color-seeing people would have to adjust to a color-blind world, just as color-blind people have to adjust to a color-seeing world today. And, in all likelihood, in this reversed world, color-seeing people would be understood as possessing a disorder of some sort and wouldn't be referred to as color-seeing (as if this is a good thing) and color-blind people wouldn't be referred to as color-blind (as if this is a bad thing). The names would change to reflect the value assumed.

Science's explanation of why some people see the same thing but different colors has experiential merit when it simply describes the existence and function of cones in the eye. Such experiences can be replicated; others can experience similar things; such descriptions are more easily experientially verified by others. But when science assumes a value difference between the two experiences, then it more easily detaches itself from ownership of the contents of the experiential structures within which scientists participate; it more easily denies or rejects the legitimacy of one group of people whose experiential contents differ from the norm while asserting the legitimacy of those constituting the norm; and it more easily views the one group as out of contact with reality (color-blindness) and the other group as in touch with reality (color-seeing). This value difference is a way to raise one group's experience above another group's experience. This makes life easier for the majority group while making it more difficult for the minority group. Both groups experience color objectively, i.e. as existing independently of their own personal experience. Both groups cannot deny their own experience of the color they see. But one group is able to determine for itself that its experience is somehow more legitimate than the other group's experience. And this group might use science to back its claim. But simply describing what cones are and how they function does little or nothing to support the claim that color-seeing is better than color-blind. It merely says that this is how these things work. It is the value that color-seeing is somehow superior to color-blind that fuels the scientist with a false notion of superiority. He experiences *his* experience to be more important, more real, and more objective than his color-blind counterpart and if he can convince his counterpart that she is somehow inferior or out of touch with reality, then his manipulations of the environment as he senses it will be easier for him to accomplish than they would be if he had to take into consideration and work to include the experience of color-blind people.

Also, the scientist fails to realize that the social world already designed according to color-seeing people creates a basis from which to judge (or actually misjudge) color-blind people. Some scientists (and many others) will argue that it is the color-blind people who need to change or adjust to the color-seeing people's world not only because of the supposed ontological reason that the color-seeing person's experience captures or reflects the objective situation but also that if they don't adjust accordingly they will experience a good deal of unnecessary hardship in life.

From the experiential point of view, the ontological reason given by science is patently false, and the practical reason given might be true but not because it is founded on a fact of nature; it is true because most people are color-seeing and have had and continue to have the social and economic power to impose their experience upon color-blind people.

Since neither the color-blind nor the color-seeing person can remove themselves from the experiential structures within which they participate, and since a scientific explanation of color-blindness and color-seeingness contains an assumed, though seemingly unrecognized, value, science's argument that one experience (i.e. color-seeing) is in touch with reality (the realistic assumption) and another experience (i.e. color-blind) is not is actually a meta-experiential construct. It distorts reality by denying or rejecting the ontological legitimacy of the experience within which the color-blind person participates. Inasmuch as the scientist is able to get the color-blind people to experience themselves as inferior to the color-seeing people and to cloak the assumed superiority inherent in his explanation in scientific terminology, scientists (and many others) are morally guilty of oppressing color-blind people. They dominate color-blind people by making them feel inferior and use science to strengthen their domination. And to the extent that color-blind people accept or affirm the superiority of color-seeing people and deny the ontological legitimacy of the experience within which they participate they assume the role of the submissive. Color-seeing people and color-blind people engage in a dominant:submissive dance.

When objectivity is understood as an integral part of experience, where experience necessarily includes the environment, then the experience within which a color-seeing person participates is just as real as the experience within which the color-blind person participates. The difference lies in their respective sensory contents. How they arrange their social and economic situation depends upon the methods they determine in relation to each other. These methods have usually involved traditional notions of objectivity and the subsequent oppression that often derives from those notions, but they need not do so. This work purports to develop, at least in a rudimentary way, methods by which society can organize itself that will dispense with oppressive, traditionally objective methods and replace them with more equitable, experientially objective methods.

Proposition 34: The basic male can impose his will upon the basic female and sustain that imposition by intentionally or unintentionally altering or distorting her identity.

Proposition 35: When the basic male distorts the identity of the basic female, he automatically alters or distorts his own identity.

Proposition 36: Identities can be altered or distorted through the creation of complex structures which are constituted by a real self, a process of self-rejection, and a false self.

Theoretical Extension: Identity and Male:Female Domination
Since males and females are alike in that each naturally desires to survive and sustain or improve their well-being, identity distortion is not something naturally chosen. It automatically reduces the max-imum amount of happiness or satisfaction achievable because the

71

happiness achieved through a distorted identity is always less in quality than that achieved through a healthy, integrated identity.

Even though the female might benefit from the protection and subsistence provided by the male, she does so at the expense of relinquishing the happiness achievable through cooperative means. She "allows" herself to be dominated by the male who forces her to comply with his demands through some form of physical, emotional, and/or sexual abuse. The abuse serves to distort her identity. The distortion creates a dominant:submissive relationship, at least in regard to that aspect of her identity being distorted.

For instance, if the male didn't want to perform a certain job required for survival or his sustained or improved well-being, he might force the female through physical abuse and subsequent intimidation to do the job. He might literally beat the female into submission. The experiential dynamics are represented as a complex structure: self-acceptance (affirmation of SSR structure), questioning of self-acceptance, repeated abuse, eventual rejection of self-acceptance, creation of a false self that accords with the wishes, will or demands of the abuser.

Once the male learns that the abuse is effective in gaining the 'cooperation' of the female without his ever having to sacrifice any happiness or undergo any pain, the egoistic door is open for continued abuse. But satisfaction alone doesn't seem adequately to account for the continued abuse and lack of assertiveness on the part of the female. We must incorporate a theory of identity which includes complex structures and meta-experiential constructs in order to better explain a pattern of continued abuse.

Persistent Probing Question: What is the original motive for the male to physically abuse the female?

Persistent Probing Question: Why should the male impose his will upon the female when his natural method of interaction would be to seek out free cooperation (e.g. negotiation) with her?

Theoretical Response: Traditional Objectivism and Impositions of Will

Human beings don't naturally want to impose their wills upon each other so as to get their way, but they do naturally want to get their way. When the imposition of will serves to accomplish the natural wish to get one's way, then the groundwork is set for distorting identities.

To get one's way is inextricably tied to one's identity. One's identity is intimately tied to traditional objectivity. We, as individuals, tend to believe that our experience is reflective of reality as it is, and if others oppose us, then we tend to judge them as somehow deficient. We experience our own experience to be the true experience, and, hence, contradictory experiences can't be true (the realist assumption). Hence, we tend to believe we have the right, even the obligation, to impose our wills upon others so that they might 'align with reality'. I'll refer to this collection of beliefs as *the realist seduction*.

If the male believes that his way of conceiving reality is reflective of reality as it is, and he has the physical capacity to impose that reality upon the female, and the female doesn't have the capacity to ward off such impositions, then the male is vulnerable to using physical force to get his way. Getting his way becomes not only a matter of increasing his perceived well-being and/or avoiding a decrease in his well-being but also a matter of being 'right'.

Being 'right' is based on traditional objective assumptions. It assumes that reality is one, that it is independent of experience, and that it is graspable by people (at least some people). When objectivity is not owned, and the capacity to impose one's will upon another is a given (e.g. physical force), then the groundwork for distortion is laid.

If the male can get the female to confirm his objective belief, which necessarily implies her deficiency if her belief conflicts with his, then the male can confirm his 'identity'.

But all of this is necessarily false or distorted. The male cannot disown his own experience (he can only believe that he can); when he imposes his own experience upon the female, he does so by force (i.e. some form of abuse); and he will tend to justify this force on traditional objective grounds, which experientially are nothing more than imaginative constructions or false selves.

When any human being believes that he has somehow captured reality as it is and is able to impose that reality upon others, and simultaneously, wards off opposing experienced realities that might conflict with his own, he is in position to create complex structures and, in turn, the meta-experiential constructs which make it possible for complex structures to be passed on from generation to generation.

Proposition 37: All people prefer doing what they want to do (though they might not do it). When their wanting to do something conflicts with another person's wanting to do something, and that conflict threatens to limit or negate their behavioral autonomy, then people will either act upon the other aggressively, assertively, or submissively.

Theoretical Extension: Responses to Domination

A child might engage in behavior that interests her, i.e. supplies her with immediate gratification, e.g. playing with a toy. Another child might want to play with that same toy and grab the toy away. The child imposed upon will either act aggressively (e.g. hit the other child, assertively (e.g. grab the toy back), or submissively (e.g. allow the other child to play with the toy). The first two responses are consistent with the child's defense of personal autonomy, whereas the third response is inconsistent but possibly consistent with one's sense of survival and personal well-being.

Some empirical studies show that children seem capable of assessing the person with whom they are interacting and of determining immediately that that person might be a threat to their well-being, if not to their survival. A considerable size difference might serve to do this. They might immediately fear the repercussions of their aggressing against the other, or even of asserting themselves in relation to the other if their past experience consists of others' intimidating them or forcing their compliance. Therefore, the personal circumstances figure into how one child might respond to another in the face of imposed will.

A child who is imposed upon might respond aggressively. Such acts tend to be expressions of dissatisfaction with the alteration of one's satisfaction level (i.e. decrease in well-being), or it might have to do with a rudimentary sense of justice infringement (i.e. involving a type of established ownership of the toy, stored for future satisfactions). Aggression in these instances tends to be the result of diminished satisfaction levels or threats of future diminished satisfaction. These acts tend to be reactive rather than proactive.

A small child will rarely force himself on the other simply to get his way. This type of behavior tends to be associated with a more sophisticated form of learned, manipulative behavior. It is the behavior of the bully, who seeks to intimidate the other in order to get his way. But the bully's behavior, as will be argued below, is expressive of a complex experiential structure, i.e. a distortion of reality and does not occur naturally or innately.

If the child in our example above takes the other child's toy and plays with it, and the other child responds by trying to grab the toy back (i.e. self-assertiveness), only to have the child who took the toy (who wants to increase his satisfaction level by playing with the toy and happens to be bigger in size than the other child) pushes the child away, and the child backs off or cries, we still do not have an example of a child naturally aggressing against another child. Rather, we have a child who seeks to increase his well-being by playing with a toy that is being played with by another child. There is no recognition of social infringement going on here, no recognition of transgressing fundamental ownership, no recognition, even, of one's part in diminishing the well-being of the other person; there is merely the wish to increase one's well-being by grabbing a toy and playing with it.

When the child cries, he expresses the displeasure he feels in having his source of satisfaction withdrawn from him. If he were already satiated from playing with the toy, or if the satisfaction gained from playing with the toy is negligible, then he might not cry at all; he might act indifferently toward the act. (Only when he is able to experience a sense of ownership in relation to the toy while he is satiated will he respond either by crying or with aggression.)

If the child responds by acting aggressively, then he could be understood to be acting in self-defense. He is defending the satisfaction he is feeling by playing with the toy; he wants the satisfaction to continue.

Nor is this type of aggressive act to be understood as a type of punishment. Punishment is an imposition of will upon someone who is judged by those doing the punishing to be at fault or guilty of some infraction. The child who takes the toy merely wants to increase his satisfaction or, in egoistic terms, maximize his self-interest. He doesn't yet know that his behavior will cause hardship to the other. When the other child cries, the child might, depending upon his level of development, feel bad for doing something that made the other cry.

He might give the toy back and forgo the increase in his well-being. The child's ability to empathize with the other child is felt as a type of pain, the pain of having harmed someone without an intention to harm. In returning the toy, the child not only eliminates his own pain but he also eliminates the pain of the other child and, hence, feels some satisfaction for doing something to reduce another's pain.

When the child acts assertively in relation to the child who has taken his toy by taking it back, prior to experiencing any sense of ownership, he is not only attempting to restore his level of satisfaction, but he is also asserting his own identity. He not only simply wants to play with the toy, but he wants to play with the toy in relation to the other child. One type of self-assertiveness is a type of self-defense. It is the confirmation of one's self in the face of intentional or unintentional domination by another.

But in some instances self-assertiveness can take on aggressive aspects. A child might push the other child away and take his toy back. So the child who has merely wanted to increase his satisfaction level by playing with the toy has his own satisfaction level diminished in two ways: 1) the toy is taken away from him and 2) he experiences the pain of being pushed (or hit, etc.) If this aggressive form of self-assertiveness is experienced by the other child as an indicator that his taking of the toy is unacceptable to the other child and will not be tolerated, then the child is in position to: 1) accept the legitimacy of the other child's playing with the toy and the illegitimacy of his taking the toy from him, or 2) impose his will upon the child or force him to surrender the toy.

The argument here is that the first impulse is a natural innate human response; the second is the product of complexification, i.e. distorted learning.

Proposition 38: No person naturally aggresses against another for the purpose of getting his or her own way.

Proposition 39: Acts of imposition of will are learned only after acts of self-defense and self-assertiveness have failed. These acts are distortions of nature. They are the product of complexification and subsequent meta-experiential construction.

Theoretical Consideration: Moyer's Classification of Aggression:
Moyer (1968) has proposed a classification of types of aggression:

1) Predatory aggression: evoked by hunger and an appropriate prey; argued that it is not really aggression (Carthy and Ebling, 1964) but an unavoidable means of getting food.

2) Competitive aggression: Also called inter-male aggression or agonistic aggression; a form of aggression exerted to achieve dominance in relation to resources and choice of females.

3) Defensive aggression: a type of fear-motivated or fear-induced aggression.

4) Irritative aggression: a form of aggression (anger) triggered by animate (e.g. people) or inanimate (e.g. weather) objects or situations.

5) Territorial aggression: an active defensive triggered by any intruder violating the boundaries of an area in which a subject, or a group of subjects, has already established living activities (Valzelli, 1981).

6) Maternal protective aggression: mothers protecting their off-spring.

7) Female social aggression: females aggressing against non-familial offspring, as evidenced in rabbits (Southern, 1948); Sears (1961) offers a "prosocial" form of female aggression, linking an unrestricted right to abortion as an unconscious form of female aggression.

8) Sex-related aggression: refers to aggression with a sexual component or sex with an aggressive component.

9) Instrumental aggression: a form of aggression used because it tends to produce positive experiences in the aggressor, i.e. it is a learned form of aggression.

We will focus on competitive or inter-male aggression because it is this form of aggression that is most subject to complexification. Valzelli argues that in humans, competitive aggression is an innate form of behavior clearly evidenced in the primate world, and also evidenced in the human world, though through euphemistic terms, e.g., "social status" has replaced "rank order"; "self-assertion" has replaced "dominance"; "assistant" has replaced "subordinate" and "immigrant" has replaced "social intruder." The fact that Valzeli argues that the first set of terms are euphemisms for the second set of

77

terms seems to indicate that he believes that the second set of terms
(i.e. rank order, dominance, subordinate, and social intruder) reflect
the actual, innate, biological, genetically-determined situation of
human society, whereas the second set of terms (i.e. social status,
self-assertion, assistant, and immigrant) reflect some sort of socially
more acceptable, watered-down version of these innate aggressive
tendencies.

Such a conception of aggression assumes that people, especially
males, are genetically predisposed to create rank orders in society and
to dominate females and other males alike. In addition to this, human
cooperation is actually equivalent to relatively stable dominant:
submissive relationships, and accepting new people into established
groups is actually "putting up with people who don't belong."

If we apply this theory to our basic social unit of the male-female
dyad, then the male should dominate the female through aggression
(dominance or "self-assertion") which creates a form of gender rank
order or "social status"), the female should submit to the male in
order to keep the peace (subordinate or "assist"), and anyone who
wants to join these two should be considered and responded to by the
pair as an invader.

These types of behaviors are supposed to be consistent with the
conception of human beings as primarily and innately competitive
and only secondarily, if at all, cooperative. If human beings are
cooperative, then that cooperation serves their basic competitiveness.
For instance, subordinates "cooperate" with superiors in order to
promote the survival and well-being of the group, a group that is
competing with other groups for resources that provide for the
group's survival and well-being.

The evolutionary perspective that accepts and promotes the idea
that human groups and the individuals that compose them are innately
competitive tends to promote a conception of human nature that pits
one human being against another (or one group against another) in its
struggle for survival and to increase its well-being. It subsumes
cooperative behavior under an innate competitive umbrella.

Such a conception of human nature finds ample empirical support
in current forms of human society. All scientists need to do is study
human interaction in most contemporary societies on earth, and they
will find empirical evidence to support their evolutionary hypotheses.
But this in no way means that such behavior is reflective of innate

human nature. If innate human nature has been altered through psychological, physical, and sexual abuse, i.e. through the alteration of human identities, then much of the observed behavior will be a reflection of those alterations. The "empirical evidence," at least in part, will actually be evidence of distorted human nature.

Theoretical Extension: Critique of Moyer's Classification of Aggression:

When the male attempts to impose his will upon the female, he does so not because he is innately or genetically determined to do so but because he wants her to do something or not do something. He experiences what she is doing or not doing as somehow diminishing his well-being or threatening his survival. Whether she is actually doing so is another matter; he need only experience her as doing so.

Also, when he succeeds in imposing his will upon her, she is not innately or genetically determined to acquiesce or submit to his behavior. At best, she is innately fearful of his outburst. If she judges that it is better for her to submit to his will, then she might well engage in submissive behavior. When submissive behavior works to relieve her of her fear and therefore promote her well-being or at least allow her not to diminish her well-being by engaging in a fight with him (an inferior form of well-being to be sure), she might come to 'accept her place in a dyadic hierarchy.'

Evolutionists seem to think that simply because a person behaves in a dominating or submissive manner that that behavior is innate. They don't seem to consider that the behavior they observe "in the field" is the result of a form of denial of what people actually experience. No person likes to be intimidated, threatened or forced to do anything. So if the male acts so as to intimidate, threaten, or force the female to do something or not do something, then the female's experiential structure will not simply be one of submission. That kind of experiential analysis would look like this:

C: 'threatening me'	C: I will do as he says
A: fear	A: submission
B: cringing $\longrightarrow$	B: submissive behavior
S: basic male	S: basic male
E: wherever	E: wherever
"I": ownership	"I": ownership

This experiential analysis is inaccurate on several counts. First, the cringing behavior in the first structure is not to be understood as a form of submissive behavior. If the male intimidates (or forces

79

through hitting, etc.) the female to act or not act, then the female will naturally tend to be fearful. She will fear for her life or safety. She is not submitting if she is cringing in an effort to protect herself.

Secondly, the movement from the first experiential structure to the second distorts the actual situation. After the female experiences fear in relation to the male outburst, she could respond in a number of ways, given her personality and her assessment of her situation. For instance, if she is an aggressive sort and she assesses the male as physically weaker or equal to herself, she might aggress in return. If she is an aggressive sort and she assesses the male as physically stronger than herself, she might back away and consider other ways to defend herself than immediate retaliation. If she is a passive sort and assesses the male as physically weaker or equal to her, then she might pause and see what the male will do next. If she is passive and assesses the male as stronger than herself, she might cry, as a baby might cry at the outburst of an angry parent.

These are just a few of the possible ways to render this situation. But any way one renders it, the immediate response by the female to a male's aggressive behavior is not one of submission. At most, it is one of fear. Submission is not the simple innate response that evolutionary theorists seem to think it is; it is a learned response. And in human societies, it is an example of distorted learning.

Likewise, the male does not aggress against the female because he wishes to dominate her. He aggresses because he wants to survive, relieve himself of pain, increase his well-being, etc. Using the list supplied to us by Moyer, the male might aggress because he fears the female, for whatever reason; this is an aggression out of self-defense. He also might aggress because he is irritated with what she is doing or not doing. In aggressing in response to her irritating behavior he is simultaneously relieving himself of pain and increasing his well-being. In aggressing in response to her not doing something, he expresses his frustration. In none of these situations does he express domination.

The human male does not seem to possess a natural or innate tendency to dominate anyone or anything. Rather, his aggression tends to be an expression of his self-defensiveness (promulgated from fear), irritation, protectiveness (territorial aggression), and jealousy (sex-related aggression). And in considering these forms of aggression further, we can reduce irritative, territorial, and sex-related aggression to forms of defensive aggression. Irritative aggression is engaged in usually to decrease pain and increase well-being. The basic male will get angry at the basic female when she acts in ways that impinge upon his well-being or refrains in acting in ways that would increase his well-being. The first response is more clearly a form of defensive behavior; the second response, though, lends itself to imposition and control. Being irritated because the female does not do something, if that something is not something already agreed upon through some form of negotiation between the two, seems to be natural and innate, but this tendency is not to be confused with a natural or innate expression of control. The male wants to control the female only when he learns that his innate wish to "get his way" is expressed in a way that actually works to serve that end. And the same is true for the female. She is innately determined to want to get her way so as to increase her well-being, and when that tendency is expressed behaviorally in a way that affects the other person in such a manner as to 'cooperate' with her wishes, she learns that such behavior will realize her wishes.

Both males and females learn that certain innate behaviors can produce behavioral responses in others that serve to realize their wishes. They learn that certain forms of aggressive behavior produce the results they want, i.e. an increase in their well-being. Once learned, these forms of aggression become examples of instrumental aggression.

The same can be argued in relation to territorial and sex-related aggression. We can understand territorial aggression to be a form of defensive aggression in that an invasion of one's living-space boundaries by another will tend to prompt fear when the invader is a serious threat and irritation (anger) when the invader is not considered to be a serious threat. The fact that Moyer defines territorial aggression as "an active defensive" indicates that this form of aggression is, at base, defensive.

Also, sex-related aggression, when understood as jealousy, can be reduced to a form of defensive aggression because the immediate experience of jealousy involves fear. The jealous mate, whether male or female, experiences fear when he or she is threatened by the actions of another male or female in relation to their mate. Men and women value the benefits they get from being with their mate; their identities are inextricably intertwined with those of their mates.

81

When another male or female is experienced as jeopardizing those benefits and that identity, then jealousy occurs. Jealously tends to manifest itself in various forms of aggression either against the perceived invader or against the mate because of a perceived betrayal. Jealousy serves to protect one's sexual interests and psychological identity and is based on fear, which characterizes defensive aggression.

Therefore, Moyer's classification of aggression can be reconstructed in this fashion:

1) Defensive aggression: the primary type of aggression; an aggression based on fear, involving threats to survival and well-being.

2) Irritative aggression: a form of aggression (anger) triggered by animate (e.g. people) or inanimate (e.g. weather) objects or situations; often occurs in response to a decrease in well-being; sometimes will occur in response to a perceived lack of cooperation by others to act in ways that are believed to increase one's well-being. The first form of irritative aggression is defensive in character; the second form is egoistic in character. Neither form of aggression admits of innate tendencies toward domination.

3) Territorial aggression: an active defensive triggered by any intruder violating the boundaries of an area in which a subject, or a group of subjects, has already established living activities; primarily a defensive form of aggression either based on fear (if the intruder is perceived as a serious threat to one's survival or well-being) or irritation (if the intruder is perceived as a minor threat to one's survival or well-being).

4) Sex-related aggression: refers to aggression with a sexual component or sex with an aggressive component; jealousy is a form of sex-related aggression; it is primarily a defensive form of aggression based on fear of loss of one's well-being that is intimately tied to perceived personal benefits and/or identity. Neither reason for jealousy (i.e. loss of benefits or identity) involves an innate tendency toward domination. Aggressive sex is a distorted form of instrumental aggression (to be discussed later).

5) Instrumental aggression: a form of aggression used because it tends to produce positive experiences in the aggressor, i.e.

it is a learned form of aggression. Learning can either be natural or distortive. Natural learning will tend to occur under the umbrella of cooperation, where competitive tendencies will serve cooperation; distortive learning will tend to occur under the umbrella of competition, where cooperative tendencies will serve competition.

6) Maternal protective aggression: mothers protecting their offspring. This is primarily a defensive form of aggression. Mothers fear the loss of and harm to their offspring and will naturally protect them when threatened. A paternal protective aggression might be added to this category.

Female social aggression: females aggressing against non-familial offspring. This is rejected as a form of aggression; it has very little empirical support from human populations.

Predatory aggression: In agreement with Carthy and Ebling, predatory aggression is not really aggression. It is an activity that involves killing prey for food. It is usually engaged in intelligently and skillfully, though when the prey is experienced as a threat to the hunter, actual shows of aggression can occur, i.e. aggression usually derived from fear and, hence, a defensive form of aggression.

Proposition 40: The urge to compete is derived from the innate, egoistic tendency toward increasing one's well-being through the affirmation of one's identity and not through the urge to decrease or threaten the survival and/or well-being of another. The latter urge is derived from a distorted form of learned aggression.

Healthy competition is the pitting of one's skills and capacities against another in an endeavor circumscribed by experientially consistent rules of engagement for the overall betterment of those individuals involved. Healthy competition is a form of self-advancement *in relation* to another and not at the expense of another. The loser can learn from the winner in healthy competitions how to better their skills and realize their capacities.

The urge to compete with others derives primarily from a need for self-affirmation. This self-affirmation can be realized in terms of survival or in terms of increased (or sustained) well-being.

People, as individuals or as collectives (e.g. countries), compete for resources in the world sometimes in terms of survival and sometimes in terms of increasing well-being. Involving survival, such competition derives from defensive aggression. Involving well-being, such competition derives from an egoistic tendency toward maintaining or increasing well-being.

When competition rests in the arena of survival, elements of identity tend to be subsumed under the need for survival. People will be less concerned with their psychological identity when their biological existence is threatened, unless their psychological identity is inextricably tied to their biological existence. When competition rests in the arena of well-being, then elements of survival tend not to be an issue of concern; rather, elements of increased happiness are paramount.

A revised list of types of aggression might look like this:

1) Defensive aggression (the primary form of innate human aggression)
   a) Irritative aggression (defensive in part; egoistic in part)
   b) Territorial aggression (primarily defensive)
   c) Sex-related aggression (primarily defensive; sometimes distorted instrumental aggression)
2) Instrumental aggression (learned aggression)
   a) Natural: primarily cooperative
   b) Distortive: primarily competitive
      1) Competitive aggression: a form of distortive instrumental aggression

Proposition 41: Unhealthy or distorted competition is a form of learned instrumental aggression, whereby one competitor seeks to force or forces another competitor into submission through the use of his skills and capacities. The satisfaction derived from such competition is based upon affirmations of a false self.

Theoretical Extension: Healthy and Unhealthy Competition

Winning is not primarily a "beating down" of an opponent but an affirmation of oneself. To the extent that this affirmation is understood to be a "raising up" of one person over another or a "beating down" of a person is the extent to which competition is distorted.

One tends to feel good about oneself when one wins a competition not because one has succeeded in exerting dominance over another but because one has successfully asserted oneself in relation to another, especially in relation to a comparable, respected opponent. When one feels good about oneself for dominating another, then one's feelings tend to derive from false self constructions.

When child A pushes away child B after child B tries to take child A's toy, child A is exhibiting an egoistic defensive aggression. He wants to continue enjoying his toy and doesn't want it taken away from him. He is "defending his territory" (i.e. his "possessions"). He doesn't do it because he likes dominating child B. It is not a natural innate human response to dominate another human being.

Even a child who hits another child who tries to take that child's toy does not hit because he wants to dominate that child. Rather, he hits either out of irritation or self-defense, though the egoistic or defensive expression might be harsh. The method of expressing irritation or self-defense would be more indicative of the personality of the child than expressive of an urge to dominate, i.e. the more aggressive child might hit whereas the less aggressive child might grab the toy back and the passive child might cry.

The urge to dominate tends to come in the wake of learning that certain aggressive behaviors have certain effects upon certain people. A child who hits another child when his toy is taken from him might learn that hitting someone can get him what he wants (e.g. his toy back, the other child to stop taking his toy, etc.) But if the child who is hit hits back, perhaps even harder, then the first child might learn to refrain from hitting when his toys are taken from him, or at least be more discriminating of whom he hits.

Child A might hit child B when child B takes his toy, and if the hitting is successful in getting the toy back, and successful in curbing any further attempts of child B to take child A's toy, and child B has no urge to retaliate, then the issue is solved. Child A will play with the toy and child B will either wait his turn or refrain from playing with that toy.

But let's say that child A not only wants to play with the toy, while he is playing with it, but also wants to keep child B from playing with it while he is not playing with it. Child A wants to keep the toy for himself and only lets others play with it if he so chooses. Child B takes exception to this and wants child A to share. When child A hits child B and successfully (though not intentionally) intimidates child B to the point that child B refrains from future attempts to play with the toy, then we could say that child A is in position to learn that his act of aggression has not only got back his toy at the moment but also has relieved him of having to aggress in the future against any attempts of child B to take his toy. He learns to dominate child B. He learns that aggressing, at least at a certain level, serves to keep his interests in tact in the present *and the future*. His original motives for acting aggressively are open to change: he can move from acting aggressively based upon self-defense (egoistic or territorial defense) to acting aggressively based upon domination.

What happens experientially might be this:

```
        Child A
C: Give me back my toy!
A: anger
B: hitting child B
S: child B
E: room
"I": ownership
   SSR
```

This experience is SSR, and, hence, real and good. The behavior might be too aggressive for the situation (e.g. a play center) or for the child being aggressed against (e.g. child B, who, let's say, is a passive sort), so people who can control the situation might step in to curb the aggression (e.g. play center worker or parent).   The natural strong aggression of one child might not be curbed by the other child who is naturally passive.

If child A and child B were innately equally aggressive, then child B might simply back off and wait his turn; but child B wouldn't simply allow child A to be the only one to play with the toy.   And if child B were more naturally aggressive than child A, or equally aggressive but physically stronger, then he might hit back with more force, thus back off child A at the moment and, possibly, in the future.

In whichever direction a natural innate expression of defensive or irritative aggression might occur, the upshot is similar: naturally aggressive acts that consist of some level of violence or force can provide the conditions for learning that such acts can be effective in controlling the behavior of others into the future. One who realizes that aggressive behavior, if expressed at sufficient strength or intensity, can bring about behavior in those to whom that behavior is directed that complies with the egoistic wishes of the person behaving in that manner will be open to continuing to act in that aggressive manner, at least in regard to people he can dominate.

The problem with this type of learning is this: the naturally passive individual does not tend to experience the naturally aggressive individual's aggressive behavior as being acceptable to him. No one likes to be harmed by others; hitting tends to harm; therefore, natural strong aggressive behaviors tend to prompt experiences of rejection rather than acceptance. The child who is hit is part of an experiential structure that looks like this:

C: Ouch!
A: surprise
B: pulling away
S: pain
E: room
"I": ownership
   SSR

which is replaced by:

C: That hurt
A: irritation
B: furrowed brow, focused eyes
S: other, room
E: room
"I": ownership
   SSR

In this brief transaction child B, the person being hit, responds to the aggression in a negative manner. At first he might be surprised by the aggressiveness of child A, but that surprise is replaced by an irritation. This irritation-experience need not contain seeds of injustice, only a repulsion of the harm child B feels. It is an example of a type of defensive aggression, i.e. child B does not want to be harmed and he is disposed to taking steps to prevent that harm from occurring; his irritation is a feeling that disposes him to act in self-defense in an offensive manner. In this sense, self-defense is not merely a "covering up" or a type of immediate "self-protection"; rather, it is a withdrawal from aggression *and* a preparation for offensive behavior that will serve to prevent future attacks. The "surprise" is a response to an unexpected expression of aggression, whereas the irritation is a militating against future expressions of aggression. This irritation-experience is also SSR: natural, real, and good.

Now, child B, who is naturally passive and who assesses the strength of child A as superior to his own, might cry. Crying, in this case, is not to be understood as an act of submission. It is a natural expression, given the situation. If the crying serves to prompt caretakers to intervene, fine. The passive child has defended himself by prompting intervention, i.e. a curbing of child A's aggressive behavior by more powerful people. But if more powerful people were not available and the children were left on their own, then child B's crying behavior might not have any curbing effect on child A's behavior. Here is where child A can learn that child B will not only surrender the toy to him but will continue to surrender the toy or, better yet from child A's point of view, never even attempt to take the toy in the future.

This learning is vulnerable to a form of abuse. Because child B does not respond to curb the aggressive behavior of child A, even if child A's behavior is originally defensive, then child A can learn to dominate child B by realizing that sufficient aggression can not only eliminate the current threatening behavior of child B but also any such future behavior.

Probing Question: Why would child A choose to use the knowledge that he could dominate child B to dominate child B when child A is naturally cooperative? Wouldn't he simply choose not to use that knowledge against child B?

Theoretical Extension: Egoism as Experiential

One possible answer to this question is: natural egoistic ten-dencies usually override natural cooperative tendencies. When it comes to questions of one's own survival, one individual will kill another if that's what it takes to survive. Likewise, when it comes to a question of sustaining or increasing one's well-being, one will harm another if that's what it takes to sustain or increase that well-being.

This answer argues that egoistic tendencies are naturally stronger than cooperative tendencies, and when one's survival or well-being is on the line, one will tend to compete with another rather than coop-erate. Cooperation will tend to reduce one's chances of survival or decrease one's well-being.

For example, if there are two people in a given area who are starving and who can't, for whatever reasons, alter their situation to save themselves from starvation, one will kill and eat the other to stay alive.

There seems to be enough empirical data to support this claim (refer to Stalin's starvation policies of the kulaks (peasants) in Ukraine which resulted in cannibalism), as well as the opposite claim, i.e. that each person will respect the integrity of the other (or even sacrifice oneself for the other) and not kill or reduce the well-being of the other even when such respect will result in an earlier death. In these situations, altruistic behavior supersedes egoistic behavior.

Empirical evidence seems to support both tendencies, i.e. egoistic (competitive) and altruistic (cooperative) behavior in survival situations. Given this, are we to conclude that human beings are naturally (innately) egoistic or altruistic? Or both? Are some of us just equipped with more "egoistic genes" and some with more "altruistic genes"? Or is this altruistic behavior the result of learning and the pressures of socialization? Or is this egoistic behavior the result of breakdowns in natural, interpersonal development? That is, if the person receives enough love and care as a child, she will naturally be more altruistic (cooperative) as an adult; whereas if she receives abuse and neglect as a child, she will tend to become more egoistic as an adult.

The contention held throughout this work is that people are naturally or innately cooperative, but in order for us to realize this characteristic, we must be raised in such a way that our physical and emotional needs are met. If our needs are not met, then our cooperative nature could develop in such a way that competitive, egoistic behaviors will tend to dominate. In this view, dominant: submissive relationships are pathological, not normal. Hierarchical organization supports dominant:submissive relationships, whereas democratic organization supports equality and healthy relationships.

In our example above, child A would not naturally or innately use the knowledge he gains that might lead him to dominate child B (i.e. his natural aggressive behavior), but he might very well use this knowledge in this way if his needs have not been met. His domination of child B becomes a source of ego-enhancement, i.e. he feels "good" about himself knowing that he can dominate child B. But such enhancement is largely false; it is delusional.

The same would hold true of people who, in desperate circumstances, killed and ate another human being in order to survive. The imposition of will upon another is indicative more of a lack of developmental needs met than a genetic disposition toward egoism.

When needs are met, respect for the life of others tends to be held in tact; people will tend to risk dying rather than taking another's life in order to sustain their own life. But when needs are not met, respect for the life of others will tend toward distortion; people will tend to kill others in order to survive. But this contention is subject to empirical support.

Applying this notion to our original social unit of basic male and basic female, though the male might realize that his show of aggression toward the female might cause her fear, he would not tend to use that knowledge to manipulate her into getting what he wants. His natural tendency would either be some form of relief or satisfaction over the fact that she either stopped doing what he didn't want her to do or was at least disposed to considering doing what he wanted her to do (i.e. her fear is prelude to backing off or cooperating with him) or he might experience his show of aggression to be a bit overboard and he might back off or apologize for his behavior, realizing that he prompted fear in her, which was not his intention.

Proposition 42: Humans do not innately intend to cause fear in others in order to get them to do or not do what they want.

Expressions of male aggression tend to be defensive and/or egoistic in nature. To the extent that they are egoistic and expressions of irritation, they are vulnerable to exploitation. The male can exploit the fear engendered in the female, but only if he in some way disregards or denies his own tendency toward cooperation. He can deny the existence of an experience he participates in that would promote his recognition of equality. Analytically, his experiential structure would look like this:

C: just do this!
A: frustration (intense irritation)
B: yelling
S: female
E: outside
"I": ownership

In this experience, the male wants the female to do something (that he, let's say, doesn't want to do but knows must be done). The healthy female's experience might look like this:

C: what?!
A: surprise/resentment
B: surprised look/resentful look
S: male
E: outside

90

"I": ownership

The healthy female (i.e. the one whose developmental needs have been met) would tend to respond to this male aggression as unjustified or illegitimate. If she did not previously agree upon a method of addressing this task, then her mate's aggression is experienced as unwarranted. She is prepared to back him off.

The unhealthy female (i.e. the one whose developmental needs have not been met) would tend to respond like this:

C: he's going to hit me!
A: fear
B: shrinking
S: male
E: outside
"I": ownership

The unhealthy female has thoughts of impending doom rather than thoughts of surprise and resentment. This might indicate that she has a developmental history of people (males and/or females) hitting her when they want her to do something (or generalized from people hitting her for not ceasing to do something they don't want her to do).

Probing Question: How did a healthy response to aggression change to an unhealthy response to aggression?

Theoretical Extension: The Inception of Physical Dominance

Human identity seems to be a fragile yet resilient phenomenon. It is fragile in that it is dependent upon others for its healthy emotional development, and others need not, and often do not, meet the emotional needs of developing individuals. It is resilient in that even if one's emotional needs are not met by others, one can still survive. Distortions of identity serve to perpetuate one's physical and emotional survival, though at the expense of one's health. 'Health' and 'well-being' take on a distorted nature, but this distorted nature is 'functional'. It works to perpetuate one's physical and emotional survival.

The male can aggress against the female in self-defense or out of egoistic motivations, but when he realizes that such naturally aggressive acts can provide for him what he wants (i.e. her cooperation), he is at a crossroads. He can act according to his own nature, which would be for him to realize that his aggression was excessive in that it produced fear, whereas it was intended only to back the female off or to engage her cooperation. In realizing that a natural aggressive act could prompt a response that could be advantageous to the male, the male "crosses the line" by denying his own nature: he "endows" his aggressive, fear-inducing act with a power it does not naturally possess: he empowers it with dominance.

Proposition 43:   Dominance is the expectation of cooperation without gaining free consent.

Once the male learns that his expressions of aggression cannot only produce fear in the female but can also be used to negate her natural rejection of his behavior, he can dominate her. On the other side, once the female allows her fear to keep her from assertively confronting the male in regard to his overly aggressive behavior, she distorts her natural disposition to stand up for herself and repel his aggression.

Proposition 44:   Dominant:submissive relationships are, at least in part, the result of humans distorting their own cooperative nature through learned abusive behavior.

Theoretical Objection: A child might hit another child simply because the other child is getting more attention from her parents, or has gotten more attention from her parents, or tends to solicit more favorable attention and loving expressions from her parents than the child himself. In other words, a child can aggress against another simply because he is jealous or envious of the other's attention gained from parents. Such an aggressive act need not be the result of a denial of his own cooperative nature but is actually an expression of his competitive nature. Sibling rivalry is an expression of innate human tendencies toward aggression and competition.

Theoretical Extension: Jealousy and Competition

If we were to analyze the experiential structures within which a jealous or envious child participates (or an adult for that matter), our conclusion might be quite different from the above. The child who experiences jealousy, much like the adult who experiences jealously, feels in some way threatened by the attention that the other child is getting from its parents. It is as if the child is caught in a dichotomous mind-set that assumes that if parental love is going out to a sibling, then it is being withheld from oneself. If a sibling is receiving love and affection from her parents, then the child experiences a loss or diminishment of self. It is the experienced loss or diminishment of self that prompts the aggressive behavior. Such behavior is self-defensive, or derived from fear of loss of self. It is not derived from an innate tendency to dominate or compete with another person.

As soon as the child is able to learn that the affection given to a sibling by the parents will not alter the affection the parents feel toward him, he will be able to accept signs of parental affection toward his sibling with acceptance, if not appreciation and repose.

Probing Question: How does a child come to accept signs of parental affection toward a sibling with appreciation and repose when it is experienced as threatening to one's own identity?

Theoretical Response: If we argue that the experiential structure within which the jealous child participates is SSR, and, hence, something to be respected and not rejected or condemned, then parents will tend not to punish the child for his jealous (and even aggressive) behavior. Rather, they will tend to protect the sibling who has been hit without aggressing against (i.e. punishing) the child who has hit his sibling. In other words, the parents will reject the aggressive behavior without rejecting the child himself. In this sense, jealously is an innate human response to parental affection being given to a sibling and not to oneself (at least at that time). When parents reject the aggressive behavior of the jealous child and protect the aggressed-against child and yet affirm the identity of the aggressor by not rejecting him (e.g. calling him bad, hitting him, punishing him, or condemning him in some way), and continue to show him affection and acceptance, then the jealous child will tend to lose his experiences of threat and, instead, experience his parents' shows of affection toward his sibling with acceptance and even equanimity or repose.

Understood in this way, sibling rivalry is not evidence of innate competition between children for the attention or love of parents. Rather, it is a form of self-defensive aggression that needs to be worked through. A child's natural, innate jealousy needs to be accepted by parents as experientially SSR and not as something to be rejected, negated or punished. When it is accepted as SSR, the

93

parents will persist in expressing signs of love and affection toward the aggressive sibling after they have made sure that the aggressed-against sibling is protected. Their methods of protection will not be punitive in relation to the aggressive child, i.e. they will not punish the aggressor (e.g. hit or verbally chastise him). Rather, they will simply protect the aggressed-against child (e.g. by separating the two, by keeping the aggressor away from the aggressed-against, etc.)

Protecting a child from aggression is not the same thing as punishing the aggressor. Protecting is a natural, innate response to perceived unwarranted aggression. Punishing a child for aggressing is a learned response to aggression. Parents learn that aggressing against (i.e. punishing) a child, whether in verbal or behavioral form, tends to produce compliance from the child. The child tends to do what the parents want him to do. And then the parents think that they have done the right thing, simply because the child behaves like they want him to, e.g. 'peacefully.' But in actuality, the parents who punish their child for being himself (i.e. for aggressing against their siblings out of jealousy) reject not only their child's behavior but the child himself. They reject the SSR structure of the experience within which the child participates by punishing the child, and, eventually, the child will reject his own SSR structure and replace it with a false self.

Summary and Conclusion: We have reached the end of the first part of this work, describing how dominant:submissive relationships might have evolved without having to invoke the socio-biological theory of evolution. We have argued, through the use of the philosophy of experientialism and the psychology of self, that the male:female dyad is the basic social unit upon which society was built. Built into the basic male and female are traits or characteristics that are genuine expressions of who they are. These expressions occur in simple, strong and right (SSR) structures that are composed of integrated cognitive, affective, behavioral, sensational, and environmental components. These components are consistent with each other and are owned. SSR structures form the basis of human identity and are to be recognized and respected as legitimate. But these structures can be distorted through emotional, physical and/or sexual force. When force is exerted (usually in some form of aggression or manipulation) over one member of the dyad (usually the female) by the other member (usually the male), the forced member's identity is subject to distortion. This distortion occurs through the formation of complex structures. Complex structures consist of an underlying SSR structure (i.e. who the person truly is), a self-rejection structure, and a false self structure. The false self structure ostensibly is in accord with the will or wishes of the forceful member but opposed to one's own nature. It is a relinquishing of oneself to another; it is the rudiment of a dominant:submissive relationship. Repeated force serves to prompt the forced member to hone her false self, thus solidifying the delusion of domination and submission being normal. Paradoxically, the false self structure could be diametrically opposed to the wishes or will of the forceful member and yet be false to one self. Such is the case with rebels.

So far we have argued that mankind is essentially a social animal and that sexual intercourse is a primary social interaction. But sexual contact is far from being the only socially necessary contact between human beings. Sexual intercourse does not occur simply as sexual intercourse, not even in cases of rape or casual sex. Elements of human identity co-exist with sexual intercourse. Emotions, feelings, thoughts, and sensations that are owned by a person are inextricably connected to the sexual behavior between two bodies. All of these components serve to constitute the person, including the environmental component. The individual person cannot be ontologically separated from the environment within which he or she exists; he or she can only be intellectually separated from that environment. The environment is necessarily a part of the identity of the person existing within it. The primordial social dyad that engages in sexual behavior consists of two continuously changing experiential structures within which each person participates and through which each person is him or herself.

The members of this primordial experiential dyad are naturally or innately disposed toward acting cooperatively with each in order to promote their survival and sustain or increase their overall well-being. These natural or innate methods of cooperation include performing tasks that are expressive of one's talents, skills, interests, and physical and psychological competencies. When conflicts between people crop up as to who does what, especially in those areas where jobs must be done in order to survive or maintain well-being, a type of

95

unforced, uncoerced, unmanipulated, cooperative agreement is struck and maintained (or renegotiated through similar methods).

Competitive urges, which are linked to egoistic self-satisfactions, are also naturally occurring, innate, expressions of self. Quite often, it seems, these egoistic urges produce impositions upon others that have to be warded off. When the male tries to impose his will upon the female, her natural response is to reject the imposition, and vice-versa. But when the female is not able to assert herself in relation to the male, then in order to survive and maintain some semblance of well-being, she distorts her identity and submits to his will. She engages in a dominant:submissive relationship. And when the male is unable or unwilling to realize that his imposition of will is a transgression of his own cooperative nature, he helps create a distortion of himself by creating a dominant false self that serves to dominate a corresponding submissive false self.

PART 2: Establishing a Primary Social Unit in the Mother-Child Bond

There is a certain arbitrariness in establishing the male:female unit as the primary unit of society because each male and female has at one time been a zygote, fetus, baby, infant, and child, thus creating a female:child social bond that could also be held as a primary social bond. It is a chicken and egg problem that we'll simply recognize, arbitrarily decide which one "comes first," and order them accordingly.

Proposition 45: Children come into being when the male sperm fertilizes the female egg.

Proposition 46: The zygote (an embryonic form of a child) is dependent upon the mother (or substituted surrogate, which could either be another woman or people in a lab) for its growth and development. If expelled from the mother, surrogate, or detached from people in a lab, it will die.

This dependency between mother and child argues against the idea that people live in a "state of nature" constituted by autonomous individuals who freely form a social contract with each other in order to ward off violence and chaos and to establish liberty and social order. A child is not an autonomous being; it is dependent upon its mother (at least) for its very survival. Yet it is a separate being (at least at birth when it is detached from the mother).   But its separateness is not the same as its autonomy.   It becomes an autonomous being when it is capable of sustaining its own existence.

Theoretical Extension: Stern's Theory of Self (excerpted from *Emotional Investment: Transforming Psychotherapeutic Assumptions*)

a) Stern's Emergent and Core Selves: The Emergent Self

Daniel Stern's notions of emergent and core selves, which he has developed in relation to both the psychoanalytic and the developmental psychology traditions, comes closer to the experiential theory than does ego and self psychology. It clarifies and rectifies some of the nebulousness and errors of the stages of development in ego psychology, and it better accommodates the holistic and analytic nature of experiential theory.

Stern argues that infants experience the world in a much more definite manner than is described in ego psychology's autistic phase of development (0 to 2 months) (see Kessen et al., 1970; Cohen and Salapetek, 1975; Kagan et al, 1978; Lamb and Sherrod, 1981; Lipsitt, 1983). Studies show that infants seek sensory stimulation and one of their most important stimuli is the human face. Infants have distinct biases or preferences in regard to sensations, and these preferences show all the signs of being innate. Also, infants appear to have a central tendency to form and test hypotheses about what is occurring in the world (Bruner, 1977). They seem constantly to be "evaluating," in the sense of asking, is this different from or the same as that? Stern concludes that infants will use this central tendency to rapidly categorize the social world into conforming and contrasting patterns, events, sets, and experiences. In addition to this, Stern argues that affective and cognitive processes cannot be readily separated. In simple learning tasks, activation builds up and falls off, indicating that cognitive learning is affect-laden. Similarly, in an intense affective moment, perception and cognition go on (Stern, 1985).

Stern sees the development of a self occurring in process from day one of the infant's life. He argues that an infant "can experience the process of emerging organization as well as the result," and that it is this experience of emerging organization that [he] calls the emergent sense of self. It is the experience of a process as well as a product" (Stern, 1985). Stern is emphatic in asserting that infants do not experience non-organization (as is claimed in the autistic phase of development). Rather, infants experience things in the world with exquisite clarity and vividness, and that the lack of relatedness between these experiences is not noticed. As these diverse experiences become somehow yoked or associated with each other, the infant experiences the emergence of organization. The sense of an emergent self concerns the process and product of forming organization. Stern believes that infants can not only organize their environments but, importantly, they can experience the organization of these experiences. It is out of the experience of organizing sense experiences that an emerging self occurs. Stern concludes that "the sense of an emergent self thus includes two components, the products of forming relations between isolated experiences and the process" (Stern, 1985).

If we were to convert Stern's notion of an emergent self, up to this point, into the experiential theory, we would hold that the sensory experiences had by the infant are, by definition, multi-componential structures in addition to being comparatively discrete or separate. That is, an infant, like an adult, will not only sense aspects of its environment and be selective about those aspects, but it will also cognize, feel, and behave within an environment.

Stern argues that infants show a seemingly innate ability to perceive amodally, i.e. to take information received in one sensory modality and translate it into another sensory modality. For example, an infant will respond in similar ways to light intensity and sound intensity. It is as if the infant is hard-wired to respond in a similar manner to intensity, whether that intensity is visual, auditory, tactile, etc. In addition to this capacity, according to Stern and developmental research, infants show signs of being innately able to cross sensory modalities and integrate information from several modalities at the same time. For example, an infant will cognize congruity between a voice and lips moving. Studies show that when the two are not in sync, the infant will show behavioral signs of preferring to look at the integrated voice-lips vs. the unintegrated voice-lips. Stern argues that at a preverbal level of consciousness, the experience of finding a cross-modal match (especially the first time) would feel like a correspondence or imbuing of present experience with something prior or familiar, a form of déjà vu event. Here, Stern is positing an affective component in relation to a sensory and a cognitive component. That is, matching sensory modalities is a cognitive function, and this cognitive function (cognition) is connected to an affective component (form of déjà vu). If we simply add the behavioral component (comportment) of the infant's looking behavior and the behavioral component (physiology) of the infant's heart rate or other bodily activity in relation to the environmental stimuli, then we will have a consciousness structure of experience. If we add to this an emerging sense of self, we will have an experiential structure.

A question arises at this point: Can an infant have a discreet sensory experience without cognitive, affective, behavioral and environmental components attached to it? Can an infant sense something without feeling it in some way, acting in relation to it in some way, and physiologically responding to it in some way?

Though Stern does not say this, his analysis of developmental studies is couched in multi-componential language. He seems to be operating within the traditional scientific linear model of theorizing by concentrating on sensation of the environment first, then moving to cognition, affect and behavior, but the language of his analyses borders on holistic and experiential theorizing. He links sensation with affect, while implying a type of cognitive function, as noted above; he links proprioception (i.e. feeling of one's own bodily existence and motions) with visual sensation by demonstrating how infants can "know" specific configurations of other people's faces by moving its face in a similar manner, and he, through Heinz Werner (1948) links sensation with affect in the phenomenon of "physiognomic" perception, or associating visual images (e.g. squiggles, smooth lines turning down, and jagged lines) with various feelings (e.g. happy, sad and angry). Such language seems to push the scientific linear model to its edge where it borders on transformation. The experiential theory pushes the language over the edge into a holistic understanding of the self and reality.

Another important idea of Stern's is his notion of "vitality affects." Vitality affects are more globalized feelings that go beyond sensory-laden ideas such as intensity level, motion, number, and rhythm and yet are not as discreet as the categorical affects of anger, sadness, happiness, etc. These are feelings like "surging," "fading away," "fleeting," "explosive," "crescendo," "decrescendo," "bursting," "drawn out," etc. These vitality affects are experienced not only by the infant but also by the adult, and they can be communicated between infant and adult and felt between person and object. For instance, these affects can be communicated by how a mother picks up a baby, felt in how the mother folds the diapers, felt and communicated by how mother grooms her hair or the baby's hair, reaches for a bottle, unbuttons her blouse, etc.

These more subtle forms of feelings that correspond nicely with peripheral (and sometimes focal) aspects of experiential structures play a vital role in the maintenance of SSR structures and a self-deceptive role in complex structures. For instance, a mother who picks up her baby roughly while believing that she is behaving in a gentle, loving manner, would be communicating the roughness to the child while contradicting that roughness by smiling (falsely). The infant who, if we are to agree with Stern, can experience the roughness and the smiling may find it difficult to integrate these two inconsistent modalities. In this example then, a mother is communicating a complex structure within which she is participating to the infant, and the infant might either disregard the inconsistency (as it does in the voice-lips studies) or somehow accommodate the inconsistency. This problem is compounded once the child gains more knowledge of smiling faces being consistent with certain types of touch. The rough touch does not match the smiling face and the child's experience is conflicting. If the self is emerging throughout these interactive processes, then the emerging self is being effected, influenced or in some sense determined by the consistent (authentic) or inconsistent (inauthentic) behavior of the parent. This notion is consistent with the experiential notion of SSR structures (authenticity) being either confirmed by others (mutual consistency), disconfirmed by others (conflicting SSR structures), or distorted by others (rejecting the rightness of one's structure). When mother smiles while handling her infant roughly, her experience could be analyzed in this fashion:

Cognition:	[I'm frustrated with you]	I'm bad for feeling this way	I'm acting lovingly
Affect:	[frustration]	self-rejection	false affection
Behavior:	[rough handling]	look down	false smile
Sensation:	[baby]	baby	baby
Environ:	[room]	room	room
"I":	[ownership]		

The baby is able to experience the surging and explosive quality of the mother's handling without necessarily understanding it as evidence of anger (vitality affect) while virtually simultaneously experiencing the drawn out pacifying smile on the mother's face. Being confronted with these inconsistent experiences, the infant might well have difficulty integrating them.

One way Stern characterizes vitality affects as different from categorical affects is by locating them within motivational states, appetites, and tensions. They are connected to the vital processes of the organism, e.g. breathing, hunger, elimination, falling asleep and waking up, feeling the coming and going of emotions and thoughts, etc. Again, the language links experiential components where breathing is categorized as a form of physiological behavior or body movement (sometimes comportment when done consciously), hunger a sensation, elimination a combination of behavior and environment, falling asleep and waking up as forms of comportments closely

101

associated with physiological movement, feeling the coming of emotions and thought a subtle type of affect, etc. Vital feelings are the feelings associated with all of these vital processes. They can serve to fill the affective component of a given experiential structure.

In the last example the vital affect can either precede a categorical affect or it can underlie the affect. So for Stern, vital affects and categorical affects are two types of affect that can co-occur. One reason Stern distinguishes these two types of affect is because, he argues, vitality affects cannot be accounted for simply by the notion of levels of activation. That is, the organism's sensory apparatus (organs plus nervous system) can be activated causing activation contours, but such activation is not the same thing as feelings. The feelings associated with these activation contours are not the same thing as the activation contours themselves. So a person can experience a rush of thoughts and feel that rush as well as think the thoughts. Experientially, this distinction makes perfect sense if we are distinguishing between cognition (thoughts) and affect (surging, bursting, etc.), but to distinguish them from other affects is more questionable unless we are using vital affects to conflict with categorical affects (as in the above example) or unless we include the vital affects as peripheral components in relation to the categorical affects. For instance, we could feel happy focally and a surging or bursting vital affect peripherally within the same experience.

For Stern the self is somehow generated within the process of organizing experience in relation to its' environment, especially human beings within its' environment. Studies show that infants tend to scan the edges or boundaries of the objects in their environment, but with human beings, they will look within the boundaries of the person's head, at facial features. The social or interpersonal connection to the formation of the self occurs in the first few months of human life.

Stern argues that "there is no reason to give any one domain of experience primacy and make it the point of departure to approach the infant's organization of experience. Several approaches can be described, all of them valid, all of them necessary, and all of them equally primary. Included in these experiential approaches are: 1 the infant's action: "self generated actions and sensations are primary experiences," 2) pleasure and unpleasure (hedonic tone), ala Freud, 3) discrete categories of affect, 4) infant states of consciousness, e.g.

drowsiness, alert activity, sleep, etc., and 5) perceptions and cognition (the route of most experimentalists) (Stern, 1985).

Experientially, the infant's actions and sensations fall under the components of behavior and sensation respectively; pleasure and unpleasure fall under the component of affect, perceptions and cognitions fall under sensations and environment (perception of external things, including one's own body) and cognition. States of consciousness would be understood as descriptions of types of experiential structures rather than primary experiences. Sleep and other unconscious states can be eliminated from "primary experience" because they are not actually experienced; their existence is inferred from evidence in conscious states. Drowsiness and other conscious states are actually experiential structures whose contents include drowsiness features.

Aside from the problem with consciousness and an implied rather than explicit connection with a physical environment (indicators of the scientific linear mind-set), Stern's conception of the infant's experience and that of an emerging self are very close to a holistic experientialist conception of reality. What remains for our discussion is Stern's sense of a core self.

(b) *Stern's Emergent and Core Selves: The Core Self*

As the infant grows and interaction with its environment increases, a core self is formed. A core self includes: 1) self-agency or authorship of one's own actions, 2) self-coherence or having a sense of being a non-fragmented, physical whole with boundaries and a locus of integrated action, 3) self-affectivity or experiencing patterned inner qualities of feeling that belong with other experiences of self, and 4) self-history or having the sense of enduring, of a continuity with one's own past. The primacy of interpersonal experience is evident within the first two months of the infant's life, and primarily out of this interpersonal experience comes a sense of a core self and core others. This process, according to Stern, does not happen over two years, ending with an individuation stage of development, as in ego psychology, but rather within two to seven months after birth. The infant does not have to go through a symbiotic stage, then hatching, practicing, and rapprochement stages to reach a sense of core self; the core self is forming within two to seven months from birth and, as explained already, is emerging earlier than that.

103

For Stern "a sense of core self results from the integration of these four basic self experiences into a social subjective perspective...The sense of a core self is thus an experiential sense of events" (Stern, 1985). For example, when an infant closes its eyes, the world gets dark. At first, an infant might not be aware of itself closing its eyes; it just closes its eyes. But it is aware of the sensation of closing its eyes, or of the burning sensation in its eyes that prompts it to close its eyes; it is aware of the relief (pleasure) of closing its eyes; it is also aware of the darkness that occurs when it closes its eyes; and it is already capable of crossing sensory modes (seeing, touching, etc.) And it is already interconnected in terms of sensation, cognition, affect, and behavior (at least in rudimentary forms). Out of this conglomeration of experiential interconnectivity comes a sense of a core self.

Specifically, agency can be broken down into three possible invariants of experience: 1) the sense of volition that precedes a motor act, 2) the proprioceptive feedback that does or does not occur during the act, and 3) the predictability of the consequences that follow the act. Stern believes that the invariant of volition is the most fundamental invariant of the core self experience. It is some 'mental registration' (usually outside of awareness) of an 'action plan', e.g. suck, gaze, etc. The physical action follows from the mental action plan. Stern argues that acts that occur above the level of reflexes are not simply performed by chance or accident; rather, they are preceded by some sort of action plan or mental representation, no matter how fleeting that plan might be.

For example, if a subject is asked to sign his name on a paper and then on a blackboard, the signatures will appear very similar though it can be shown that different groups of muscles are used to complete each act. This points to the idea that there exists some sort of mental 'action plan' that is executed by different parts of the body to produce similar results. This notion of action plans is similar to Piaget's and Beck's notion of cognitive schemas, and it falls neatly within the scientific linear conception of reality.

Experientially, cognitions do not precede action; rather, they co-occur with action (behavior). The 'action plan', if within experience, registers either in focal or peripheral cognition. If focal, the infant (or adult) is clearly aware of it, and the strength of the structure is relatively strong. If peripheral, the infant's awareness of it is less clear, and the strength of the structure is relatively weak. If it occurs outside of experience within which the infant participates, then its existence is inconsequential in relation to it. It is equivalent to non-existent. It may very well be consequential in relation to those who are interacting with the infant, those conceiving of the notion of 'action plans' in relation to infant (and adult) behavior, but if such 'action plans' occur outside of infant awareness, then their existence cannot be connected to a developing core self because there is nothing being experientially processed by the infant. Processes are occurring in the infant from another person's perspective (e.g. researcher's), but to claim that the infant's developing core self depends upon processes of which the infant is completely unaware, without owning that claim, is to create a meta-experiential construct, or to distort reality. In order for Stern's notion of 'action plan' to carry experiential weight, it must either be experienced in some way (focally or peripherally) by the infant or believed in by the infant through trusting another person. And, of course, since this trust cannot be the product of theoretical exchange, it seems that it needs to be the result of basic interaction between infant and adult. The notion of 'action plan' might contribute directly to the behavior of the researcher, but it means to the infant only what is being communicated through the behavior of the researcher (or those participating in the research).

Experientially, Stern's notion of 'action plan' is similar to Beck's notion of 'cognitive schema', and the same analysis can be applied to each. An action plan is a cognition, and cognitions occur in conjunction with a behavior, not in a prerequisite or semi-causative role. An analysis of it would look like this:

Cognition: suck thumb (pre-linguistic)
Affect: anticipated pleasure
Behavior: body preparing to move
Sensation: body, environ
Environ: room
("I"):   ownership
           SSR

which changes to:

Cognition: moving thumb to mouth (pre-linguistic)
Affect: confidence
Behavior: moving thumb toward mouth
Sensation: body, environment
Environ: room
("I")   ownership
           SSR

which ends in:

```
Cognition: sucking thumb (pre-linguistic)
Affect:    pleasure
Behavior:  sucking
Sensation: thumb, environment
Environ:   room
("I"):     ownership
           SSR
```

This analysis argues that there is no 'action plan' that precedes the action but rather that several relatively discreet experiences occur in relation to each other. The 'action plan' notion is actually a cognitive component of the initial experience. It is accompanied by the behavior of the body's preparation to move. In other words, there already exists an action or a behavior prior to the behavior of moving the thumb toward the mouth; it is the body preparing itself to alter its current movements. As the thumb moves toward the mouth, a new cognition occurs: moving thumb toward mouth (pre-linguistic). Here the infant cognizes its own body motion. It is confident in relation to this motion. If the thumb should miss the mouth and therefore conflict with the anticipated pleasure felt in the initial experience, then slight irritation might occur and slightly diminished confidence, and probably a continuation or persistence of motion toward the mouth (until the skill is learned into habit).

The initial experiential structure is strong enough to prompt the next structure, and there are no conflicting experiential structures vying for expression, e.g. the infant is not attending to a pain in its foot, which might bypass thumb sucking and move directly into crying. The prompting of movement of the thumb toward the mouth is already happening in the prior experience where the body is preparing to move. Whether the movement of the thumb toward the mouth occurs is not a function of volition (will); rather, it is a function of experience. If the experience is strong enough and there are no significantly strong conflicting experiential structures (and these seem to be reciprocal notions, i.e. strength to alter flow of current experience depends upon strength of conflicting experiences), then the act will occur.

Viewed in this way, "volition" is not a mental phenomenon that somehow converts mentality into physical movement; rather, it is either a meta-experiential construct or a short-cut way of referring to an experiential process. If the former, it will be rejected by exper-ientialism; if the latter, it will be accepted as an effective heuristic concept.

106

Stern's second invariant property of proprioceptive feedback converts nicely into peripheral experiential contents and focal experience when a skill is first being learned. The infant will initiate movement of its thumb toward its mouth and be peripherally aware of the accuracy of its movement through proprioceptive feedback. Experientially, proprioceptive feedback consists of a set of experiences in relation to the task at hand. Initial learning might entail confidence-persistence-irritation experiences until the skill becomes automatic; then confidence will prevail and become peripheral.

Stern's third invariant is consequence of action. This also converts nicely into experiential structures. It refers to the experiences that follow a given act. For instance, if the movement of the thumb to the mouth is successful and is followed by various sense-pleasure experiences, then the infant can begin to recognize its efficacy in moving its body. The pleasure reinforces its efforts and helps create a sense of a core self.

In converting Stern's notion of agency into experiential theory, an initial thumb sucking experiential structure might look like this:

Cognition: this is agitating (pre-linguistic)
Affect: agitation
Behavior: body moving in agitated manner
Sensation: body (hunger possibly), environ
Environ: room
("I"):   ownership
            SSR

which changes to:

Cognition: suck thumb (pre-linguistic)
Affect: urge
Behavior: body preparing to move
Sensation: body, environ
Environ: room
("I"):   ownership
            SSR

which changes to:

Cognition: moving thumb to mouth (pre-linguistic)
Affect: confidence
Behavior: moving thumb toward mouth
Sensation: body, environment
Environ: room
("I")   ownership
            SSR

which ends in:

Cognition: sucking thumb (pre-linguistic)
Affect: pleasure
Behavior: sucking

107

```
Sensation: thumb, environment
Environ:   room
("I"):     ownership
           SSR
```

If we posit that the initial urge to suck one's thumb is innate, possibly generalized from the innate sucking of the nipple, and is prompted by some form of bodily agitation or discomfort (e.g. hunger, etc.), then we can locate agency within the cognitive component of experience rather than in the mind. Agency becomes a property of experience and splitting experience into cognition (mind) and behavior (body) is either unnecessary or misleading.

The signature example above can be explained without resorting to a mind before body (linear) explanation. For instance, each experiential set accounting for each type of signature (i.e. desk vs. board) consists of its own set of components. They might look like this:

```
Cognition:    sign name on desk          : sign name on board
Affect:       confidence                 : confidence
Behavior:     body preparing to sign     : body preparing to sign
Sensation:    pen, desk                  : chalk, board
Environ:      room                       : room
("I"):        ownership                  : ownership
                 SSR                         SSR

Cognition:    signing name on desk       : signing name board
Affect:       confidence                 : confidence
Behavior:     body signing               : body signing
Sensation:    pen, desk                  : chalk, board
Environ:      room                       : room
("I"):        ownership                  : ownership
                 SSR                         SSR

Cognition:    completed signature        : completed signature
Affect:       confidence                 : confidence
Behavior:     looking at signature       : looking at signature
Sensation:    pen, desk                  : chalk, board
Environ:      room                       : room
("I"):        ownership                  : ownership
                 SSR                         SSR
```

If we can assume that the desk signature preceded the board signature and that the person already knows how the signature looks and feels while and after he signs it, then we can hypothesize that his proprioceptive feedback can sufficiently inform him that his board signature is 'right' (close in appearance to his desk signature). The muscles used are not different enough to produce dissimilar signatures. But all he might have to do is sign his name with his other hand to show that any 'action plan' or 'cognitive schema', if present, is either very faulty in its conversion to action or that it will take time and practice to get one signature to look like the other. If the former is the case, then an 'action plan' seems to be a relatively impotent notion, and if the latter is the case, then 'action plan' can be replaced altogether by a learning explanation, i.e. recognizing how one's signature looks and feels and making sure the new signature looks and feels similarly.

So rather than locate volition (agency) within an 'action plan', which is located within the mind, and which precedes an action, experientialism would locate it within the cognitive component of experience, which is inextricably connected to the other components, and which co-occurs with behavior and evolves into other experiential structures, also, possibly, containing agency.

Stern argues that self-coherence helps develop a core self in an infant. Self-coherence is established by determining a unity of locus, coherence of motion, coherence of temporal structure, coherence of intensity structure and coherence of form. Briefly, the unity of locus refers to the idea that "a coherent entity ought to be in one place at one time, and its various actions should emanate from one locus" (Stern, 1985). Coherence of motion refers to the idea that things that move coherently in time belong together. Coherence of temporal structure refers to the idea that many behaviors that are performed simultaneously by one person share a common temporal structure. Coherence of intensity structure refers to the idea that behavioral intensities of one person generally match the intensities of another. Coherence of form refers to the idea that one's form or configuration "belongs" to oneself or another.

So the notion of coherence applies to both the infant and to other persons (or entities). An infant can recognize coherent patterns of behavior, affect, and sensations within itself and in relation to others and is able to differentiate these patterns as discrete. The self-other differentiation occurs early in life as these patterns are recognized and matched between the infant and others. For instance, infants are able "to conserve the identity of a particular face across the various transformations of that face in different facial expressions" (Stern, 1985). They are able to keep track of the identity of an object in spite of changes in size or distance, its orientation or position of presentation, its degree of shading, etc.

In addition to self-coherence, Stern argues that self-affectivity is critical in helping form the core self. Self-affectivity refers to the emotions felt by the infant and how these emotions are separated into discrete categories. Stern argues that each emotion consists of three invariants: 1) proprioceptive feedback from face, respiration, vocal aspects, etc., 2) arousal or activation, and 3) emotion-specific qualities of feeling. For instance, parents and others can communicate joy to an infant by making faces, tossing it up in the air and catching it, playing with it, smiling, laughing, etc. The infant will respond in kind.

Eckman's (2003) studies of adult human beings indicate that emotional expressions seem to be universal, i.e. that all humans know how to feel discrete emotions and recognize them in others. Apply the same notion to infants and we have an affective and innate form of core self development. Infants can recognize their own emotions and others' emotions through expressions of those emotions by others and proprioceptive feedback within themselves.

Finally, self-history refers to the ability of infants (and adults) to remember the other core self invariants: agency, coherence and affect. They are able to connect things they've done in the past (agency), with discrete and understandable sets of experience (coherence), and with their feelings connected to themselves and others. Memory gives continuity to other core self invariants. It locates infants (and adults) in time and space over time.

All of these core self invariants discussed by Stern, for the exception of those aspects of agency already discussed, fit well into the experiential analysis of reality. The relationship between the caregiver(s) and the infant is crucial in the development of the core self and the core other. The infant's attention, curiosity and cognitive engagement with the world are regulated by both the infant and the caregiver. Both respond to each other; the relationship is reciprocal but not symmetrical, i.e. the caregiver can stimulate the interest of the infant, and the infant can stimulate the interest of the caregiver, but the caregiver brings much more experience to the interaction than does the infant. The same applies to the satiation of interest and involvement.

Again, these interactions, according to Stern, are relatively discrete. The core self of the infant forms in relation to a process composed of relatively discrete experiences and not through alternating fusion and separation states in relation to the caregiver as posited by ego psychology.

Developmental psychology's integration with psychoanalytic and attachment theory seems to have produced a theory of a self that aligns quite well with the ideas constituting the notion of self in experiential theory. In experiential theory the notion of "I" as ownership refers to the cognitive linkage between one's thoughts, feelings, behaviors, sensations and one's own body as the object of sensations as one's own, i.e. "mine". Though neither experiential theory nor Stern's development/psychoanalytic theory can explain exactly how this ownership occurs, Stern's theory of emergent self comes close. As interactions with one's environment occur, especially with the caregivers in one's environment, the infant is able to process these interactions and develop a distinct core self and a distinct core other. Symbiotic and separation stages are replaced or analyzed into relatively discrete experiences involving at first sensual representations, intensities, rhythms, physiognomic perceptions and vitality affects (emerging self) which eventually help form a variety of self-invariants which integrate to form a core self.

Viewed through an experiential lens, the infant engages in numerous SSR experiences very early in life. Though it is unclear as to how exactly the infant comes to own self-indicating components of consciousness (e.g. my thumb, my hunger, my pain, etc.), it seems that it does so at a very early age and primarily in conjunction with a caregiver. Those experiences that Stern refers to as self-regulated by the infant (interest moving to satiation moving to irritation, etc.) are representative of SSR experiences and are, experientially, when integrated, formative of the core self.

For example, when an infant is interested in a caregiver's face, its attention is on that face. When the caregiver responds in kind to the infant, then the infant's interest-experience is confirmed by the caregiver. In effect, the caregiver is approving the rightness of the infant's experience. The infant's core self, realized in the SSR structure of its interest-experience, is strengthened and affirmed by the SSR structure of the caregiver's interest-experience. But when the infant's interest-experience is not responded to in kind, then the infant's core self is not confirmed; but neither need it be rejected. The caregiver might not be in the mood to confirm the interest-experience of the infant. Hence, the experience plays itself out and the infant's attention shifts. But if the caregiver rejects the interest-experience of the infant and communicates something like, "Oh, don't look at me, you terrible baby," then the rightness of the experiential structure is rejected, and the infant's core self is altered. As far as the infant is concerned (we'll hypothesize), its' interest in the caregiver is a sincere expression of who the infant is at this time; as such, it is SSR, real, and good. But when the caregiver rejects the legitimacy of the experiential structure within which the infant participates, then the immediate response would be something like:

Cognition: I am wrong, bad? (pre-linguistic)
Affect: confusion
Behavior: slightly puzzled look
Sensation: caregiver
Environ: room
"I":   ownership

which eventually shifts to (after repeated like experiences)

Cognition: I am wrong, bad. (pre-linguistic)
Affect: self-rejection
Behavior: vacant stare
Sensation: caregiver
Environ: room
"I":   ownership

The rightness of the infant's experience was rejected by the caregiver and the infant was made to respond as if its natural (sincere) self-expression was wrong. Since it experiences its experience as perfectly right, it is initially confused in relation to the caregiver's response. Because of the disparity of power between the caregiver and the infant, the infant can do little else than adjust to the caregiver's rejection of the rightness of its experiential structure (it's self) and accept the caregiver's rejection and deny its own self-acceptance. Its experiential structure becomes complex and its identity has been distorted.

If Stern is correct about the early development of a self in infancy, and experiential theory is correct about the formation of complex structures, then false self structures can form very early in life, thus creating emotional dependencies on caregivers in the form of identity alterations due to, in this case, emotional or psychological abuse. Add to this physical and sexual abuse and we have the rudiments for the development of a variety of psychological disorders and pathological social situations.

Proposition 47: The self is integral to all traditional ontological objective claims.

Theoretical Extension: The Realistic Experience and the Self

When a child is capable of self-reflection, and can form a core self, he will tend to experience a wide variety of phenomena realistically. That is, he will experience objects in his environment as separate from himself, as having an existence of their own (i.e. object-constancy), and as having properties of their own (e.g. volume-constancy, color, taste, etc.) It is realistic experiences that form the ground for the identity of the child. They consist of SSR experiences, which include an environmental component, within which the child participates, and are characterized by clarity and certainty. For instance, a child might look at a ball and the experience might look like this:

```
     Focal                Peripheral
C:   object               orientated, object-as-solid, object-as-constant
A:   interest             familiar, comfortable
B:   looking (at ball)    moving body parts, breathing, etc.
S:   ball                 objects in room, smells in room, tastes, etc.
E:   room                 world beyond room of which child could be aware
"I": ownership
     SSR
```

In this typical realistic experience, the child is aware of a ball as a "something," i.e. as an object in relation to other objects (like a floor, walls, etc.) The child need not participate in an experience of this sort. For instance, it might not be clear to the child that what is being perceived is a solid object that will not suddenly disappear. The ball could be experienced as a type of hallucinatory object or a solid object that could disappear. But we will say that its experience is so constituted. Such an experience is experienced as real or true not only for the child but for everyone, as far as the child is concerned. The experience is so clear that it must reflect reality as it is and not simply as the child experiences it to be.

This type of experience is akin to Descartes' idea of "clear and distinct idea," i.e. an idea that is indubitable or undoubtable (Descartes,1993). The child cannot doubt the reality of what it perceives. Such tends to be the nature of realistic experiences: because an object is experienced to be real, it must be real (i.e. exist outside of experience). But when experience is conceived as a necessary combination of components which include cognition and the environment, we need not affirm the realistic existence of objects

113

simply because we cognize them as existing-beyond-experience. Cognizing them as existing-beyond-experience is enough. For the child, the ball exists beyond its experience of it because the experience within which he participates is so constituted. Whether or not the ball 'actually' exists beyond the experience which dictates that it does so exist is completely irrelevant or inconsequential. If it cannot be experienced in any way other than how it is experienced at that time, then any existence of the ball other than the one happening in experience is of no consequence, no concern, and no relevance to the child. If this is so, then realistic experiences are just that: experiences constituted by realistic contents (e.g. object-constancy, volume-constancy, solidity, etc.) Beyond this we cannot go.

This is why realistic experiences tend to constitute the basis for identity in people, children as well as adults. They *appear* to cross the experiential boundary into an objective world that is somehow detached from experience. Objects in these experiences tend to be so real to us that we assume that they are similarly, if not identically, real to everyone else. When we run across someone who experiences those objects differently from us (e.g. color-blind vs. color-seeing), we are fundamentally and essentially perplexed. We tend to doubt the veracity of their claims. We do so because the experiential structures within which we participate consist of our ownership of all of that structure's contents. We cannot escape owning the contents of the experiential structures within which we participate. The realistic components are ours and, hence, they constitute, at least in part, us.

Even when we experience objects to be real beyond the experience within which we, as individuals, participate, we remain within the limits of experience: we can still own our own experience. For example, one might hold that a painting is beautiful and assume, at least to some degree, that it would, or at least should, be experienced as beautiful by everybody. We would be, to some degree, surprised if others didn't think it was beautiful. But we would not be willing to prohibit or prevent others from holding their beliefs or acting upon them by, let's say, writing articles that refute any claims of beauty in the painting. When others refute or contradict our experience, and we can grant some degree of legitimacy to their counter-claims, then we can more clearly own our own claim. Legitimate counter-claims (contradictory to our own) tend to relativize our own objective claims.

This phenomenon is referred to as the *relativization* of traditional objective claims: what has been assumed to be objective for one has been contradicted by another, and the other's claim seems to be legitimate to the one whose experience is contradicted.

The contradiction initially creates a form of disorientation or confusion. If the person experiencing the contradiction is healthy, that is, if the experiential structures within which he participates are simple, strong and right, he will tend to experience the contradiction as curious or odd and will tend to pursue clarification and legitimization from the other. But a person whose experiential structures are complex will tend to experience the contradiction as threatening to his identity (and hence, his reality) and will seek to de-legitimize the experience of the other, sometimes to the point of exerting force.

In the case of color-blind and color-seeing experiences, the color-seeing individual will tend to see a particular color in the object being perceived. When a color-blind person contradicts that experience, the color-seeing person will initially be disoriented or confused. This would be a typical response to contradiction to one's own assumed objective reality. The healthy person's response would tend to be one of curiosity. He would be grounded in his own objective experience and own that objective experience as an individual person enough so that a contradiction to his experience is not threatening to his identity. The contradiction might "knock him a bit off-kilter," "give him pause," or "strike him as curious or odd," but it wouldn't activate his defensive emotions or his repertoire of defensive behaviors. Rather, it would tend to attract him to the other. He would tend to pursue clarification and legitimization of the other's claim, e.g. "Why do you think this object is gray, when it's obviously red?" If, upon investigation, one comes to believe that the other is honest in his communication of his experience, then one's objective world that was limited to one's own experience is broadened or widened. It now includes the fact that some people (at least this particular person) actually sees the color of the physical world differently from oneself, and that one's own experience might not be the only one reflective of the world as it is outside of one's experience of it.

This recognition can admit of a pluralism within an objective world, which is deeply contradictory, or it can admit of a world defined by and limited to experience itself, where experience is defined as a necessary combination of cognition, affect, behavior, sensation, the environment, and the "I", and be deeply consistent.

When pluralism admits of multiple legitimate points of view given the backdrop or assumption of a traditional objective world, it is deeply contradictory. For example, the person who claims to adhere to "one true belief" but is willing to admit of contradictory beliefs as 'legitimate' is either guilty of making an untrue claim or is unable to realize his own rejection of the 'legitimacy' of the other's claim. If one adheres to a traditional objective stance, which, by definition, allows only one true claim, which is supposed to correspond with the one true reality, and yet is willing to admit some form of legitimacy to counter or contradictory claims, while still retaining a traditional objective assumptional framework, then one is either guilty of lying or is deceiving himself into thinking that counter or contradictory claims have the same legitimacy as his own objective claim. If one operates from an assumptional framework holding that there is but one true reality and that contradictory realities can never be legitimate and yet holds certain contradictory realities as legitimate, then one is deeply inconsistent with oneself.

But when the claim to objectivity is less amenable to legitimate refutation, then the ability to own one's own claim becomes less evident. For example, we might hold that slavery is morally wrong and assume, at least to some degree, that such a claim would be experienced as wrong by everyone. We would not only be surprised but appalled if someone believed otherwise. We might very well be willing to prohibit or prevent those who believed otherwise either from voicing their opinions or from acting upon them. If we live in a democracy where free speech is valued, then we might not be able to prevent them from voicing their beliefs, but we probably would be able to prevent them from acting upon their beliefs by creating enforceable laws prohibiting them from doing so. In this case, and in cases like this, objectivity in experience is less amenable to ownership. It is more difficult for us to own objective claims that involve strong emotion and moral conviction. It is as if the strength of our emotions or moral convictions transport us outside of the experience within which we are participating and into an 'objective realm', a realm that we, of course, have access to, whereas those disagreeing with us are prevented access.

It is much more difficult for us to own our own objective claim because of the claim's interconnectedness with our identity. Counter-claims tend not to be given legitimacy, especially when those claims are acted upon. Therefore, we will tend to report people who own slaves and prosecute them in courts of law.

But even these objective claims can be owned: they are our beliefs, whether they reflect an objective reality or not. It doesn't matter if there is an objective reality out there beyond our own experience; it is our own experience that we hold to be applicable to everyone. "If *you* don't hold a similar belief, then *we* will tend to reject the legitimacy of your opposing belief and stop you from acting upon that belief; but we will be responsible for our actions. Our preventing you from owning your own slaves says something about us and not something about an absolute, objective reality that exists beyond experience."

Even though we tend to understand our traditional objective claims to be reflective of a world detached from us (i.e. realism), the fact (experiential fact) is, we cannot detach ourselves from any objective claim that we make. All objective claims are our own. They form an essential part of our selves. We tend to ground ourselves, i.e. our identities, in those claims. For example, a Catholic tends to see herself as a Catholic and not simply as a person who believes in doctrines taught by the Catholic Church.

The distinction is subtle though, I think, important. A Catholic, at the far end of the "identity spectrum," will tend to orient herself toward the world *through* her traditional objective beliefs. She will tend to filter perceptual data through the strainer of Catholicism. Such a Catholic might be considered orthodox or conservative.

A Catholic who is plotted more toward the middle of the "identity spectrum" might affirm her belief in the doctrines of Catholicism, while simultaneously affirming some form of legitimacy of opposing traditional objective belief systems (e.g. Baptist, Jewish). This type of person would be considered to be of the ecumenical sort. She would tend to let others believe what they want to believe, even though their beliefs differed from her own. She would be willing to live with others peacefully though their beliefs contradicted her own.

At the other end of the "identity spectrum" lies the individual who is not only willing to allow others their own point of view (even when it contradicts her own) but is also willing to let them act upon

117

their beliefs. These people tend to be liberal and accepting of difference, even when that difference is rejected by them individually.

If we assume a traditional objective stance, and this stance conflicts with other stances, then it seems contradictory and disingenuous of us to accept, either in theory or practice, opposing claims and actions. If there is but one world, and if we (or some of us) can understand that world as it is and not simply as we understand it to be, and if we do, in fact, understanding that world as it is, and others oppose that understanding or profess a conflicting understanding, then a traditional logic dictates that the opposing stances are wrong. If we were to accept the legitimacy of opposing objective beliefs, while affirming the legitimacy of our own objective beliefs, then, given the nature of traditional objective beliefs, we would be deluding or lying to ourselves: we would be deeply hypocritical. And this claim can be borne out in experiential analysis.

When an ecumenist first hears an opposing viewpoint, the experience within which he participates would tend to look like this:

C: "opposing belief"
A: slight repulsion
B: reflective stare
S: environment including other person
E: other person in room
"I": ownership

which is replaced by:

C: I'm bad for feeling repulsed (I am unaccepting, unloving, intolerant, etc.)
A: self-rejection
B: vacant stare or actually looking away or down
S: environment including other person
E: other person in room
"I": ownership

which is replaced by:

C: I'm acting good
A: false confidence
B: false head nod
S: other person
E: other person in room
"I": ownership

Because the ecumenist assumes a traditional objective orientation, and because the issue at stake is intimately tied to his identity, his immediate response to a contradictory claim would tend to be one of rejection. The strength of that rejection might be tied to the amount of threat that one might feel in relation to the person making the conflicting claim: the more threatening, the stronger the rejection. Given the traditional objective framework within which the person operates, some form of rejection is the most honest response. But because this person, let's say, has been judged by others in his society as being too narrow or judgmental in his thinking (i.e. a type of rejection) and is pressured to be more tolerant, he accedes to the pressure by rejecting the legitimacy of his own repulsion-experience and develops the false self of acting good. He is able to judge his nodding behavior as an indicator of his tolerance, and, hence, his goodness. The false self of the ecumenist is born within the development of a complex structure. It only needs to be honed into a deep form of hypocrisy.

Theoretical Objection: The ecumenist might argue that not all ecumenical orientations are hypocritical, that some ecumenists can hold an objective belief while simultaneously affirming one's right to differ. Here the ecumenist joins forces with the democrat who affirms the first amendment to the Constitution which affirms the right of people to express beliefs even when those beliefs conflict with their own beliefs. In this case the ecumenist might argue that he is affirming the person's *right* to believe what he chooses over and above affirming the belief itself. In a sense, then, it is the person he affirms and not his belief.

Theoretical Response: This argument might carry some weight if the ecumenist were to be operating from an experientially-objective orientation where he could sincerely affirm the legitimacy of the other's perspective even though it conflicts with his own (e.g. a color-seeing person sincerely accepting the objective legitimacy of the color-blind person's claim), but then he would no longer be an ecumenist. By definition, an ecumenist holds some form of traditional objective belief and traditional objective beliefs, if accurate, reflect an understanding of the world as it is. An opposing belief cannot be affirmed if one is to avoid contradiction. And if the ecumenist says he can affirm the person and not the person's belief, then the experiential structures within which he participates would be similar to those of the color-seeing person's affirmation of the color-blind person's claim. They might look like this:

C: I see this object as red; you say you see it as gray
A: curiosity
B: looking at object, talking
S: person
E: room

119

"I": ownership
    SSR

which shifts to:

C: You consistently maintain that the object is gray, and all of your
    behavior indicates that you see it as gray
A: growing confidence and trust
B: observing, thinking, talking
S: person in various locations
E: various locations
"I": ownership
    SSR

which shifts to:

C: Therefore, I believe you actually see this object as gray
A: confidence
B: looking at object
S: object in room
E: room
"I": ownership
    SSR

All of these experiences are SSR. The person's curiosity (and the rejection and doubt we can assume preceded it) is replaced by confidence and trust in the person's claim but only after consistent claims and consistent behavior by the color-blind person and the growing belief by the color-seeing person that this person is telling the truth; he actually does see the object as gray.

The difference between this series of experiences and a series of experiences which would usually characterize an ecumenist's affirmation of the person or at least the person's right to hold conflicting beliefs is significant.

In order to make this distinction clear, we'll have to analyze the structure of traditional objective claims that cannot be verified through observation. Claims of God's existence and many other religious claims are more complex and complicated than are claims of the color of an object.

In order to address this problem, we'll have to speculate as to what the experiential structure containing the first claim of God's existence might have looked like.

Theoretical Application: Supernatural vs. Natural Objective Claims

In the Bible, the first recorded words of God purportedly were: "Let there be light (Genesis: 1:3)." But at this time the heavens and the earth were formless, empty and dark, so there was no one to hear these words, except, perhaps, God himself. So the "voice" of God was already making itself manifest before there was anyone or anything to "hear" it. No people were around to claim God's existence at this point. But right after God made Adam and Eve, he blessed them and said to them, "Be fruitful and increase in number; fill the earth and subdue it. Rule over the fish of the sea and the birds of the air and over every living creature that moves on the ground" (Genesis: 1:28). Then God talked about giving them seed-bearing plants and beasts of the earth.

Perhaps the first human beings didn't ever claim God's existence; perhaps they simply experienced his existence, much like a baby experiences the existence of its parents. But since God, as opposed to parents, is non-sensible, such an experience would have to be much different from our sensible experiences. Perhaps Adam and Eve didn't really hear God saying these words, but they understood his saying them somehow. But why should we believe that Adam and Eve understood God's words without ever having learned a language, given that God spoke a language? Or why should we believe that God might have spoken in a non-linguistic manner and the only way the writers of the Bible could convey this way of speaking was through their own words? And how is it that Adam and Eve were never babies who at some point in their development learned a language like the rest of the human species? Were they created as adults fully equipped with a spoken language?

Many accounts in the Bible dramatically contradict human experience of the natural world: humans are born as babies and are not created as adults; humans are made of flesh, blood, and bones, not formed from clay; humans are created through sexual intercourse (sperm and egg) and not from a supernatural being who implants zygotes in people's wombs, etc. Cognitive contents of experiential structures can remain fairly consistent between human beings when observations are limited to the natural world. Scientific methods have debunked many of the accounts in the Bible and have relegated them to the status of myth.

Once we get beyond our experience of natural, sensible phenomena and begin to posit the existence of non-sensible phen-omena, the tendencies of our senses to achieve some form of agreement between human beings is given up in favor of whatever the imagination might concoct. When immediate experience, which is necessarily constituted in part by the environment (i.e. natural world), consists of cognitive components that are not immediately connected to the environmental components, then the content of those cognitive components is limited only by the power of our imagination. This imagination might be grounded to some extent in sensible experience, as is the imaginative creation of a wealth of "sub-atomic participles," i.e. phenomena that, for the possible exception of a single photon or light particle, escape sensibility, or the imaginative creation of "strings" in string theory to account for many sensible and some non-sensible phenomena.

When we shift experience from the sensible to the theoretical, we open the door for the imaginative. Experientially, imaginative experience, which includes the theoretical that seeks to explain the sensible, is just as real as sensible experience, but no more real. All experience, whether sensible or non-sensible (sensible or imaginative and/or theoretical) are equally real inasmuch as they are constituted by the components of cognition, affect, behavior, sensation, and the environment, and are owned.

In the foregoing, experience has been divided into two categories: 1) sensible and 2) non-sensible. Sensible experience includes all those experiences consisting of an environmental component that is immediately connected to the cognitive component. For example, in this experience,

C: This is a tree
A: confidence
B: looking at tree
S: tree
E: tree outside
"I": ownership

the cognitive component "this is a tree" is immediately connected to the environmental component "tree outside." The focal aspect of the experience consists of a cognitive and an environmental component that are immediately connected to each other.

But in the following experience:

C: trees are made of sub-atomic particles
A: confidence
B: talking
S: tree
E: tree outside
"I": ownership

the cognitive component is not immediately connected to the environmental component. The person does not perceive anything referred to as sub-atomic particles. Rather, he perceives a tree. The "fact" that trees are made of sub-atomic particles lies in his imagination. He cannot sense sub-atomic particles as he perceives the tree; therefore such experiences are non-sensible experiences. All non-sensible experiences are imaginative. Rather than perceiving a phen-omenon in the natural world, we conjure an image through our imagination and connect that image somehow to the natural world. How we do this is an historical, experiential fact.

When Democritus posited that objects in nature were constituted by indivisible, indestructible objects called atoms, he did so while not being able to sense these atoms. He could not see, feel, taste, smell or hear the tiny objects he claimed to be the ultimate constituents of what he did see, feel, taste, smell and hear. His notion of atoms being the ultimate constituents of natural objects was an imagination. An imagination, defined experientially, is a cognitive component of experience not directly connected to the environmental component of that same experience.

These imagination experiences tend to be either 1) theoretical or 2) fictional. Theoretical imagination-experiences are those exper-iences that attempt to account for sensible experiences, especially contradictory sensible experiences. For example, we might posit that there are components of the eye that are directly involved in the phenomenal experience of certain colors. Prior to experimenting with the eye's anatomy and physiology and their connection to the environment, scientists posited or imagined that there was something about the eye that was directly connected to the sensible experience that dictated that some people see the same object differently as far as color was concerned. This hypothesis, as are all hypotheses, is an imagination-experience, but it is an imagination-experience aimed in the direction of non-fiction, as opposed to the direction of fiction.

Non-fictional imagination-experiences constitute the bulk of scientific theory. When the non-fictional imagination-experiences shift to sensible-experiences, the cognitive components of experience are immediately attached to the environmental components, and the idea becomes a part of the scientific corpus (as observable facts). In our example, what was once an imagination-experience (e.g. something in the eye can account for this discrepancy in phenomenal experience) is replaced eventually (through many experimental experiences) with the observation of objects in the eye called cones and the hypothesis that these cones are directly related to the perception of color in objects in nature. The inference is a type of experience that connects the sensible experiences (e.g. observations) of people's responses to objects in the environment, given the respective anatomical structures of their eyes. People whose cones are such and such in number (anatomy) and function (physiology) will see one color, whereas people whose cones are different in number and function will see another color. The number and function of cones will be experienced as directly connected to the phenomenal experiences of each individual. Scientists will tend to experience such a direct connection as a type of causation, i.e. that such and such a number and function of cones in the eye causes a person to see one color as opposed to another.

If God is a non-sensible being, then he cannot constitute the content of any environmental component of experience. He must either be a fictional imagination cognition connected to, or co-existent with, some sensible environmental component or a theoretical imagination cognition also connected to, or co-existent with, some sensible environmental component. As a fictional imagination cognition, "God" does not refer to anything in the environment. As a theoretical imagination cognition, "God" is believed to refer to something beyond the human mind, something that is non-sensible, and something that is extra-environmental (i.e. beyond the universe). In one sense, "God" is used in a similar manner as is "sub-atomic particles": neither "God" nor "sub-atomic particles," for the possible exception of photons, is immediately connected to an environmental content that can be identified as them. The environmental content is always identified as something else. For example, "God" might occur in experiences that contain natural environmental content like:

C: This is the power of God
A: fear
B: talking
S: storm
E: outside
"I": ownership

In this example, "God" is used in direct connection to a natural storm. The idea of there being a God who is directing or causing the storm is an imagination: it is the idea of God being the cause of the storm. The same is true for many scientific theoretical cognitions. For example, in this experience:

C: That is a pi-meson
A: interest
B: looking at bubble chamber
S: bubble chamber

S: room
E: "I": ownership

In this experience "pi-meson" refers not to an actual sub-atomic particle but to a trajectory in a bubble chamber. The pi-meson is itself an imagination: it is imagined that there is such a thing as a pi-meson that corresponds not only to the trajectory in the bubble chamber but is the cause of the trajectory. But whether or not that observed trajectory was actually caused by a sub-atomic particle called a pi-meson is wholly inconsequential. What is consequential is that we believe that there is an actual sub-atomic particle that causes the trajectory we observe.

Also, when we consider a more common experience like this:

C: Blood is flowing through my lung capillaries right now
A: confidence
B: talking
S: person
E: room
"I": ownership

the cognition, as a component of experience, is not connected to the actual blood flow into one's capillaries but to the person to whom one is talking. The "fact" that blood is flowing through one's capillaries in one's lungs is a non-fictional imagination: it is a belief. We tend to incorporate that belief and many others like it into our corpus of "facts" not because we have actually seen lung capillaries and blood flowing through them but because we trust that others have actually seen such things. We tend to trust their honesty in relation to their experience. Most of our worlds are comprised of imagination-experiences that are founded upon trusting the direct experiences of others.

When supernatural entities constitute cognitive components of experience, they are, by definition, extra-experiential referents. Since the environmental component of experience consists only of what we call the physical world or sensible objects, the word "God" cannot refer to anything in the environment. "God" must refer to that which is considered to be either fictional or non-fictional. As referring to a fictional referent, "God" is a cognition known not to refer to anything in the physical environment. As referring to a non-fictional referent, "God" is a cognition believed to refer to something in the environment, though not to anything in the immediate physical environment (i.e. sensual or environmental components of experience) and not to anything in any physical environment. For a person who does not believe that there is a God outside of one's mind, "God" would be a

125

content of the cognitive component of experience without a referent outside of one's mind (i.e. a fiction), and for a person who does believe that there is a God outside of one's mind, "God" would be a content of the cognitive component of experience with an imagined referent outside of one's mind (i.e. a belief). Both "God" and "pi meson" are imaginations; the difference between the two is that "God" is an imagination believed to refer to an actual non-physical being and "pi meson" is an imagination believed to refer to an actual physical being, though neither referent is sensible. Also, for most people "blood flowing through my lung capillaries" is an imagination believed to refer to an actual physical event, though that event is not an immediate component of experience. In fact, "blood flowing through my lung capillaries" is overwhelmingly an imagination and not ever simply a cognition connected to a sensual and environmental component. We would rarely if ever actually see blood flowing through our capillaries in our lungs. Rather, we would tend either to see blood flowing through someone else's capillaries (if we are in the medical profession) or simply trust others who claim to have witnessed such things. Based on this trust, we infer that we, who are human like those whose lungs have been seen, also have blood flowing through our lung capillaries. The inference is also content of a cognitive component of experience that is usually connected to some sensual and environmental content that is not that to which we are inferring.

Since "God," by definition, cannot be immediately connected to anything in the sensual or environmental components of experience, then it must be an imagination. The first experience of God, then, must have been an imagination-experience. Whether there was a being in a non-physical realm that corresponded to the word or idea "God" is wholly inconsequential not only because all traditional objective claims are experientially inconsequential but also because its referent is, by definition, incapable of being sensed.

So it seems that when we speculate about the first experience of God, we seem to be limited to 1) that that experience occurred in nature (i.e. in a physical environment), 2) that the content of the cognitive component of experience must have been an imagination, and 3) that the content of the sensual and environmental components must not have been that to which the cognitive content immediately referred. And this seems to be so not only of the first experience of

God but of all experiences in which "God" is a part of the cognitive component. "God" and God can never exist in the same experiential structure. Only phenomena in the physical world can co-exist with their corresponding cognition.

If this is so, then God is an imagination similar in kind to pi meson and blood flowing through my capillaries. All are contents of cognitive components of experience; the first two are by definition non-sensible and the third is sensible but is usually not sensed by the person participating in the experience of which it is the cognitive content.

Since God is non-sensible, he can never be the content of a sensual or environmental component of experience. If the first experience of God occurred in nature, and God is non-sensible by definition, then the idea of God was probably conjured in the mind in response to nature, as opposed to being implanted in the mind by God. We can support this contention by observing the behavior of children. Prior to being taught by adults that there is a God, children seem incapable of coming up with the idea on their own. Their cognitive components are filled with immediate needs and wants, all in reference to the natural environment. A possible exception to this general observation might be when children are abused and they tend to create an imaginary friend whom they seem to believe exists in the physical environment though is not a physical being. But this imaginary friend is usually like other people and not a supernatural, meta-physical, all powerful being.

The same can be said about atoms. Democritus probably conjured the thought of an atom in response to his experience of nature. He never observed an atom, so the atom could not have constituted the sensual and environmental components of any experience in which he might have participated. At best, an atom was an imagination that accounted for the existence of objects in the environment that remained in the environment when people weren't observing them.

A similar thing could be said about those philosophers who conjured the idea of substance being a something to which all objects of a certain type can be reduced or into which they can be analyzed. There is no direct apprehension of a substance or, to put it experientially, the idea of "substance" as a cognitive constituent never occurs in the same experience as its referent. Rather, a substance is a cognitive content that accounts for the existence of objects of a certain type that don't seem to go out of existence when one is not sensing them.

The argument over the existence of God does not lie in the experiential fact that God is an imagination; even the theist must admit this. The argument lies in whether or not "God," as an imagination, refers to a fictional or non-fictional being. The same argument exists in relation to "pi-mason" and "blood flowing through my lung capillaries." The difference between these three forms of imagination is that "God" will never be connected to the sensual and environmental components of experience simply because God is, by definition, non-sensible; whereas a pi mason, though at present non-sensible, is at least possibly sensible given the appropriate mediating sensing technology (unless we accept Heisenberg's uncertainty principle and claim that all observations of sub-atomic particles will not be sensations of particles as-they-are but only as-they-were or as-they-are-changing-into-something-else or as-they-are-moving-else-where); and "blood flowing through my capillaries" is immediately sensible given the proper sensing circumstances.

The closer we get to the possibility of being able to immediately sense that which we cognize, the stronger the possibility of having other people's experience match that of our own. This is why science has been more successful than religion in gaining universal affirmation of its claims. Conversely, the further away we get from the possibility of being able to immediately sense that which we cognize, the weaker the possibility of other people's experience matching that of our own. When the cognitive component of experience is ruled out from ever matching the sensual and environ-mental components of experience, then we push into the realm of fiction.

Thoughts and feelings have traditionally been understood as personal or interior phenomena, not subject to observation or sensation from another person. People can think and feel without those thoughts and feelings being detected by anyone. But when analyzed experientially, all thoughts correspond to some feeling, which corresponds to some behavior that is able to be observed by others. Even the most mundane of thoughts, e.g. $1+1=2$, corresponds with some feeling, e.g. confidence, and some behavior, e.g. reflective comportment. Thinking, while listening to someone speaking during a conversation, is accompanied by various levels of attentive and reflective behavior, and that behavior is observable by others. Each word need not match or correspond to anything discrete within the environment; most words used do not correspond to anything in the immediate environment. This is why Wittgenstein's attempt to map language onto the physical world failed (Wittgenstein, 1997). But when words do match objects and relations between objects in the environment, then we have a powerful common denominator for creating universal affirmation of experience between human beings.

But even though thoughts might be necessarily connected to a behavior, that behavior might be so ambiguous as to make it nearly impossible at times to know what one is thinking. A reflective stare could be associated with a great variety of thoughts. One might have to know the thought habits of a person very well to be able to determine with any degree of accuracy what one might be thinking in association with a reflective stare.

Add to that false self construction, which is limited only by imagination, and we can multiply the ambiguity greatly by reaching into the realm of delusion.

So not only does much of the language we employ either in thought, speech or writing not match with the world around us in any discrete manner, it also is not associated with behavior in any one-to-one correspondence. This ambiguity gives thought its private quality. We often don't know what other people are thinking unless they tell us. And then it is a question of trusting what they say.

With the inroads into the anatomy and physiology of the brain and the invention of psychotropic drugs, science has even been able, to some degree, to sense thoughts and feelings, if we accept the materialistic claim that thoughts and feelings are reducible to neuron activity in the brain (in combination with the chemistry of the body inasmuch as it affects the brain). Through microscopic viewing, science can see cells in the brain (i.e. neurons). Through magnetic resonance imaging, science can see which areas of a brain are being stimulated by a given stimulus.

But at this stage in its development, neuroscience can only discern gross brain functions. It cannot isolate neural networks that correspond to phenomenal thoughts. So individual thoughts are not able to "be seen" in the world outside of one's own mind. Only through introspection can thoughts "be seen."

So when it comes to thoughts like "God," we are barred, at least at present, from sensing any version of what that thought might correspond to or match with in the sensual and environmental components of experience. If future work in neuroscience were to reveal a correspondence between discrete neural networks in the brain and the phenomenal thought of God in the mind, then we might have at least some type of sensual and environmental content that can be directly associated with the thought of God, though the association would still not be one of identity; the cognition of "this neural network is my thought of God" can never occur in conjunction with the observed neural network. Like with Heisenberg's uncertainty principle, the immediate observation of neural networks cannot completely capture the cognition associated with it. The associated cognition will always be in the past and the immediate cognition will be unobservable as it occurs.

So if the thought of God can, by definition, never be associated with the immediate sensation of God or the immediate environment, and the thought of God cannot be immediately connected to discrete neural networks in the brain because we cannot get outside of consciousness to make good any traditional objective claim that we might make, and at best, the thought of God can only be associated with, or believed to be represented by, specific neural networks in the brain, God as a thought was probably imagined in response to the direct experience of nature. God is an imagination believed to refer to a non-fictional being that can never be sensed in a physical environment, but it must be an imagination that occurs in relation to a physical environment because all imaginations (as cognitions) must occur in relation to a physical environment.

Probing Question: Can God be an imagination that refers to a non-fictional being that can be experienced, whether directly or indirectly, through one's mind or spirit?

Theoretical Extension: Experience and God
In order to avoid the accusation of God being a delusion, it seems that "God" must refer to some sort of non-fictional being that can be experienced in some way, either directly or indirectly, through one's mind or spirit since he cannot be experienced directly through the senses.

Descartes offered several arguments for believing that the thought of God entered the human mind not indirectly through responses to experiences of the forces of nature but because God himself must have put the idea of himself into our minds. He argued that because we are finite beings, the only way we could conceive an idea of an infinite being is if an infinite being put the idea of himself into our minds; hence, God exists because we, as finite beings, can conceive of him (Descartes, 1993). But since the idea of infinity can be conceived in relation to many different things, e.g. numbers, space, time, etc., and we do not have to conclude from this that these things have put the idea of their infinitude into our minds, then it seems more plausible to hold that we are types of beings capable of conceiving of infinity, even though we are finite beings. Being finite does not seem to bar us from conceiving of infinity.

Here we can shift into considerations of the claimed mystical experience of God. Many mystics will argue that they have experienced God in the oneness of the manifold things of the world or a union of the many into a transcendent whole. But such experiences can take place without any reference to or belief in God whatsoever. Substitute "Nature" for "God" and the natural mystic can experience the oneness of manifold nature and never subscribe to a belief in God. If the natural mystic's experience is the same as or similar to the theistic mystic, then the theistic mystic just adds another experience to a natural mystical experience, an experience that is unnecessary or possibly misleading to the natural mystic. This set of experiences might look like this:

Cognition:	All things in the world are one	All nature is one in God
Affect:	awe	love, contentment
Behavior:	reflective, meditative posture ➤	smile of contentment
Sensation:	object in the natural world	objects in natural world
Environ:	outside	outside
"I":	ownership	ownership

The first experience is all that is necessary for the mystic to experience the oneness of nature. The second experience moves away from an awe felt in relation to nature and is replaced by an experience which connects oneself in a personal way to a supernatural being. It reiterates the oneness of nature and therefore is redundant, but it also adds to that a personal connection to a supernatural being (at least the idea of a supernatural being). The oneness of an impersonal nature is transformed into a personalized impersonal nature, as if the impersonal nature has been created by a being who loves us.

131

In the first experience the cognition is directly connected to the sensual and environmental components. In the second experience the cognition is partially disconnected from the sensual and environmental components in that "God" is not connected to any content in the sensual and environmental components of the experience. Forcing a connection between a supernatural being and the physical world (environment) seems to have no basis in the physical world; its basis seems to be psychological, i.e. believing that nature is one in God has psychological benefits. It allows a person to be loved by a powerful being.

A similar argument can be made of the prayerful person. For instance, a person often prays to God for some sort of guidance in her decision-making. Such prayers can be delivered on her knees, while walking through the woods, or in some other reflective environment. The non-theist might opt to reflect during his decision-making process by walking through the woods, on a beach, or in some other natural environment conducive to reflection. What occurs in both situations is reflection: considering options, weighing one's response to the options, waiting for clarity, dealing with anxiety, etc. Often times, the theist will give their will over to God, which, to the naturalist is equivalent to allowing nature to take its course.

Believing in the guiding force of nature and the guiding force of God is rendered the same or similar by the naturalist. Conceiving of nature as a guiding force in decision-making is an imagination believed to refer to something non-fictional and sensible, though indirectly sensible. The guiding force of nature is not the same as a tree. We can sense a tree as we cognize it as a tree. We cannot sense the guiding force of nature as we sense objects and events in nature. At best we can sense natural objects and events that produce or allow us to generate a solution to our problems. Once a solution is generated, and we are at peace with that solution, then we might attribute that solution to the power of nature.

Likewise, the theist will not directly sense the guiding power of God in the objects and events in nature. Rather, she will at best sense natural objects and events that she imagines are under God's control in an orderly universe, which, at this time in her life, is not so apparent to her. She will call upon that imagined being to re-order her life, to guide her in deciding what's best for her to do. And once she reaches a decision that produces peace in her, she will tend to attribute her decision and the peace she experiences to the power of God.

It seems that the two processes are similar, especially in their results, i.e. a peace-producing decision, but there seems to be some important differences. One imagines a force behind objects and events that can be directly sensed, whereas the other imagines a force behind a force behind objects and events that can be directly sensed. Why imagine a force behind a force when the force of nature seems to be sufficient to obtain a peace-producing decision?

Meister Eckhart argued that the ultimate human achievement is the total submission of one's will to that of God and that a true and full love of God admitted of no will other than that of God (Eckhart, 1994). He assumed not only that God existed but that he was all-good, and therefore, any human being who submitted his will to the will of God was adopting an all-good will and that only good behavior proceeded from such a will. Hence, any human being who submitted his will to that of God was not so much God's instrument to do his will but rather a soul consistent with Goodness. Any behavior that was not good was relegated to human self-will, and any behavior that was good was not so much to the credit of the human but rather a manifestation of the goodness of God.

If we understand God as an imagination conceived in response to an uncaring or neglectful, fear-inducing power of nature and the identity-altering effect of abusive human behavior, whether or not that imagination refers to anything in the physical or a meta-physical world, then the God of Eckhart becomes the imagination of the antithesis of fear and abuse. That is, he becomes pure love. God is an endless source of love in a world with limited expressions of such love. The human soul can align itself with the boundless love of God by submitting itself to the will of God.

Probing Question: Does the imagination of the power of God exist in addition to the imagination of the forces of nature because the imagination of the power of God offers us a way to influence the forces of nature?

Theoretical Response: The forces of nature seem overwhelmingly to be indifferent to human hopes and concerns. A tornado doesn't consider who it is killing or whose property it is destroying. All in its path will be affected, rich or poor, good or bad, old or young. Cancer will affect a wide variety of people, whether those people do anything directly to bring about the cancer or not. But a personal God is not indifferent to humanity. A personal God can be called upon to help us, can be moved to action in our behalf by our petitions, can be influenced to control the power of nature in order to preserve our lives, promote our health, and help us decide what is best for us to do. A personal God supplies us with what nature does not: care.

Theoretical Extension: The Need for God

The imagination of a personal God might well have been conceived in response to a seemingly impersonal nature and the destructive forces inherent within it, but that alone doesn't seem to explain why people have lost or abandoned their faith in the forces of nature. Though nature possesses life-ending qualities, it also possesses life-sustaining and life-flourishing qualities. How is it that the naturalist can allow nature to take its course without ever petitioning a personal God to make sure that nature does his or her bidding?

A possible answer to this question might lie in the way people have treated each other from the time people have come into existence. Once it was discovered that acts of aggression, whether physical, emotional, or sexual, had an effect on others so as to make them submit to the aggressor, trust in people, as a part of nature, was abrogated. Our trust in the forces of nature was broken, at least in part, by the abusive behavior of some people toward other people. The genuine care of people for people in nature was replaced by a type of false care that was inextricably connected to an imagined meta-experiential construct that, it was believed, would respond favorably to the petitions of people. A personal God was conceived in response to a seemingly indifferent and often life-threatening nature and an abusive treatment of humans by other humans. Nature cannot supply humans with the care needed for their natural development, and humans have broken the trust needed for them to be at home in nature through their abusive behavior toward each other. A personal God became necessary for humans to live in a physically uncaring and humanly abusive world.

Proposition 48: The self is integral to claims of theism.

Theoretical Extension: The Experience of God

Any claim of God's existence that a human being might make occurs within the natural, physical environment; it occurs within an experiential structure. Moreover, the theist cannot get outside of that structure ever to make good or "prove" that claim. Therefore, any objectivity awarded that claim must occur within the experiential structure itself. Experientially, objectivity consists of the actual contents of the experiential structure itself. Experientially objective contents are either SSR (simple, strong and right) or complex, allowing for expressions of each along a continuum. Claims that are made of God's existence to be independent of the experiential structures within which those claims exist are to be owned by each claimant. In owning a traditional objective claim, the claimant relativizes the claim and objectivizes the cognition simultaneously. Such a claim might look like this:

C: God exists
A: confidence
B: talking
S: environment
E: wherever
"I": ownership

Whether or not the cognition captures or refers to an actual being is inconsequential. What is important here is whether or not the cognition occurs within an SSR or a complex experience. If SSR, the claim is valid and should be respected by others and the person should be accommodated within society. If complex, the claim should be assertively confronted as a false self construction while affirming the underlying real self.

When a claim of a personal God is made, the validity of that claim lies in the actual structure of the experience within which the claim exists. In order to determine whether or not a claim for a personal God is simple, strong and right (i.e. authentic, valid, real, good) one must rule out complexity. But if we accept the argument that any claim of God's personal existence must occur in a physical environment, and that such claims are imaginations, and that such claims occur in response to events in a natural, physical environment, and that specific events in that environment produce tremendous fear in us, and that human beings, despite their efforts to care for each other, have a long history of abusing each other, then we would probably find claims of the existence of a personal God as being a meta-experiential construct, i.e. a false self cognition, joined by other

135

like-thinking false selves, and institutionalized into a traditional objective ideology passed down from generation to generation through the coercive power of social hierarchy.

Such an experience might look like this:

C: this is life-threatening	I am weak (compared to nature)	I am strong (with God's help)
A: fear	self-rejection	false confidence
B: fearful behavior	looking down	false compliance
S: natural event	environment	environment
E: wherever	wherever	wherever
"I": ownership	ownership	ownership
SSR		

The above experience is a rendering of a rather sophisticated idea. Prior to the sophistication of theism we might posit a type of pagan experience, where the natural events themselves or the objects in nature that were believed to cause such events would have constituted the cognitive component of the experiential structure. For instance,

C: this is life-threatening	I am weak (compared to nature)	I am strong (with Zeus's help)
A: fear	self-rejection	false confidence
B: fearful behavior	looking down	false compliance
S: natural event	environment	environment
E: wherever	wherever	wherever
"I": ownership	ownership	ownership
SSR		

In this situation the ancient Greek and Roman will reject their own abilities to deal productively with the power of nature and create a false self constituted by an imagination of a being behind the natural event that can control those types of events. They can call upon Zeus, the god of all gods and a pre-curser to theism, to influence nature to prevent all sorts of natural disasters, or they can call upon specific gods like Neptune to calm the seas and watch over them on their journeys. Or they can call upon more psychological gods like Apollo to guide them in their intellectual pursuits and appreciation of music; or Dionysus to allow them to express their inner feelings of anger and revelry. Humans either rejected or didn't realize their own power to deal productively with the power of nature, so they imagined a power behind the power of nature in order to influence that imagined power on their behalf. Likewise, in the psychological realm, humans either rejected or didn't realize their own power to deal productively with the feelings they felt that produced behavior that proved problematic for them, so they imagined a being that could influence those feelings on their behalf.

Eventually, these various imaginations were consolidated into one being that controlled or influenced all aspects of nature, both external and internal. The God of theism became an all-powerful imagination who could, at least in theory, be influenced to control nature, both external and internal, on our behalf.

The God of Judaism could not only control or influence natural events but could also bring justice to Judaism's oppressors, i.e. people who dominated their existence or imposed their wills upon them in some manner. That God could protect them to some degree from natural disasters and from interpersonal pain due to abusive human behavior.

On the interpersonal level, the Old Testament God is a God of justice, a protector against injustice, a giver of power to overcome injustice and enforce justice. It is a forceful, vengeful and sometimes violent God. It is a decidedly masculine God.

The God of Christianity continues to possess all of the above qualities though tempered by the qualities of mercy, forgiveness and love. Jesus, as the son of God, reinstitutes the care that has been subordinated to justice in the God of the Old Testament. The God of the New Testament in the person of Jesus can be understood as evidence of human movement toward the re-capturing of mankind's ability to care for each other and to mend the damage done to each other by each other when they learned that abusive behavior could get for them what they wanted. In the urgings to love one another as oneself and to love one's enemy, Jesus attempts to transcend the boundaries that parcel humans into competing groups. He looks past what divides human beings, i.e. their opposing beliefs of some sort of traditional objective reality and towards what unites them, i.e. their humanness. The shift in focus is away from traditional objective ideological constructions like paganism and Judaism and toward a union of people as people, i.e. what today might be considered a biological position. Despite our opposing religious (read super-natural) differences, we share a fundamental biological similarity. In our biological similarity we are, at least to a great degree, united. We can recognize humanness in each of us because we share, to a great extent, similar genetic structures. Such recognition can dispose us to care for one another.

But Jesus, like any human being, was a product of his time in addition to being an original thinker and moral revolutionary. He didn't know about biology as we do today; he had no idea of what genes were; he never conceived of neurons or neurotransmitters in the brain. Rather, he understood human similarity in metaphysical and literary terms. But the result is the same: all human beings are capable of caring for and being cared for by others, regardless of family, group, or societal connections.

Proposition 49: The self is integral to claims of biology

Theoretical Extension: Identity and Biology

Just as we cannot remove ourselves from experience to capture a traditional objective supernatural reality, so too are we unable to remove ourselves from experience to capture a traditional objective natural reality. The biologist is just as limited to experience as is the theist. Claims that reduce supernatural ideas to neuron transmissions in the brain are themselves cognitive components of experience. Some of them occur simultaneously with matching sensational and environmental components (e.g. surgeon looking at heart) and some (most) occur without matching the content of those components. The latter are imaginations. Some of these imaginations refer to physical objects and events outside of the immediate experiential structure (e.g. blood filling our own capillaries); some refer to past events either in the form of memory or in the form of historical accounts (e.g "I saw the movie, *Lincoln*, last night" and "Lincoln was assassinated while in office"); some refer to types of things, events, or states of being (e.g. chairs, concerts, democracy) and are known as concepts; some refer to things believed to exist in the physical world but cannot or are not sensed either through our senses or through our senses aided by technology (e.g. atoms); some refer to nothing that exists in the physical world and are referred to as fictions (e.g. unicorns, Huckleberry Finn); some refer to nothing that exists in the physical world but are sometimes believed to exist in the physical world (e.g. hallucinations); some refer to nothing that can be sensed in the physical world but are believed to exist in a metaphysical world in conjunction with the physical world (e.g. ghosts, God, soul); some refer to people, events or motives that are believed to exist in the physical world when they do not so exist (e.g. delusions).

This variety of imaginations constitutes the bulk of human reality. The imaginations that we're concerned with in biology are those that refer to objects and events in the physical world, including our own brains (e.g. blood in our capillaries experienced directly or indirectly through trusting the experiences of others, neurons in our brain experienced directly through a microscope or indirectly through trust) and objects that are believed to exist in the physical world but are difficult to sense clearly (e.g. neurotransmitters).

Direct observations of biological phenomena are not considered here to be imaginations. Rather they are cognitive components of experience that co-constitute experiences consisting of sensual and environmental components that connect to, or correspond with, the cognitive component. So when a biologist sees a neuron through a microscope, he cognizes it as a neuron as he senses its size, shape, etc.

But each biological phenomenon has a history behind its development. The discovery of the neuron was preceded by speculation in relation to the microscopic structures of brain tissue. These speculations were imaginations; they were conjured in the head and thought to exist outside of one's cognition and in the physical brain itself. When neurons were first observed through a microscope, the "neuron" shifted from an imaginative content of cognition to a cognitive content directly connected to, or associated with, sensual and environmental content. This experience was communicated to others who could verify these observations (other biologists, neurologists, etc.) and to the general public. The general public, who usually will not look though a microscope to see a neuron, will tend to accept the existence of such things on faith (or trust). In this sense, most of human reality is based on faith or trust in other human beings.

No matter how convinced the biologist is in believing that what he is observing (discovering) exists in a world independent of him, he must circle back and admit that such a belief is a part of experience. Whether or not a biological phenomenon is an existent beyond experience is inconsequential or irrelevant. What is consequential is that he believes or experiences it to be something independent of him.

Experiences of traditional objectivity have a better chance of being confirmed by others when the cognitive component of an experience is connected to the sensual and environmental components of that experience. Biologists who observe a neuron through a microscope have a better chance of convincing others of the validity of their experience if others can participate in a similar experience. As more and more people participate in similar experiences, the reality of the neuron becomes more and more accepted, until it is fully accepted into the corpus of "traditional objective reality".

Most biologists tend to be realists and they tend overwhelmingly to understand what they are observing to be independent of their observations, even though their observations are exactly that, i.e. *their* observations. It is an experiential contention that no biologist can detach himself from experience to discover anything that might exist in a traditional objective world. Rather, his experience at one time might be constituted by a cognition (e.g. "neuron") and a sensation (e.g. neuron cell structure) and an environment (neuron cell structure of brain tissue, under microscope, in lab, etc.) and at other times by the imagination of "neuron" (in the form of memory) in connection to other sensual and environmental components. This experience is communicated to others and they can participate in similar experiences if desired. At no point in this process is the integrity of experience pierced so that one might enter an "objective world." It is only *assumed* that one has entered an objective world.

The color-seeing person assumes that the leaves on the tree he is observing are green; the color-blind person also assumes that the same leaves are some shade of gray. Each would tend toward thinking that any person would see it the way he or she sees it. Each person's experience consists of a traditional objective content. We're arguing that that content is located in the peripheral aspect of the cognitive component of experience and its necessary connection to the environmental component and not in the environmental component itself, nor in any environment disconnected from experience. Whether or not the leaves are green or gray is of no consequence.

The color-blind person's 'failure' to distinguish between green and gray or red and gray, seeing both as shades of gray, tends to be understood by the biologist as a 'disorder', that such a person is 'missing' cone structures in the eye which process light so as to see color. But such a viewpoint only reflects the ego-centricity of biologically-oriented people. Simply because most people possess the cone structures necessary to see red/green distinctions does not mean that the world outside their perception of it is actually red/green. If most people in the world did not possess those cone structures and saw reds and greens as shades of gray, then shades of gray would be what they are, and the environment would be understood accordingly, leaving the color-seeing people to be the disordered, too-many-cone-structured people who have to expend extra energy to adjust to a color-blind world, i.e. people who would be prevented from obtaining certain jobs that required accurate distinctions between shades of gray and not between red and green.

Most biological claims, it seems, can be corroborated by others because others are equipped to experience phenomena in the same way, and this capacity allows biology its strong position in determining 'objective reality.' But some biological claims (e.g. color-blind:color-seeing) admit of difference that cannot be explained away except by the establishment of complex structures. In order to conform to a one-world, realistic view, biologists must reject the validity of the experience of those people who go against the norm and cast them into the realm of abnormality and deficiency. If they can get those whose experience differs from the majority to believe that they are 'in fact' disordered or deficient, then they have succeeded in imposing their own experience upon others, and the world they've manipulated goes on relatively unperturbed. It is the color-blind people who must adjust to the color-seeing world, not the reverse.

Only recently has the experience of biologically "different" people been recognized as legitimate. Society is taking steps to adjust to the experience of these people by requiring ramps for wheel chairs, schools for the deaf, reading for the blind, etc. But it seems we've got a long way to go before we recognize other legitimate biological experience.

Proposition 50: Biology is an experiential enterprise.

Theoretical Extension: Experience and Biology
In general theory and practice biology is a realistic enterprise. Biologists tend to assume not only the existence of a traditional objective world but that that world can be perceived, reached, grasped, or understood by the human being. So when biologists make claims, they tend to make them as cognitions that correspond with an environment that is detached from that cognition. But if we accept the experiential tenet that cognitions cannot be ontologically separated from the environment, then biologists are forced to own their own claims, and their understanding of their environment

141

becomes individualized or particularized. Churchland, a philosopher of neuroscience who assumes the validity of traditional realism, argues for the individuality of biological organisms. He says that each of us is biologically constituted in our own unique way (genetically, hormonally, chemically, etc.) and that we each interact with an environment that is slightly different from each other by virtue of our necessarily occupying slightly different space in relation to others (Churchland, 1995).

This individual constitution is subject to biological investigation. Biologists, at least in theory, can understand exactly what each body is made of, how the parts of each body interact with each other, and what effects the environment has upon those bodies.

While retaining the traditional objectivity of their objects of investigation, biologists (as materialists) can also maintain a radical relativism in that each of our world views (cognitions) is reducible to neuron networks in the brain. The neuroscientist will investigate neural networks as the equivalent of beliefs, propositions, understandings, and world views. It is in the anatomy and physiology of the brain that lie cognitions of any sort. To manipulate neural networks is to manipulate people's understanding of, and response to, the environment. This is evident in noting the effect that psychotropic drugs have on people: some can make people paranoid; some can relieve them of paranoia.

If our world views are reducible to neural networks in the brain, and our brains are independent of each other and are themselves the result of individual genetic structures and individual interactions with aspects of the environment, then each of us is determined to possess an individual world view. And that world view (i.e. neural networks in the brain) is subject to scientific investigation. In this way, biologists can determine the objective contents of color-blind and color-seeing people's eyes and the effects those contents have upon the brain and explain why color-blind and color-seeing people see red/green the way they do.

But if world views are so particularized and determined by biological phenomena and forces, then are the biologist's realistic assumptions compromised? After all, the biologist's neural networks are, at least in theory, subject to the same scrutiny. He could study his own neural networks and manipulate them so as to change his world view. Is the biologist caught in a circle like the experientialist?

Must his world view that is equivalent to the neural networks in his brain be individualized and relative to the world views of others? Can he ever remove himself from his own brain and understand the environment (including his own brain) as it is and not simply as he understands it to be?

It seems that he cannot. If world views (i.e. cognitions in the form of beliefs, propositions, etc.) are equivalent to specific neural network activity in the brain and no one can remove him or herself from his or her own brain, then the biologist's world view (and all propositions that constitute it) are relative to others. By arguing for the reducibility of cognitions to neural networks in the brain, materialistic biologists are caught in a contradiction. Each person's brain is constituted as it is and acts as it does, and each person's brain (including that of the biologist) is subject to realistic investigation; yet no one (including the biologist) can get outside of their brain activity to determine what their brain activity is or what constitutes their environment. The materialistic biologist's understanding of the 'objective world' seems, inevitably, to circle back on itself and encapsulate itself in the brain of individuals.

This, in and of itself, presents no problem for the experientialist because the experientialist has brought traditional objective reality inside experience and owns traditional objective claims. Relativizing traditional objective reality is the result. But since the biologist tends to adhere to a traditional objective assumption about reality, he is caught in a contradiction. How can world views be reducible to neural networks in the brain while these neural networks in the brain are subject to objective research? How can anyone who cannot get outside of his own brain activity determine his own brain activity in a traditional objective manner? If the biologist cannot do this, then he, like the experientialist, must own his own objective claims.

Proposition 51: All traditional objective claims must be owned in order to avoid contradiction.

Proposition 52: The owning of all traditional objective claims allows legitimate contradictory views of reality.

Theoretical Extension: A Critique of Traditional Objective Systems of Thought

143

When the theist and the biologist (and anyone who adheres to a traditionally objective system of thought) own their own claims, they relativize traditional objective reality, rendering *what* they say to be of less importance than *how* they say it. If what they say is said in the context of an SSR or authentic structure, then the claim is legitimate and needs to be respected by others. Conversely, if what they say is said in the context of a complex structure, then the claim is illegitimate and needs to be assertively confronted and exposed as false while affirming the real structure that underlies the false structure.

Theists who adhere to a traditional objective system of thought, believing that they have somehow captured or grasped objective reality, must either deny their own beliefs when they affirm the legitimacy of contradictory beliefs through the creation of complex structures or reject the legitimacy of others' beliefs and act to repress or punish those who hold them, thus subjecting themselves to accusations of bigotry and intolerance. In other words, a consistent theist living in a pluralistic society must be either deeply hypocritical or intolerantly bigoted.

But when one rejects traditional objectivity and accepts experiential objectivity, then one can consistently accept contradictory or differing reality claims without being guilty of hypocrisy, and one can reject contradictory claims without being guilty of bigotry. In fact, one is morally obligated to accept contradictory claims if they are made within SSR experiential structures, and one is morally obligated to reject contradictory claims if those claims are made within complex experiential structures.

Likewise, biologists who adhere to a traditional objective system of thought, believing that they have somehow captured or grasped objective reality, must either deny their own beliefs when they affirm the legitimacy of contradictory beliefs through the creation of complex structures (e.g. color-blindness as a human deficiency) or reject the legitimacy of others' beliefs and act to repress or punish those who hold them (e.g. denial of tenure because of 'illegitimate research'), thus subjecting themselves to accusations of bigotry and intolerance. In other words, a consistent biologist living in a pluralistic society must be either deeply hypocritical or intolerantly bigoted.

But if the biologist owns his own traditional objective claims, he might avoid accusations of hypocrisy and bigotry by recognizing the biological plurality (individuality) of human organisms and their inextricable connection to their particular physical environment and that his own understanding of those diverse organisms is itself reducible to specific neural networks in his brain, the reality of which must be recognized even on realistic biological grounds. The diversity inherent in the biological constitution of human organisms requires biologists to accept a type of relativism because that relativism ultimately rests upon objective biological contents and processes. Experientialism requires the biologist to go one step further. It requires that the biologist relativize even pluralistic objective claims by owning his own traditional objective claims. Biological realism is thus reduced to a process of historical development, practical learning, inter-human trust, and the transmission of knowledge from generation to generation rather than a realistic, objective, overarching reality used by the few to dominate the many.

When traditional objectivism is rejected and experiential objecttivism is embraced, human beings are on equal ground. Reality claims become relative to the individual and objectivity lies not in the content of the claim but in the structure of experience. When experiential structures are simple, strong and right or authentic, they are real; when they are complex, they are distorted.

Experientially, reality is real or distorted; there is no such thing as "unreal" or "not real." To claim that something is not real is to confuse either:

1. The fact that something exists for one but not for another, e.g. a person might feel love for another, while the other does not believe this is so

2. That something exists at one time and not at another, e.g. Lincoln died at the end of the Civil War; he no longer exists

3. That something exists "in one's head" and not "in the world," e.g. he experienced an hallucination

In all of these areas, existence is relative to something: to another person, to history, or to the physical world. Each aspect of each area exists: the love exists for the lover whether or not the beloved believes this; Lincoln existed at one time and no longer exists, i.e. his physical body is no longer observable but his memory and, later, stories of him exist; a hallucination is just as real as the physical environment within which the person hallucinating exists.

Rejecting traditional objectivism and accepting experiential objectivism transforms the focus of ontological questions from the physical world of nature (and the supernatural) to human experience, which necessarily includes the physical world (environment). Claims of the physical world are made within experiential structures. If these structures are SSR, then the claim is authentic and real (as opposed to distorted), regardless of whether or not the content of the claim is rejected and replaced by another claim at some point. The structure of the experience within which the claim exists supersedes the traditional accuracy of that claim. Traditional accuracy becomes a matter of prudence and not ontology, a practical concern rather than a reality issue, a matter of trust rather than conformity to a reality devoid of human contact.

Proposition 53: Human reality is particular to the individual.

It seems to be, on both experiential and materialistic grounds, that reality claims are particular to individuals. The individual human being occupies his or her own physical space, and does not share that physical space with another. The human body is spatially integrated and individual. Materialistic science recognizes this as so.

But psychologically, human reality is social. The self does not seem to exist in a vacuum, nor does it exist completely independently of others. The individual physical body might well exist independently of others but only when the human is capable of a hermit-like existence. Developmentally, the human body requires other human bodies (or at least other animal bodies) to care for and nurture it to adulthood; without that care the body dies or fails to thrive.

Proposition 54: Human reality is inherently interpersonal.

Since we cannot extricate ourselves from our own experience, any reality claims we might make are experiential. Since we are social animals, and our identities are formed socially, and our identities are inextricably connected to nature, any reality claims that we make in relation to nature are products of society. The biologist and the physicist derive their interests and passions not only from their individual biology but also from their sociology. Their identities can be understood as bio-psycho-social. Without the biology, there is no body. Without the psycho, there is no private world. Without the social, there is no interpersonal world. In order for a human being to understand himself within the world he exists, he must interact with others. And others play a crucial role in the development of that individual, biologically, psychologically and socially.

Proposition 55: The human self develops as a balance between the personal (biological and psychological) and the interpersonal (social).

When the individual person asserts himself amidst others (e.g. parents), he realizes himself through SSR experiences. When others accept the legitimacy of those experiences, the individual self develops. When others reject the legitimacy of those experiences, the individual self is in position to become distorted. If the individual does not possess the capacity to defend himself from rejection or, in other words, assert himself in relation to others, he will tend to reject the legitimacy of his own experience and accept the 'legitimacy' of others' experience. This is the essence of complex structures and reality distortion.

Probing Question: What do we do when the biological and psychological aspects of an individual come into conflict with the social aspects of that individual?

Theoretical Extension: Experiential Consistency

Experiential consistency is the experientially objective core of experiential thought. Experiential consistency occurs on individual as well as interpersonal levels. The individual level can be divided into two levels: 1) intra-experiential and 2) inter-experiential. The intra-experiential level of consistency refers to individual SSR structures. Each experiential "frame" or "structure" consists of experiential components. Each component consists of focal and peripheral aspects. The contents of these aspects need not be consistent with each other in order to have a consistent structure, but the structure itself needs to be SSR or authentic in order to be consistent.

For example, a woman might be in conflict over whether or not abortion is good or bad. She might have believed most of her life that abortion is bad, the killing of an innocent life, etc., but when her friend gets raped and lands up getting an abortion, she goes through a series of experiences involving her friend, her own feelings of love for her, and her own beliefs about abortion, and she eventually comes to a determination that abortion, though wrong in instances of convenience, might be right or at least morally acceptable if under-taken in rape situations. At some points in this development, an individual experiential structure might be constituted in this fashion:

Focal	Peripheral
C: Abortion might be right when raped	Abortion is wrong in all situations
A: confidence/doubt	confidence
B: thinking	thinking
S: environment	environment
E: room	room

In this experiential structure, the woman is thinking that abortion might be right when raped, but she is aware that she also thinks it is wrong, even when raped. Her previously held belief that abortion is wrong in all instances is being challenged by her growing new belief that it might be acceptable in rape situations. At this point, the old belief has receded into the periphery of consciousness, but it still possesses strength of its own; it is strong enough to exist as a peripheral aspect of the cognitive component of an individual experiential structure for some length of time.

The content of "abortion is wrong in all instances" conflicts with the content of "abortion might be acceptable in rape situations," but this conflict does not render the structure inconsistent. Rather, the individual is in conflict. She is moving from one belief to another, and such movement will often consist of conflict, if not ambivalence.

"Conflict" is defined as conflicting claims on the same or different levels of consciousness. Such conflicts might not produce recognizable or observable ambivalence. Rather, they tend to register as doubt, hesitation, reticence, insecurity, un-sureness, etc. "Ambivalence" is defined as recognizable or observable conflict. This level of conflict usually occurs on the inter-experiential level of consistency.

Inter-experiential consistency occurs when two or more experiential structures or "frames" are consistent not only in their content but also in their structure. For instance, a belief might start out as a weak SSR structure and grow in strength over time, as more SSR structures of like content occur (e.g. "abortion might be morally right when raped" changes to "abortion is morally right when raped.") Inter-experiential conflict occurs when the content of two or more experiential structures are in conflict with each other. Often times, the conflicting content that exists within the peripheral aspect of consciousness shifts into the focal aspect, thus pushing the conflicting focal aspect into the periphery. Such development will tend to appear to others (and to oneself) as ambivalence.

But ambivalence is not to be considered experientially inconsistent. Rather, ambivalence, at least the type of ambivalence discussed here, is evidence of two SSR structures in conflict with each other, the outcome to be determined at some point in the future.

Experiential inconsistency occurs when one SSR structure is denied, negated, altered, or rejected in favor of another person's value, judgment, or world view. The result of such a replacement has been referred to as complexification.

Complexification occurs (usually) on the interpersonal level of consciousness. It is here where the biological and psychological meet the sociological. Experientially, the biological and the psychological are two aspects of the same experience; the biological cannot be divided from the psychological. Experientially, the biological is rendered in the sensation and behavior components of experience, whereas the psychological is rendered in the cognitive and affective components of experience. The sociological is rendered in the environment component of experience. When another person occupies some aspect of the content of the environmental component of the experience within which one participates, one is an actively social being. When that person seeks to negate the legitimacy of the rightness of the SSR structure within which one is participating, and one is vulnerable to that force, one will negate the rightness of one's own structure (and any belief that occupies the cognitive component of that experience at the time).

Probing Question: How are we to distinguish from conflicting experiential structures that result in learning and those that result in complexification?

Theoretical Extension: Learning vs. Complexification

If the structures in conflict are SSR, then the result will be one of learning; if the structures are complex, then the result will be one of complexification. The difficulty is knowing which is which.

For instance, when mother asserts herself by preventing her son from exercising his curiosity by sticking his finger in a light socket, the son participates in conflicting experiential structures. As far as he is concerned, he is not doing anything wrong or bad; he is simply acting on his curiosity. But mother knows better in this instance. So she imposes her will upon the child, creating a conflict within him. To the degree that the son accepts the imposition as legitimate, i.e. as in his best interest where this best interest aligns with his own sense of self-interest, the son learns to stay away from light sockets.

The same is true for learning chemistry. Initially, a student's experience does not admit of microscopes and the images that can be experienced with them. Objects in the environment appear as they are perceived through his senses. But when objects are perceived through a microscope, a conflict exists between experience of objects through one's senses and experience of the same objects through a microscope. But the conflict is resolved by the coordination of the two sets of experiences. This coordination occurs in an experience like:

C: These microscopic images are occurring when I observe this
    object through my unaided senses
A: confidence
B: looking at microscopic images
S: microscopic images
E: lab
"I": ownership

All of the experiential structures within which the person participates throughout this analysis are SSR (we'll say) in structure. That is, the original perception of the object is SSR; the conflicting microscopic images are SSR, and the coordinating experience of linking the original experiences with the microscope experiences is also SSR. The coordinating experience, in this example, is facilitated by the knowledge (or, originally, the belief) that a microscope will render co-occurring images of the same object. When the coordinating experience occurs, learning takes place. We learn that microscopic events are occurring in objects that normally (with our senses) we do not perceive. The conflict is resolved through a process of coordinated integration.

A similar thing occurs when the son grapples with his mother's imposition of will upon him in regard to sticking his finger in the light socket. His original set of curiosity experiences come in conflict with mother's imposition of will. Eventually, he resolves the conflict by integrating the two sets of experiences into one overriding experience:

light sockets are off limits in regard to his curiosity. Learning has occurred.

But when complexification occurs, the conflict between experiential structures is different from those structures constituting learning experiences. When father imposes his will upon son by hitting him and calling him an idiot for sticking his finger in a light socket, son's experience consists of a negation or denial of the legitimacy of the SSR experience within which he participates. Rather than integrate the conflicting sets of experiences, he, himself, disintegrates. He 'resolves' the conflict through submission or (the flip side of submission) rebellion. His identity disintegrates, at least in reference to this conflict.

So if father rejects the curiosity of his son by smacking him and calling him a stupid idiot, over time son will reject the legitimacy of his own curiosity and replace it with (usually) how father judges his son to be, i.e. a stupid idiot whose natural curiosity is bad. Once son accepts that he is a "stupid idiot" and deserving of being hit, at least in reference to his curiosity, his self becomes distorted. He understands himself not as he is but as his father understands him to be.

This complex structure, or distortion of identity, requires some sort of strength in order to become a 'viable' part of his identity. But since the strength is not rooted in himself (as SSR structures which are "covered over" by a false self structure), and his beliefs in relation to himself (self-appraisals) are skewed toward that of his father, the false self that is created will tend to align with the judgment of the father (or be rebelled against) and the belief constituting the cognitive component of his new, false self structure will be ripped from its identity mooring and constitute a delusional aspect of a now complexified identity structure. The child will believe, at least in relation to his curiosity, and, more particularly, in relation to his curiosity in relation to his father, that he is a stupid idiot deserving of being hit. A part of the child's identity has been distorted.

A biological and a psychological aspect of the child's identity is rejected in favor of another person's judgment of the child (i.e. father's) and a hole now exists within the identity structure (and the reality) of the child. His natural development has been altered. Who he is is, in part, constituted by what his father judges him to be and not by his own natural self-acceptance (SSR structure).

151

The problem now becomes how to recover that aspect of one's self that has been "lost" or covered over by a false self. In the father's presence, the child will tend to exhibit the false self, in this case, a self that is acceptable to father. Around other people, i.e. those who would accept an expression of his real self, he would tend, at least for a while, to be himself. But it seems to be the nature of identity that when one aspect of one's identity has been distorted, that distortion becomes a focus of attention for the child. It is as if the child knows at a deep level that something is wrong with the way he acts around his father, whereas around others who would accept that aspect of himself, he senses only consistency in his self-expression. This dynamic addresses the reason why children who are abused will often form seemingly strong (overly strong) bonds to the abuser. The abuser has distorted the child's self (through the inadvertent complicity of the child), creating a hole in the child's identity. Now the identity must be filled in. The problem must be fixed. But does the child possess the ability to fix it? Most likely not. He does not possess the ability to assertively confront his father, to reject his father's judgment of himself, to accept the legitimacy of his own judgment of himself, and to be himself in relation to his father, at least concerning the issue at hand (i.e. curiosity). Rather, he tends overwhelmingly to reject that aspect of himself that his father rejects.

When the child replaces his self-judgment with his father's judgment of him, he develops a false self. He judges himself through the eyes of his father, so to speak. When his true self expresses itself as SSR experience, it is immediately denied or rejected and replaced by the false self that is consistent with (or in the case of rebellion, totally opposite) the judgment of him by his father. The experience, in condensed form, will look like this:

C: [What is that?]	I am stupid, bad, etc.	I am good.
A: [curiosity]	self-rejection	false confidence
B: [looking at X]	looking down	false compliance (or rebellion)
S: [father]	father	father
E: [room]	room	room
Real Self	Real Self rejection	False Self

When the false self is created, the ground for the child's identity (and reality) becomes "detached from its mooring." An aspect of his identity is, at it were, floating on the ocean or floating in space. It has no real anchor. He has lost touch with himself. A hole in his identity is created and that hole must be filled. But with what? Once the real self is rejected, what is there to replace it with?

Herein lies the basis for the creation of traditional objective realities that are unhinged or 'detached' from ownership. Cognitive contents are created by one's imagination and are limited only by the limits of one's imagination. One's experience is no longer limited to the natural world. Any world can be created through one's imagination.

Once the child rejects the rightness of his own experience, he unhooks himself from himself (at least in part) and hooks himself to something false. Because that which he comes to accept about himself is false, he cannot achieve real strength. He cannot stand alone, as it were. He cannot assert himself as he is and be able to withstand contrary points of view or opinions. Therefore, in order to feel some sense of strength, he attaches himself to other false selves, i.e. other people who have been abused or neglected and have created false selves in the wake of it.

Probing Question: How does someone who has been abused or neglected "find" others who have been abused or neglected?

Probing Question: Why is someone who has been abused or neglected attracted to others who have been abused or neglected?

Theoretical Extension: Abuse and the Spread of Complexity

If abuse creates a hole in the SSR development of a given individual's identity, then that individual becomes dependent (identity-ontologically) upon a source outside him or herself for his or her self-fulfillment. One cannot be satisfied with oneself if one is not in some sense, 'being' (or at least acting) in accordance with the judgment of someone else. So in order to become satisfied, one engages in behavior that is believed will satisfy the other upon whom one is dependent. In turn, one will be satisfied with oneself because the other is satisfied with one, and only because the other is satisfied with one.

But the other's satisfaction is ultimately false. In our example, the father's satisfaction with the son is dependent upon the son's rejection on his real curiosity and 'acceptance' of his submissive behavior. When the son is submissive, the father 'accepts' him, thus reinforcing the son's false self. But the father's acceptance of his son's submissive behavior is based on the father's own inability to

153

accept his son's true self, i.e. his son's natural expression of who he is.

The father's response to the child's behavior might be SSR (genuine) if the father simply doesn't understand the child's behavior; the behavior is too foreign to him for him to understand. Such behavior would be akin to a color-seeing person's inability to accept or affirm the behavior of a color-blind person saying that the color he is looking at is not close to the color that the color-seeing person sees. One simply can't affirm the legitimacy of the other person's claim because it contradicts the experience of, or is too foreign to, the person. The lack of affirmation is SSR or genuine. The person is consistent with himself.

But being unable to accept the legitimacy of a given behavior is not the same as rejecting that behavior. Not affirming a behavior is usually characterized by confusion, doubt, caution, curiosity, etc. and not condemnation or rejection. Not affirming a behavior gives the benefit of the doubt to the actor. One suspends judgment and tends to allow the behavior without making a definite judgment either way of that behavior. The doubt or confusion is SSR or authentic.

But when the response is one of rejection or condemnation and the son is not in position to assertively confront his father and, hence, reject his judgment of him, then the father's judgment of the son is inculcated into the identity structure of the son through complexification of the experiential structure within which the son participates.

When complexification occurs, and the son's false self that is more aligned with his father's judgment of him rather than his own, then the son becomes dependent upon the acceptance of the father in order to accept himself. When that acceptance is not forthcoming, the son's self-acceptance does not obtain. The son is now on a treadmill. He can obtain his father's acceptance if he acts ingenuously, but when he acts ingenuously, he cannot ground his behavior in himself; he cannot genuinely accept his own behavior. So if father does not for any reason whatsoever show acceptance of son's behavior, then son's self-acceptance is compromised. A dominant:submissive relationship is created.

Once a false self covers over a real self, not only does behavior become ingenuous, the cognitive component of the false self experience must be filled with content. That content is limited only by the limits of imagination. When self-rejection occurs, the cognitive content of experience (usually something like "I'm bad; I'm weak; I'm wrong") must be replaced with content that is functionally acceptable to the individual. Often that content will align with that of the dominating person.

For instance, if father rejects the rightness of his son's experience by his abusive behavior, then he can offer his own behavior as model for the son to inculcate into his identity, i.e. father is critical and unaccepting; son becomes critical and unaccepting. In this case, the son learns directly from the father how to respond to the curious behavior of his own children, if not (through generalization) others beyond his own family.

But the reverse could also occur. The son could reject his own natural curiosity and adopt a submissive, 'non-critical' false self. So instead of becoming critical like his father, he becomes 'non-critical' and 'accepting', but this behavior is false. His 'passive conforming' behavior is acceptable to the father on a superficial level, but the whole transaction between father and son is false. Son 'submits' to father (but resents that submission); father 'accepts' son (but resents that acceptance). Now father and son are on a treadmill. No matter how much the son behaves so as to please the father, he will fail. No matter how much the father seeks to produce an acceptable son, he will fail. Both father and son are engaged in false self interaction. The relationship, at least in regard to this issue, becomes dominant: submissive.

In the first instance, son will rebel against his father by adopting his father's behavior and directing it back toward him or others. In the second instance, son will conform to father's demands and seek to gain father's acceptance through more overtly submissive behavior. Either way, the false behavior, whether overt or covert, requires justification, at least to the individual self. The rebellious son must justify his own critical, unaccepting, aggressive behavior in order for him to 'accept' himself; the conforming son must do likewise. Since the behavior is false, and detached from its natural grounding, the content of the cognitive component within which the behavioral component exists need not be consistent with its natural setting (environment). One could conjure up any cognition (idea) that will serve to justify one's false self construction.

For instance, the son could believe his passive behavior is morally good, that he is being a dutiful son, and that other sons who act rebelliously or assertively are bad in some way. In order for him to sustain such a belief, he will 'naturally' seek out like-thinking people, people who are 'repulsed' by rebellious or what seems to them to be aggressive behavior in children. These like-thinking individuals will tend to band together, reinforcing each other's false self, giving themselves a semblance of strength. And they will tend to codify their justificatory belief (e.g. "obey your parents," "filial piety," etc.) so it can be taught not only to others (spatially spreading the word) but generationally (temporally spreading the word). But the strength is false, and the code that carries it is also false.

Likewise, the rebellious son will believe that his father is a tyrant and that his critical aggressive behavior is morally justifiable. He will tend to seek out or be attracted to like-thinking individuals. This group will tend to reinforce each other's critical, unaccepting, rebellious behavior and develop for themselves some semblance of strength. But the strength is false. They will also tend to codify their justificatory belief (e.g. "might makes right"; "spare the rod, spoil the child", etc.) and pass those beliefs on from generation to generation. The codification of complexity is referred to as meta-experiential construction.

PART 3: Distorting Human Cooperation

Proposition 56: When divested of ownership, objective realities tend to become ideological instruments (i.e. meta-experiential constructs) born out of personal, familial, and group complexification of identities.

Theoretical Extension: Democracy and Evolution

Elucidating the path from familial complexification to meta-experiential construction requires philosophical extension, empirical data, and historical speculation.

As mentioned earlier, anthropologists generally agree that human society began with bands of hunter-gatherers consisting of networks of families with more-or-less nuclear boundaries. These bands were generally egalitarian in social structure. Individuals acted as they saw fit, made agreements with each other as they saw fit, and tended to punish those who violated group mores or customs and "upstarts" who tried to force their will upon others in the group. But some anthropologists tend to believe that though the group politics was egalitarian, family politics was more hierarchical, with the male as the dominant figure. The evidence for this conclusion is based upon relatively modern-day research in relation to contemporary hunter-gatherer groups, e.g. the Kalahari Bushmen.

Speculating about the past based on present-day groups of people has its inherent problems. Simply because there are present-day hunter-gatherers doesn't mean that hunter-gatherers dominated past human existence; nor does it mean that present-day egalitarian behavior in a minority of human groups represented by hunter-gatherers is indicative of the "true nature" of human beings that might have gotten distorted at some point in history, i.e. when agriculture was supposed to have introduced private property into human social life. But if we accept some of these anthropological theories as a true, or as actually 'capturing' historical reality, then we must accept at least the possibility that human beings are, at least to a good degree, naturally cooperative and egalitarian in nature.

But even if we are skeptical in regard to anthropological theories that assert a primal, biological egalitarian inclination among human beings, we are more hard-put to rid ourselves skeptically of human equality given recent history's growing development and spread of democracy throughout the world. The push to move away from monarchies, totalitarian regimes, oligarchies, and committee-run socialisms to democratic political structures offers strong empirical support for the idea that human beings are, at base, egalitarian or cooperative and that we are just now in history trying, en masse, to reconnect to our natural roots through our strong push for democracy throughout the world.

This push toward democracy throughout the world is the most difficult phenomenon for evolutionists and socio-biologists to explain. For if human beings are biologically determined to structure themselves hierarchically, then why are so many of us pushing to establish a political structure that is non-hierarchical or egalitarian, as in democracy? On this issue, evolutionists remain nearly completely silent.

The best attempt to explain this phenomenon is that democratic practices, whenever they have occurred in history, are the result of genetic mutations that will not survive the pressures of natural selection. Democracy is at best an unstable biological anomaly that will be marginalized in the same way that web-toes are marginalized, i.e. the genetic blueprint for it might exist, the gene structures that bring it about might be passed on from generation to generation because the genotype has not negated procreation, but it will not proliferate in the world because the social structure that it gives rise to (democracy) is too unstable to allow individuals to live long enough to promote those genes. What this amounts to is that tendencies toward democracy are only going to be marginally and/or temporarily successful. They will last until they are shown to be ineffective in promoting the life of the offspring that are generated within such systems of human society or until those possessing hierarchical genetic structures simply overpower and kill off those possessing democratic genetic structures, or the genetic structures will continue to express themselves in the population (as do web toes) but only in a marginalized way. In this sense, all democratic movements occur under the forceful umbrella of some type of hierarchical structure, whether it is monarchy, totalitarianism, oligarchy, aristocracy, or committee-run socialism.

Theoretical Extension: A Note on Anthropological Skepticism

We offer no argument against the idea that human society started out as egalitarian hunter-gatherer bands, only a caution not to accept this idea as actual without more empirical evidence and more sound critical argument. The idea, though, does fit with the thesis of this work. If human society started out with an egalitarian social structure, then what happened? Why did we, as egalitarian social beings, change so drastically? Why did we adopt hierarchical social structures so thoroughly? Or, in deference to those anthropologists who hold that hunter-gatherer political systems were egalitarian but families were hierarchical, why did the family system usurp the political system? And, to complicate things even more, why is democracy such a strongly held political system in the contemporary world? Even if we hold to a mixed theory of human nature and maintain that humans are both egalitarian and hierarchical in nature, then why has hierarchy so dominated recorded human history and egalitarianism so dominated pre-recorded human history (as spec-ulated) and is resurging now through the proliferation of democratic political structures throughout the world (as actual or empirical)?

Theoretical criticism: Critique of Private Property

In order to address this question, first it seems very unlikely that private property was simply the result of the discovery of agriculture. Private property was always a phenomenon in human existence. Almost all children in all families exhibit the phenomenon of private property in the notion of "mine." Even at mother's breast a child can exhibit private property behavior. The child will cry when separated from the breast when not satiated. Whether it is mother or another child who prevents the child from feeding, the behavior will tend to be forthcoming.

If we accept Stern's thesis that self-reflectiveness occurs around the age of six months, then the child's behavior, prior to that time would be understood not as indicative of "mine" but as one of biological egoism where the source of one's pleasure has been withdrawn before one is satiated and one seems to be disturbed by its withdrawal (crying) and wants it back (grasping, biting, etc.) But once self-reflection occurs, then the notion of "mine" can be applied, and the removal of a pleasure source might well be construed as a personal thing. This idea can be applied to anything to which a child might attach pleasure or happiness. This "mine" in childhood seems the more likely candidate for the source of private property than does the discovery of agriculture.

Long before the development of agriculture, the notion of private property existed. It was very much a part of the hunter-gatherer societies inasmuch as the notion of "mine" existed as a human experience. Prior to self-reflection, children seem to be unaware of themselves as something different from the various objects that make up their environment. This is not to say that they are somehow "melted into" or experience themselves as "one with the objects in their environment." Rather, it means that they have not yet recognized themselves as a force that can alter their environment. They merely react to their environment, including their own body. So when their environment produces pain in them, they respond. When their body feels pain or pleasure, they act accordingly. But they do not seem able purposefully to act upon their environment until they are able to self-reflect. When they self-reflect, they are able to learn that their behavior produces certain responses, some of which are wanted (e.g. happiness, satiation), some of which are not wanted (e.g. pain). When they are able to self-reflect, they are able not only to attach themselves to objects in their environment, including their own body, but also to act in ways that produce certain desired or undesired consequences. They seem to become agents in the world, i.e. self-conscious do-ers.

At this point in development most humans seem to become capable of owning not only objects in the environment but also their own thoughts, feelings, behaviors and sensations. At this point the experiential structures within which they participate, probably for the rest of their lives, obtain. Once components of consciousness are owned, experience exists for that individual: prior sensations become *my* sensations; prior behaviors become *my* behaviors, etc. This same primordial notion of ownership can apply to objects in one's environment, especially parts of one's body.

When a part of one's body (e.g. mouth) is attached to something independent of one's body (e.g. mother's breast), the independent object, though cognized as independent when separated from oneself, could easily be artificially assimilated with one's own body, as if the breast becomes an extension of one's own body. One way in which ownership could have come about then would be in the symbiotic

160

experience of "owning" an extension of one's body (i.e. mother's breast). In this sense, the crying behavior of the infant when mother's breast is withdrawn before satiation could be understood as a response to some artificial aspect of its own body being removed from the rest of its body, as if a part of its own body has been separated from it.

But this assimilation or symbiosis (Hamilton, 1990) is artificial. The breast does not actually become part of the infant's body. The assimilation is imaginary. But, depending upon the developmental stage of the infant, the imagination that the breast is an extension of one's own body might or might not be self-conscious. If un-self-conscious (i.e. prior to self-reflection), the imagination might very well "blend into" or "become one with" the environmental object. The infant's mouth and the mother's breast are "attached," as experienced by the infant, and the removal of it constitutes a separation of one part of oneself. But such a separation would be similar to separating a body part of an insect from the main body. The insect might respond behaviorally to the separation, but we would be hard put to argue that such behavior is the result of a primordial notion of self-reflection (i.e. "mine"). Rather, we would tend to argue that the behavior is a biological response to the removal of the body part.

But once self-reflection occurs in the infant, the infant is capable of understanding itself (and parts of itself) as separate from objects in its environment. At this point, mother's breast becomes an independent object to the infant and its mouth becomes an object that it owns. In order for the infant to "blend into" or "become one with" the independent object now it must employ its imagination. It must imagine that the breast is an extension of its own mouth. But if it does so, it creates an illusion for itself. When that illusion is broken, i.e. when mother withdraws her breast, then the crying behavior ensues.

But such speculation might be considered fanciful or too metaphysical for the realistic mind. After all, we really don't know what's going on in the mind of the infant. Perhaps it cries when mother removes her breast before satiation simply because its "happiness trajectory" (course of happy or satiety experiences) has been rudely interrupted. When an infant (or any human for that matter) has its course of satisfying experiences suddenly interrupted, it will often exhibit disturbed behavior. Its experiential flow was suddenly disturbed; its agitated response is only natural. Such a response is more akin to egoism and the maximization of self-interest than to an alteration of a meta-physical construction of identity. But such behavior would be 'self-interested' without the self (if prior to self-reflection). It would be 'egoism' without the ego. So perhaps at the pre-self-reflective stage of development, crying behavior at the withdrawal of mother's breast might be attributed to a biologically determined reflexive response. But when self-reflection obtains, crying might be interpreted, at least in some instances, as an agented expression of dissatisfaction, i.e. an interruption in one's flow of satisfaction experiences to which one takes exception. It is at this point that "mine" takes on experiential ontological significance.

Whether an infant's crying is a biological response to an alteration of patterns of satisfaction, a response to a symbiotic identity disruption, a response to a non-symbiotic identity disruption, or an agented expression of dissatisfaction, the phenomenon of "mine" either is or is coming to be crucial to the experience. When self-reflection occurs, we have the basis for ownership.

At first, we own the components that constitute the experiential structures within which we participate. A child will own its own cognitions, affect, behavior, sensations and the immediate environment within which it operates. Obviously, this type of ownership, when applied to the environment that is not one's body, is not a legal ownership; an infant will not legally own the objects within its environment. Rather, it is an experiential ontological ownership of the contents of those components that constitute the experiential structures within which one is participating.

For instance, an infant will own its own fingers and toes (bodily environment), its own feelings of pain and pleasure (sensations), its own feelings of joy and contentment (affect), and its own movements of its hands and feet (behavior). These components of experience (i.e. cognition, affect, behavior, sensation, and bodily environment) comprise the set of components that constitute the core of an individual's identity. The rest of the environment, which consists of everything outside of one's own body, including other people, constitutes the remainder of the environmental component of experience. The remainder of the environmental component of experience confirms (actively supports), is neutral to (passively supports), or disconfirms (actively rejects) the core self of the individual.

From this analysis we might well conclude that ownership in humans is inextricably connected to the ability to self-reflect. Once that ability is actuated, we own components of experience. Included in those components is the environmental component, which includes our own body as well as all of the objects and the space surrounding it that constitutes our immediate environment. The "mine" which characterizes the "I" component of experience applies to all objects and space that are connected to the other components of experience.

For instance, in the experience:

	Focal Consciousness	Peripheral Consciousness
Cognition:	(prelinguistic "object")	
Affect:	interest	
Behavior:	looking at object	
Sensation:	ball	objects in room, odors, bodily sensations, etc.
Environ:	room	objects, odors, sounds, etc. in room
"I":	ownership	

the ball, which constitutes the focal aspect of the environmental component of experience, is owned by the child. The entire sensory field of the child, as it can be cognized, is owned by the child. This notion is often conveyed by the use of the term, "my space." The entire space and its contents, as it can be cognized, felt, acted upon or sensed, is owned by the child.

Proposition 57: Private property originates in the phenomenon of self-reflection.

Theoretical Extension: The Origin of Private Property

Those components that constitute the core of a person's self (i.e. cognition, affect, behavior, sensation, and bodily environment) are intimately owned. Not only are these components inextricably intertwined, but they are also cognized as aspects of oneself. The remainder of the aspect of the environmental component (i.e. objects, space, people, etc.) is cognized as separate from the individual. The separateness of this aspect of the environment decreases the strength of ownership that exists between the individual and that aspect. In other words, the objects in one's immediate environment and the space that surrounds them are simultaneously owned by the individual and shared by others (or potential others, including other objects, animals, people, etc.), whereas cognitions, feelings, behaviors, sensetions and body parts are owned exclusively by the individual. This exclusivity of ownership coincides with strength of ownership. The more intimately something is connected to our identity, the stronger is the bond between it and us. Objects in our environment are less intimately connected to our identity; they are separate from our self and in a public world, to use Bertrand Russell's term (Russell, 1988). But these objects, and the space that situates them, are, nevertheless, owned by us. The environmental component, which includes all objects in it, is *my* component.

Proposition 58: All individuals own all contents of all components of all experiences within which they participate.

As soon as a hunter-gatherer senses a berry, she owns that berry experientially. It is a part of the experience within which she, and only she, participates. She cannot remove herself from the experience within which she participates in order to divest herself from experientially owning that berry.

But since we share this planet with other human beings, animals, and plants, etc., the odds of that kind of exclusive ownership happening are slim. Therefore, the chances of achieving that kind of ownership are extremely rare. The chances of maintaining that kind of ownership are even rarer. Someone or something is bound to sense that berry (or more accurately, those berries) along with her. Once it is sensed by someone or something else, then it becomes a component of the experience within which he/she/it exists (inasmuch as animals can experience), and then what person or what procedure determines how that resource is to be acted upon becomes a source of concern.

Theoretical Critique: Locke's Theory of Justice in Acquisition

Locke posited that the various resources of the world, which include plants, animals, and minerals (and, I'd like to add), air and water, and anything else that might constitute an environment, can be owned when one mixes labor with those resources. Simply put, if we pick the berry, it is our berry. If we till the land, it is our land. Etc. Owning or acquiring an unclaimed resource requires that we apply labor in relation to that resource, and once we apply our labor, that resource is legitimately ours.

Using this definition of private property, a hunter-gatherer would have only to pick the berry to own it. Therefore, even within contemporary political theory, the discovery of agriculture would not have been the beginning of private property. Even hunter-gatherers who never tilled the land could lay ownership claims to resources simply by mixing labor with those resources.

But so far we have argued that even prior to acting upon a resource in such a way (i.e. picking it), the resource is already owned experientially: it is in the individual's field of vision (or some other sensory field). But it is (probably) also in other people's field of vision (or other sensory field). Therefore, it is subject to the same ownership claims by others. Now it becomes a matter of who can legitimately claim it to be his or hers, or theirs (in reference to groups of people).

One method of determining ownership of a resource is who senses it first; it is a first come, first serve notion. The first person to come into sensual contact with a resource can own it. This seems to be absolutely true on the individual experiential level. But on the interpersonal experiential level, there are multiple "absolutes" interacting with each other. And each of these individuals might need this resource in order to live.

Probing Question: If there is only one berry for two people to live on, and one person sees the berry first, can the person claim ownership of the berry, simply by seeing it first?

Theoretical Response: A Critique of Locke's Theory of Justice in Acquisition

A distinction must be made between owning something simply if that something is a content of the environmental component of experience and owning something to the exclusion of others so owning it. The first type of owning is an experiential-ontological ownership. It occurs by virtue of the structure of experience and is the root of all forms of ownership. The second type of owning is social, legal, or political. It occurs for other reasons.

According to Locke's theory of acquisition, social ownership occurs by virtue of mixing labor with the resource. Anyone who can sense an object can own that object experientially, but not anyone can secure that object for their own use exclusively of others. Not anyone can remove that item from general experiential ownership and put conditions on its use by anyone else. In order to be able to do this, one must work for it, or mix one's labor with it. The mixing of labor with a resource provides an intuitive justification for making that resource one's exclusive property.

This would mean that the person who senses the berry would not be able to lay claim to it as property. She must first pick it; then she can lay claim to it. But if she labored to *find* the berry in the first place, then she might claim ownership of the berry just by sight.

It has been hypothesized that the reason one might intuitively and justifiably lay claim to a resource by mixing labor with it is because our body is already owned, and that includes the behavior of that body. Extending that behavior into the environment is just an extension of owning one's body.

This would be similar to the infant in the above analysis intuiting ownership of mother's breast or a ball, but not quite the same thing. In the infant example, the ownership is not established through labor. Simply because the infant acts upon the object in the environment does not make the object his. Simply because he grabs at or sucks the nipple does not mean that he can lay claim to the contents therein. It doesn't seem likely that an infant would object to the withdrawal of the breast or the ball as an unjust act, i.e. as taking away something that one has worked for. It seems more likely that the infant would object for biological egoistic reasons. Nor does this address the issue of exclusivity or the right to own that object and to do with it as one sees fit, especially those objects that are a part of someone else's body.

Therefore, sensing an object might well be enough to determine experiential ownership, but it is not enough to establish exclusivity of ownership. Also, to act upon an object in the environment is not sufficient to establish exclusive ownership of that object. Simply because a child plays with a ball at a daycare center does not make the ball hers. But there is some intuitive appeal to the notion that acting upon an object puts one closer to ownership of the object than does the mere sensing of it. In the case of berry picking, acting upon the berry by picking it seems to put one more in position to claim ownership of it, at least much more so than just seeing the berry.

Probing Questions: Wherein lies the distinction between acting upon an object and mixing labor with the object? Is labor just one form of action that one can perform in relation to an object (resource)?

Probing Questions: If one were to pick a berry and play with it (not eat it), then can one claim ownership of it? Must there be some specific form of action done in relation to an object in the environment for that object to be owned, to the exclusion of other people? Does the action of picking a berry constitute work only if the object of the action is eating, i.e. aimed at survival? If the goal of picking the berry is to play with it, then is the picking not work? If so, does this lessen one's claim of ownership of the berry?

Theoretical Response: It seems clear that seeing (or sensing) a berry (something separate from one self), constitutes several components of experience (i.e. the sensual and the environmental components) and, hence, are owned; and the contents of these components differ fundamentally from other contents of the same components that help comprise the individual identity (e.g. mother's breast). On the intra- and inter-experiential levels, ownership of the components of experience is a necessary starting point for any other form of ownership.

The self-reflective infant owns all of the contents of the components of each experience within which it participates on the intra- and inter-experiential levels of experience. But only those contents that constitute its identity are automatically owned. That is, only those environmental contents that are intimately connected to oneself (e.g. one's own body parts and processes) are owned exclusively, as given by experience. All other environmental contents, which are separate from oneself, are automatically owned by the individual but not exclusively. They are necessarily a part of the experience within which the individual participates, but they are also experienced as separate from one's identity. How one can claim exclusive ownership of any of these separate contents of experience differs fundamentally from how one can claim ownership of one's own bodily contents. We can more readily apply "mine" to our own cognitions, affect, behavior, sensations and body parts than we can to separate objects in the environment.

In summary, we own:

1) cognitions, affects, behaviors, sensations and body parts as integral to our self
2) objects (and processes) in the environment that constitute immediate experiences within which we participate, and this is reflected in the idea of "my own space" and consists of the full range of environmental contents constituting all experiences within which we participate, and
3) objects (and processes) in the environment within which we immediately participate and act upon in such a way as to secure those contents (objects, etc.) for our exclusive use.

Probing Question: How do we move from owning "our own space" to owning any of those contents therein exclusively?

Theoretical Response: Experientially, we don't seem to experience objects in the public world in the same way we experience objects in our private world (e.g. cognitions, behaviors, body parts, etc.) The latter experience usually consists of knowledge of the inextricable connection between the content and our self. For instance, we usually cannot separate a cognition, affect, or body part from being "ours" (though there are experiences where this seems to be done, e.g. types of dissociation, forms of hallucination, and various brain lesion-induced disorders, etc.) But normally, these contents are inextricably connected to our identity. But most contents in the environmental component of experience tend to be experienced as separate from our own identity. There are the exceptions where separate objects might seem to "blend into" our self, e.g. childhood symbiotic experiences with mother, some forms of love (passionate love for a person, mystical love for a supernatural being, maternal love for a child), some forms of superstitious unions (cannibalism, transubstantiation, snake bite ceremonies), etc., but these "exceptions" seem to involve some degree of imaginative manipulation of experiential contents (to be discussed later).

Those contents that are generally experienced as being separate from one's own identity represent those items that Locke argues can be owned exclusively by people simply by mixing one's labor with them. Using this idea, the first person to pick the berry in the above example with the intention of eating it, and, hence, surviving, can claim exclusive ownership of the berry, leaving everyone else to find their own berries. If there is only one berry and two people needing it for survival, then the person to pick it rightly and justly owns it and can do with it as she sees fit.

But Locke includes a proviso in his theory of acquisition: one can acquire any resource as long as one doesn't worsen another person's situation by doing so. Does the person who picks the berry worsen the other person's situation? Both people's situation, prior to the picking of the berry, is the same: starving. Simply by picking the berry and owning it (and doing with it as one sees fit) does not mean that the other person's situation is any worse than it was: he is still starving, perhaps a little more than before but that's not due to the other person picking (and eating) the berry. To make the other person's situation worse, one might tie the other person up or harm him in some way so he can't pick the berry, but simply picking and eating the berry doesn't seem to make the other person's situation any worse. It just makes the first person's situation better.

One might argue that picking and eating the berry might cause the other person psychological harm (e.g. depression, frustration, envy, etc.), but this seems avoidable if the person who picks the berry does so in private and never tells the other person. One could conceivably horde any resource as long as he does so outside the experiential realm of others.

Nozick argues that a person could not justifiably own the only water hole in a desert and charge others what he wants (or just drink it all himself) because in doing so he is making other people's situations worse off, i.e. he is violating Locke's proviso. But why would this be so? If the person drills the hole and finds the water, then hasn't he mixed his labor with the water and, hence, can justly claim ownership of it and do with it as he sees fit? After all, he hasn't prevented the others in any way (we'll say) from looking for and finding water themselves. They simply didn't do it, or they looked in the wrong places. He hasn't done anything to harm them; he has only done something to help himself. His discovery doesn't worsen their situation; but neither does it help their situation. It is neutral to their situation. Nozick seems to admit this when he argues in a footnote that if a person labors to preserve his water hole when others have allowed their water holes to dry up, he might justifiably claim ownership of that water hole and do with it as he sees fit (Nozick, 1974).

Even if we argue that the other people's situation is worse off because they don't have access to water in that area of the world and that all the water is being monopolized by this individual, it still doesn't mean that their situations are made worse off by the person who discovers the water. If no one had discovered water, their situation would be exactly the same as it is.

Even the psychological argument seems to carry little weight. The other people might suffer psychologically if the person who discovers the water through his own efforts claims that water for himself, to do with as he sees fit, thus worsening others' situations by adding psychological pain to their physical situation. But if this is so, then the door is open again for all such acts being a violation of Locke's proviso. For instance, a chemical company that works to discover a new drug that will cure a disease and claims ownership of the drug (patent laws) and does with the drug as it sees fit (e.g. sells it, throws it out, etc.) violates the proviso because it causes psychological harm to those people who don't have access to the drug, cannot afford it, etc. They know it's out there, and they can't have it.

The argument in the latter case is that the drug company does not horde all the resources that went into creating the drug; others can access those resources and make their own drug (never mind patent laws which prohibit that from happening, at least for a period of time). But this argument can also be applied to the water hole situation. The person who discovers a water hole is not hording all the water in the world. There's plenty of water elsewhere, and anyone who wants it can go get it (never mind the pain and effort it requires to do so).

The argument can also be made that when anyone acquires a resource simply by mixing his labor with it, he extracts a percentage of the total amount of the resource in the world, thus reducing the accessible amount of that resource. If the resource is material and situated geographically, then that reduction of availability of that resource could be said to make other people's situations worse off in that it would cause them to exert more energy to acquire that resource from another part of the world.

This argument can be extended, at least in reference to material resources, by saying that any exclusive ownership of any material resource makes other people's situations worse off because it limits opportunity for them to acquire that resource. Even a person who catches a fish in a river limits, if ever so slightly, the next person's chances of catching his own fish because there is one less fish for him to catch. The limitation might well be negligible, but when fishing becomes an industry and one large company has a large fleet of fishing boats and secures for itself a significant percentage of the accessible fish in a given area, then opportunity for others to make a living at fishing is significantly diminished. Their situation becomes worse because one company is grabbing up most of the fish in the area and for them to fish elsewhere would require a good deal of time, energy and expense on their part.

Proposition 59: When anyone exclusively owns a fixed, limited resource, he automatically makes the other person's situation worse off by reducing his or her opportunity to access that resource simply because there's less of the resource to access.

How much worse a situation is made is determined on a case by case basis. For instance, securing ownership of much of the gold in California makes it very difficult for others to make a living at golddigging in California, whereas securing ownership of much of the fish in a river might not make it so difficult for others to make a living at fishing in that river if enough fish are left to multiply and thus resupply the river with fish. Much depends upon the nature of the limited resource.

Any securing of ownership of a limited resource automatically fails a strict interpretation of Locke's proviso, even if no one recognizes his more limited opportunities to secure a share of that resource.

Theoretical Objection: A Loose Interpretation of Locke's Proviso and Response

It could be argued that Locke's proviso should only be interpreted loosely. He says, in effect, that you can own whatever resource you want (if you mix labor with it) as long as you leave enough of it for others to live on. Hence, a person who discovers a water hole can own a portion of it as long as there's enough for others to live on.

But how would this work? Would the person say, "Since I discovered this water hole through my own labor, I will claim 'X' amount of it for my personal use; everyone else in the area who might want it to live on can determine for themselves what to do with the rest.

There are a number of problems with this tack. First, how much water is there in this water hole? Is it strictly limited? Is it continuously resupplied at a certain rate? Is that rate dependent upon other factors like rainfall, snowfall, seepage, etc.? How is one to determine how much water is in the water hole? How much water is needed by each individual in the area who wants access to the water hole? It seems that these things need to be known before one is able to determine just what portion of the water they can legitimately claim as their own without creating hardship for others.

At best, the libertarian thesis which holds that people should be free to acquire whatever resource they want as long as they work for it and leave enough for others (i.e. do not make others' situations worse) is extremely vague in practice and is pragmatically impossible to implement. At worst, it provides philosophical justification for greed and exploitation.

It is extremely vague and pragmatically impossible to implement because in order to determine just how one's acquisition of a resource affects others requires knowledge of 1) how much of that resource exists in the world, 2) how well-informed others are of the existence of that resource, 3) what type of resource it is (does it replenish itself relatively quickly (e.g. water) or slowly (e.g. oil) 4) how many people there are who need (survival) the resource to live on, 5) how many people there are who would benefit (well-being) from using the resource, and 6) how much effort it would take for people to access the resource.

In order to gain this knowledge, one must engage, at the very least, in some sort of *impact analysis*. An impact analysis includes information about how the extraction of a resource from the total amount of that resource (i.e. exclusive ownership) affects others in terms of their opportunity to extract that resource for their own use (survival, well-being, trade, gift, etc.) This would require a person to know, at least, how many people there are who want that resource, whether they want it to survive or to increase their well-being, how much of it they want (or need), and how much difficulty they would have in acquiring some portion of that resource.

Simply engaging in a cost/benefit analysis, as is the practice of most businesses, is not enough. A cost/benefit analysis will provide information about how much resource acquisition, transformation of those resources into products (manufacturing), and marketing of the products will cost a company in relation to how much the company will benefit from the sale of the products (operating costs plus profit). This does nothing to address the impact that the company's actions (ownerships) have on others.

Using our example of the water hole, the person who drills for the water would have to know the impact on others of his ownership of the water. He'd have to know how much water exists at least in that area (in others areas too if water can be piped to that area from other areas), how many people need the water for survival or well-being, and how difficult it would be for them to access that unclaimed water.

Since it would probably be very difficult, bordering on impossible, to find out exactly how much water exists in the area (and surrounding areas) without engaging in an unreasonable amount of labor, that information would, at best, be an estimate based on as much knowledge as could be gathered by people. But in order to obtain that knowledge, people involved in the discovery and delivery of well water would have to share their knowledge with others. Businesses that claim a resource for their own tend overwhelmingly not to share knowledge with others as to how to access and distribute a resource for the obvious reason that it encourages competition with them. Rather, they tend to horde that information so they might be able to expand their business in the future, if so desired. This makes it even more difficult for people who want to acquire that resource to actually acquire it. This supports the argument that any ownership of any fixed or limited resource will automatically put others who want to acquire that resource at a disadvantage. It will be more difficult for them to acquire the resource, given that someone has already acquired some portion of it, no matter how small that portion. As the acquired portion becomes larger, the difficulty for acquiring a portion of it becomes greater. This puts everyone who wants a portion of the resource at a disadvantage: it will require more labor for them to own a portion of that resource than that expended by the current owners of that resource. Had the current owners of that resource not ever claimed ownership of that resource, then everyone, at least in the immediate area, would be on equal footing: anyone could mix their labor with that resource, and the amount of labor would be relatively the same. But when some people grab up ownership of that resource in the area, then others might have to go to great pains to access that resource by other means (e.g. moving to other locals). This puts them at a disadvantage in regard to resource acquisition.

If this is so, then any acquisition of any limited resource will probably cause the position of any other person who is interested in acquiring the resource to worsen. Locke's proviso fails to obtain, not because one has been negligent in making sure that others aren't worse off by their resource acquisition (though this might certainly be so), but because it is impossible to acquire exclusive ownership of any fixed, limited resource without making other people's situation worse off.

Since obtaining information necessary to determine the total quantity of a resource available would be, at least in many cases, extremely difficult, most people who claim ownership of those resources through labor do so without knowing how their behavior might affect other people. Also, other people might not know that a person has claimed a portion of that resource for his own use. Hence, the act of claiming a resource (or a portion thereof) through labor is a unilateral act that assumes a form of ignorance of others due either to a lack of money or energy to obtain the knowledge necessary to judge the effect that one's ownership claim has on others or to a lack of interest in how it affects others. These forms of ignorance constitute the vagueness and pragmatic inapplicability of Locke's proviso.

Because of the vagueness of Locke's proviso, people who grab up resources through labor, without ever performing an impact analysis, and can justify their negligence by simply "believing" that they have not made others worse off by doing so, put themselves in a position to exploit others. They justify their own acquisitions by arguing that "others can do what I did." But the fact is, other can't do what they did without expending more energy than they did simply because there is not the same amount of resource available to them.

This difference might be altogether negligible at first, but it still exists. Just like one factory putting out smoke into the air might be negligible to the community at first, but as more factories do so, the cumulative effect becomes great (and very noticeable), so too will the effect of one who grabs up a resource not be noticeable at first, but as more of that resource is grabbed up, the effects become more noticeable. But when the effect of grabbing up resources is not noticed by others, then those who do acquire them do so with the supposed justification for their acquisition to be one of satisfying Locke's proviso: "I left enough for you to do just as I did, so you can't complain." But the inescapable fact is: the amount of resource has been diminished by the person's acquisition of some portion of it, and that fact alone makes it more difficult for the next person to access that resource, even if that difficulty is not noticed at first.

So when the first person grabs up a resource and others don't notice the effect that it has upon them in their efforts to grab up some portion of that resource, the first person gets accustomed to thinking that his acquisition is just: "If no one complains, then I must be justified in doing what I'm doing." When it comes time to notice that the effort it takes for others to claim some portion of that resource which has already been claimed by some (large portions by the few or small portions by the many), far exceeds the effort that the current owners of that resource have expended in their drive for ownership, then it is too late. Others have already claimed a significant portion of that resource for themselves and have devised laws to protect that claim. If anyone else wanted to do likewise, they would have to expend an exorbitant amount of effort to do so. If they did not notice that disadvantage, then they are subject to exploitation, even if that exploitation is unintended. Moreover, if they are convinced that someone else's ownership of a resource is fully justified simply because they have worked for it, they participate in their own exploitation. Others can now say that "You can work for it, just like I did." The fact that it is more difficult to own that resource is conveniently pushed under the rug, or, less metaphorically, not recognized under the law.

Theoretical Criticism: Locke's "Second Proviso"

What many libertarian thinkers like Nozick tend not to mention is Locke's contention that not only must one who acquires a resource through labor leave enough for others, but they must also not take more than they need. In regard to perishable resources, they must not take more than they could eat or use immediately. Acquiring the resource, only to let it rot or die, is not permitted in Locke's thinking. Hence, the buffalo hunters on the early American frontier who killed buffalo for their hides, leaving the rest to rot, were at least partially guilty of violating Locke's second proviso. They used a portion of the buffalo for their own use, but left the rest to rot, when Indians

175

could have used much more of the buffalo for their survival and well-being.

This condition aligns pretty well with Christianity's Natural Law, which, through reason, determines that humans are: 1) the caretakers of the world and its resources (God is the real owner), 2) equal to each other in the eyes of God, and 3) have equal right to those resources. Natural Law argues that people should value eternal things like goodness, justice, knowledge, virtues, etc. more than temporal things like possessions (resources), money, power, the body, etc. We should use temporal things in order to obtain or achieve eternal things and not the reverse. For example, using money to obtain goodness is fine, but using knowledge to obtain money would be an inversion or a perversion of Natural Law. Such prescriptions indicate that we should use only that much of God's resources to survive and achieve a sufficient amount of well-being (read health and happiness). We should own only that amount of the totality of resources that will allow us to survive and be healthy (which includes a reasonable degree of happiness). Owning any more inverts the Natural Law; it makes ownership of temporal things more important or valuable than ownership of eternal things.

Locke's second proviso of using only as much of a resource as one needs seems to be overlooked by many libertarian thinkers today. But even Locke dispensed with this proviso when he noted that when it comes to non-perishable resources (like silver and gold) and substitutes for resources altogether (like money), the naturalistic limitation of rotting or dying is lifted. With these resources, the sky is the limit, i.e. there is no limit as to how much one can own.

But when we shift into the realm of non-perishable resources, and especially into the area of money, we are more subject to the criticism of violating Locke's first proviso of not making other people's situations worse by claiming ownership of a resource, whether the resource is perishable or not.

For instance, a farmer who claims ownership of the seeds he plants and the crops he cultivates extracts a portion of the total amount of seeds available for planting and uses them for his own use. This extraction automatically makes it more difficult for other farmers (even if only slightly) to access those seeds simply because there are less seeds available. (For a replenishable resource like seeds, this difficulty might be so slight as to be unrecognizable. But it adds up and becomes very noticeable when those owning the seeds become great in number or the seeds owned become great in number).

What the farmer does now is convert a perishable resource (crops) into a non-perishable resource (money) by selling his crops to others (retailers) who, in turn, sell them to others (consumers) or by selling them directly to others. This conversion from a perishable resource to a non-perishable resource (money) allows the farmer to transcend Locke's second proviso of owning only as much as you can use for your own survival and well-being. One can grow as many crops as one is able to sell.

If the requirement to eat only as much as you need is applicable at all, it would now apply to the consumer (i.e. buy only as much as you need to eat). So Locke's second proviso is inapplicable to most people who claim ownership of resources through labor because money, silver, gold, etc. are non-perishable and can be accumulated without limit (not including its natural fixed limits), and perishable resources can be accumulated and converted to money in the market, thus relieving the owner of the moral duty to own only as much as he needs. He can sell as much as he wants.

Also, the conversion of a perishable resource into a non-perishable resource, like money, makes it possible for the farmer to claim his ownership of seeds to be unlimited. He can own as many seeds as he can afford. This escape from the conditions of Locke's second proviso allows the farmer to buy up as many seeds as he can, which, of course, limits the amount of seeds available to others, which, in turn, makes it more difficult for others to own seeds, which means that the conditions for satisfying Locke's first proviso have not been met.

In conclusion, Locke's theory of justice in acquisition, being defined by mixing labor with whatever resource is claimed, is extremely opportunistic; anyone can claim ownership of any unclaimed resource as long as one, in some way, works for it. Simply under this rule, a person could dig a hole and discover water and claim the entirety of that water for himself, regardless of others' needs.

Locke's proviso (i.e. first proviso) is designed to set limits on the acquisition of a resource by ruling out that the acquisition of that resource makes anyone else's situation worse off. But the proviso is not only extremely vague in that it sets no conditions by which one can determine the effects of one's acquisition upon others, but it also allows one to oppress others through capitalizing on the ignorance of all persons involved (both present and future) in the ownership of that resource.

Locke's second proviso is designed to set limits on the acquisition of perishable resources, but this proviso is easily avoided when perishable resources are converted into non-perishable resources through the implementation of money. Once the conversation occurs, the moral requirement disappears or is, at best, pushed onto the consumer of the products made from the resources.

The entire attempt to establish justice by establishing justice in acquisition of resources through labor is faulty at best, exploitative at worst.

Probing Question: If a resource is not claimed by anyone, and if it is extremely difficult, if not impossible, for one to determine just how much of that resource is available to everyone, and it is extremely difficult, if not impossible, to determine how the claiming of that resource will affect others, then why can't one just grab up that resource by mixing labor with it as long as it is not obvious that one is making others' situations worse off?

Theoretical Response: The Libertarian Thesis
This, I dare say, is the exact logic used by libertarians of the Lockean tradition to justify their resource acquisitions in the name of freedom. Why would one want to grab up more resources than one needs to live on? Why do companies want to maximize their profits when those profits exceed what is necessary for them to operate? The standard answer given is: competition or, more accurately, economic and, eventually, physical survival. If a company wants to compete with other companies for a share of the market and survive as a company, then it must maximize its profits. But a company need not maximize its profits in order to continue its existence; it need only make enough profit to sustain its existence. The standard response to this is that if a company only seeks enough profit to sustain its existence, other companies will run it out of business because those companies will seek to maximize their profits and not simply sustain their existence. So if it is to exist as a company, it *must*, at the very minimum, seek to maximize its profits. Whether its methods of doing

so are effective or not remains to be seen, but it is incumbent upon the company to try.

Proposition 60: Any acquisition of any fixed, limited resource removes that part of the resource from the total amount of that resource available to others.

Proposition 61: Any removal of any part of a fixed, limited resource from the total amount of that resource makes it more difficult for others to acquire some part of that resource, even if that difficulty is initially unnoticed by others.

Proposition 62 (a concluding theoretical proposition): Any removal of any part of a fixed, limited resource from the total amount of that resource fails Locke's (first) proviso. It automatically makes others' positions worse off because it automatically prevents them from acquiring that part of the resource that has already been acquired, i.e. that part which would have been available to them prior to being acquired.

Conclusion: Locke's (first) proviso is logically unsustainable and empty of substantial meaning; it is theoretical and cannot be applied practically. Simply because we mix our labor with something does not mean that we should, or have any right to, own it exclusively.

Theoretical Support: Capitalism as a System in Violation of Locke's Theory of Justice in Acquisition
This contention has ample empirical support, if by "empirical support" we mean sensible evidence of the detachment of labor from ownership in the world. Throughout capitalism, owners of capital and the means of production are overwhelmingly *not* the people who mix their labor with the resources. Overwhelmingly, those who mix labor with resources do so because the owners of those resources (and/or the means to make products derived from those resources) have hired them to do so.

Seen from this perspective, Locke's (first) proviso for his theory of justice in acquisition fails to obtain in most capitalistic ventures. The owners of capital and the means of production are often, though not always, involved with resources only in an indirect way. They

179

tend not to mix their labor with the resources directly, as would a laborer. Rather, they mix their labor with intellectual, methodological, and interpersonal phenomena (i.e. managerial duties). The only thing tangible that they might mix their labor with is money, and usually even this is not tangible (i.e. it is rendered as numbers). It is the laborers who directly mix their labor with the resources, yet they usually have no claim on those resources. They don't own that with which they mix their labor. In capitalistic businesses, the people who directly mix their labor with resources, overwhelmingly don't own the resources and cannot, by law, claim ownership of those resources. The only way they can own the resources is by purchasing stock in the company within which they labor. But this type of ownership has nothing to do with mixing labor with resources. Rather, it has to do with "owning" the labor of those who actually do mix their labor with the resources. In this sense, a person who owns stock in the company within which he labors owns his own labor and the resources with which he mixes his labor not because he mixes his labor with those resources but because he participates in a system of ownership that is divorced from the idea of Locke's theory of acquisition. He owns the resources of the company not because he works with the resources but because he joins others who buy part of the company. Buying part of a company constitutes ownership in capitalistic ventures, not mixing one's labor with the resources "belonging" to that company.

Theoretical Objection: It might be argued that the original owners of the resources actually mixed their labor with those resources. Hence, they deserve to own them exclusively of others. They have simply freely chosen to contract with others to mix their own form of labor (manufacturing) with the resources and paid them for their labor.

For instance, the original owner of an oil well might have actually dug that well with his own hands or used equipment to dig the well that he manufactured with his own hands or justly purchased from others who manufactured the equipment themselves and pulled those resources out of the earth with his own hands. This sequence of events would seem to satisfy Locke's justice in acquisition of resources (ignoring the argument that it can never be satisfied); it just doesn't come close to being an example of how capitalistic business ventures actually work.

Theoretical Response: More Problems with Locke's Theory of Justice in Acquisition

What labor, exactly, has been mixed with the resource of oil in this instance? If we understand "labor" to be equivalent to a type of "behavior" and, in relation to fixed, limited resources, "behavior-as-physical-contact-with-the-resource," then the digger of an oil well is mixing his labor only with that part of the ground that he physically comes into contact with; he can only own that part of the ground that he is digging in. When he finds oil at the end of the hole he digs, he can labor to remove some or all of it from the earth; he can claim only that which he labors to remove. It seems that the rest of the oil in that well should still be up for grabs as long as others are willing to dig their own holes and remove the oil.

The digger of the original hole might argue that the entire well of oil is his, even though he didn't mix his labor with all of it. He *plans* to mix his labor with all of it; therefore all of it is his. Or, similarly, because it was his *idea* that there was an oil well in the earth where he was digging, then he is entitled to the entire well. It was the entire well that he was digging for, not just the parts with which he immediately mixed his labor.

Here, it seems, we have a problem identifying just what constitutes a resource. A minor mining for gold in a river bed or side of a mountain in California can claim only the gold he physically removes from the river bed or mountain. He can't claim the entire supply of gold in the river or the mountain simply because he has the *idea* of extracting the entire supply from that source.

Likewise, a person who invents a light bulb will actually mix his labor with a relatively small amount of resources, but once the bulb is discovered and made to work, he claims exclusive ownership of his idea (i.e. method involved in manufacturing a light bulb), which prevents others from using those resources to manufacture their own light bulbs and sell them, even if they mix their labor with those resources.

There seems to be a great variety of types of resources which include, but are not limited to: 1) physical, fixed, limited resources like gold, diamonds, and land (though there might be some question as to how deep below the surface of the land one's ownership might extend), 2) physical, fixed, replenishable resources like fish, game, and crops, 3) physical, fluid, quickly replenishable resources like water and blood and 4) physical, fluid, slowly replenishable resources like oil, 5) physical gaseous, quickly replenishable resources like air, hydrogen, nitrogen, etc., 6) non-physical ideas that can be converted into a template for manufacture and copy. like inventions, creative works, and drugs, 7) semi-physical, semi-fixed, semi-replenishable resources that are not actual resources but substitutes for actual resources like money, stocks, bonds, and numbers that reflect money, 8) non-physical, non-fixed, replenishable resources like ideas, concepts, expressions, etc. There seems to be no limit to defining what constitutes a resource.

There also seems to be problems in defining just what constitutes mixing one's labor with a resource. Does the digger for oil mix his labor with the oil in the well that he does not (yet) extract from the ground? Does anyone mix his labor with the air space above his land? Does anyone mix her labor with the ideas she thinks up, i.e. is thinking a form of labor? Does anyone mix her labor with her own body and the physiological processes that make it up? Can a person mix his labor by thinking of something and therefore owning that something he thinks about?

Despite all the difficulties we seem to have in regard to defining just what constitutes a resource, and what constitutes labor, and what constitutes the process of mixing our labor with a resource, we have somehow managed to divide up the resources of the world into exclusive compartments. We have claimed resources for our own use; we have designed and implemented laws to protect our current claims and any future claims; and we have developed a rationale for all of the above, no matter how superficial that rationale might be.

In other words, in the name of freedom we have parceled out a great number of resources and left only a percentage of those resources for others to use, making it much more difficult for them to own those resources simply because there is less of those resources to own. We have justified our ownership of those resources without knowing what constitutes a resource, what constitutes labor in relation to a resource, and what constitutes a relationship between labor and a resource.

Theoretical Extension: The Origin of Property and a Critique of Entitlement

No one is *entitled* to unclaimed natural resources; they (including animals, etc.) need or want those resources for their survival and well-being, but they aren't entitled to them. "Entitlement" is a term used in connection with a person's, or a group of people's, efforts (labor) to acquire resources and keep them exclusively of others.   In a state of unclaimed resources, people act upon their needs/wants for those resources; they want to survive or be well; justice does not apply. Justice only occurs when more than one person wants/needs the resource, but only one person claims ownership of that resource. Justice occurs when exclusiveness in acquisition of resources occurs.

People have grabbed up resources for their exclusive use not because they have mixed their labor with them, as if that alone gives them a right to exclusive ownership of the resource, but simply because they wanted the resource, they didn't want to share the resource with others, and they were able to defend their exclusive ownership of the resource from others who might try to grab up a share of that resource for their own use. In other words, they simply took it, and no one objected enough to make any difference. Their defense of their acquisitions might have been physical, logical, legal, theoretical, psychological, etc., but somehow they were able to defend the fact that they acquired some part of the world of resources for their own use, exclusive of anyone else's possible claim on it. Locke's theory of acquisition was created in the wake of business already completed. People had already grabbed up resources for their own use and were able to defend their exclusive ownership of those resources. Locke's theory gave them some sort of moral justification for their actions and helped convince others that they had a right to claim exclusive ownership of those resources as long as they worked for them.

Theoretical Objection: It might be argued that most capitalistic owners of oil don't simply start digging in unclaimed land but they purchase the land that they think will provide them with oil underneath the surface. They buy land that is already owned by others, privately or publicly. Others freely sell their land to oil speculators (capitalists). If the transfer (sale) of land is just (i.e. freely engaged in and not coerced or fraudulent in any way), then the buyer can do anything he wants with the land (within the current laws). He owns not only the surface of the land but everything underneath that surface (how far underneath might vary depending on how their actions in relation to their interests affect others).

Theoretical Response: In relation to Locke's theory of justice in acquisition, if we assume that the original owner of the land actually worked the land in question and, hence, could 'legitimately' claim ownership of it, and that he freely sold his land to an oil speculator, then the oil speculator's claim to the land, though not made on the grounds of mixing his labor with the land, could be made on the grounds of justice in transfer, i.e. the owner is free to transfer (sell, trade, give away) his land to whomever he wants, and anyone can purchase the land for whatever they want to do with it (within the law). But the oil speculator is only interested in that part of the land he decides to drill in. He is not a farmer wishing to plow and cultivate most of the land. He only wants to use that part of the land that will provide him with access to the oil he believes exists underneath the surface. So he buys up more land than that with which he intends to mix his labor and more land than he needs. But since he doesn't know exactly where the oil is under the surface, he wants to make sure he buys up enough land to cover his risk.

At the inception of the purchase, the oil speculator's ownership of the land fails Locke's conditions for justice in acquisition. He does not mix his labor with all the land he owns; he simply buys the land. He does not even *intend* to mix his labor with all the land he owns; he intends to mix his labor only with those areas of the land he thinks will yield the oil. If the land is cultivatable, than his purchase of it makes it more difficult for farmers to own cultivatable land because now that part of the earth is unavailable to them; hence, his purchase violates Locke's (first) proviso of not making other's situations worse off. Also, the oil speculator has no intention of using the oil for his own consumption; rather, he intends fully to sell his oil to others on the market and make as much money as he can in doing so. Hence, he violates Locke's (second) proviso of not grabbing more resources than you can use for your own survival and well-being.

This example is very typical of capitalistic ventures, and at each step it fails to meet Locke's conditions for justice in acquisition, even if those conditions were acceptable to establish private property.

But as already argued, simply because one mixes one's labor with resources doesn't mean that one is entitled to own those resources. The entire edifice of capitalism argues against this claim. Few people in capitalism who actually mix their labor with resources own those resources. And when they do "own the resources," (i.e. own stock in their own company), their ownership is devoid of actual labor. Most capitalist ventures do not involve mixing labor with resources; they involve buying and selling commodities for the capitalist's own use. All capitalist ventures fail Locke's (first) proviso simply because they usurp resources that were at one time available for use by others, thus making it more difficult for others to access those resources; most capitalist ventures fail Locke's (second) proviso of using only as much of the resource as one needs. By converting resources into money, i.e. assigning a money value to each resource, people have virtually eliminated "perishable" resources from the earth by converting them into marketable commodities. As marketable commodities, perishable resources are not limited to the immediate use of the individuals claiming ownership of the resources through their labor. They become commodities for sale on the market. Any vestige of a moral use of those resources is passed on to the consumer (e.g. buy only as much as you can eat). The business of growing and selling those commodities becomes magically exempt from having to adhere to Locke's (second) proviso.

Theoretical Objection: Certainly claiming exclusive ownership of resources with which one has mixed one's labor has more intuitive appeal than claiming ownership of those resources without having mixed one's labor with them. People deserve to own those resources they work for, and people who don't work for those resources don't deserve to own them, or any part of them.

Theoretical Response: This is the typical libertarian thesis which, in effect, is a way to justify ownership of resources simply through taking the initiative to mix labor with or work for those resources.

If a berry gatherer spots an unclaimed berry bush 100 feet away, she can take the initiative to traverse the 100 feet and pick the berries. This alone, according to Locke's justice in acquisition (minus the provisos) would qualify her to own the berries (at least those she actually picks), and she can do with them as she sees fit (e.g. eat them, sell them, etc.) But let's say that there are two berry gatherers who spot the same bush at the same time, and both of them take the initiative to traverse the 100 feet to pick the berries. But one of them is physically built like a sprinter and is naturally faster than the other, and she gets to the bush more quickly, and is able to pick all the berries before the other gets there. Is the physically quicker one entitled to all the berries because she has actually picked them, whereas even though the other might need or want the berries, or some portion of them, she is not so entitled to them because she hasn't actually mixed her labor with them?

Theoretical Argument: The Libertarian Response

Libertarians tend to answer this question with a resounding "yes." One can use whatever advantage one naturally has over another to acquire any unclaimed resource for his own use. This is argued again in the name of freedom. The faster person should not be penalized for her speed. Simply because she is faster than another person doesn't mean that she is any more or any less entitled to those resources. It merely means that she has been equipped by nature to mix her labor with those resources more quickly than another, other things being equal. She should neither be penalized nor rewarded for her speed. Her speed is morally neutral. It is merely a physical fact. If she had to share her berries with the slower person simply because the slower person might need or want them, or some portion of them, her freedom to acquire those berries through her labor would be infringed upon.

In other words libertarians like Nozick contend that inequality will exist in regard to resource acquisition based on: 1) individual initiative of actually mixing one's labor with the resources (some will and some won't take the initiative) and 2) natural differences in characteristics of individual people (some will naturally be better in doing so than others). If both people in our example have the initiative to work toward acquiring the resource, then both are in position to justly acquire the resource. If one does not have the initiative to traverse the 100 feet, then one will not do what is necessary to acquire the resource (picking the berries), and, hence, will not be entitled to it, or any part of it. If both have the initiative, but only one has greater speed and can reach the resource more quickly than the other, then only one will actually mix her labor with the resource (i.e. pick the berries); therefore, only one is entitled to that resource. The advantage of speed would be a morally neutral fact of nature. Hence, Nozick's justice is based on initiative and work (direct and indirect) and is represented (probably) by unequal distribution. Natural differences are morally neutral.

Theoretical Response: The Welfare Liberalist

Rawls argues that since people aren't for the most part responsible for their natural endowments, they cannot morally lay claim to resources simply because they possess the natural characteristics that dispose them to take the initiative and to mix their labor with the resources over and against others (i.e. they have a naturally competitive advantage). In other words, simply because one is naturally able to reach the berry bush more quickly than another (or pick berries more quickly, etc.) does not entitle one to own those berries. Natural endowments are morally neutral, yes, but when they result in unequal acquisition of resources, then a method of distribution must be employed in order for that acquisition to be just. Naturally endowed resource-acquirers cannot horde all the resources; they must share, and not exploit others in doing so. For Rawls, the richer resource-acquirers must share with the poorer ones, if only as much as would make the poorer ones better off than they were before the richer ones got richer. Even when the richest get richer by their own labor, they must share their spoils with the poorest so they don't worsen the poorest people's situation relative to them (Rawls, 1999).

Theoretical Argument: The Libertarian and the Welfare Liberalist

Nozick and the libertarians want to protect absolute freedom, a supposed condition of a supposed state of nature (primal human society). But even Nozick recognizes that a state of nature is a fiction, though this does not prevent him from using the idea as a heuristic basis for his theory of entitlement.

For Locke, a state of nature refers to a time when human beings were free to roam the earth and acquire any resource they wanted or were able to acquire for their own use. This idea presupposes an intense egoism on the part of every human being as well as instant adulthood. Imbedded in the state of nature idea is the idea that all human beings, at the inception of human beings on earth, were egoistic adults capable of acquiring resources at will. They might not have been equal in their natural endowments toward those resources, but they were at least equal in their capability of acquiring those resources. In other words, all people in the state of nature *could* acquire resources, but they could also get beat out by others who were better endowed to acquire those resources.

This libertarian thesis aligns well with the evolutionary idea of survival of the fittest. In evolutionary theory those people who inherit genetic structures that provide them with the natural endowments to acquire resources more quickly or efficiently than others will tend to obtain those resources more quickly than others. And given Locke's theory of justice in acquisition, their acquisitions will be just if they mix their labor with those resources.

Hence, it is not only natural but just for those biologically advantaged to acquire resources and not be forced to share them with others. In fact, forcing them to share with others violates their right to own them exclusively of others (i.e. it violates their right to liberty and property).

The welfare liberalists, including Rawls, will argue for some version of what Nozick calls an "end-state theory," where some sort of distribution of resources is necessary in order for acquisitions to be just. Simply because some people are naturally endowed to obtain resources more effectively than others and choose to do so does not mean that they can justly keep all the resources, making life more difficult for others. They must share those resources. How they do so is determined by the various "end-state" theories of justice, i.e. by people who make arguments in relation to justice in acquisition of resources, like Rawls.

Theoretical Extension: Rejecting Locke's Theory of Justice in Acquisition:

If Locke's theory of justice in acquisition of resources entails mixing one's labor with those resources as long as the proviso of not making other people's situations worse off is impossible to achieve because any acquisition of any resource will automatically make someone else's situation worse off (though it might not be noticed at first), then the entire libertarian thesis of people having a right to acquire resources simply by mixing their labor with them must be rejected.

Regardless of the strong psychological appeal of wanting to own that which one works for, the fact is, any ownership of any resource is going to be made at the expense of others simply because it makes it more difficult for others to own that resource. Locke's theory of justice in acquisition is self-contradictory. It is impossible for it to be realized in practice (unless one is simply not aware of the problems it permits).

In addition to this, Locke's theory of a state of nature has already been roundly criticized by communitarian arguments that point out that early groups of people were constituted by families, where children were dependent upon parents for their very survival. It takes years of nurturance for human children to grow into viable adults. We aren't all born adults as the original state of nature idea seems to imply. Rather, we are, as children, dependent upon adults for our very survival and well-being. We cannot supply ourselves with these things. If our parents don't nurture us, we die. If our parents nurture us badly, we are unhappy. Hence, we are not all resource-acquirers at all times, capable of acquiring resources at will. It is hoped that children who are initially dependent upon parents for their survival and well-being will, given proper care, develop into adults who will not be dependent upon their parents in any way but can fend for themselves in the world. If "fending for themselves" entails resource acquisition, then we hope that our children will be able to acquire resources for their own survival and well-being.

When understood from the developmental point of view, people in a "state of nature" are far from free to do whatever they want. Children cannot do whatever they want simply because they need their parents to do for them. Freedom to grab up the resources that surround them is extremely limited for children.

According to anthropologists, even as hunter-gatherers, people were not free to do as they pleased. In keeping their children safe, parents often prevented them from doing as they pleased. People who crossed personal and group boundaries were often punished in some manner, discouraging them from crossing those boundaries again. Upstarts who tried to impose their wills upon others were shunned, chastised, banished, and sometimes even killed.

Only when society (from family to state) breaks down do we see rampant, uncontrolled egoism producing a chaotic, "every person for himself," intensely competitive social structure. Only when personal boundaries are not caringly enforced in the family do we see children "running wild" or overrunning their parents. Only when states cannot come to agree with their methods of making and enforcing laws do we see people scrapping for themselves. Far from being a primordial state of human society, the state of nature, as unbridled freedom to do as one sees fit in relation to the resources that surround them, is, if attainable at all, the result of interpersonal break down.

Also, Locke's (second) proviso of limiting the amount of one's acquired resources to that which one can use immediately for survival and well-being is, in modern capitalist societies, avoided simply by transforming the value of those resources into money. Money does not need to be used immediately (i.e. it is not perishable in the same way food is perishable); it can be accumulated without limit.

Probing Question: If we accept the thesis that private property has its roots in human experience, where cognitions, affects, behaviors, sensations and the various environments within which each of us participates, are owned, then how do we move from owned components of consciousness, which are necessarily personal, to owning aspects of experience that are not personal but rather public or interpersonal?

Theoretical Response: The Phenomenon of Altruism

An answer to this question has already been offered: we take those resources we want and/or need and defend our exclusive use of them from encroachment by others.

But this answer does not belie the rampant egoism constituting a state of nature. Rather, it belies a communitarian interdependence that consists of both egoistic and altruistic tendencies.

The berry-gatherer in our example usually does not live alone; she is part of a group, whether that group is her natural family or her social, hunter-gatherer group. As such, she is already disposed to share her berries with others, possibly only her family but also, possibly, the entire group.

Evolutionists argue that such acts of altruism are genetically-based human traits. Parents (especially mothers) will naturally tend toward nurturing their children. Socio-biologists refer to this as parental investment. Mothers show stronger evidence of this trait than do fathers. If the berry-gatherer in our example has children, then, biologically, she will be disposed toward sharing those berries with her children. She will be less disposed toward sharing those berries with others outside of her own family, but still more disposed than sharing with strangers. The theory is that genetic structures dispose people to share primarily with family, secondarily with members of one's group, and thirdly with strangers.

An alternative theory (i.e. a learning theory) that accounts for the same results argues that parents will establish intimate relationships with their children (in nuclear family societies) and that this relationship accounts for why they want to share the fruits of their labor (forgive the pun) with their children, why their children before members of their group, and why members of their group before strangers. The distinction lies in the emotional bonds forged between people. More emotional bonds are forged between parents and children than between parents and group members or parents and strangers.

This theory holds that we are altruistic toward those whose existence we come to value, either in themselves (i.e. love) or inasmuch as they benefit us (i.e. reciprocal altruism). In family situations any biological disposition toward caring for others over and above caring for ourselves, at least in some instances (i.e. altruism) and the attendant guilt that would accompany our inability or unwillingness to do so, could be overridden by social and environmental (i.e. learned) conditions. For example, mothers who can't take care of their children might put them up for adoption and be able to live with their decision with minimal pain. Fathers can abandon their children in certain situations while experiencing minimal pain. Parents can maximize their self-interest at some expense to their children as long as that expense is within acceptable limits. The value that parents have of their children is based on the acceptance and love that they feel for them, and vice-versa. In this situation mutual acceptance and love create the value of the relationship and explain the altruistic behavior that might ensue. Parents sacrifice for their children because they love them and not because they are genetically programmed to do so.

Another theory, the one endorsed in this work, holds that there are genetic factors that dispose parents to sacrifice (within limits) for their children and will prompt urges in prospective parents to have and nurture children, but this disposition is relatively weak and can be overridden by emotional concerns. For instance, if parents who want children but cannot, for whatever reason, handle the raising of those children, give them up for adoption do so because they have not been able or are unwilling to establish (for whatever reasons) the bonds necessary to continue that relationship. If the emotional bond between parent and child does not obtain, then the genetic disposition to have and nurture children can be overridden.

This theory holds that there are two underlying sources of altruistic behavior in parents: 1) genetic disposition (and its chemical correlates) and 2) emotional bonding. The genetic disposition tends to be relatively weak; the emotional bonding tends to be relatively strong. Altruistic behavior toward children would then manifest itself primarily when genetic disposition and emotional bonds are strong, secondarily when emotional bonds are strong and genetic dispositions weak, thirdly when genetic disposition is strong but emotional bonds are weak, and fourthly when genetic disposition is weak and emotional bonds are weak.

In this theory the idea of genes disposing us to want children and feel strong urges to nurture them aligns well with other animals that exhibit the same or similar behavior; the theory has evolutionary support. But there is considerable evidence to support the idea that simply because people are related by blood does not mean that they are willing to act altruistically toward their children over and above anyone else. There is a wealth of evidence to support the idea that friends and lovers will trump family when it comes to altruistic acts. This is because those "strangers" have established stronger emotional bonds than those bonds established with family members or that pair bonding will trump kin altruism. Kin altruism will trump friend altruism only when the necessary emotional bonds are established between kin. Without emotional bonding between kin, kin altruism is weak.

This mixed theory also accounts for love bonds between males and females being stronger (often times) than family bonds. Individuating from family and starting one's own family with a relative stranger requires a strong emotional bond to be established with that stranger. In these (normal) situations a relative stranger wins out over family in regard to altruistic behaviors. Genetic disposition might account for the initial sexual attraction between lovers, but emotional bonding is usually needed for altruism between lovers to occur. The lovers need to have more value to their relationship than sexual attraction. When emotional bonds are formed, sexual attraction becomes a part of the relationship and not merely its instigator.

Theoretical Extension: Integrating Altruism into Property Ownership

If we understand altruism to mean "giving to others what one *could* take for oneself," and not its usual meaning of "sacrificing one's own well-being (or survival) for the well-being or survival of another," then we can integrate altruism into the experiential democratic theory being developed here.

If we accept that the original hunter-gatherers did not act independently (i.e. egoistically) but rather interdependently (i.e. at least kin altruistically and, probably, group altruistically), we can better understand how private property came about and what has happened since its inception. If the original hunter-gatherers were constituted by a network of families, and if those families consisted of interdependent members possessing some degree of (kin) altruism (rather than individuals who just happened to be using each other for their own survival and well-being), and if the families were interdependent, possessing some degree of (group) altruism (rather than individual families who just happened to be using each other for their own survival and well-being), then we can hypothesize that owning resources exclusively of others originated in the experiential structures within which we all participated but was actuated by others' acceptance or rejection of the legitimacy of such ownership claims.

If the original berry-gatherer gathered berries not merely for herself but for her family and (probably) her group in addition to herself, then her experiential ownership of the berries (being objects constituting the environmental component within which she participates) extends to kin and group ownership. If another hunter-gatherer band sought to take the berries gathered by the berry-gatherer, then the berry-gatherer might try to defend the exclusivity of her ownership by warding off the others in some manner. But this seems plausible only when there are enough berries left for the other hunter-gatherer band to claim for their own survival and well-being. If the other hunter-gatherer band could simply pick the other berries remaining for their own use, then the original hunter-gatherer band would be ostensibly justified in their defense of their already picked berries. But if the original hunter-gatherer band picked the berry bushes clean, then the other band is put into a position of having to forage elsewhere for their berries, which might pose a considerable expenditure of effort. It might be easier for them to take some or all of the berries already acquired by the original band. What's to prevent them from doing so? The answer offered is nothing but the original band members themselves.

In this scenario the original band claims ownership of the berries because they picked the berries (i.e. mixed their labor with the resources) and they value (love, like, depend upon) those with whom they want to share them. The second band claims a right to the berries, but that that right has been usurped or pre-empted by the original band. The original band at least needs to share the berries with the second band.

If we were to adhere to Locke's theory of justice in acquisition, then the original band is fully justified in its acquisition of the berries if they leave enough for others. But who are these others? If the others are not around at the time of the picking, or if no one in the original band is aware of them being around, then does the original band fail to meet Locke's (first) proviso if they pick the berry bushes clean? If the second band happens upon the berry bushes only to find them picked clean, then are they justified in their demands, granting knowledge of who picked the berries, that the original band share the berries with them?

Is this a matter of "first come, first serve?" Or is this a matter of "equal access to resources?" The argument in favor of the former says that it would be asking too much for the original band to know who is in the area that could access those resources before they could act on acquiring them. They cannot conduct an "impact analysis" before they can acquire the resources for their exclusive use, which in this case, might consist of a search to determine just who is in the area. Hence, they are justified in acting in accordance with their own needs and wants at that time. The argument in favor of the latter says that even if you cannot feasibly conduct an impact analysis, you must recognize that those (unclaimed) resources are for everyone's use and not just yours. Nature provides the resources; humans utilize them. But *all* humans can ostensibly use them, not just *some* humans.

194

When some humans use them, exclusive other others, then they automatically make others' situations worse off. Just because they might not know that they make other people's situations worse off, and even if those whose situations are made worse off by their actions are unaware that this is so, does not mean that they are justified in claiming exclusive ownership of the resource. Once it is determined that one's exclusive ownership of the resource is made at the expense of another, then the one who claimed the resource must share that resource with the other. Natural resources are to be used by all people for their survival and well-being (read health and happiness).

This line of argument implies that: If there is a limited amount of a given resource and that resource is needed by all people for their survival or well-being (health and happiness), then all people are entitled to that amount of the resource that will ensure their survival and well-being. This implies that no one is entitled to more of any limited resource than one needs to live on and to be healthy and reasonably happy, though one might take more of that resource than one needs if everyone else's needs are already met.

Though Locke's (first) proviso is impossible to achieve, and, hence, cannot be used to argue for entitlement to resources, his (second) proviso is not only achievable but it is a natural limitation to resource acquisition. It is consistent with a long-held Christian value of "taking no more than you need."

For example, if we agree that oil is a limited resource (absolutely or very slow in being replenished) and that some people will need (want) more oil for their survival and well-being than others (i.e. their economy depends greatly upon oil, whereas others' economies do not), then they will be entitled to that amount and only that amount of oil that will provide for their survival and well-being. The same is so for all the others.

Here, entitlement is linked primarily to survival and well-being (i.e. the right to life and health) and secondarily to work (i.e. the right to property). I could dig the only water hole in the area, and I might feel that since I was the only one in my community (granting I live in a community) who took the initiative to dig that hole and discover the water that I own the water and can do with it as I want. This is the crux of the libertarian ethos: it is based on a *feeling* of entitlement. But simply because one *feels* entitled to something does not mean that he or she *is* entitled to it. Others in my community might feel entitled to that resource too simply because they need it to live on. This feeling is linked to the notion of a right to life. One has a biological need to survive, surpassed only in special situations like suicide and self-sacrifice.

For example, one needs water to survive. If there is water in a given area, then all those in that area will need that water to survive. This biological fact supersedes the psychological feeling that one is entitled to that water if one works for it. This is why others in the community will expect and demand that that water be distributed among them. And if the person who discovers it is unwilling to allow such a distribution, he will be forced by the others to overcome or relinquish his resistance.

This expectation or demand has nothing to do with the fact that their situations are not made worse off by the acquisition of the water by the individual who dug the hole. This expectation or demand has everything to do with the biological need for survival and well-being. Community members will expect the other to share the valuable resource with them based on their biological need for it, and if the member is resistant, then the community will overcome that resistance and, in some way, force the other to share. This is the essential position of the welfare liberalists who are in favor of government intervention in the free market, e.g. taxing the rich and distributing the money to the poor.

Probing Question: If no one can actually determine how much of a limited resource there is (e.g. oil), then can one justly be prevented from taking what one needs by working for it, even if it might limit access to that resource by others? Should we not opt for freedom to grab up a resource when the opportunity presents itself as long as it doesn't obviously hurt someone else? Is this not the only practical solution?

Theoretical Response: Toward an Egalitarian Division of Resources in a Free Market
We *can* know how much of a limited resource exists for human consumption if we limit "amount" to the "amount in use." We might not know how much of the resource actually exists (i.e. that which is in use plus that which is not in use), but we can know how much of the resource is currently in use. We can tabulate the exact amount of

the resource that has been accessed by all those who have accessed it. But such tabulations would rest upon cooperation between all the businesses that use the resource; such information would have to be shared. This would greatly alter the competitive ground upon which capitalism supposedly rests.

Also, we *can* know how many people there are who want the resource for their survival or well-being. For example, we can tabulate the quantity of oil in use around the world by consulting business records, and we can tabulate the number of people (individuals, groups, countries) who want the oil for their well-being (granting that oil is not needed for survival) by consulting consumption records. What is much more difficult, though, is to determine how much oil each person or group or society needs for their well-being.

Libertarians argue for the freedom of individuals to grab up resources through labor and to transfer those resources (now private property) to others as they see fit (i.e. trade, sell, give away, etc.) For them there should be no central body (e.g. government) to distribute these resources in whatever manner it sees fit. Distribution is to occur naturally and probably unequally because only some people take on the risk and responsibility of ownership of those resources.

Welfare liberalists argue that when people are free to grab up resources through labor and to transfer them to others as they see fit, they will often times exploit others for their own benefit either by grabbing up too many resources or by transferring them in ways that exclude or take advantage of others. These inherent flaws in the free enterprise system require government intervention to protect those who do not own or control the resources.

But when libertarian freedom is synthesized with welfare liberalist equality and resources are grabbed up by all those constituting the business-as-situated-in-a-social-context, then we will, I believe, witness a transformation of hierarchy in business into democracy in business and a transformation of human organization consisting of competition-requiring-cooperation into a structure consisting of cooperation-requiring-competition.

Theoretical Extension: Equal Entitlement: Resource entitlement is a theoretical justification for some people grabbing up resources to the exclusion of others and for some people to take resources from others so that yet others can share in them. Libertarians use "entitlement" to justify grabbing up resources through labor. Welfare liberalists use it to distribute resources to all equally (or some variation thereof).

Most, if not all, human beings want to survive and be well (healthy and happy). Hence, most people are uniform in their resource need for survival and health (and some degree of happiness). But humans are variable in their wants in regard to property that will afford them well-being. The invariability of the need for resources for survival and health and reasonable happiness trumps the claim that mixing one's labor with a resource entitles that person to the resource because claiming resources exclusive of others will automatically make others' situations worse off.

An infant needs resources that will provide it with survival and well-being even if it doesn't "work" for them. For instance, an infant need not *crawl* or *flail* to get at mother's breast and *suck* at the nipple in order to be "entitled" to the milk inside; it simply needs the milk in order to survive and be healthy. A child need not *do chores* in order to earn resources that will allow it to survive and be healthy; it simply needs those resources to live and be healthy.

Likewise, adults need resources that will provide them with survival and well-being. An adult need not labor in relation to those resources in order to get them, as if labor somehow justifies their getting them. They simply need them in order to survive and be healthy and happy and others either will or will not supply them with those resources.

If every human being needs resources in order to survive and live well, and there are only so many resources available, then how these resources get distributed is of great concern to all human beings. If the number of human beings who need these resources is determined in good part by the sexual activity of humans already existing, then can the sexual activity of some put an unwanted strain upon others in regard to resource needs, and, hence, compromise the notion of equal entitlement?

The answer to these questions and possible solutions to these problems must be left for Volume 3 of this work.

Proposition 63: All human beings need natural resources that will provide them with survival and well-being.

Proposition 64: All human beings need food (including water), shelter from natural elements (variable, depending upon climate), and clothing to protect their bodies from natural elements (variable, depending upon climate).

These two propositions entail that if our berry-gatherer does pick the berry bush clean before another band of hunter-gatherers comes into their area searching for food, and the berries have not already been eaten, then they need to share the berries with the other band, if the other band's search for berries is authentic (SSR). The other band has worked for the berries (i.e. searched them out) but have come up short because the first band beat them to it. Simply by being the first ones to the berry bushes does not mean that the first band is entitled to all the berries they can pick and can do with those berries at they see fit, including hording the berries for themselves.

This is where the need for survival and well-being trumps exclusive ownership of resources through work. All people need resources to live and be well, but not all people need to work for resources in order to live and be well.

Proposition 65: All people need resources to live and be well, but not all people need to work for resources in order to live and be well.

Some resources are there for people even if they do not work for them, e.g. air and land. People are born into air and on land and utilize these resources whether they work for them or not. But the same is true for all other resources. People are born into the world of resources whether they work for them or not. All people need these resources in order to survive and live well. But not all people are able to work for those resources. And some people might be able to work for those resources but are not as able to do so because others beat them to the resources.

Proposition 66: Working for resources does not mean that one is entitled to those resources. It simply means that one works for (acts upon) the resources one needs in order to survive and live well.

Is an adult entitled to the resources provided by nature even if he can't work (hard enough) for them in relation to others? Are all human beings entitled to resources for their survival and well-being regardless of whether or not they mix their labor with those resources? If they are not so entitled, then are all adults who, for whatever reason, cannot work for a living, not entitled to have the resources necessary for them to live and be healthy and happy? And are all adults who can work for those resources but choose not to not entitled to those resources?

The libertarian theory seems to require a Darwinian "survival of the fittest" method of justice. The hard-core libertarian will argue that all those who can or choose to work for a living can acquire the resources necessary for their survival and well-being; all those who cannot or choose not to work for those resources will suffer or die. The soft-core libertarian will argue that all those who cannot work for a living should be supported by others because they would work if they could, and hence, deserve to live and be well. But those who can work but choose not to work will suffer and die. In effect, they deserve to suffer, if not die.

The welfare liberalist theory holds that all adult human beings are entitled to the resources that nature provides though, depending upon the specific theory under the general umbrella of liberal theory, those resources will be distributed in some "just" manner.

Theoretical Argument: The libertarian's main squabble is not with infants, children, and disabled adults; these people, supposedly, can be subsidized by able adults who are responsible for them (e.g. relatives) or by charity (in preference to being subsidized by taxpayers). Libertarians have a problem with able adults who choose not to work for a living and live off government subsidies (i.e. tax money coming from other people). They don't think it's fair that able-bodied people who can work for a living do not and, instead, rely on the government (everybody else) to provide the resources necessary for their survival and well-being.

The welfare liberalist's position on this is that if all human beings, which include all able adults, are entitled to resources for their survival and well-being, then government is obliged to provide them with those resources if they are not able to do so themselves and if their wills have been so impeded by the free market so as to make it

200

extremely difficult for them to do so. They don't want to provide resources for those who simply refuse to work (even though this might occur within the government subsidy system).

Theoretical Extension: Natural Acquisition of Resources

If we accept that movement from experiential ownership of environmental components of consciousness and the totality of contents that lie therein to exclusive ownership of some of those environmental contents is determined by individual initiative to acquire those resources derived from a need for those resources, though the initiative is often, though not always, associated with others (kin, group), then we can legitimately posit that exclusive ownership of any contents of the environmental component of consciousness (i.e. resources) is determined, if there are no competing others in the area that one is aware of, by one's initiative (labor) in relation to those resources. This answers to the immediate needs of those who acquire resources.

But if others make themselves known or are able to be known by those acquiring the resources of their need (or want) of those resources for their survival and well-being, then those who acquire those resources, even if through their own labor, are in position either to defend their resources from others or to share them with others. But are they "obligated" to defend or share those resources?

The "obligation" to defend the resources lies primarily in one's need for survival for oneself and one's family and/or one's group inasmuch as emotional bonds are created between members of one's family and/or group.

The "obligation" to share the resources derives from the needs of all human beings, i.e. the need for resources for their survival and well-being. This obligation is reflected in the rights to life and health.

Proposition 67: The rights to life and health trump the right to property, even if that property is necessary for life and health.

Theoretical Extension: The Rights to Life, Health and Property

The rights to life and health are integral to experience. They are anchored in human biology. Most human beings are biologically determined to strive for survival and well-being. But most human beings do not strive for property. Rather, they strive for resources that will provide them with their survival and well-being. Berry gatherers pick berries not to own property but to survive and be well. Most human beings (with few exceptions) act upon resources for that same reason.

It is only when those actions come into conflict with others that the issue of justice even surfaces. The original berry-gatherer picked the berries without a thought as to the justice of it. The berries were there; the people needed them to survive; therefore, they picked and ate the berries. If no one else was around to want or need the berries to live on, then the picking of the berries would go down as an act of survival. Whether it was just or not was not a factor.

The conversion from acting upon resources in order to survive and be well to determining that those resources so acted upon are one's exclusive property is a conversion based on one's natural tendencies to take and keep or to take and share.

Some people take resources for their own survival and well-being and are ready and willing to defend their acquisitions from others. Here, ownership is derived from work (for acquiring the resource) and force (ability to defend the acquisition from others). In this sense, ownership is not a matter of justice in acquisition through labor; it is a matter of acquisition (work) and defense (repelling force).

Some people take resources for their own survival and well-being but are ready and willing to share their acquisitions with others if others need them. Here, ownership is derived from work (for acquiring the resources) but is trumped by the recognition that others also need those resources to live and be well. The amount of resources shared will depend upon the need or want for oneself, one's family and one's group. Sharing is a function of the strength of egoistic needs and wants and the emotional bonds created between family and group members.

The original resource acquirers acquired resources because they needed them to live on and be well. They automatically (experientially) owned the resources inasmuch as those resources were contents of the environmental components of experience within which they participated. They acted upon those resources because the resources didn't just come to them. They wouldn't have acquired them if they didn't act upon them. If others did not act upon them (either because they couldn't or just chose not to), then they did not acquire the resources. Those who acquired the resources could lay no claim to exclusive ownership of the resources; they merely acquired them and, if they so desired, defended their acquisition from others, or, if they so desired, shared their resources with others. If they defended their acquisition from others, then they might have had to deal with others trying to take some or all of those resources from them, because others would, just like them, act in accordance with their need for survival and well-being. If they shared their acquisition with others, then they might have had to settle for less of the resources than they needed or wanted, but such a choice was theirs to make.

If some people who are not naturally inclined to share their resources with others (i.e. egoistic people or takers) and can defend their resource acquisitions from others with minimal effort, then they will do so. If too much effort is required to defend their resource acquisitions from others, then they might decide to share, at least enough to appease those who make demands on them.

If some people who are naturally inclined to share their resources with others (i.e. altruistic people or givers) and are able to live with less than they would have if others were not in need of those resources, then they would do so. They might limit their sharing to a level that does not compromise their survival or minimal well-being. If pushed by others to compromise their survival or minimal well-being, they might naturally defend their resource acquisitions. Some altruistic people might go further and sacrifice their survival by sharing their acquired resources with others.

The issue of entitlement never comes up throughout these exchanges. The issue of rights at this basic level is a non-issue. But the practical issue of needing resources to survive and live well does surface. Hence, the egoists who defend their acquisitions from others will have to deal with others when those others try to grab up their resources, or portions thereof. And those altruists who share their resources will not have to defend their acquisitions as much as the egoists, but they will have to live with less resource for their survival and well-being.

Those who don't share their resources will have to contend with those scrapping for their survival; they will, in all likelihood, have to defend themselves from theft or personal injury because the need for survival will tend to outweigh respect for property, regardless of how much work went into the acquisition of that property. Sharing the resources might be easier than defending them from theft. In this circumstance, even egoistic persons will act 'altruistically', even if only behaviorally, because it is to their advantage to do so.

Another option for people is to barter their resources for the resources of others. The second band of hunter-gatherers could trade clothes or trinkets for berries instead of stealing from the first band, especially if the first band can easily defend itself and its resources from the second band. But such bartering is subject to the needs or whims of the more powerful band. The first band could easily refuse to barter and simply keep their resources for themselves. But if the barter items are attractive enough to the first band, and the loss of some of their resources does not outweigh the gain from the trade, then the first band will trade.

Another option for people is to expend the necessary energy to acquire resources from other sources. The first band could refuse to share their berries with the second band, and the second band might not be able (actually or perceived) forcibly to take some or all of the berries from the first band, so the second band could search for other resources in nearby areas. Since the second band will not know (we'll say) if there are any other resources in the area that would sustain their existence, then a decision to search for other resources would be, at best, risky. But that risk (actual or perceived) would be less than the risk of trying to take resources from others.

Probing Questions: Is the first band of hunter-gatherers obligated to share their berries with the second band? Is the first band's primary obligation to themselves and secondary obligation, if any, to strangers? Is one's obligation to one's self primary in regard to one's survival and secondary in regard to one's well-being (e.g. might be hungry if they share but they won't die by sharing)? Is there any obligation to do or not do anything in relation to anyone?

Theoretical Response: If one possesses a biological urge to protect oneself from harm and to sustain one's survival and well-being (Proposition 3); and if one possesses a biological urge to have sex with another (Proposition 2); and if one naturally forms an emotional bond with that other (Proposition 5), then one will feel an obligation to protect and provide for the survival and well-being of that other person. Mates in a pair bond or, less anthropologically, spouses in a marriage, will feel a need to protect and provide for their partner. Inasmuch as they act to satisfy this need, they are consistent with themselves. Inasmuch as they fail to act, they will tend to feel shame. Shame is the feeling that results from acting inconsistently with one's self.

Probing Question: Is one socially or ethically required to act so as to protect and provide for one's spouse or partner?   Is there a universal ethical mandate for a partner to protect and provide for his or her spouse that trumps any lack of biological urge to do so?

Theoretical Extension: Biological Mandates and Social Leaning

Inasmuch as social or ethical (i.e. universal) mandates are consistent with biological dispositions, then there do seem to be social or ethical mandates for people to provide for their partners and children. But when those mandates are inconsistent with biological dispositions, then those mandates are either meta-experiential constructs and they need to be assertively confronted, grappled with, and eliminated, or they legitimately conflict with others' biological dispositions and therefore must be recognized as legitimate courses of action, at least on the biological level.

For example, if some people are biologically disposed (i.e. genetically determined) to feel strong urges to protect and provide for their partner and children, then acting otherwise would probably be experienced as shameful. But if one is not biologically disposed to feel those urges, then acting otherwise will tend not to be experienced as shameful. A male might be biologically disposed to be attracted to a female other than his spouse and to leave his spouse and children for that female. But this biological urge would need to be empirically connected to genetic structures in order to have any weight in regard to being moral. Simply arguing, as socio-biologists do, that because this phenomenon is pervasive in the world it must be genetically motivated is not enough to make a case for morality.

Socio-biologists who argue that parental investment tends to be lower in males than females, i.e. that males tend to be genetically determined to leave their spouse (and children) for another without feeling much shame (i.e. serial monogamy), while failing to determine the genetic structure causing the urge to do so, are probably

205

creating a meta-experiential construct to 'justify' male sexual be-havior.

Experientially, if the male is genetically so determined, then he will tend, overwhelmingly, to act in accordance with that determination. For society to fight that tendency with universal, ethical mandates would be futile at best, oppressive at worst. Socially imposed ethical mandates, foisted upon biological dispositions, if effective, will tend to result in false compliance by the individual, often times attained by socially-induced guilt (internal) or socially-induced force (external).

But if the male *is* genetically determined to stay with one's partner but opts to act against his biological disposition, for whatever reason, and shame does not prompt him to correct his behavior, then we will hypothesize that his 'explanation' and 'justification' for his behavior is a meta-experiential construct. Those who are biologically disposed to protect and provide for their partner and offspring and yet do not (i.e. those who abandon their partner and offspring) can seek 'solace' in the socio-biological theory that they, being men, are not biologically disposed to sticking around and raising offspring. But such 'solace' is actually the result of seeking out other people (and theories) that agree with their wish to override their biological disposition and to justify the override. Here is where society can provide an ethical demand (e.g. protect and provide for your partner and offspring) that aligns with a biological disposition (i.e. protect and provide for your partner and offspring), and where shame can be assuaged in 'favor' of a bogus 'universal' theory (i.e. that men tend to have sex with a variety of women (are sexually promiscuous) and possess low parental investment (will tend to abandon or neglect their children).

If we can accept the truth of Proposition 5 that it is natural (i.e. most people are biologically disposed) to not only be attracted to and have sex with another but to form an emotional bond with that person, then the reason men would leave their spouse and children for another woman would probably lie in the quality of emotional bonding and not in a biological disposition. If the biological disposition to leave one's spouse and children cannot be empirically grounded in genetic determinations, then rather than assuming that at some time in the future such genetic connections will be made, it is probably more prudent (and accurate) to look for the historical creation of meta-experiential constructs.

In this case we would be looking for historical creations of complex structures. Why would men (or anyone) posit that men leave their spouse and children because they are genetically determined to do so? What might be their motivating factors for doing so? One obvious answer is that it serves their purposes to come up with this explanation: they are not to be held responsible for their actions if they are genetically determined to act in this manner. It gives them a "green light" to get out of their current situation.

But such an explanation seems to address only the superficial aspect of the situation. Experientially, we can't just demonize the male who abandons his wife and children (for another woman). If the abandoning behavior is a part of a complex structure (i.e. a false self), then there must lie a real self that underlies a false self. Such a complex structure might look like this:

C: my spouse doesn't want to have sex with me	C: I'm not worthy	C: Other woman wants me
A: dejected	A: self-rejection	A: attraction
B: looking at spouse	B: looking down	B: fantasizing of other woman
S: spouse	S: room	S: room
E: room	S: room	E: room
"I": ownership		
SSR		

In this experiential analysis a male who feels rejected by his spouse rejects himself. He doesn't assert himself in response to his wife's behavior; rather he allows her behavior to determine his self-worth by rejecting the legitimacy of the SSR structure within which he participates. Whether or not his wife rejected him is not at issue; what is at issue is his determination (cognition) that she rejected him. He feels dejected because of his spouse's behavior. But instead of exposing his interpretation of her behavior to conflict by letting her know how he feels, he simply rejects himself. In this sense, it is easier for him to reject himself than it is to assertively confront his spouse with his insecure feelings. Such a confrontation would admit of vulnerability. He might be wrong about her motivation. Maybe there are other reasons she doesn't want to have sex with him. Or he might be right about her motivation and doesn't want to accept the fact that she doesn't find him sexually attractive (or some other personal reason). So he avoids confronting her and opts for self-rejection instead. His self-rejection initiates the construction of a false self, which in this case has its origins in the fantasizing of another woman. In order for a false self to appear to have strength it must seek out justification for its being (i.e. by connecting with other like-thinking people (if possible), creating explanations that 'justify' itself). In this case, the male 'justifies' his fantasizing about another woman by talking about his fantasies with other men who might think like he does, e.g. that men are biologically determined to seek variety in women, that marriage (monogamy) is against their nature, that wives are cold and sexless, etc. He gains bogus confirmation experiences, confirming only the false self being constructed. As his false self becomes honed (and more 'justified'), he lands up leaving his wife and children for the other woman; and he doesn't feel much shame in doing so.

But it would be inaccurate to say that he doesn't feel any shame. He actually does feel shame, but he is able to cover up that shame with a false self that enables him to 'justify' his current situation (i.e. leaving his wife and children for another woman). Such a construction might look like this:

C: I feel rejected by you]	[I've never told you my feelings]	I want other woman
A: [rejected]	[shame]	false desire
B: [looking down]	[looking down]	telling wife
S: [wife]	[room]	wife
E: [room]	[room]	room
"I": ownership		
Real Self	Real Self	False Self

In this analysis the man has, historically, felt rejected in relation to his wife (probably on numerous occasions). Instead of confronting her with his feelings, he constructs a false self by rejecting the legitimacy of his own feelings of rejection and constructing an experience that covers up those feelings of dejection and self-rejection. Buried under the self-rejection is a natural shame. The man has actually gone against his biological disposition to stay with his spouse and children by constructing a false self. The false self has allowed him to 'justify' his abandonment. But his justification is false. He actually feels shame for not having confronted his spouse with his feelings of rejection. His shame lies in his inability to assertively confront his wife about his feelings of rejection, and not in his leaving his wife for another woman. This shame is buried so deep that he (probably) doesn't even know that it's there. It has become so distorted that he is 'unaware' of it. But, in fact, he is aware of it, but only slightly, and in a "nagging" way.

This is but one example of how people can cover up their biological dispositions. Another is offered, paradoxically, yet again by socio-biology. Many socio-biologists argue that men are genetically disposed to have sex with a variety of females and that emotions need not play much if any part in their sexual behavior. These two phenomena – casual sex and promiscuity – are linked. It is easier to have sex with many partners if you're emotionally uninvolved; it is much more difficult to do so when you are emotionally involved with someone.

Those purely sexual contacts (e.g. "hook-ups") that are virtually devoid of emotional bonding, more often than not, can be understood as biological overrides, 'justified' through the use of meta-experiential constructs (e.g. that's just the way men are).

If most people are biologically disposed to form emotional bonds with those with whom they have sex, and yet they are able to have sex 'without forming an emotional bond' and then 'justify' that sex, then they are simply deceiving themselves. Emotional bonding is actually a part of their sexual activity, but they, for whatever reason, refuse to admit it, deny it, or minimize it.

The foregoing argues that many of the socio-biological theories about male and female sexuality are probably meta-experiential constructs that seek to 'justify' male promiscuity, serial monogamy, mid-life crises, and sex without emotional bonding.

Another example: Socio-biologists will argue that males like variety in sex and will seek out that variety even if they are committed to one person because it is their nature to do so; the biological need for variety in sex trumps emotional bonding. Under this theory, men who cheat on their wives are only acting consistently with their biological (i.e. genetic) dispositions.

But when these acts are analyzed experientially, we tend to find something different. The man who cheats on his wife might experience a sexual attraction to another woman, but that attraction occurs in conjunction with a disposition for emotional bonding, though that bonding might be very weak. A man who finds another woman sexually attractive and acts upon that attraction to the extent of having sex must experience the woman not simply as a combination of sexually stimulating parts but at least as a whole person constituted in part by sexually stimulating parts. In other words, the "wholeness" of a woman cannot be separated from "the parts" of that woman. It is a *woman* to whom the man is sexually attracted and not simply a combination of sexual parts.

The woman is an experiential being; she participates in experiences constituted by cognitive, affective, behavioral, sensual and environmental components, as owned. Optimally, though certainly not necessarily, she participates in SSR structures and expresses who she actually is to her male partner. If she is an experiential being in this more narrow sense in her sexual encounter, then the male might well retreat from acting on his biological urges because such vulnerability would be threatening to him. If he were to take advantage of her and have sex with her, he would feel genuine shame. But if she is operating out of a complex structure, then the male, who is operating out of a complex structure of his own, might well be motivated to have sex and not feel shame in doing so. But such sexual encounters are usually constituted by an unrecognized aggressive component, and the shame is experienced but is immediately denied.

A typical set of experiential structures in "hook ups" or casual sex situations might look like this:

C: sexy body	C: she feels for me	C: I'm weak	C: she's weak
A: desire	A: trepidation	A: self-reject	A: disgust
B: looking at body	B: looking at eyes	B: looking down	B: looking at eyes
S: sexual stimulation other's body parts	S: her eyes	S: environment	S: eyes, sexual stimulation
E: room	E: room	E: room	E: room
"I": ownership			
Real self	Real self	------	False self

In this situation the male initially feels sexual desire while looking at certain body parts of the female (SSR). His feelings of desire correspond with his stimulated body parts. But when he looks at the female's eyes, he detects vulnerability in her, i.e. an emotional bonding with him. This corresponds with his feeling of trepidation in relation to her. He immediately assesses his own trepidation as evidence of weakness and rejects it. Now he is able to look at her eyes and see weakness and feel disgust. Since this man has been taught that women exist for men's sexual pleasure (meta-experiential construct), he is able to reject his own fear and cover it up with a false self (disgust-experience). The false self not only allows him *not* to feel vulnerable, but it also allows him to 'justify' his renewed sexual stimulation. But this false self entails an aggression against the female (she's weak, disgust, etc.) He's able to objectify her in the construction of his false self. Now he can align his behavior with his natural sexual stimulation without having to recognize his emotional involvement. Now he can seek out or be amenable to a meta-experiential construct that would 'justify' his sexual behavior (e.g. women exist for men's sexual pleasure, men do not get romantic, men are in sexual control, etc.) Also, if he had not done this, he might have lost his sexual stimulation (e.g. erection) and thought of himself as 'less than a man' (another meta-experiential construct).

This is only one example of how a male can rid himself of emotional content while having sex with a partner. Women can perform similar "slights of mind" if they have reason to avoid emotional involvement while having sex, and they are subject to the same processes of complexification as are men.

If both partners are operating out of complex structures, then their experiential structures might look like this:

Male's experiential structure:

C: sexy body	C: she feels for me	C: I'm weak	C: she's weak
A: desire	A: trepidation	A: self-reject	A: disgust
B: looking at body	B: looking at eyes	B: looking down	B: looking at eyes
S: sexual stimulation other's body parts	S: her eyes	S: environment	S: eyes, sexual stimulation
E: room	E: room	E: room	E: room
"I": ownership			
Real self	Real self	------	False self

Female's experiential structure:

C: he wants my body not me	C: I'm not good enough	C: I'm desirable	
A: insulted	A: self-rejection	A: false confidence	
B: looking at man	B: looking aside	B: falsely touching man's body, "moaning", etc.	
S: man touching body	S: wall	S: man's body	
E: room	E: room	E: room	
"I": ownership			
Real self	-----	False self	

An analysis of the female's experiential structure reveals that she initially (we'll say) experiences the man's behavior as insulting, i.e. that he doesn't really know "her," that he just wants her body for sex. Because she has been trained to think that women need to satisfy men's sexual desires or be sexually desirable to men (both meta-experiential constructs), she rejects the legitimacy of her own feelings of insult by thinking that she is not worthy of being loved. Then she covers up her self-rejection (and her feeling of insult) by believing that she is desirable. She judges herself by the behavior of another (the man), even when that behavior is false itself. Hence, her confidence in her self-estimation is false and she feigns sexual involvement.   Both people come out of this experience deeply unsatisfied, but superficially 'satisfied.'

With the inculcation of meta-experiential constructs, men can not only 'justify' their relatively emotionless sexual contacts with women, but they can also 'justify' their abandoning females and offspring, either outright or for another female. Because they are able to employ a false self to cover up their fear, they are able to minimize and distort their emotional involvement, thus stultifying their identity development.   They can leave without feeling too much shame because they 1) have not allowed themselves to be emotionally vulnerable and 2) have found a meta-experiential construct to 'justify' (read "excuse") their behavior (e.g. she's just a clingy woman, real men don't get emotional, etc.)

The problem is being able to distinguish between experiences associated with natural genetic dispositions (and those learned in natural situations) and those associated with experiential complexification and meta-experiential construction.   How can we tell when one is being oneself and when one is acting as a false self?

Proposition 68:   "Entitlement" is a term created in order to justify people grabbing up resources for their own use and not wanting to share them with others. "Entitlement" is often used as a meta-experiential construct.

Theoretical Extension: Entitlement as a Meta-Experiential Construct

The original hunter hunts down and kills a deer. He does this because he needs food. He probably also does this to provide food for his family. He might also do it to provide food for his group.

Relative to other people who are not a part of his group, he feels entitled to the deer because he has labored in relation to it. If others were to try to take the deer from him, he would probably prevent them from doing so, if he could. Not only would he prevent them from taking the deer because he needs it to survive or be well, but he also would feel that they didn't work for it like he did; therefore, they don't deserve it.

But is this so? The thief could be said to work for the deer but not by hunting, rather by taking. Taking could be construed as a form of labor; it's just not the same form as is hunting. Even thieves might well feel a sense of entitlement to a resource after they've acquired it. Both the hunter and the thief will tend to feel entitled to the resource when they've mixed their labor with that resource.

But "feeling" entitled and "being" entitled are two different things. Individually, we might all feel entitled to that which we work for. The hunter claims ownership, either implicitly or explicitly, of the deer. He doesn't want anyone else taking it from him primarily because he needs it to live on and secondarily because he has worked for it (and the other has not). He will tend to share it with those who are important to him, e.g. family, group members, but he wants to do this freely and not because of some imposed obligation or external force. Inasmuch as his genetics and his emotional bonds dispose him to share, he will share.

But if someone who is neither genetically nor emotionally bonded to him makes demands upon him for some portion (or all) of his deer, his ownership of that deer becomes explicit and he is willing and, possibly, able to defend his ownership by force, if necessary. If he is willing and able to defend his exclusive ownership of the deer, he will do so, at the expense of the other, who is viewed as an interloper or thief.

If there is ample game in the area, the hunter feels fully justified in owning and defending his deer from others (i.e. satisfying Locke's proviso). He feels entitled to the deer, and he feels justified in defending his ownership of that deer, inasmuch as his methods of defense align with his natural tendencies and moral determinations.

But *is* he entitled to the deer? If a person is disabled and cannot hunt or is simply a horrible hunter, and he is not connected to a family that has a few good hunters as members who could provide for him, but he is a part of the group (i.e. band of hunter-gatherers), then is he at all entitled to some of the deer?

If the hunter is genetically disposed to share the deer with members of his group (i.e. group altruism), then he would probably share the deer with the disabled person. If the hunter is also emotionally bonded to this member of the group, then he is even more disposed to share the deer. But what if his genetic disposition to share with this member of the group is weak, and if his emotional bond with him is also weak? Then is he morally required to share the deer?

If one can recognize another as a member of one's group, whether that group is one's family, one's social group, one's state, one's country, or one's species, then one is bound to the other through identity. Experientially, this boundedness is often realized in experiences of empathy. Many people experience others, even if strangers to them, as "the same as them" and can not only recognize that sameness but be moved to supportive action in relation to them. Experiencing a member of one's group who cannot provide for himself will often move other members to compassion. This compassion will prompt them to share resources with them. To act against such an experience would be a source of shame.

This extends a biological disposition toward caring for one's fellow humans into groups that can be as wide-ranging as one's species. Many people can be moved to compassion for people whom they've never met (e.g. helping the poor, helping those experiencing natural disasters, helping the disabled and impaired.) And these people might feel shame if they do not act in relation to their disposition toward compassion.

But is there a moral rule that requires us to help others even if we are not moved to compassion, even if we do not experience empathy toward others, even if we do not recognize the sameness of the other with ourselves?

Nussbaum criticizes Rawls' theory of justice because Rawls seems to have no place for the disabled and impaired in his society's methods of determining just laws to govern their behavior (Nussbaum, 2006). Rawls' system requires rational adults to put themselves under a veil of ignorance before determining just principles that will govern their behavior (Rawls, 1999). The problem, says Nussbaum, is that the disabled and impaired are left out of that group of rational adults. Rational adults must make decisions of justice *for* the disable and impaired because they are not able to make those decisions themselves.

This criticism is similar to the criticism levied against Kant's deontological theory of ethics. Kant requires universal affirmation of principles and imperatives in order to determine moral rules. All people are subject to any universal rule or principle, inasmuch as they are people. But for Kant, "people" means "rational people," which means "rational adults." All rational adults should be able to affirm a universal moral rule or principle because all people are similar to each other, or equal in essential ways.

Kant has the same problem as Rawls. Can moral rules or principles be determined, at least in part, by the disabled and impaired? Are the disabled and impaired rational? Can, or should, their input (i.e. vote) be accepted as vital, important or even credible? Do the disabled and impaired have a claim to resources acquired by others' labor and should their opinion on the matter be accepted as equal to the voices of normal rational adults?

Gilligan argues that such considerations are masculine considerations (Gilligan, 1982). Men are concerned with reason and justice on an abstract, universal level. Men think it's important or imperative to transcend personal concerns and to subordinate those concerns to universal concerns. Women, on the other hand, tend to care for those close to them, i.e. those to whom they are emotionally attached. The web of care starts with the family but it extends outward into the group and eventually includes the stranger. Failures to care for people, whether family, friends, or strangers, are moral failures.

Many feminists criticize Kant's deontology not because it is inaccurate or domineering but because it is myopic. It sees morality only through the narrow eyes of cold reason. It fails to recognize the legitimacy of the more feminine experience of care.

Sometimes reason is a function of care, and not the reverse. For instance, when Kohlberg presented the dilemma of Heinz, who considers whether or not to steal a drug which he cannot afford to buy in order to save the life of his wife, to an eleven year-old boy and an eleven year-old girl, he found that the boy's answer revealed abstract rational thinking, arguing that the principle of saving lives is more important than the principle of not stealing, and therefore, it was moral to steal in these instances; whereas the girl did not think it would be moral to steal the drug because the person would probably be caught and go to prison, leaving his wife and family without a father (Kohlberg, 1996). She thought that Heinz and his wife should get together and come up with an alternative to stealing which would result in the same outcome, i.e. obtain the drug without breaking the law.

In this example, Kohlberg, who is, in one sense, quite Kantian in his thinking, argued that the boy had achieved a higher level of moral reasoning than the girl by being able to think in abstract terms and principles and that the girl thought at a lower moral level, only considering the act in terms of relationships, i.e., submitting to authority, consequences in regard to others, etc.

Gilligan argues that the girl's answer was indicative of a lower level of moral reasoning only if one assumed that abstract, principle-oriented thinking was the highest level of reasoning. If one conceived of reasoning as a multi-faceted phenomenon and that it can be applied in a variety of ways to a variety of problems, then Heinz and his wife could reason with each other about an alternative to stealing in order to get the drug. At the very least, this form of reasoning is more creative than the boy's solution. Also, it is legal.

So, is the wife, who, let's say, finds herself in the category of disabled or impaired, to be considered a rational adult? Can she have an equal say in the construction of moral principles by which one could be held accountable? Can she claim entitlement to resources if she can't provide those resources for herself?

This problem typifies the problem of justice and human organization: Is justice determined by traditional objective methods or is it determined by individuals in relation to each other?

Christianity developed a morality based on the idea that God, a supernatural and supreme being, has imparted to us through word (i.e. scripture) and reason (a moral faculty to supplement scripture), a system of moral rules that are universally binding, whether one is biologically disposed to such actions or not, whether one is emotionally bonded to others or not.

Kant developed a system of morality based on the idea that reason, a faculty every human possesses (at least every adult human), if used properly, could discern moral rules that are universally binding, whether one is biologically disposed to such actions or not, whether one is emotionally bonded to others or not.

Both Christianity and Kantian deontology are basically traditional objective moral systems. Christianity is absolutely objective in that the moral laws are equivalent to God's eternal law, which is transcendent to the determinations of human reason. It is conditionally objective also in that human reason can transcend parochial religious beliefs and determine morality independent of revelation. But even these determinations, if done properly, are consistent with God's eternal law (that is not laid down in scriptures). Deontology is

216

conditionally objective in that human reason can be faulty, according to Kant. It is not an absolute determiner of moral rules. But it is the best thing we have to help us know right from wrong. And if used properly, we can determine universal moral rules that are equally binding for all rational people. So like science that maintains that the scientific method is not perfect (absolute) in that it won't necessarily render reality as it is (i.e. it's the best thing we have to determine reality), so too does Kant's reason determine moral reality in the best way humans can.

Compare utilitarianism which argues that moral rules are determined by the consequences of our actions. Those actions that produce the most happiness for the most people or decrease (or prevent) pain for the most people are good moral actions. Those actions that produce allot of pain for allot of people or decrease (or prevent) happiness for allot of people tend to be bad actions. In this system moral rules are determined after the actions have occurred and are dependent upon our abilities to calculate and quantify people's happiness and pain. In this system reason is a faculty of mind that determines happiness:pain ratios, either though prediction or through monitoring.

If happiness and pain are objective phenomena, then utilitarianism is an objective moral system. But those developing the theory didn't seem to spend much time arguing this issue. They just tended to assume that people can determine for themselves what makes them happy and what makes them pained. Hence, utilitarianism tends to be understood as a relative theory: what actions make some people happy might make other people pained.

Feminists who have developed care theory, like Gilligan, will fall more in line with utilitarian than deontological thought. First, we tend naturally to care for members of our family; second, we care for intimate group members; third, we care for members of larger groups (e.g. state, country, and species). Care theory admits of priorities: family relationship often take precedence over group relationships, etc.

Care theory aligns well with that aspect of evolutionary theory promoted by socio-biologists that argues for the human genetic disposition toward altruism. Evolutionary theory also admits of priorities: sacrifice for family first, group second, larger group third.

217

Care theory is aligned with both socio-biological and utilitarian theories in that the object of care tends to be some form of happiness (e.g. acceptance, fulfillment, satisfaction, etc.) Females think in terms of relationship over abstract principles. They will tend to bring those who are directly involved in the moral situation (i.e. the principals) together, process their thoughts and feelings about the situation, and, optimally, come to some sort of consensus for action. At the very least, the principals must be able to accept or be satisfied with the determinations made by those involved in the process. This acceptance or satisfaction is often times determined by utilitarian considerations: how will others feel about the action? And unlike deontology which subsumes emotion under reason, care theory subsumes reason under emotion (in the form of care). For care theorists care determines the framework within which reason can operate most effectively.

Experientially, reason is neither a moral faculty that determines (though imperfectly) moral rules (imperatives, principles, duty) as in deontology nor a mental faculty that determines happiness:pain ratios, which, in turn, determine moral rules, as in consequential theories. In fact, experientially, reason, as it is used in deontology, more often than not, is a meta-experiential construct; and as it is used in utilitarianism it is vulnerable to complexification.

Theoretical Extension: Reason as Conflicting Sets of Experiential Structures

Reason has a long and noble history in Western philosophy of being understood and thoroughly accepted as a mental faculty with three central functions: 1) it determines right from wrong (Christianity, deontology), 2) it determines which course of action will provide us with survival and well-being (utilitarianism, evolution, care theory, etc.), and 3) it helps us think more clearly by pointing out and eliminating contradictions and fallacies (traditional logic).

Christian and deontological use of reason has been severely challenged by the more practical utilitarian use. Utilitarianism argues that morality is derived not from any mental faculty but from human experiences of happiness and pain. We learn what makes us happy and pained by experiencing the consequences of any given act. We use reason to place individual acts into categories or types (e.g.

stealing, killing, etc.) and determine the consequences of each type (collection of individual acts) to judge whether or not those acts should be considered moral or immoral. We construct rules (laws, imperatives, principles, and commandments) so that we can teach our young to do or not do "x" because it will cause allot of people happiness or pain, respectively. In all of this there is no moral function of reason. Mill rejected the idea that there ever was any moral faculty called reason (Mill, 1987).

Another severe challenge to the moral function of reason was the Holocaust during World War II. The Nazis were rational in their determinations of how to kill the Jews of Europe and Russia. They believed that killing Jews would help them survive and be well. And they deliberated at each step of dealing with the "Jewish question" as to how to accomplish their task. But not many people today would ever say that the Nazis were moral in trying to annihilate the Jews. They were rational in their deliberations, but they based their rationality on immoral grounds. It was not how to get a job done that was immoral; it was the job itself.

The same argument has been used against the use of reason as a moral faculty in the creation and use of technology in warfare. The creation of armaments that will destroy millions of people was an intensely rational endeavor. Science valorizes reason as a practical and logical faculty, but it tends to separate itself and its use of reason from ethical concerns. Reason can be employed to create weapons of mass destruction, but it is not used to judge whether or not the creation and use of those weapons are moral or not.

In many circles reason is no longer accepted as a moral faculty. Its intuitive quality lends itself to relativization: one person's moral act is another person's immoral act. Hitler was convinced that the Jews needed to be eliminated (intuition); it was just a matter of how to do it (reasoning). Hitler, as evidenced by his final recorded words, believed up to his suicide in the bunker that he was acting morally by killing the Jews, but believing (i.e. intuiting) that "x" is moral does not mean that "x" is moral.

Experientially, beliefs are relative to those who believe, but only those beliefs that are constitutive of SSR or authentic structures are moral. Experientially, Hitler's belief was clearly a distortion of reality, the result of complexification of experience (in his personal development) and the passage of meta-experiential constructs from previous generations. Reason, as a practical faculty, as applied to the decisions pertaining to the holocaust, was used to determine courses of action based upon faulty, distorted moral grounds.

Experientially, reason is a set of conflicting experiential structures and has nothing to do with being a moral or practical faculty employed by humans to do anything. All people reason inasmuch as they participate in experiential processes constituted by conflicting sets of experiential structures.

For instance, Heinz, in the above example, considers whether or not it is moral for him to steal the drug to save his wife. Two experiences conflict with each other:
1) this drug will save my wife (I want to save her)
2) stealing in most instances is wrong

Let's say that both experiences are SSR (natural, authentic, real, and moral). Heinz values his wife's life and wants her to live; the drug is available but he can't afford it; the drug is believed to be life-saving. Heinz also believes (intuits) that stealing is generally wrong; only in some particular instances might it be right; this might be one of those instances.

Christian reasoning might look like this:

I want my wife to live	The drug will save her	I can't afford the drug	I can steal the drug
desire	confidence	confidence	confidence
thinking	thinking	thinking	thinking
environ	environ	environ	environ
room	room	room	room
SSR, 9.5	SSR, 8	SSR, 9	SSR,7

Stealing is immoral	It is against God's law	I'll think of getting the drug another way
condemnation	confidence	confidence
thinking	thinking	deciding
environ	environ	environ
room	room	room
SSR, 9.5	SSR, 9.7	SSR, 9.8

In this analysis (though superficial and simplified), the conflict is resolved with minimal reasoning. The idea of stealing the drug (moral act) is overridden by the idea of stealing being immoral. The idea of it being against God's law supports or strengthens one's moral condemnation of the act. We can assume that the strength of the conflicting experience (e.g. I can steal the drug) was initially relatively weak in relation to the condemnation-experience. This would probably admit of a peripheral existence of the condemnation of stealing in the stealing-experience, which would naturally lessen the strength of the stealing-experience and allow that experience to be overridden by the last experience of committing to think of getting the drug another way. *

Deontological reasoning might look like this:

I want my wife to live	The drug will save her	I can't afford the drug	I can steal the drug
desire	confidence	confidence	confidence
thinking	thinking	thinking	thinking
environ	environ	environ	environ
room	room	room	room
SSR, 9.5	SSR, 8	SSR, 9	SSR,7

Stealing is immoral	It violates a moral imperative	I'll think of an alternative
condemnation	confidence	confidence
thinking	thinking	deciding
environ	environ	environ
room	room	room
SSR, 9.5	SSR, 9.7	SSR, 9.8

In this analysis, which is similar to the Christian example in many ways, the conflict is resolved with minimal reasoning. The idea of stealing the drug (moral act) is overridden by the idea of stealing being immoral. The idea of it being a violation of a moral imperative supports or strengthens one's moral condemnation of the act. We can assume that the strength of the conflicting experience (e.g. I can steal the drug) was initially relatively weak in relation to the condemnation-experience. This would probably admit of a peripheral existence of the condemnation of stealing in the stealing-experience, which would naturally lessen the strength of the stealing-experience and allow that experience to be overridden by the last experience of committing to think of getting the drug another way. **

Utilitarian reasoning might look like this:

I want my wife to live	The drug will save her	I can't afford the drug	I can steal the drug
desire	confidence	confidence	confidence
thinking	thinking	thinking	thinking
environ	environ	environ	environ
room	room	room	room
SSR, 9.5	SSR, 8	SSR, 9	SSR,7

*This example is complicated by the probability that such reasoning is distorted and not SSR. The use of God to justify one's behavior, whether affirming or negating that behavior while affirming or negating some other behavior, is likely to be the result of historical complexity and contemporary meta-experiential construction.

**This example is complicated by the probability that such reasoning is distorted and not SSR. The use of an objective moral imperative, whether affirming or negating that behavior while affirming or negating some other behavior, is likely to be the result of historical complexity and contemporary meta-experiential construction.

221

Stealing is usually immoral It tends to cause allot of people pain.

condemnation	confidence
thinking	thinking
environ	environ
room	room
SSR, 9.5	SSR, 8.5

But in this case my stealing the drug would cause the druggist little pain, while causing me and my wife (and others) a good deal of happiness.
confidence
thinking
environ
room
SSR, 9.8

Stealing the drug would be moral in this instance
confidence
deciding
environ
room
SSR, 9.8

In this analysis the conflicting experiential structures are the same (steal the drug or not), but the solution is different. In this instance, rather than realize the pre-determined moral way to act (either by realizing God's law or by recognizing the moral imperative and connected moral principles), the moral solution is determined by considering who will be hurt and how will they be hurt versus who will benefit and how they will benefit. If the happiness:pain ratio is in favor of stealing the drug, then stealing would be moral; if the reverse, then not. In this instance, it was determined to be moral.

Care theory's reasoning might look like this:

I want my wife to live	The drug will save her	I can't afford the drug	I can steal the drug
desire	confidence	confidence	confidence
thinking	thinking	thinking	thinking
environ	environ	environ	environ
room	room	room	room
SSR, 9.5	SSR, 8	SSR, 9	SSR,7

I would go to prison	My family would have to struggle	I should think of another way to get the drug
confidence	hurt	
thinking	thinking	confidence
environ	environ	thinking
room	room	room
SSR, 9.5	SSR, 8.5	SSR, 9.8

In this analysis the possible consequences of the act of stealing the drug are considered. If the theft would result in imprisonment (which the person is confident that it will), then what are the repercussions of this act on others, especially wife and family? The feelings of others are vital; relationships need to be maintained, if possible; keeping the network of relationships together is important. The moral worth of the act itself (Christianity, deontology) serves the end of keeping relationships intact.

In none of these analyses is there anything like a mental faculty of reason. There is no metaphysical thing that performs the reasoning that goes on. Rather, the reasoning that goes on is the actual process of conflicting experiential structures that work themselves out to some sort of conclusion. If there were no conflict in thinking (no multiple possible courses of action), then there would be no reasoning. And simply because there is a conflict in thinking does not mean that there is something behind the conflict that is working out the conflict.

In each of these analyses there is supposed to be some sort of 'entity', 'phenomenon', or 'faculty' that is doing the reasoning (working out the conflict). Historically, men have supposedly been naturally in possession of great amounts of this faculty, whereas women have either less amounts of it, are faulty in their use of it, or simply have none at all. Therefore, it is argued, that men should be in positions of power in society; they know how to make rational decisions, whereas women's decisions tend to be irrational or emotional.

But experiential analysis, even in this oversimplified rendering, shows that there is no faculty that reasons; rather, reasoning occurs as a function of experience, in particular conflicting experiences. Every human being participates in this process inasmuch as every human being participates in conflicting experiential structures. Men might favor an experiential process that is aimed at universal (objective) applications of morality; women might favor an experiential process that is aimed at particular (relative) applications of morality; but all human beings reason, inasmuch as they experience conflict in possible courses of action (e.g. future actions), conflict in discriminating moral from immoral acts, and conflict in entertaining logically inconsistent ideas (based upon traditional objective ontological assumptions).

Theoretical Extension: Reason as Moral Intuition

Historically in philosophy intuition has been used to "ground" moral decisions. We simply appeal to each other as rational beings in order to agree on which actions are moral and which are not and try to support our appeal with reasons that can be universally accepted. Inasmuch as we succeed, we derive a set of universal principles or moral laws which guide, if not determine, our behavior (e.g. natural law, deontology).

Experientially, intuition is nothing other than certain types of experiential structures. When someone conceives the thought that murder is wrong and can gain universal or near universal affirmation of this idea, it doesn't mean that there is some sort of metaphysical thing or entity called intuition that has the capacity to connect human thinking to an objective reality outside of the mind. It simply means that our cognition aligns with other components of experience that might or might not be constitutive of SSR structures which tend to be affirmed by many other people. Just because a majority of people see an object as red while a minority sees it as a shade of gray does not mean that the object is one or the other and that someone is wrong or deficient in some way in their perception. Both perceptions, if constitutive of SSR structures, are right or real and need to be recognized as such. Likewise, if moral determinations based on intuition are constitutive of SSR structures, then those determinations need to be recognized as right or real.

Parallels, if not equations, can be drawn between intuition and patterns of neurological networks in the brain. Neuroscientists tend to conceive of brain activity as divided into interconnected areas consisting of: cognition (primarily the cerebral cortex), affect (primarily the limbic system), behavior (primarily the motor area), and sensual areas and areas that synthesize the input from the various senses; each of these areas correspond to the components of experience (minus the environment and the "I"). Neural networks run to and from each of these areas to all other areas, some directions more dense in neurons than others. If neuroscience were able to isolate neural networks as combinations of specific cognitive, affective, behavioral, and sensual neural activity, it might be able to render intuition in terms of neurological networks.

For instance, if a human witnesses a murder of a child, his experiential structure might look like this:

C: horrible
A: repulsion
B: seeing murder
S: murderous behavior
E: room
"I": ownership

SSR

Inasmuch as the structure is SSR (not complex), the moral determination is real and right for that person; it needs to be respected as such by others. But inasmuch as it is complex, it is a distortion of reality and a moral wrong. Such an experiential structure might look like this:

C: [why is he doing that to that child?]	I'm bad	horrible
A: [curious]	self-rejection	false confidence
B: [seeing murder]	looking down	false affirmation
S: [murderous behavior]	environ	environ
E: [room]	room	room
"I": [ownership]		
SSR (real self)	(self-rejection)	(false self)

In this experiential structure the real self consists of the person feeling curiosity about the event he is witnessing and not horror. Though few people might feel this way about a murder of a child, it is possible for there to be some who do. Since no person can escape the experiential structures within which he or she participates, the content of that structure is reality. The fact is that the person does not experience horror in relation to this event; he experiences curiosity. From most other people's point of view, such a response to such an event would be considered odd, bizarre, pathological or possibly depraved. But such interpretations are relative to one's own experience and (possibly) the collective experiences of many others. They are not to reflect an inversion or deficiency in relation to some objective reality. Relative to most people, such a response would be odd, bizarre, etc. But the fact is, this person experiences this event in this way, just like the color-blind person experiences red as a shade of gray. When others respond to the 'odd' person in a rejecting manner (e.g. odd, bizarre, pathological, or depraved in relation to an assumed objective reality), and that rejection is communicated over and over to this individual, the individual, in order to survive and be at least somewhat well in this community of people, rejects the legitimacy of his own experience and alters himself by affirming (though falsely) the horror responses of others. He spouts their reality but does not experience it. Hence, paradoxically, it would be immoral for this person to affirm a belief reflecting a felt horror and intuitive rejection of an event that he does not experience. And, likewise paradoxically, it would be immoral for others to condemn this person for his 'odd' response to the event. Odd though it might be in relation to others, it is still real and right, not only for that person but for that person in relation to everyone else; others must recognize its legitimacy. Just

225

because color-seeing people tend to experience color-blind people's experience as odd, bizarre, or pathological (in a physiological sense) doesn't mean that color-blind people's experience is any less real than that of color-seeing people. It is what it is; the contents of experience are what they are. Rejecting the legitimacy of such content is to deny that reality. Such denials tend to create complex structures and distortions of reality.

Theoretical Extension: Reason as Practical

Consequentialist theories of reason hold that reason is a mental faculty that is used to determine courses of action that will provide an individual (egoism), closely-related or otherwise emotionally connected people (care theory), or groups of people (utilitarianism) with the most happiness over pain. From a consequentialist perspective, moral acts are not the direct result of the functioning of reason but the indirect result of such functioning. For consequentialist thinkers reason is a mental faculty that, if used properly, will provide direction for the individual when conflicting courses of action occur for that individual.

This direction could be rendered in moral or practical terms. That is, consequentialist decisions range from whether or not to steal to which food to eat. Both types of decision are based on happiness:pain ratios. Once those ratios are known (through empirical verification), then moral and practical guidelines are created which are passed on from generation to generation.

Experientially, reason is a process involving conflicting experiential structures that work themselves out to some sort of conclusion (i.e. course of action). There is no faculty performing the process; it simply occurs in the wake of conflicting experiential structures. Each conclusion or course of action rendered from the process is subject to experiential validation and revision: did the course of action produce happiness or pain? was the course of action effective in reaching its goal? Etc. Experientially, reason is an experiential process engaged in by all (or most) human beings who are acting in the world in order to survive and live well and not a meta-physical faculty of mind.

Theoretical Extension: Reason as Logical

Historically, reason has also been equated with logic. Logic is the business of clear thinking. Clear thinking is defined as thinking that aligns with actual physical (natural) reality. Logic, as traditionally conceived in philosophy, is thinking that assumes the existence of a traditional objective world and the ability of at least one human being to understand that world as it is and not simply as it is experienced to be; it is a traditionally objective enterprise.

One function of logic has been to rid humanity of mythical thinking, superstition and delusion. If we make a necessary connection between our thinking and the physical (sensual) reality outside of our minds, then any reality claims we might make have to be grounded in this physical world. Metaphysical claims like "God created the world" become suspect because we can't sense God and, hence, no one has ever witnessed creation. All metaphysical claims become suspect. The objective reality of traditional logic is that reality that can be sensed. Reality claims can be universally accepted if we keep the claim necessarily linked to the physical world. Once we get beyond this connection and start making reality claims that are not necessarily linked to the physical world, then problems crop up.

Hence, if someone makes a reality claim like "the leaf is red," others can verify that claim simply by looking at the leaf. Since reality is objective for the logician, if the claim that the leaf is red is true (i.e. objectively real), then any claim that posits something else is necessarily false (untrue). Such claims would be considered illogical and irrational. Hence, unfortunately from the experientialist perspective, the color-blind person who sees the leaf as a shade of gray would, in the traditional logician's world, be illogical or irrational.

But linking mental statements to physical reality isn't the only function of logic in philosophy. It also deals with words, placement of those words, and the rules for placement. We can make claims (propositions) and draw conclusions from those claims that have little to do with observation or sensation of a physical world.

For instance, we can say that "all gimjabs are flipple"; "jerkej is a gimjab"; therefore, "jerkej is flipple." We can know this to be true even if we have never seen a gimjab, don't know what a gimjab is, and know that we have just made up the word out of thin air. The very structure of our language can render truths that must be universally accepted. Clear thinking here is more the product of language rules than of making necessary links between language (thinking) and the physical world. It would be inconsistent (i.e. illogical) for us to say that: "all gimjabs are flipple"; "jerkej is a gimjab"; therefore, "jerkej is not flipple", if, of course, we know what "not" means.

But can we know of nouns, verbs, and adjectives without ever being sensually attached to a physical world? If we have never experienced a "thing" in the physical world, would we ever know what a "thing" was? If we had never experienced an action (things in motion) or similarities and differences between things (adjectives) or between motions (adverbs), would we ever know what a verb, an adverb, or an adjective was? Is language not rooted in, and a product of, our necessary connection to our environment? If we were never sensually connected to our environment, would we have a language at all?

From this perspective rational thinking would involve an understanding of lexicon and rules of grammar and syntax. We'd have to know that "gimjabs" are nouns (persons, places, things, concepts), "flipple" is adjectival or descriptive of nouns (if we already know that the absence of an article like "a" or "an" before a word lessons the likelihood that the word is a noun), that nouns in this language are usually placed before a verb, and that "is" is a verb of a transitive sort, etc.

We know that a "gimjab" is a noun because we are familiar with the rules of English. We are familiar with the rules of English (or any other language) because we live in a world of changing things. If there were never any world of changing things, then we (if we would exist at all) would know of no categories such as nouns, verbs, adjectives and adverbs. Nouns are persons, places, things and concepts (or ideas). Persons, places and things are clearly in the changing physical world. Concepts or ideas are either reflective of things in the changing physical world (e.g. tree) or things in the changing mental world (e.g. soul). But any word reflecting anything in the mental world must have been conceived *in* a physical world of changing things. I was able to create the word "gimjab" not because I've sensed a gimjab in the world of changing things but because I live in, and have sensed, changing things in the world and am able to categorize my experience of those things in order to communicate my experience to others. If there never were any changing things that I

228

could sense, I would never conceive of anything. A gimjab is a noun because a tree is a noun, and not the reverse.

Science has relegated allot of "gimjabs" to the category of myth, but myths are still nouns, just not ones reflective of things in the changing physical world. They are reflective of things in a changing mental world. But everything in the changing mental world would not exist without our connection to the physical world. If we could annihilate what we refer to as the physical world, we would, in effect, annihilate ourselves because without the physical world, we are no more.

The foregoing has argued in favor of logic's necessary connection between the mind (ideas, words, language, rules of language, etc.) and the physical world, but it rejects logic's acceptance of objective reality as something detached from the person. We know that a gimjab is a noun, but that doesn't mean that the (mental) category of "noun" exists apart from physical things in a changing world of physical things. Rather, it exists only in conjunction with those changing physical things. Likewise, concepts, ideas and imaginations exist only in conjunction with changing physical things.

The concepts, ideas and imaginations need not reflect things in the changing physical world, but they need take place or occur in a changing physical world. As long as imaginations are recognized as imaginations and not as something reflective of the changing physical world, they offer no serious problems to our living in a changing physical world. But as soon as imaginations are conflated with things in the changing physical world, then we are subject to fantasy constructions and myth-making. The reality of a changing physical world tends to uproot and debunk such constructions and myths. Science has done so with many religious myths.

But when science replaces religious absolutism with scientific objectivity, it does little more than religion to avoid meta-experiential construction. Scientific claims, when objective, are equally subject to the criticism of being mata-experiential constructs or distortions of reality.

Once traditional objective thinking (and assumptions) are rejected and replaced by experientially-determined reality, the 'clear thinking' function of reason becomes not only suspect but problematic. Experientially, the syllogism:

Premise: All gimjabs are flipple
Premise: Jerkej is a gimjab
Conclusion: Therefore: Jerkej is flipple
is logically consistent in regard to language use if one accepts the rules of language in certain ways. If we accept that nouns are persons, places, things, and concepts that follow adjectives like "all" either immediately or eventually, that verbs of action or being follow nouns either immediately or eventually, and that adjectives could either precede a noun or come after a verb but refer to a noun that precedes the verb, then we might understand the sentence, "All gimjabs are flipple."

But if our language is not so ruled, then we might have great difficulty understanding what the sentence means. It might appear as gibberish to us until we are able to understand the grammatical and syntactic rules of the language.

Even when we consider the simple logical rule of identity as in: $A=A$, we need to accept the rules of this construction before we are able to understand and accept it. For instance, we must recognize that the symbol "A" that precedes the equal sign is the same thing as the "A" that follows the equal sign. There is nothing to stop us from understanding the first "A" to be something totally different from the second "A" and then to maintain that $A=A$ would be illogical.

Likewise, we have to first accept the integrity of categories such as nouns, verbs, and adjectives as well as the rules of grammar and syntax of the language if we are to accept the legitimacy of the syllogism above. What's to stop us from conceiving of nouns as words that refer to "spiritual substances represented in material and non-material forms"? Our understanding of a concept of a "tree" would differ considerably from our current Western understanding of a noun. Also, what if we understood these nouns to be imbedded in symbols that are much more complex than the symbols (letters) we use? For instance, let's say that a certain collection of lines (similar to those employed in Chinese languages) contains the symbol for "tree" but only when attached to other lines which indicate something relevant to the symbol for "tree." In other words, the symbol for "tree" never exists without some other "qualifier." This might indicate that the language in use does not possess symbols that reflect discrete things in the physical world but only things-in-conjunction-with-qualifiers. Understanding nouns as relatively complicated symbols makes it very difficult for the speakers of the two languages to accept the logic of the other, unless the rules and symbol-references are clearly understood and accepted.

If the logic of language is necessarily connected to language's connection to the physical world; and if people's connection to the physical world is reflected in their language; and if such connections vary in fundamental ways; then any logical construction is subject to acceptance or rejection of those rules of language through which that construction is made manifest.

Logic is not reflective of some absolute, universal mind that somehow imposes itself upon the changing physical world. Nor is it a genetically-determined disposition to experience the environment (changing physical world) within which one acts as objective (singular and privy to human experience). Rather, logic is the experience of understanding the language symbols and rules of the group within which one operates.

For example, a color-seeing person will say: X is red. A color-blind person will say: X is a shade of gray. Each person will accept the language rule of identity, agreeing that the X in "X is red" is the same as the X in "X is a shade of gray." If the underlying assumption of these people is one of traditional objectivism, then one person, at least, is wrong. There cannot be two accurate renderings of one reality when those renderings are in conflict.

Traditional logic is based in a traditional objective understanding (assumption) of reality. Hence, it is able to argue that rules of identity supersede and condition experience of changing physical things. After all, there is only one physical world; hence, one's understanding (experience) of that world has to match the world as it is. But when the traditional objective world is rejected in favor of an experientially objective world, which includes the probability of multiple objective worlds, then the rules of logic are likewise rejected (or at least accepted only relative to the language systems within which they exist).

An experientially objective logical language is a language based upon accepted rules of use. The language and its rules are as "organic" as the people who use them. Rationalist attempts to argue for the pre-existence of grammatical and syntactical rules (e.g. Chomsky), whether these rules are meta-physically or physically (i.e. genetically) imposed represent one side of the traditional objective coin. The other side is represented by the empiricists' attempts to derive the rules of language strictly from experience with the physical world. In the empiricist's world, the rules of grammar and syntax have come about in response to our interaction with the physical environment.

These opposing arguments result from accepting a traditional objective approach to reality. When reality is equal to experience, where "experience" is defined as a necessary combination of "mental" and "physical" components, then the battle between rationalism and empiricism transforms into an integration of "mind" and "body." The rules of language are now seen as the result of an integration of the traditional "mental" with the traditional "physical." "Mental" arguments for the existence of rules of language cannot win out over "physical" arguments, and vice-versa, once traditional objective assumptions are rejected. Understanding reality as a necessary combination of "mental" and "physical" components places the battle between the mental and the physical squarely within the experiential. Some experiences reflect the mental, others the physical; both are real. The question is: which experiences are SSR (i.e. authentic, real, or moral) and which are complex (i.e. inauthentic, distortions of reality or immoral)?

The object of ontological investigation is experience: what is its structure? What are its contents? What is the relationship between the components that constitute it? The tool for ontological invest-tigation is also experience: how does experience understand itself? Is explanatory experience (e.g. theory, explanation) consistent with immediate experience (e.g. observation, imagination)? The logic of experiential objectivity (as opposed to traditional, dualistic object-tivity) lies in consistency between SSR structures and not between the correspondence between the 'mental' world and the 'physical' world or in the acceptance of 'universal rules of language'. When viewed experientially, traditional logic is transformed into an experiential logic; the "mental" is integrated with the "physical"; traditional objective reality is brought inside experience and kept there; all traditional objective claims are owned; and consistency in experience replaces consistency between a discrete mental world and a discrete physical world. In this sense the separation of mental and physical and its subsequent need for alignment that is so important to traditional objectivity is replaced by an integration of the 'mental' and

232

the 'physical' into components of experience, whereby the need for alignment between "mental" and "physical" disappears. Such an alignment becomes a matter of practical concern. Also, in this sense, the acceptance of universal rules of grammar, whether derived from rational or empirical sources, is replaced by authentic and consistent experiential structures on all levels of experience (i.e. intra- and inter-experiential, mutual, group, societal, and inter-societal levels of consistency). What is logical becomes what is componentially consistent; what is illogical becomes what is componentially complex.

A traditional logical problem viewed through the lens of experientialism would look like this:

Focal	Peripheral
C: Lincoln is the 16th president of the U.S.	orientation, things in room, own body, etc.
A: confidence	comfort, familiarity, etc.
B: talking	standing, pacing
S: students	students
E: room	room
"I": ownership	
SSR	

As long as the experiential structure is SSR, the statement is considered logical. Since the traditional objective world has been brought inside experience, it is no longer a basis upon which every true statement must rest. Experientially, it doesn't matter if the statement reflects an actual state of affairs (or, in this case, a past state of affairs). What matters is that the statement (as cognition) be consistent with the other components of experience. If there is no complexity within the structure, then the structure is real, right, and true. Reality, morality, and logic are united into one basic structure.

Therefore, if I believe:

Focal	Peripheral
C: Lincoln is the 15th president of the U.S.	orientation, things in room, own body, etc.
A: confidence	comfort, familiarity, etc.
B: talking	standing, pacing
S: students	students
E: room	room
"I": ownership	
SSR	

then I would be making a true statement for me. Now, others might disagree with me and show me a list of U.S. presidents and convince me that I am wrong. If I accept the validity of such evidence to support their contention, then I will admit that I was wrong before and I will now hold that Lincoln is the 16th president of the U.S.

This might sound ridiculous to those who assume that at least one person can discern reality (historical or otherwise) as it is and therefore make claims that reflect or capture that reality in words. But once we admit that experience is inescapable, any belief is just as real as any other. Experientially, a belief is a cognitive component of experience that is necessarily connected to other components. Getting beyond any environment within which one exists at this moment is ontologically impossible. A statement about an historical event is made in a current environment, and we can't get beyond the current environment to make good our claim. We believe the claim is true, i.e. that Lincoln existed and was the 16th president of the U.S. because we trust what we've been taught. We trust that there actually were people who knew Lincoln, wrote about him, talked about him, etc. and convinced others who never saw him that he existed and was the 16th president. Whether or not he actually existed, and whether or not he was the 16th president of the U.S. is of absolutely no consequence to us. We believe that he did exist and that he was the 16th president of the U.S. Our belief (cognition) is very consequential to us. It is an integral part of what we hold to be real.

If I maintain that a man named Vertogline invented the light bulb ten years before Edison did, then promptly destroyed his work and died, and that this bit of information was passed down to me from previous generations in my family, and I trusted the veracity of those individuals, then I might believe, even if most people disagree with me, that Vertogline invented the light bulb. If I saw the need, I might try to convince others of the truth (correspondence with reality) of my belief. If I couldn't convince them or if I didn't see the need to do so, I could go to my grave believing that it was so. Whether it was so or not would probably not matter to anyone other than me and, possibly, some people in my family. Life would go on and history would be recorded again and again with Edison (with some serious controversy over this though not including anyone named Vertogline) as the inventor of the light bulb.

Once traditional objective reality becomes relativized, it no longer is illogical for someone to make a statement that does not reflect what most people hold to be true, even if they can get millions of others to hold the same thing. (Again, consider the color-blind:color-seeing example).

234

An experiential analysis of logic as applied to language construction might look like this:

C: Lincoln is Lincoln	orientation, things in room, own body, etc.
A: confidence	comfort, familiarity, etc.
B: talking	standing, pacing
S: students	students
E: room	room
"I": ownership	
SSR	
C: Lincoln is not Roosevelt	orientation, things in room, own body, etc.
A: confidence	comfort, familiarity, etc.
B: talking	standing, pacing
S: students	students
E: room	room
"I": ownership	
SSR	

The speaker has assumed that the first "Lincoln" in his statement refers to the same person that the second "Lincoln" refers to; he is confident in what he is saying because it is so obvious to him that this is so (law of identity). This statement is true even if no one named Lincoln actually existed. Even if "Lincoln" referred to a dog, a plant, or a fictional character, the statement would still be true because the speaker accepts that his first "Lincoln" refers to the same thing as does his second "Lincoln."

But if the speaker assumes that his first "Lincoln" refers to the 16th president of the U.S. and the second "Lincoln" refers to his dog, then he might have trouble feeling confident in saying this. For him the 16th president is not his dog and hence, "Lincoln is Lincoln" is not true. Rather, his second statement is true. If his interlocutors know who he was referring to with each "Lincoln," then they would probably agree with him, i.e. that "Lincoln is not Lincoln" is a true statement.

Analyzed experientially, this might look like:

C: Lincoln is Lincoln	1st Lincoln" as 16th president; 2nd Lincoln as dog ; orientated, things in room, own body, etc.
A: confused	comfort, familiarity, etc.
B: talking	standing, pacing
S: students	students
E: room	room
"I": ownership	
SSR	

In this experience, the speaker is saying "Lincoln is Lincoln" but he is thinking that his first "Lincoln" refers to the 16th president; whereas the second "Lincoln" refers to his dog. The statement might strike him as bizarre; hence, the confusion. So even though the logician might unequivocally agree with the statement, the speaker is not so convinced.

And when the following occurs:

C: Lincoln is not Roosevelt	orientation, things in room, own body, etc.
A: confidence	comfort, familiarity, etc.
B: talking	standing, pacing
S: students	students
E: room	room
"I": ownership	
SSR	

If the speaker assumes that "Lincoln" refers to the 16th president and "Roosevelt" refers to the 32nd president of the U.S., then he might well feel confidence in stating this, granting that he knows these historical bits of information. But if the speaker assumes that "Lincoln" refers to the 16th president, whereas "Roosevelt" refers to his dog, then his confidence might not realize itself for long. He might wonder why he said such a thing.

Now, if "Lincoln" referred to the 16th president and "Roosevelt" to his dog, then his statement "Lincoln is not Roosevelt" is true for him. And it would be true for his interlocutors too if they knew what the words referred to. The only ones who might disagree with him would be the logicians.

Likewise, if each of the speaker's "Lincoln"'s refers to a particular configuration of ink on paper, then "Lincoln is Lincoln" is true, but not for the reasons the logician would maintain. It would be similar to saying that "xpzif is xpzif." In this case, if the speaker assumes that "is" means "looks identical to," then he might speak confidently. But if he assumes "is" means "refers to the same thing," he might be puzzled by his statement because he doesn't know what "xpzif" refers to. Even if he knows that "xpzif" refers to itself as a configuration of ink on paper, he might not be clear on this because the first "xpzif" takes up a different space than does the second "xpzif." Something might not be something else unless it is that something else, in which case something is not something else; it is only itself.

What is logical depends upon what the speakers, writers, or thinkers mean by the words they use to express or realize themselves. They make sense to others inasmuch as others know what the words they use refer to, what the organization of their words means, and whether or not their references are a part of their own experience. The words themselves would tend to constitute the focal aspect of experience for the experientialist; but there is a great deal of meaning

236

within the periphery of experience (e.g. motivation, assumption) that the surface words don't often include.

In conclusion, traditional logic, which is based on traditional objective assumptions about reality and rationalistic, metaphysical grounds for logic must be rejected in favor of an experiential logic, which is based on experiential objective assumptions, the explication of experiential processes and the contents of the structures therein, and a relativistic manifestation of language with some universal tendencies.

Theoretical Extension: Experiential Reasoning and Entitlement

Once reason is understood to be an experiential process and not a moral, practical or logical faculty inextricably linked to a traditional objective world, it is easier to see how the terms "reason" and "entitlement" can be used as meta-experiential constructs.

One of the most obvious uses of reason in the past is that it is a faculty owned either exclusively or at least developed to the highest degree in men rather than women. This use 'justifies', at least in part, male domination in all socio-economic areas of life, especially in those areas where hierarchy is the preferred organizational structure. If men are more rational than women, either naturally (i.e. genetically) or developmentally (i.e. through training or learning), and if reason is required to make practical decisions that determine the course of one's life (or others' lives), then it behooves humanity to place men at the top of hierarchies so we all might survive and live well.

As already argued, this use of reason has exploded in the wake of two world wars, the holocaust, Stalin's starvation policy of the kulaks (peasants), genocidal 'cleansing' of all sorts, holy wars between religions, etc. How men have been "rational" is not only indicated in the development of science, mathematics and technology but also in their penchant for killing each other by aligning themselves with ideologies that 'justify' mass murder, torture, and annihilation. The latter uses of reason hardly merit praise.

To claim that men are rational beings, as opposed to women, who are emotional beings, is to use reason as a meta-experiential construct. As already argued, a meta-experiential construct is an idea (construct) that came about, at least in part, because of the complexification of experience; the complexification of experience rests upon

237

the development of a false self created in the wake of physical, sexual, and/or emotional abuse (or as the result of natural trauma, unresolved grief, etc.)

In order to support this claim in relation to reason, we need to entertain the possible motives for the claim that men are more rational beings than women, but we need to do this in an historical context. Why would early man ever come up with the idea that men can think better than women in regard to knowing what course of action to take when confronted with alternatives that would promote survival and/or advance the well-being of themselves and others, when women, even in ancient history (we might reasonably surmise), determined, on a daily basis, just what actions they should engage in to promote the survival and well-being of their family members and showed considerable accuracy in doing so? Do we honestly think that early men naturally possessed a capacity to reason in this manner far superior to women when women had exhibited this capacity, with significant accuracy, every day in nurturing their young? If they did, then why did men entrust women with the daily job of raising their children when they knew that their rational capacities were faulty?

Now what is more likely, it seems, is that men tended to perform jobs that required more physical speed and strength (jobs based on physical endowment, e.g. hunting) and women tended to perform jobs that required less physical strength and more physical nurturing (jobs based on physical endowments, e.g. berry-picking, tending to and feeding children). This aligns with the extended premises to premise #13. So far, no problem. The question is: why did men come to dominate women in their choice (tendency toward) jobs? Is hunting intrinsically more important than raising a family? Are women in-capable of hunting? When agriculture was discovered, was farming intrinsically more important than raising a family? Were women incapable of farming?

There seems to be no reason to think that women are incapable of hunting and farming. They might not be able to do it as well as men because men tend to be stronger than women and these activities might be better accomplished by stronger people, but they, overall, possess the strength necessary to do the job.

The division of labor between men and women on the grounds of natural endowments makes allot of rational and practical sense. Men can do the jobs that require more physical strength better than women; therefore, when men and women form pair bonds, it makes more sense for men to do the jobs requiring more strength, if they are physically capable of it, possess some skill and interest in doing it, etc.

But this does not address why men have come to dominate women in this regard. Cooperation has been replaced by domination. Why? Is it simply more rational for women to let men dominate them because men's jobs in relation to survival and well-being are more important than women's jobs? Have women realized the prudence of letting men dominate them because men have the job of providing the lion's share of the resources for their survival and well-being and the survival and well-being of their children, and challenging that domination would result in death to them and their family?

This question belies a capitulation, an accepted subordination of will, and a rejection of the equality between men and women. It states that simply because men earn the lion's share of the resources for survival and well-being, they *deserve* or *are entitled to* dominant status in social (family) situations. It says that male domination is a prudent decision, made by rational people, in order to best achieve the survival and well-being of everyone involved.

Or has the natural emotional strength of women to stand up for themselves been sapped by the natural expressions of men's physical endowments in the form of aggression realized in physical, sexual and emotional abuse in early human social development; and has this sapping of emotional strength become institutionalized into ideologies and social organizations through the creation and implementation of meta-experiential constructs? This work is an argument in support of the latter.

It is irrational to think that men are more rational than women, given the history of women's capacity to make decisions daily that provide for the survival and well-being of themselves and their children. This irrationality, passed off as rationality, is a meta-experiential construct or a distortion of reality. It is rationality, made irrational, which, in turn, is made 'rational'. In other words, the 'rational' contention that men are more rational than women is evidence of a false self, a false self that occurred in the history of human social development, and that was transformed into a meta-experiential construct and passed on from generation to generation through the construction of institutions and ideologies that facilitate this passage.

The history of male domination and entitlement is, to a good extent, founded upon a distortion of reason. The thinking goes: When survival and well-being are dependent upon choices made that will or will not support survival and well-being, those choices need to be made by people who are best equipped to make them. Who is best equipped to make those choices that will provide for the survival and well-being of a person or a group of people? Is it the individual him or herself? Is it males (generally)? Is it adult males (generally)? Is it intelligent people, men or women? Is it physically strong people, men (usually) or women (sometimes)? Is it rich people, men or women? Is it willful people, men or women? Is it knowledgeable people, men or women? Is it wise people, men or women?

If reason is an experiential process and not a moral, practical or logical faculty of mind connected to objective reality and a process engaged in on a daily basis by women as well as men, with relatively good success, then at least both male and female adults are, on the whole, equally qualified to make decisions that will determine survival and well-being of themselves and those in their care.

This places parents (and not simply the father) as joint deciders of courses of action in relation to themselves and their offspring. Parents tend to decide who does what in the family because parents have learned how to negotiate the world around them without killing themselves off (knowledgeable, wise). Children have to learn how to do this. Children are dependent upon parents (or other care-givers) to help them learn how to fend for themselves (and eventually their offspring). Impaired adults are likewise dependent upon others to help them fend for themselves (i.e. be autonomous as possible). Some children and adults will be dependent upon others for most if not all of their lives. This dependency is not a matter of choice but a determination of nature.

When parents disagree as to how to accomplish the task of surviving and creating well-being for themselves and their children, they do not naturally opt for one of them to impose his will upon the other in order to get his way and expect to get away with it. The male might well try to impose his will upon the female out of frustration, but he does not *expect* the female to submit to his imposition of will. No one who tries to impose his or her will upon another person naturally expects the other person to submit to such an imposition unless his or her experience has already been distorted. Such an expectation is the result of complexification and not a natural disposition (genetic structure) toward domination. Arguing that it is, in 'fact', a natural (genetic) disposition is to engage in meta-experiential construction.

If we hypothesize that the original impositions of will by males in relation to females were actual experiences engaged in by actual men and women early in the history of humanity, then these attempted impositions were probably constituted by some form of aggression, as opposed to intelligent discourse. When men wanted to get their way, they aggressed. So when early man wanted to do X or didn't want to do Y, and yet knew that X could be done better by the woman and that Y needed to be done by someone for survival and well-being, then he could easily (naturally) *try* to impose his will on the female and prevent her from doing X or make her do Y by aggressing against her. It is *the attempt* to impose one's will on anther that seems to be natural in the biological sense. We can observe such behavior throughout all stages of human development.

But such aggression would naturally be rejected by the female. She might respond in a variety of ways, depending upon her personality and her social situation. For instance, if she were personally disposed to being intimidated by acts of aggression (personality), she might tend to be watchful of her mate's actions, fearing another bout of aggression; she might catch herself before being forceful with her opinion next time the confrontation occurs, etc. If she were disposed to being assertive, she might tell her mate to refrain from attempts to impose his will on her, tell him how it makes her feels when he does so, withhold future cooperation from the male (e.g. no sex, no shows of affection, and not as a way to retaliate but as a natural unwillingness to cooperate) or she might avoid him. If she were disposed to being aggressive herself, she might return his aggression, even to the point of brawling or worse.

It is not natural for anyone to submit to the imposition of anyone else's will upon them. Allowing someone to force their will upon oneself requires a distortion of experience. It requires one to want to do X, while 'having' to do Y, or at least not wanting to do Y, while 'having' to do Y. One's affect (at least) will not align or be supported by one's behavior. People land up doing all sorts of things they don't want to do.

When the first man imposed his will upon the first woman, the first woman didn't simply accept such behavior. Such an experiential set would look like this:

C: "he's dragging me by the hair
    to get me to do X"
A: respect/appreciate/like/love, etc.
B: smiling/respectful glance/petting the male affectionately, etc.
S: pain, male
E: outside
"I": ownership

In this experience the affect simply does not support the cognition or the sensation. Feeling pain is usually not accompanied by feelings of respect/appreciation/like/love in relation to the person imposing the pain.

When anyone imposes their will upon anyone else (e.g. parent-child, man-woman, man-man), those who are imposed upon will, unless each person's wills are similar (and, hence, the "imposition" is not understood as an imposition but perhaps as guidance or training), reject the legitimacy of the imposition.

If person A wants person B to do (or not do) X, and person B does not want to do (or not do) X, then person B will simply convey to person A that she doesn't want to do X. If that settles the matter, then fine. But if person A demands that person B do (or not do) X, and person B does not want to do (or not do) it, then person B's experience will conflict with that of person A not only in regard to the activity under consideration but also in the way person A is acting.

An expression of want in reference to the behavior (cooperation) of another usually is not experienced as imposing to another. (Sometimes, especially with those who tend to be more sensitive to the wants and needs of others, people might experience a sense of duty or obligation to respond to an expressed want of another.) On the other hand, a demand tends to be experienced as imposing. A demand (command, order, etc.) requires at least a particular behavior from the person being ordered that is consistent with the demand. But in order for the experiential structure of the person being ordered to be SSR, all components must be supportive of each other. The behavior must align with the affect and the cognition. If the person ordered does not agree with the demand or does not want to behave in this way, then her cognition and affect will not align with her

242

behavior, and she will have to create a false self in order to execute the order.

If the man simply wants the woman to do (or not do) X, her experiential structure might look like this:

C: (to do X?)	I don't want to do X
A: interest	repulsion
B: listening to question	talking
S: man	man
E: outside	outside
"I": ownership	
SSR	SSR

In this analysis the woman at first, we'll say, is interested in what the man is saying to her, but once she understands him, her immediate response is one of repulsion in regard to his expression of want. If the experiential structure is SSR, then she is acting as an experiential being and the man needs to respect that.

If the man, for whatever reason, does not simply express his want but instead demands that she do X, then her experiential structure might look like this:

C: (do X!)	I don't want to do X	I should say 'no'	He might hurt me if I don't
A: fear	repulsion	confidence	fear
B: fearful look	grimacing, thinking	confident look	fearful look
S: man	man	man	man
E: outside	outside	outside	outside
"I": ownership			
SSR	SSR		
Real self	Real self	Real self	Real self

C: I'm weak	I'm doing X
A: self-rejection	resentment
B: looking down	doing X
S: environ	environ
E: outside	outside
"I": ownership	
	False self

In this analysis the demand prompts a fearful response in the woman (it need not, depending upon the woman, the forcefulness of the demand, etc.) Her repulsion-experience is couched in or influenced by the first fear-experience; she knows she doesn't want to do X, but she also knows that he is threatening her. She considers a response of saying 'no' (acting in accord with the strength of her repulsion-experience, but the fear-experience that follows overtakes her say-no-experience. Up to this point, she is herself; all experiences are SSR. But she is in conflict with herself. The overall structure is characterized as compound.

The question is: wherein lies the strength of experience? Is the say-no-experience (assertiveness) stronger than the fear-of-being-hurt-experience? If so, she should say "no" and be prepared to deal with the consequences. If she is not ready at this point to deal with the consequences, or if she doesn't quite know what those consequences would be, then she would act so as to gain more information, until she felt confident in her saying "no". The strength of experience lies in assertiveness.

But if she allows his expression of demand to overpower or dominate her own sense of self, then a complex structure is formed. She rejects her own identity (I'm weak) in favor of his demand on her. Her identity becomes dependent upon his values as expressed in his demand. She condemns herself as weak and she now orients herself in relation to him through fear. Her interactions with him that follow tend to be characterized as false; they are tinged with fear and resentment.

Herein lies one way the male can dominate the female. He can prompt fear in her through intimidating behavior. If she is the type to be sensitive to intimidation and feel fear quite easily, she might be disposed to allowing the creation of complex structures. If she is naturally more resistant or less sensitive to intimidation, she might assert herself in relation to the male immediately. If he responds to her assertiveness by ramping up his intimidation, perhaps to the point of violence, then she might allow complexification in order to survive and 'be well' within this situation.

Probing Question: Why would the male ramp up his intimidating behavior if the female assertively confronted him in relation to his demand? Do men naturally get more demanding when their initial demands are rejected? Does this support the idea that men are genetically determined to dominate?

Theoretical Extension: Natural Personalities
Some men might naturally be more disposed to express themselves more aggressively than others. Some women might naturally be disposed to be more intimidated by shows of aggression than others. When paired these two types might be a feeding ground for complexification.

In other situations men might naturally be disposed to be less aggressive but more assertive. These men would not tend to try to dominate others but would not allow themselves to be dominated by others. Also, women might be the same. When paired this group would tend to be respectful of each other, consider each other's point of view, confront each other when the other tries to impose his or her will upon him or her, and make decisions consensually.

Then there might be other men who are naturally passive and women who are naturally aggressive. When paired we have the reverse of the first type. The female imposes her will upon the male through complexification.

But to argue, as do evolutionists, especially of the sociobiological persuasion, that such impositions are biologically natural is to fly in the face of actual experience. Many people can behave in a submissive manner, but this does not mean that they want to do so. Initially, people of all sizes and shapes will at least balk when someone tries to impose his will upon them. In our previous example, when the mother who imposes her will upon her child for fear of harming himself, her behavior is met with resistance. Until the child can understand that what is being done to him is for his own good, then such impositions, even when judged clearly from the mother's point of view as necessary, are resisted. It takes time to process information and assimilate it into one's identity.

Likewise, many people can act in a dominant manner, but this does not mean that domination is a biologically natural, and hence inevitable, relationship structure. We've argued that *attempts* to impose one's will upon others will be naturally engaged in; all people seem to have these urges from time to time, especially when those in their care are difficult to interact with. Parents are especially vulnerable to such impositions and children are especially vulnerable to submission. But often times the cost of allowing impositions of will to occur is complexifation or the alteration of one's identity. Unless the imposition is in natural accord with the identity (read "will") of the person being imposed upon, the behavior that aligns with the imposition will be inconsistent with the other components of experience, and the experience will be complex.

Probing Question: Do all people reason in the same manner? Or do men reason 'better' than women? Do adults reason 'better' than

245

children? Do unimpaired individuals reason "better" then impaired individuals?

Theoretical Extension: Differential Reasoning

If women are very capable of sound practical reasoning (vs. moral or logical reasoning), as evidenced over millennia in their child-rearing decisions that promote the survival and well-being of their children; and if such skills are transferable to groups of people other than their families (via group altruism, whether genetic or learned), then there seems to be no good reason to think that that skill cannot be transferred to business situations. Women can "care for" members of their business as well as for their own children. The care might not be as emotion-laden or strong as it would be for members of their own family, but the rational skills employed could be equally effective or accurate.

Generally speaking, range and depth of experience in the world will put adults in position to reason better than children. They simply know better how the world works; they have more data with which to reason. They tend to be more reflective and thoughtful in relation to their decisions. They tend to think more critically, looking at situations from multiple points of view and opting for those alternatives they believe will be fruitful.

But this is not to say that children do not reason or, when they do, reason badly. Children reason when they assess whether or not an animal will harm them, what actions will result in negative and positive responses from parents, what actions will take them outside of their comfort zone, etc. Children will often have a keen sense of what is good for their survival and well-being, and they will act to promote that survival and well-being. But since they are unfamiliar with many things in their environment, including the ways of people, their reasoning tends to be less accurate than that of most adults. Also, because children tend to act more impulsively than adults, or have less ability to check their behavior when experiencing strong emotions, they will tend to reason less accurately than adults. Similar arguments can be made for impaired people, depending upon the nature of the impairment.

When reason is conceived as a process rooted in survival and well-being and not as a faculty of mind to be aligned with objective reality, then it can be seen as something all human beings engage in, most of the times effectively, sometimes not. Its effectiveness lies in it resulting in promoting the survival and well-being of the individual, the group, the society, etc. But when one's survival and well-being is obtained at the expense of another, reason can be used as a meta-experiential construct which would tend to 'raise' one person, group, or nation above another where acquiring resources becomes a competition rather than a cooperation, and self-defense becomes the 'rational' line of justification.

Theoretical Extension: Entitlement and Reason as Not Natural

Entitlement and reason complement each other in their use. A rational being wants to promote his survival and well-being; resources are required to promote that survival and well-being; he acquires resources in order to promote his survival and well-being; he is intimately connected to others (especially family) in his efforts to survive and live well; he wants to acquire enough resources to ensure his family's (and possibly his group's) survival and well-being; there is a limited amount of many of the resources (some are replenishable and, hence, approach unlimited); every time he acquires a limited resource, he makes it more difficult for anyone else to acquire that resource (even if not noticed at first). In all of this, there is no talk of entitlement.

The biological world (as opposed to the social world) does not involve entitlement. It involves acquiring resources for survival and well-being. Reason is a process whereby resources are acquired in order to promote survival and well-being. Humans learn which resources are beneficial to them and which are not. Science enlightens us as to why some resources are beneficial and others not, which allows us to refine our trial-and-error learning methods so as not to harm ourselves unnecessarily and to promote our survival and well-being more effectively than simple trial-and-error.

Acquiring resources to the exclusion of others (private property) is a matter of acting rationally to promote one's survival and well-being. But such actions usually do not occur in a vacuum. There are other people who need or want those resources for their survival and well-being. If someone acquires allot of a given needed resource, then others are at a disadvantage in acquiring that resource. But the need and want for the resource are still there. How far do they go to acquire that resource? Do they just take it from those who have acquired it? Do they somehow force the others to share the resource with them equally? Do they somehow force the others to share the resource unequally? Do they somehow force the others to share the resource based on individual need/want or some other principle? Do they negotiate with others and determine an acceptable sharing of the resource?

Again, in all of this seemingly natural interaction, there is no question of entitlement. Rather, there's a question of who gets what. How much does one get in order to ensure one's survival and well-being? Once one acquires resources to meet one's needs and wants, then how does one deal with others who want to meet their needs and wants in relation to those resources one has acquired? Does one share according to some agreed upon method of sharing? Or does one defend one's acquisitions from being taken by others?

Pure capitalism is based on the notion that acquisition of resources is just only if those resources were acquired by work and only if the acquisition of those resources did not make other people's positions worse off. We've already shown how Locke's proviso fails to be a practical or logical way to operate in the world by showing that every acquisition of any limited resource will automatically make it more difficult for anyone else to acquire that resource and, hence, make their situations worse off. Locke's proviso cannot be met. Therefore, capitalism must be based on grounds other than freedom to act in one's best interest. It is offered here that capitalism is based on one's felt entitlement to those resources for which one works. This sense of entitlement allows us to protect from others that which we have acquired through labor; it disposes us to justify that entitlement through physical violence, ideas, argument, and laws, and to create a society based on such entitlements and their justifications.

Probing Question: How does that feeling of entitlement come about? Is it natural or biologically derived (i.e innate)? Do we naturally feel entitled to that which we work for? Do we naturally feel entitled to resources simply because we need them to survive and they are there for the taking? Or do we somehow learn to feel entitled to that which we work for or are related to by being born into it?

Theoretical Extension: Takers, Self-Asserters, and Givers
If two hunters track the same deer and expend the same amount of energy doing so, and both hunters shoot an arrow into the deer,

both hitting the deer's heart at the same time, which hunter, if either, is entitled to the deer? Both worked equally for the deer; it's not a question of degree of work. Is it a matter of degree of need? Let's say that both hunters need the deer equally for survival, that both have three children and a wife to feed, that all family members need roughly the same amount of food to survive, etc. Is the stronger of the two entitled to the deer simple because he is the stronger; or maybe the reverse: the weaker is entitled simply because he is the weaker? Are they equally entitled because they both worked for it equally and have the same need conditions? Should they share the deer according to some agreed upon or objective rule of distribution? Will those naturally disposed to acquiring and defending their resource do so, at the expense of the other? Will those naturally disposed to sharing do so, at possible expense to themselves? Will those naturally disposed to giving do so, at expense to themselves?

If there are people who are naturally disposed to taking and defending their resources, then two takers might land up fighting each other for the deer. One taker and one self-asserter will land up with the taker trying to impose his will upon the self-asserter and the self-asserter defending himself from the imposition, moving the "negotiation" toward some form of sharing. If one is a taker and the other a giver, then the taker will simply take and the giver will go without. But the giver will be watchful of the taker and less willing to give next time. The giver might have to align himself with other givers and self-asserters to prevent the taker from taking. If both are self-asserters, then negotiation will tend to occur as to how the deer will be shared or, in special circumstances, who might give to whom. If both are givers, then both will be disposed to letting the other take the deer, yet both will know that they need some of the deer to survive. Hence, givers will tend to negotiate a sharing method, both wanting the other to take the lion's share.

We don't see many pure givers because they wouldn't last long enough to perpetuate their genes. Most givers, it seems, possess a healthy degree of egoism; they want to live and be well. Hence, most givers will tend toward negotiation in regard to sharing; they just won't tend to take much.

We see quite a few self-asserters in the world, but this seems to be a relatively new phenomenon or an old phenomenon (hunter-gatherer egalitarianism) being revived in modern times (democratic revolutions). And we tend to see this in the political world, but not in business. What we tend to see mostly in business is relatively few takers and relatively many givers. But the takers tend to be dominators, and the givers tend to be submitters. This form of interaction dominates the business world.

A taker acquires a resource because he wants/needs the resource. The fact that he worked for it is of secondary concern. It would be odd or slightly pathological if a taker shot a deer, really didn't want or need it, and fought another to have it exclusively. The want/need has to be naturally connected to the acquisitive behavior. If there were no other hunters around, our hunter would simply shoot and take the deer for himself and his family. He would never think that he was entitled to the deer. Entitlement only surfaces when another person wants/needs the same deer. If both hunters in our example want/need the deer, and both shoot it at the same time, and both are takers, and both assess each other to be of equal strength, then the idea of having labored for the deer might surface. Both hunters will feel they deserve the deer not simply because they are humans in need of food but also because they worked for it. Entitlement surfaces as a reason for grabbing up resources *to the exclusion of others.*

All things being equal, the only thing that might put one hunter over another in regard to the deer is that one hunter is a natural aggressive taker who expends his aggression through intimidation or abuse and is not challenged or backed off by the other. If there is no check on natural aggression, by the aggressor (self-checking) or by the other, this opens the door for the natural aggressor to learn that his or her aggression if effective in getting him or her what he or she wants. Natural aggressors learn to dominate.

Also, if the natural aggressor aggresses against the self-asserter, when the self-asserter is isolated from others and is physically or mentally weaker than the aggressor, then the self-asserter is in position to be dominated by the aggressor (complexified). If the self-asserter is among other self-asserters, while being physically or mentally weaker than the aggressor, he can solicit the help of other self-asserters and they, as a group, can prevent the aggressor from imposing his will on them (e.g. egalitarianism in hunter-gatherer situations).

But when the self-asserters are complexified, they develop a false self in order to survive and live relatively well with the natural aggressor, who has become the dominator. The natural aggressor has transformed himself into a dominator, through a rejection of himself and a creation of a false self. Such a phenomenon might look like this:

C: (hitting person)	I'm ashamed for hitting person	person doesn't object	I'm right for hitting person
A: frustration	shame	puzzled	false confidence
B: hitting person	shamed behavior	puzzled behavior	false behavior
S: person	person	person	person
E: outside	outside	outside	outside
"I": ownership			

In this analysis the natural aggressor hits the other person. This experience could be SSR, if the aggression is done out of frustration and not domination. Most, if not all, people can get frustrated to the point of aggression. Most any parent can attest to this. Even a naturally passive giver can get "pushed to her limit" and become aggressive in the right circumstances. And most anyone could become legitimately aggressive anytime they are violated by another person. Aggression is not the culprit here; dominant aggression is.

Hence, when a natural aggressor hits another person, the other person's response becomes vital to how the aggressor might understand his aggressive behavior. If she responds aggressively, then the aggressor knows either that he's in for a battle or that he has crossed the line and has imposed himself on the other illegitimately. If he interprets her aggressive retaliation as illegitimate, then he has probably denied his own shame and has created a false self that is one of aggression: he will understand his aggression as right, i.e. not only effective but morally justified. If he interprets her aggression as justified, then he has probably recognized and felt his shame (i.e. grappled with himself) and is in position to apologize and mend his ways.

If the victim of the aggression responds in an assertive manner (e.g. tells the aggressor how she felt about his aggression, refuses to meaningfully engage the aggressor, refuses to show affection, etc.), then the aggressor is in good position to recognize his own shame and apologize for his behavior.

If the victim of the aggression responds in a passive (i.e. giver) manner, while retaining some resentment (i.e. natural egoism), then she is in position either to gain support from others to defend herself from further aggression (acts self-assertively) or to submit to the aggressor by developing a false self.

251

Theoretical Extension: Nazi Germany, Reason and Entitlement

One of the best examples of reason being understood as a mental faculty that is supposed to align with an objective reality that includes the notions of entitlement and self-defense is Nazi Germany in twentieth century Europe. Hitler was able to appeal to an objective ideology of Aryan supremacy and tried to create a pure German race that was entitled to the resources of most of continental Europe and the Soviet Union at least up to the Urals. The ideology 'justified' the extermination of the Jews, many Slavs, and many of the elderly, disabled and infirm in Europe and the Soviet Union. Hitler also appealed to the objective ideology of evolution and its tenet of survival of the fittest to 'justify' his actions. He maintained this ideology up until the time he committed suicide; he just 'realized' that the Germans were not 'the fittest' after all.

At each step in Hitler's rise to power, he had reasons for his actions. His purge of the SA (the paramilitary arm of the national socialist party) was 'justified' on the grounds that the SA supposedly threatened a takeover of power. Kristallnacht (wholesale destruction of Jewish property) was 'justified' on the grounds that the Jews were believed to be behind bolshevism and capitalism and that bolshevism sought to destroy Germany; so killing Jews and Slavs was believed to be an act of self-defense.

Because of the Germanic people's historical accomplishments in the sciences, philosophy and the arts, Germany (and Austria, etc) enjoyed a very high place in world culture. After WWI, Germany suffered a reversal of fortune and found itself having to submit to the wills of others through the Treaty of Versailles. If you couple that with serious socio-economic problems, then Germany was ripe for a restoration of its elite world status, but this time through its military domination.

With Aryan supremacy and survival of the fittest through a will to power as objective ideological goals, Hitler's genocidal methods, at least until the German war machine was halted, were rational. His actions to re-militarize the Rhineland, to take the Sudetenland, and even to invade Poland and the Soviet Union, though considered risky, were calculated to succeed. As long as he was successful, Hitler acted in ways that seemed to promote the survival and well-being of the German people. In other words, he acted rationally.

The problem was not the Nazi's rational capacity to achieve a goal; the problem was the goal itself. Any traditional objective ideology lends itself to distortion because it necessarily limits reality and is very prone to elitism. It claims understanding of reality as it is, and assumes that that reality is one. When one believes that one has captured reality as it is, and that belief conflicts with others' beliefs, then, rationally (logically), others' beliefs must be wrong. And if one has the capacity and is inclined to impose one's reality upon others, then one will. And in order to justify this imposition of will, one will claim entitlement based on the overriding accuracy of one's grasp of 'objective' reality.

Hitler thought he was right up until his suicide. He believed that the Jews manipulated bolshevism and, to a good degree, capitalism, and that they needed to be annihilated; he did, though, seem to lose his faith in the German people, believing that they didn't deserve to be the rulers of Europe because they either betrayed him or didn't live up to his expectations.

Understanding reason to be a morally neutral mental faculty that is used to connect human beings (i.e. minds) with (objective) reality is to open the door for pathological distortions of reality (or meta-experiential construction). The objective reality becomes the goal, as well as the guiding force, of human behavior. Reason, as a supposed neutral faculty of mind, is used to achieve that goal, while simultaneously being guided by that goal. A person's rationality is determined by its effectiveness. Hitler used Aryan supremacy ('purified' German nationalism) and evolution's notion of "survival of the fittest" to justify his racial cleansing. The idea was his goal, and that goal guided his actions. His justification for his actions was determined by the success (effectiveness) of those actions. As long as he was successful in achieving what he and the German people considered to be survival, happiness and well-being, then his actions were considered rational, at least by a particular group of people. Only when the tide changed, and the Soviet Union turned back the German invasion, did many of the German people think that Hitler's actions might not be rational.

The idea of reason as a faculty of mind receives its meaning in the wake of practical success. If the individual's or group's actions promote survival and well-being, then those actions are considered to be rational. But if they produce the reverse, then they are considered to be irrational. Thinking in this manner, Hitler was acting rationally, at least for the German people, up until the time the Soviet Union stopped his army and reversed the tide of the war. He was even acting rationally for many British, French, and American people when he re-militarized the Rhineland and took over Austria and the Sudetenland. Hitler's reasons for doing so aligned with his objective ideology: he wanted to unify the German people. Austrians and the Sudetenland in Czechoslovakia were essentially Germanic. A Germanic identity made some sense to Britain, France and the United States, all having a certain definable identity themselves. And none of those actions by Germany prompted a military response from any of the allied countries. They were, generally, seen as rational and understandable actions. Such actions promoted group identification, and, as such, were done to promote survival and well-being of a group of people who were (at least to some degree) 'willing' to be indentified in this manner. But when Germany went further and took over all of Czechoslovakia, Hitler went beyond the rationale of German identity, as far as Britain, France, and the United States were concerned. But the allied countries didn't do anything about it. Since the Czechoslovakian government seemed to 'allow' Germany to take over their country, the allied countries just let it happen. But they were not settled on this issue. They became very suspect of Germany's intention to impose itself and started thinking more in terms of Germany's actions as being illegitimately aggressive. When Germany invaded Poland, the allies recognized the intentions of Germany to be illegitimately aggressive rather than assertive, and some of them declared war on Germany.

As soon as one's own survival and well-being are perceived to be challenged by another's actions, the actions of others are subject to accusations of irrationality. German actions in relation to the re-militarization of the Rhineland, their taking over Austria (which many Austrians seemed to appreciate), and their taking of the Sudetenland in Czechoslovakia were all considered to be at least somewhat rational by the British, the French, and the Americans. The German people wanted a German nation. Austria was basically German, so it would easily integrate with Germany, and Slavic Czechoslovakia could remain itself while German Czechoslovakia (Sudetenland) would assimilate into Germany. This seemed to make some sense to the allies. And none of these actions threatened the survival and well-being of any of the allied countries. But when Germany took over the entire country of Czechoslovakia, the allies became more suspicious of German intentions. Could Germany be a threat to them? Is it simply asserting itself and becoming a true nation, with peaceful intentions, or is it trying to impose its will upon others who don't really want that imposition? Poland was not ambiguous in regard to Germany's invasion (i.e. imposition) of that country. They not only did *not* want Germany to take over Poland, but they were also prepared to resist such an invasion. The allies were no longer suspicious of German intentions; they knew them. The possibility of Germany's intentions to impose its will upon others became a probability, if not a certainty. Hence, once Germany's actions became a challenge to the survival and well-being of England and France, the "rational" actions of Germany became "irrational."

"Reason" is a term used in relation to the practical concerns of survival and well-being. It is meaningful inasmuch as actions tend to bring about survival and well-being for those acting. When those actions become detrimental to one's survival and well-being, and are still engaged in, then they are considered to be irrational.

As applied to the physical world, "rational" is any action that promotes consistency between the way people think and act and the way the physical world is, so long as those actions promote one's survival and well-being. Likewise, as applied to the social world, "rational" is any action that promotes consistency between the way people think and act and the way the social world is, so long as those actions promote one's survival and well-being. The difference is: the physical world seems to have little or no intentions behind or aligned with its "actions." Animals might, to some extent, intend to kill a human being, but such intentions are usually understood to be determined by genes and are relatively transparent. Even the most intelligent animals will not tend to falsely engage in 'benign' interaction with others (animals or humans) with the intention of setting that animal or human up for the kill. They might act stealthily before pouncing, but such stealth is usually not understood to be intentionally false behavior. Falsity seems to be a human phenomenon. Plants and minerals seem to possess nothing in the way of "intention" to help or harm other plants, minerals, animals, or humans. Intention seems to be a predominantly human phenomenon.

The Nazis were good liars. In Hitler's *Mein Kampf*, he extolled lying as a laudable practice, if not a virtue. One can hide one's intentions as long as one's behavior serves to gain what one wants. Hitler wanted survival and well-being (and world domination to ensure that survival and well-being).

Since reason, in the practical utilitarian sense, is traditionally understood to be a morally neutral faculty of mind, its function is determined by its effectiveness in achieving the person's goals. The goals tend toward happiness and away from pain, or to put it biologically, toward survival and well-being. If one achieves survival and well-being in relation to others, one is acting rationally. If one does not, then one's actions are irrational. Germany was acting rationally up to a point, then irrationally after that.

Theoretical Extension: Reason as Process

Experientially, rationality is defined as a necessary experiential structure or a structure within a set of experiential structures. When understood as an experiential process, reason is subject to experiential analysis. One doesn't simply choose action A or action B as if one could get outside of one's experiential structures, select option A or B, put that option into one's experiential flow, jump back into the flow of experience, and experience it. Rather, one must move with the flow of experience. One's self and one's reality are determined by the flow of experience. The question is: do our choices align with who we are and who we a coming to be at each moment, with each decision?

Experientially, rational choices are those that align with who each person is and who each person is coming to be. Who each person is, and who each person is coming to be are determined by consistent experiential structures. These experiential structures necessarily involve motives for actions. Motive structures must align with action structures in order for any action to be rational, even when rationality is understood in traditional terms.

For instance, when a woman is hungry and seeks out what she could eat in the refrigerator, she might spy a piece of pie. The pie might appeal to her. But then she might think that she wants to lose some weight and eating the pie will not achieve that goal. She has conflicting wants: the want to eat the pie and the want not to gain weight. The conflicting experiential structures, let's say, are equal in strength. And both experiential structures are SSR. The stalemate prompts her too look around the refrigerator for other possibilities. She sees some carrots. The carrots attract her but only mildly. She leans toward the pie. She thinks, "I could go running after eating the pie." This experience is also SSR and quite strong. It answers to her not wanting to gain weight while wanting to eat the pie. The experience is SSR. She is not deceiving herself in relation to eating the pie. So she eats the pie and goes running afterwards. She monitors the results of her actions by weighing herself and adjusts her actions accordingly.

In this analysis, experientialism overlaps with empiricism, or, more accurately, empirical experiences serve to frame her behavior in this matter. The woman values being a certain weight; she also values eating pie. Her well-being is intimately involved in both values, even though these values might at times conflict. She reasons that she could eat the pie if she goes running afterwards to burn off the calories she takes in and not gain weight. The experiential structure is stronger than all the preceding structures, so she moves in that direction. But will her actions bear out in the future? Will her running after eating the pie serve to keep her weight the same (maintain her well-being)? She weighs herself to make this determination. If she weighs the same, then she believes she made a rational decision in eating the pie and running afterwards. If she gains weight, she might investigate why. There might be all sorts of reasons, other than eating the pie, as to why she has gained weight. If she determines that the pie is probably the cause of the weight gain, she adjusts her values next time she wants to eat pie and not gain weight, perhaps eat less, run more, etc.

In this example, reasoning is not determined by actions that align with 'reality' outside of one's experience. That reality has already been dispensed with; we cannot get beyond experience to reach it. Therefore, empirical methods, which consist of hypothesis (eat pie and run will not result in gaining weight), testing (eat pie, run, check weight), and conclusion (weight gain; no weight gain?), serve practical ends but do not determine whether or not she is acting rationally.

For example, if her value of not gaining weight is the result of prior complexification of experience, then the results of the testing (conclusion), though traditionally 'rational', will not be experientially rational. If her natural tendencies to eat pie in the past have prompted others to condemn or criticize her for her behavior, and she internalizes that criticism (e.g. I'm bad, wrong, weak, etc.), and she creates a false self so she can deal with her social situation (whatever that is), then that false self is expressed as a false value (e.g. I'm good when I sacrifice pie and keep my weight low). Any amount of empirical data gathering and verification will not determine the rationality of her behavior because the value itself upon which the empirical methods are based is convoluted or complex (i.e. experientially irrational or inconsistent).

Such values are often revealed in motive structures. In our first example, the woman's value structure, "I want pie," is SSR; the value structure, "I don't want to gain weight," is also SSR. She comes up with a plan that she experiences as satisfying to address both values (i.e. eat and run). The decision was rational. Even if she determines afterward that she gained weight from eating the pie, despite her running, her decision was still rational. Even if she were to decide in the future to do the same thing and eat the pie and run but gain some weight, the decision might still be rational if her values of eating pie and not gaining weight were to shift toward valuing the pie over the amount of weight gained. But if her future decision should go against her own value structures and she, let's say, values not gaining weight over eating pie, and she knows that eating pie will cause her to gain weight, yet she still eats the pie, then her behavior might be considered to be irrational. But not because she is acting against her own well-being; rather it is because she is acting inconsistently with herself and who she is coming to be. At this point she needs to look at herself, get a better understanding of who she is and what her values are (as opposed to what others tend to impose upon her), and act according to her real values.

The distinction between reason-as-faculty and reason-as-process might be clearer when we consider the second example above. When the value is convoluted or complex, the experiential structure containing the 'value' is the false self structure; and the motive for the behavioral component of the false self structure lies in the complexification of experience itself.

For example, the woman whose experience has been complexified might have a complex structure looking like this:

C: I want pie	I'm fat (bad)	I'm good
A: desire	self-rejection	false confidence

B: looking at pie   looking down   reaching for carrots
S: pie   environ   carrots
E: room   room   room
    SSR

In this case the woman legitimately wants to eat the pie, but she rejects that want by rejecting herself in relation to the want. She has internalized a value imposed upon her from someone else (e.g. individual, group, culture, etc.) So she creates a false self which rejects the legitimacy of the real self and opts for the carrots. In doing so, she thinks she is acting 'rationally'. When she checks her weight, her 'rational' act is confirmed: she has not gained weight. She is 'happy'. Empirically, she passes the rational test. She has acted in a way that has made her happy (i.e. increased her well-being).

Experientially, she has acted irrationally. Her happiness is distorted. Her happiness depends upon the approval of others. She doesn't possess the value of not wanting to gain weight. She doesn't really have any problem with gaining some weight. But she has been imposed upon by others. Others would reject (or have rejected) her for gaining weight, and she is not strong enough to ward off their judgments (impositions) and assert herself in relation to them, so she creates a false self to "manage" the situation. She avoids conflict, stays in the good graces of others, and is able to survive and live somewhat well by adjusting to the values of others.

Empirically, she would appear rational by eating the carrots rather than the pie. But experientially, her motive for eating the carrots is based on the values of others, not herself. Her happiness in regard to her results of no weight gain is false, but she doesn't recognize the falsity of it. She considers herself as strong for having resisted the temptation to eat the pie. But her judgment is false. Her confidence in her judgment is false. So in order to gain some semblance of strength, she has to seek out others who think like she does, i.e. other false selves who are supported by ideologies (i.e. meta-experiential constructs) that support their false selves. In our society, such meta-experiential constructs abound. Modern American women don't seem to know themselves very well at all in regard to their natural weight. American men seem to want their women a certain way, and they don't hold back about conveying that want to them. And American women tend to internalize the judgment of American men, creating false selves in order to remain accepted by them, and seeking out like-thinking women to bolster their flagging self-confidence.

Hence, the plethora of diets, spas, pills and psychological disorders revolving around weight. *

When reason is understood as an experiential process rather than a faculty of mind, the criteria upon which rational judgments are based (i.e. happiness:pain, or survival and well-being) become exposed as sometimes false. Not all people experience "true" happiness; they accept a false happiness for true happiness. This false happiness is determined by the values of others rather than themselves. Hence, much of the data of empirical research involving people in relation to people (as opposed to people in relation to the natural world of animals, plants, and minerals) consists of false reports. The data is tainted. Objectivity is distorted. What appears to be rational empirically might actually be irrational.

Theoretical Extension: Reason and Entitlement

The connection between reason and entitlement is an intimate one. When answering the question of why the original hunter kept the deer for himself (and his family, etc.) to the exclusion of others, the hunter can offer: "I worked for it; you didn't." But in our example where the second hunter stalks and shoots the deer at the same time as the first hunter, that reason seems not so convincing. Both hunters worked for it. Even in those situations where the first hunter shoots the deer and the second hunter, unbeknownst to the first hunter, is seeking the deer but not finding it until the first hunter already shoots it, the second hunter might claim a right to the deer simply because he, like the first hunter, has been looking for it (i.e. working for it).

Extended out further, all people are looking for resources in order to survive and live well, but not all people find resources at the same time; nor do all people know how to find them; nor are all people

---

• This does not mean that all attempts to control weight are the result of complex structures. The obesity problem in the United States seems to be real, experientially and scientifically. But the solution to this problem does not lie in empirical research, when the data of empirical research is false to begin with. Rather, the solution lies in knowing oneself, being oneself, and being prepared to deal with the consequence of being oneself.

equally capable of finding them; nor are all people living in proximity to certain resources; nor do all people possess the technology to access those resources; etc.

With all of these variables to consider, how does one person claim ownership of any resource, exclusive of others, simply based on working for it? How is a person entitled to a resource simply because he has worked for it?

The answer is: he is not so entitled. Entitlement is not an objective state of being conceived by an enlightened objective faculty of mind (i.e. reason) pronouncing that all human beings are entitled to natural resources, and, hence, everyone should be provided those resources in one way or another (e.g. Christianity, welfare liberalism, etc.). Nor is it an objective state of being determined by mixing one's labor with those resources one happens to need or want. No one is entitled to any resource simply because he works for it, no matter how strongly he feels about it. Certainly, people take resources and defend them from others. But they do so because they need or want the resources, not because they have worked for them. It's only when others challenge their taking of the resources that people argue for entitlement.

If our hunter argues that he is not sharing the deer with another hunter who has come upon the scene a little late because our hunter has shot the deer and not the other hunter, the other hunter might accept that reason if the first hunter is bigger than he and can harm him if he tried to force some form of sharing. Also, he might even accept that argument if there are more deer for him to shoot in the area, appreciating the first hunter's efforts. But if the first hunter has bagged most of the deer in the area and is keeping them for himself (and his family, group, etc.), then the second hunter will probably not be very "reasonable" with the first hunter. Survival and well-being will trump "reasonableness" and the second hunter will do what he has to do to survive and live well. This puts the first hunter into a defensive mode, if he is a taker. Survival and well-being become a competition. When survival and well-being become a competition, entitlement becomes a reason for exclusive ownership. But if the hunter is a self-asserter, he will tend to share the deer with the other hunter after negotiating equitable terms of sharing. If he is a giver, he will tend to share the deer even if the terms of sharing are less equitable for him.

Theoretical Extension: Managerial Capitalism

For takers, reason is used to calculate decisions in terms of competitive success. "What must I do to keep this resource without being harmed?" "What must I do to protect my exclusive ownership of this resource?" "What must I do to convince others that I deserve this resource, and they do not?"

If there are natural takers in the world, then they will be biologically disposed to taking resources and keeping them for themselves, regardless of how it might affect others. They might be limited in their taking by the responses of others who might rebel in some manner and demand at least a share of the resources for themselves. This describes egoism in its purest form.

The theoretical justification for such behavior lies in Locke's theory of acquisition of resources. As long as one works for those resources, one can keep them and protect them from being taken by others. Locke's proviso was meant to cover the problems created by the "regardless of how it might affect others" clause of egoism. The proviso was meant to soften one's egoistic pursuits and recognize, at least to some degree, the feelings and welfare of others. Pure egoism would incorporate some form of the proviso, but it would look more like this: "You can take whatever you work for and not share any of it with others as long as others don't harm you for what you've done. If they can harm you, you might want to share a little, but only enough to calm them down."

It has already been argued that Locke's proviso is impossible to follow, so any limitation upon egoism is achieved either by other egoists (through a series of purges, take-overs, overthrows, oppressive monopolies, etc. at worst, or striking a competitive balance with others at best, or by self-asserters who form egalitarian systems that curb egoists' pursuits and force them to share, or by givers (utilitarians, Christians) who also form egalitarian systems but are usually willing to give more of their resources to others than are the self-asserters, even when they've worked for them.

The takers' world, if successfully imposed upon others, is the world of managerial capitalism. Self-asserters and givers do not possess any natural tendency to take resources and not share them with others who might also need them. Adam Smith argued that if left alone (i.e. to be free to act without government interference), people will strive to survive and improve their well-being. Their freedom to acquire what they need for their survival and what they want for their well-being would somehow allow the group (society, nation, species, etc.) to create the most happiness for everybody involved. This happiness is created indirectly rather than directly. That is, it is not the individual's intention to make others happy (as in utilitarian thinking); rather, by intending their own happiness (egoism), they will create the circumstances whereby others will benefit. Hence, individual entrepreneurs will create businesses whereby they will not only benefit themselves but also others through the creation of jobs, networks of suppliers and retailers, and customers who value the products. Any egoistic actions that might hurt their efforts to benefit themselves and hurt others (e.g. oppressive working conditions, faulty products, fraudulent behavior, etc.) will tend to be limited because they will tend ultimately to hurt the entrepreneur. When everybody acts in their own self-interest, an "invisible hand" will operate, allowing each individual to maximize his or her self interest and minimize the harm he or she causes others.

Viewed through the eyes of experientialism, this notion is extremely naïve, but viewed through the eyes of history, it is a definite advance over the monarchical systems of economics in the past. When monarchies determined economies, the group's (nation's) ways of acquiring and distributing resources was the province of the monarchy. The monarchy had the money. One person, in conjunction with advisors and elites, was ultimately in charge of deciding who could acquire what, how much they could acquire, how much of what they acquired went to the monarchy, etc. But when the monarchy gave (or loaned) money to individual merchants to acquire resources, it not only took a good portion of the acquisitions for itself but it also let individual merchants prosper. Individual merchants were able to acquire capital. As individual merchants acquired capital, they were able to act somewhat independently of the monarchy to improve their well-being. By the time Adam Smith's notion of the "invisible hand" occurred in print, individual merchants had already developed a considerable degree of economic inde-pendence from the monarchy. Individual initiative and capital development was seen as an end in itself rather than a means to an end. Egoism was set free from dependence upon the monarchy and individual people were able to determine for themselves (at least to some degree) what they wanted to do, what they wanted to acquire, and how they wanted to use their acquisitions. They didn't have to get permission (and money) from the king in order to prosper or, to put it another way, that "permission" was granted by the laws created and enforced. They could accrue enough money (capital) to provide for their survival and well-being independently of the monarchy. Individual people's dependence upon the monarchy was transcended and people started, through their own initiative, to create an economy somewhat independent of the control of the monarchy.

In its early days capitalism marked a move toward economic democracy. More people had the freedom to create economic units (i.e. companies) that developed their own capital (though taxed by the government), and, hence, more people could direct their own lives rather than have them directed by the monarchy. By the time Adam Smith came along (Smith, 2003), this freedom to direct one's own economic future was a reality in need of an ideological explanation and justification. Smith provided what was needed. What was already happening in the world (i.e. the democratization of the economy and its flip side of independence from monarchical economic domination) was given expression in Smith's economic philosophy.

Under Smith's philosophy, though still very connected to and influenced by the Christian moral ideals of the time, egoism was given credibility, releasing it from the dictates of the Christian anti-egoistic hierarchy and the controls of the political monarchy. Egoism (read "individuality") was made morally acceptable. The shift from monarchy-controlled mercantilism to merchant-controlled mercantilism set the stage for the acceptance of egoism as a viable "ethic." Smith's "invisible hand" sanctioned egoism through its utilitarian outcome, i.e. more people will be happy if the economy is substantially independent of government control and individuals are allowed to act freely in their formation of companies. If individuals are allowed to act freely to acquire resources and to do with their resources as they see fit, then people will be motivated to acquire those resources by creating acquiring and producing groups (i.e. companies) that would consist of a number of individuals who would benefit from their association. It was a win-win situation, at least relative to feudal economics.

Theoretical Extension: The Protestant Revolution

Several centuries before Adam Smith's democratization of economics came Martin Luther's democratization of religion (1483-1546). The protestant revolution challenged the hierarchical authority of the Roman Catholic Church, setting the stage for the development of many individual Christian religions. The autocratic authority of the pope was replaced by many individual leaders appealing to, and developing, ideologies that supported variations of the Christian religion, all claiming to be Christian, and all claiming objectivity. Objective religious unity became decentralized, though each separate religion still held on to its respective objective claims.

The splitting into objective religious factions represents the democratization of religion by allowing room for self-determination, but the traditional objective ideologies helped maintain a traditional objective focus for each of the religious factions. The one Christian religion became relativized, but each group formed their own Christian religion which competed with each other for the ultimate claim to objectivity.

What was done in religion was reiterated in economics several hundred years later. Smith's democractization of economics provided ideological expression for the already underway creation of individual, self-determined, self-supporting companies that challenged the economic authority and control of the monarchy. And each of these companies was headed by a person with unilateral power over the workforce that constituted the company. Policy and procedure was the province of the company head, owner, or manager. Power was held by one person or a small group of people, and the power was unilateral, i.e. it was imposed upon others. The unified economic system headed by the monarch was replaced by many individual companies headed by individual owners or managers. Business policy and procedure paralleled the separate religious belief systems of Protestantism.

Theoretical Extension: The Development of Science

Likewise, the Copernican revolution (1473-1543) ushered into history the democratization of knowledge or reality. Copernicus challenged the authority of the Church to explain how the physical universe was constituted. Later, Darwin (1809-1882) challenged the authority of the Church to explain how people got here. The scientific revolution opened the door for individual people to determine what was real and what was not inasmuch as the scientific method could be engaged in by any intelligent person. One did not need papal approval to investigate the nature of physical reality. Science could align itself with government for funding initially and eventually with business. As government became democratized in the time of Adam Smith, so too did economics. Science was able to get funding from each of these sources and did not depend upon religion.

But science, like religion, tended to be objective in its orientation. It threatened religion because it offered another explanation of how and why human beings came to exist and what their 'purpose' was in life, an explanation that did not require an all powerful God. In effect, it replaced God with Nature. The laws of Nature become the new objective reality, a battle still going on today. The scientific method has become *the* method for determining objective (or at least quasi-objective) reality in the modern world.

Science developed into the various sciences (physics, astronomy, biology, etc.) just as religion developed into its various religions, just as economics developed into its various businesses. Each science had its own areas of investigation, and each science pushed for validation of itself (i.e. parity with the Church) or supremacy (over the Church) in regard to objective reality claims. Logically, simple parity with the Church would render a form of relativity and would more truly democratize knowledge, but inasmuch as science wanted to replace religion in certain areas, it wouldn't settle for parity. It would require supremacy: when scientific claims conflicted with religious claims, scientific claims would win out because they were closer to the 'truth (reality)'.

Theoretical Extension: Political Revolutions

Democratic revolutions occurred in England, America and France in the 17th and 18th centuries, all in response to monarchies or the strong influence of monarchies. Democracies were tried in Germany and the Soviet Union but gave way to fascist and communist regimes, respectively, only to be again replaced by democratic governments, though a very weak one in the Soviet Union's case. Democracies are developing in countries throughout the world at such a rate that one might well posit that there exists a movement toward self-government around the globe.

Like in all the other shifts toward democracy (i.e. religion, economics, and reality in general), the shift toward democracy in politics empowers the individual, allowing more self-direction than the individual ever had in recorded history. But also like these other areas of life, people are put into or attain positions of power in relation to others. Depending upon the structure of the democracy, that power of the individual is usually curbed by law (constitution) and is subject to a system of checks and balances.

Theoretical Extension: Parallel Developments in Democracy

This distinguishes political democracies from the democratization of economics, religion and knowledge (reality). The democratization of economics is practically devoid of checks and balances on the power of the CEO and board of a typical corporation or the President/CEO of a typical sole proprietorship. In corporations, the CEO and board have to "answer to" the stockholders, but they are rarely subject to the power of the stockholders to determine their behavior. Most managerial decisions are made without stockholder input. Stockholders will retain power to vote board members out of office, but this is a relatively rare phenomenon.

Refined a little further, often times the board acts merely as a "rubber stamp" for the CEO and will approve the decisions of the CEO as long as they think those decisions won't hurt the company. And many board members are not inclined to challenge the decisions of the CEO because they either do not know enough about the business to challenge him or, more cynically (realistically?), they will trust the CEO to make the decisions that will allow them to benefit from their being on the board.

In effect the CEO of most corporations possesses a great deal of power, and the system of checks and balances on that power is relatively impotent. In the case of the sole proprietor, the system of checks and balances is even less evident. There is no board to approve one's decisions. Often times there are no stockholders to "answer to." In sole proprietorships the owner is virtually king (or sometimes queen).

Of course, the government acts as a check and balance to both corporate power and sole proprietorships, perhaps the most powerful check and balance.

Religious democratization was achieved in the West with the Protestant revolution (it was greatly aided by the invention of the printing press). But the democratization consisted of the formation of many smaller hierarchies, where pastors were put in positions of authority and often times acted as rulers of their flock. But this type of hierarchy did not usually possess a realistic (physical) system of government (force) to back up the influence of the pastor. Such influence was primarily ideological (i.e. psychological). Pastors were able to enforce their decisions through psychological force based on ideological beliefs. Physical force to conform tended to be against the democratic underpinnings of the Protestant revolution, at least in relation to its believers.

Hence, the hierarchies that developed in the wake of the democratization of religion by the Protestant revolution were, primarily, ideological hierarchies, and their forcefulness was determined primarily by the ideas that governed everybody involved in that particular branch of the Christian religion.

The democratization of knowledge (reality) that resulted from the scientific revolution (historically, the Enlightenment) occurred over against the domination of reality by religion (i.e. Christianity). But it, like the others areas of human life, did not produce a pure form of democracy in its wake. Rather, it developed factions of science with their own hierarchical structures and their own objective or quasi-objective methodologies.

Though science tends to boast of its superiority over the narrow absolutism of religion by incorporating an inherent skepticism in regard to reality determinations, it very often crosses its own boundaries and realizes itself as the dispenser of reality as it is and not simply as reality as scientists understand it to be.

In sum, historically, knowledge of reality was democratized with the development of science, but science split into factions, each with its own objective or quasi-objective assumptions. Historically, religion was democratized by the Protestant revolution, but each religion spawned by the revolution maintained an objective ideology that competed with other objective ideologies for supremacy. Historically, economics was democratized by the development of capitalism, but each economic enterprise was ruled by a capitalist.

Historically, people seem to have pushed for democratization of all areas of human endeavor, but they seem unable or at least unwilling to let go of traditional objective thinking and democratization has stopped at the group level. Groups still maintain their hierarchies along with their corresponding objective or quasi-objective ideologies. Why?

Theoretical Extension: Capitalism and Hierarchy

Though recorded history seems to indicate a movement in many areas of human life toward democracy in the form of individual self-determination, such self-determination is limited to groups. It has not penetrated down to the individual yet. Capitalism expresses self-determination in the form of group-determination. It is the group (e.g. business, company, or firm) that acts as a self. And that group is overwhelmingly structured hierarchically.

If by capitalism we mean the accrual of profit by a company so that that profit can be used to reinvest and grow the company so that that company can survive and increase its well-being, often times, though not necessarily, in competition with others, then capitalism does not entail hierarchy. This form of capitalism could be practiced by democratically structured companies.

But capitalism, as defined above, is overwhelmingly structured hierarchically, so much so that capitalism and hierarchy seem to go hand in hand. In fact, no business enterprise in the United States can legally be formed without being hierarchical in its structure. The business can opt to conduct itself in an egalitarian fashion, but it has to structure itself hierarchically in order to be legal.

It is the hierarchical structure of capitalism that is problematic from an experiential point of view. It is why experientialism would criticize Smith's "invisible hand" as being naïve. To think that natural egoism will limit its excesses simply because people will retaliate against those excesses, thus balancing power between people is to assume that 1) all people are able to affirm their own experience in relation to others, 2) all people have the natural capacity to assert themselves in relation to those who seek to impose their will upon them, and 3) all people are equally capable of grappling (or working through) their assertive confrontations, when such confrontations are made.

If people can legitimately be divided into three somewhat broad, overlapping categories consisting of takers, self-asserters, and givers, then takers will have an advantage over the others unless the others can cooperate with each other to curb the excesses of the takers. This aligns with the anthropologists' claim that hunter-gatherers would cooperate with each other to punish the "upstart" for trying to impose his will upon others.

If the original hunter-gatherers were naturally more disposed to being self-asserters or givers, then they would tend to share resources rather than keeping them all for themselves. In this case, the berry-gatherers who picked the berry bushes clean would tend to share the berries with those who came upon the scene late and were hungry and with those who were incapable of picking berries altogether. Sharing would serve not only to express who the self-asserters and givers were, biologically speaking, but also indirectly to keep the others from taking at least some of the berries in order to survive. In this sense, sharing prevents theft or cooperation averts competition.

If the original hunter-gatherers were naturally more cooperative than competitive, more egalitarian than hierarchical, then something happened to upset human nature because recorded history is replete with evidence of hierarchical organizational structures, with men being overwhelmingly at the top of those hierarchies. The contention in this work is that abuse happened: physical, sexual, and emotional abuse, through, in part, the natural urges to get one's way in relation to others and to act upon those urges. Things went wrong when those natural aggressive actions by some were not repelled by others, when the aggressor became the dominator and the bully, when those aggressed against became the submissive or the bullied. When others could not assertively confront those attempting to impose themselves upon them and therefore back off the imposers, they tended to create complex structures and false selves in order to survive. Egalitarian cooperation was insidiously replaced by hierarchical competition.

The group of people most vulnerable to impositions of will is children. Even if most children are naturally self-asserters, they will tend to form complex identities when confronted by more powerful adults. Adults who naturally act to get their way in relation to children will tend to find an area of exploitation in the natural power imbalance between them and children. Here is where natural takers can proliferate. Natural takers will naturally try to get their way in relation to their own children by acting aggressively or manipulatively. The aggression or manipulation will tend to prompt the children to deny some natural aspects of themselves and force them to create false selves in order to survive and live somewhat well. The false self, being false, requires ideological support in order to exist and proliferate. The false self requires meta-experiential construction. Meta-experiential construction is 'naturally' linked to hierarchy.

Theoretical Extension: Meta-Experiential Constructs and Hierarchy

Meta-experiential constructs are limited only by the imagination. Entire imaginative worlds can be created that will serve to raise some people above others in the quest for grasping reality and justifying one's being. Feuerbach criticized religions that lay great stock in faith in an ideology because such faith separates people from each other (Feuerbach, 1989). It 'raises' one group above another and 'allows' that group, if they are so capable and inclined, to impose that ideology upon others. Such impositions are 'justified,' ostensibly, by the faith that the ideology is aligned with objective reality.

When objective reality is believed to transcend the physical world (i.e. nature), a world that most people can access in a similar manner, interpersonal validation of that objective reality is subject to personal experience. Entities and processes 'beyond' the physical world can be introduced into objective reality, and those entities and processes can be believed to be hierarchically structured in relation to nature. For example, the supernatural can have unilateral power over the natural. When this happens, those constructing, developing and maintaining supernatural ontological systems can conceive just about any idea and endow that idea with any amount of power as one deems appropriate. God can have infinite power; Yahweh can be all just; Allah can be infinitely merciful, etc.

Metaphysical conceptions of God and entire apparatuses of subordinate metaphysical beings (e.g. souls, angels, demons, spirits, etc.) can be conceived as objective entities controlling, or at least influencing, nature and the human beings in nature. Such conceptions are subject, as are all conceptions, to human experience. If one human being conceives the idea and can convince others to accept

271

that idea as objectively true, then a metaphysical reality is created, i.e. an ideology that guides, if not conditions, thought and action within its scope), and is able to be passed down from generation to generation.

Such metaphysical, ontological systems include, though are not limited to, Christianity, Judaism, Islam, Mormonism and any other theistic system of thought. But there are a number of non-religious metaphysical, ontological systems that act in a similar manner. These include, though are not limited to, a variety of autocratic and oligarchic regimes, e.g. monarchies, communisms, committee-run socialisms, military or religious totalitarian regimes, fascisms and, to some extent, even representative democracies. Even science that might eschew a great deal of historical metaphysics is subject to being a metaphysical, ontological system when scientific claims are not owned.

Any ideology that claims to have access, unique or not, to objective reality without accepting ownership (and responsibility) for those claims is subject to suspicion or intense scrutiny, because the tendency to convert such claims into active impositions upon others is so great (at least for some people, e.g. takers), and the vulnerability to submit to those impositions is so great (at least for some people, e.g. givers), and the natural possibility of creating social forces to support ideological impositions upon others through complexification and meta-experiential construction is so great that efforts to stand up for oneself, to be oneself in the face of imposition of another's will of any sort (e.g. religious, political, economic, etc.) can be rendered ineffective.

The connection between meta-experiential construction and hierarchy is an intimate one. Metaphysical ideologies, whether religious, political, economic or scientific, are prone to complexification and meta-experiential construction. Complexification is, by its nature, intimate. It occurs between father and son, mother and daughter, husband and wife, employer and employee, etc. Complexification is the result of physical, sexual and emotional abuse (imposition of will). Meta-experiential construction is based upon and derived from complexification. It is the ideological 'justification' for such impositions of will. Hierarchy is the organizational structure that co-creates, proliferates, and sustains meta-experiential constructs.

Probing Questions: If human beings are to act cooperatively with each other and make necessary and important decisions in regard to future actions, wouldn't hierarchy be the organization of choice to achieve the desired results? Individual human beings might be able to decide certain things for themselves if individual action is sufficient to meet one's needs, but when meeting one's needs requires cooperation from others, then isn't it more expedient, if not necessary, to empower one person or a small group of people to make those decisions and to force others to implement those decisions?

Theoretical Extension: Aristocratic Reasoning

These questions underlie the essential argument for aristocracy and fly in the very face of democracy. The aristocratic argument maintains that there are some people who know better than others what to do in a given situation, and that these people should be not only able to decide what to do but be empowered *over* others so that their decisions will be implemented. This addresses not only the idea that decisions are made by knowledgeable people (i.e. the right people), but also the idea that these decisions will be carried out by others (under the threat of punishment if necessary).

The aristocratic argument, similar to the argument justifying monarchies, totalitarian regimes, and communistic committees, has in many countries that have opted for some form of democracy, formed a co-existent relationship with that democracy.

For example, American representative democracy shares its democratic principles and practices with the aristocratic principles and practices of business. This is especially evident in the government's linkage with business. Inasmuch as business, with its overwhelmingly hierarchical structure, supports or influences government elections and decisions, the aristocratic principles and practices of business share power with the democratic principles and practices of government. Inasmuch as a democratic government benefits from, or is influenced by, business, it is prone to represent business concerns over public concerns. When it represents business (a minority of the people) over the majority of the people (public), it functions at best as an aristocracy and at worst as a plutocracy, but it does not function as a democracy.

Theoretical Extension: Rousseauean Democracy

Rousseau argued back in the 18th century that representative democracy was just another form of slavery, one where the people are free one day of the year (or one every two or six years, depending upon the elections of representatives) to vote for the people who are empowered to frame (write up) and ratify (vote on) laws without the people's direct consent and to enforce those laws as they see fit. When the power to ratify laws is kept by the lawmakers themselves, Rousseau argued, some form of tyranny results. In this view, American representative democracy is a form of limited tyranny, limited only by the lifetime of representatives, subject to periodic voting. In this sense, American representative democracy is a form of limited tyranny by consent of the people, an idea that strains credibility but is nevertheless true. Americans 'accept' the limited tyranny of their government. The reason they do is the same reason that underlies aristocracy: let the people with knowledge, skills and intelligence rule and everybody else will comply or be punished. In this way, groups (nations) of people can get things done rather than continually arguing and fighting over who decides what, where nothing gets done (Rousseau, 1987).

A minority of the people (i.e. representatives) is allowed to frame and ratify laws without direct input from the majority of the people (i.e. the public). The only power the people have is to vote their representatives out of office (or sometimes to impeach them). For Rousseau, this would be a form of tyranny. In order to protect ourselves from tyranny, according to Rousseau, Americans would have to divest Congress of its power to ratify laws while allowing it to retain its power to frame (write up) the laws. Congress would use its knowledge, skills and intelligence to frame laws but the people (general public) would have the power to ratify those laws. In this sense, Congress would lead and the people would either agree or disagree with their leadership.

Rousseau also argued that the general will (i.e. the ultimate determiner of any justifiable government) is not achievable in a democracy that grants the power of framing and ratifying laws to a select group. What will happen is that the select group will, like everybody else, seek to advance its own survival and well-being. And if its survival and well-being is at least in good part dependent upon a select group of others (i.e. businesses), then they will frame and ratify laws that are consistent with those upon whom they are dependent.

The general public, on the other hand, if free to assemble as it sees fit, will tend to form groups (i.e. interest groups) that are designed to influence the will of the lawmakers. The interest groups and the lawmakers will form an aristocratic bond, so when the lawmakers frame and ratify laws, the laws will tend to be in support of the interest groups that have supported the lawmakers. The interest groups are usually connected to some form of business. Business, as hierarchical, is already aristocratic. Hence, aristocracy in the form of business significantly influences the lawmakers who, in the American system, already have the power to frame and ratify laws.

Rousseau wanted to separate the power to frame laws from the power to ratify them and to give the power to frame laws to the lawmakers and to ratify them to the people. But "the people" needed to be a people free from the distorting influence of interest groups. Even in a democracy where the people voted on the laws directly, the tendency to form interest groups would exist. But these interest groups would aim not at the lawmakers but at the people themselves, because in Rousseau's democracy, the people would have the power to ratify the laws. Even in this situation, Rousseau believed that the interest groups would need to be neutralized by making them equal to each other so that when the members of the interest groups went to vote, they would cancel each other out, and the general will would be rendered.

In a Rousseauian democracy Congress would be elected by the people to frame laws. The people (public) would be empowered to ratify those laws. Interest groups would form to influence the people to vote their way, but these interest groups would be equalized by law and, hence, cancel each other out come voting time. And then the vote will reflect the general will. And, for Rousseau, the general will, if achieved, is infallible, though subject to change. And it is the only justification for government.

Rousseau challenges the aristocratic argument by separating the power to frame laws from the power to ratify them. He gives the power of ruling to the people; the people put themselves under their own rules. But in enforcing those rules, the magistracy (law enforcement and courts) would be structured hierarchically.

But the aristocrat objects, saying that the people are not capable of ratifying laws; they aren't even capable of understanding those laws (bills). Hence, lawmakers should consist of people with the intelligence and skills to frame and ratify laws (supposedly for the good of all), and the people should obey those laws (again supposedly for the good of all).

Theoretical Extension: Rousseauean Democracy in Business

If we extend Rousseau's thinking into the organization of businesses, we might (and sometimes have already done) construct businesses democratically.   But here is where the aristocratic argument tends to carry a lot of weight. Should not those who are equipped with the personality, skills, knowledge and intelligence to "see the big picture," to make decisions that will turn out positively all the time (optimally) in the quest for survival and well-being in the world of business, be allowed to rule a company? After all, businesses have to compete with other businesses (often times), and most people are not skilled or intelligent enough to make the decisions that will promote the survival and well-being of the company. And, for that matter, most people don't *want* to make those decisions; they don't want the responsibility it entails.

A democratic rebuttal to this is that if businesses were structured democratically, then competition would soon transform itself into cooperation.

For example, the theater business in America today is predominately hierarchical in its basic structure. A single artistic director (or similar name) acts like a CEO of a private company. He (let's say) has power to make critical decisions in relation to the theater company (e.g. select plays, select directors, etc.) and to enforce those decisions through punishment (firing, demoting, etc.) He usually has to answer to a governing board, often made up of elite members of the community. He works in conjunction with the board to make and enforce his decisions. Most theater companies are structured in this manner.

But if the theater business were to be structured democratically, the "big picture" would look entirely different. A core group of facilitators (vs. officers) would be elected by the entire membership of the association (vs. company) to facilitate (vs. run or manage) the association. These facilitators would have to "answer to" an

276

agreement (or constitution) whereby policy and some procedure are set out and agreed upon by all members even before the association starts up, i.e. they would have to "answer to" their collective selves. A board, in this type of association, if necessary at all (i.e. demanded by law), would act more as a consulting group and arbiter in times of conflict and stagnation. Some decisions would be made by those empowered to make those kinds of decisions based on the agreement; other decisions would be made by the entire membership through an agreed upon majority vote.

Funds would be accrued primarily by membership fees, and each member (except children) would have to recruit and maintain a small list of patron members (i.e. theater goers); this would be akin to a large sales force. Other funds would come from traditional sources like grants, charitable contributions, endowments, and non-membership patron attendance, etc., as long as none of these latter sources bring about any form of controlling interest in the association.

This form of organization is designed to recruit the entire play-making and theater-going community in any given geographical region. A central source of funds is created for all professional members to access and is distributed in an equitable manner by the core facilitators in accordance with the policies set down in the agreement. Term limits for all facilitators are pre-determined, and new elections would be held at the end of each term. Facilitators could be terminated at any time according to due process.

As this form of organization grows, smaller, independent organizations stop competing with each other for a share of the market. The competition for funding goes *inside* the association. Independent theaters compete against others in a similar way that members of a baseball team compete against each other for playing on the starting team. But instead of competing for a share of the market, they would be competing for centralized funds distributed according to agreement rules established by every professional member constituting the association.

For example, if theater company A develops a history of producing plays in genre X that are attended by a high percentage of the total number of people who like those kinds of plays, and theater company B develops a history of low percentage attendance for the same type of play, then the core facilitators will probably fund a play of that genre from theater company A over theater company B when that kind of decision must be made. This is similar to a pitcher on a baseball team who develops a winning record and one who develops a losing record. The manager will tend to select the one with winning record over the one with the losing record when that decision must be made.

But since the association is democratically structured, and most of the funds for production are internally and centrally located, theater company A will not be able to use "its share of the market" to control the system of power that develops in the wake of capitalistic freedom. It will not be able to establish itself as the "top dog" or the "king of the hill" in relation to other competing theater companies or individuals. Rather, it, like all other companies and all other individual members of the association, would have to compete for funds based on association rules and not based on the company's influence and ability to accrue money (i.e. to establish elite status). They will have to establish status based solely on their ability to produce quality plays that are appreciated by many people who like those sorts of plays. This places competition on the level of quality productions and not on the level of accruing money (and power) that makes it easier for the company to produce quality productions over and against their competition.

When competition is internalized, quality goes up. When it is externalized and left to the forces of traditional capitalism, competition tends to secure money and power for those who are willing to use their money and power to maintain their survival and to increase their well-being, often at the expense of others. When others are not able to compete with the "top dog" for a share of the market, their productions tend to be of lower quality. This serves the purposes of the "top dog," because it means that most people will attend their plays.

When the business of theater is democratized, and funds are distributed to companies (established or transient) based on availability and agreed upon rules of competition (e.g. attendance rates for given genres), then good plays can come from just about anywhere in the association and are not limited to the "top dog" theater(s) in the area.

In addition to this, theater companies will tend to become more fluid in their construction. For instance, an actor might want to produce a play. Instead of getting permission from the artistic director (which often times is not granted) to produce the play, she could form her own theater group by using the pre-established data banks available to her in the association. If the combination of producer, director, actors, etc. that she is able to put together produces a quality play that gleans high attendance in that genre, then she is on track to developing a name for herself in the association and is in better position to complete for funds when such competition is necessary (i.e. when funds are scarce). These production groups could develop anywhere at any time.

This fluidity of action will tend to break down traditional company allegiances and focus on quality productions that will satisfy the play-going public overall rather than the play-going public that can afford to go to plays produced by the "top dog" theater(s). Traditional ownership of theaters and the exclusivity of company membership will give way to a fluid creation of production companies competing for stages and spaces for productions. Since the funds for production are centrally located and dispensed democratically, traditional owners of theaters and theater companies will come to cooperate with other theater owners, other companies, and all other individual members of the association in order to produce the best quality plays for the most people.

Instead of forming individual companies that are hierarchically structured and that compete with each other for a share of the market, more often than not creating an unequal balance in power and a decrease in overall production quality (because of lack of funds for the competition), a democratic theater business will serve to centrally locate the funds, subject those funds to democractically-agreed upon methods of distribution, internalize competition thus driving up the quality of productions for the entire theater community, and energize the play-making community by equalizing opportunity for project funding.

A democratically-structured business would tend toward creating a cooperative "big picture" where hierarchically-structured competition between hierarchically-structured businesses would be replaced by a cooperatively-structured association of some relatively stable and some relatively fluid organizations, all of which can access central funds (and any other funds they can) in order to produce their product. Methods of distributing those funds would be democratically-determined, thus avoiding the formation of committee-run forms of socialism. Change in the association would be determined by vote according to agreement; the vote on issues would be direct, thus avoiding Rousseau's limited tyranny criticism. The powers of the facilitators would be subject to agreement, and any violation of the agreement would be subject to punishment. Enforcement of the agreement would be handled by due process laid out in the agreement, ultimately resting, when necessary, with the direct vote from members of the association.

In such an association, the "big picture" is not the entire field of competition as it is in traditional capitalistic businesses but a coordinated and cooperative enterprise between all members of the association, regardless of their group affiliations or lack thereof. Such a business would truly be "of the people, by the people and for the people."

In response to Rousseau's criticism that interest groups will tend to form, even in direct democracies, and these interest groups will seek to influence the people (e.g. all voting members of the association), policies would be in place in the agreement that would equalize the power of such groups, thus canceling out their influence come voting time. The ability for one group to dominate others would be curbed or even possibly eliminated through legislation. (More details and arguments in relation to democratically-structured businesses will be available in Volume 3 of this treatise).

PART 4: Economics and Hierarchy

Let's return to our speculative beginnings and develop an economics based on experience, where "experience" is defined as a necessary combination of cognition, affect, behavior, sensation and the environment, as owned. Experientially, thoughts, feelings, behaviors, sensations and environments are owned by the individual who is participating in the experience. Usually, we would have no problems accepting the idea that the individual owns his own thoughts, feelings, behaviors and sensations as long as these phenomena occur in conscious, self-reflective states, but ownership of environments and all contents therein must be qualified. As already argued, the experiential ownership of environments is limited to that environment that constitutes immediate experience.

For example, we own a tree that we are looking at inasmuch as the tree constitutes an aspect of the environmental component of the experience within which we participate. If seeing the tree causes pleasure in us, then another person or thing that comes in the way of our seeing the tree will tend to prompt a negative response in us, in a similar way that a child will respond negatively to another child taking his toy: the pleasure trajectory has been interrupted and not by our own will.

Another example: we might be enjoying the silence we experience while sitting on our porch, only the have that silence interrupted by the loud barking of a dog. Experientially, we own the space that surrounds us within immediate experience and an alteration of that space that is not willed by us will tend to prompt some sort of response. If the alteration is experienced negatively (as pain or cessation of happiness or pleasure), then we will tend to respond negatively (e.g. with irritation, anger, etc.) If positive, we will tend to respond positively.

Another example: we are talking to a person who has just eaten onions and we are offended by his breath. Experientially, we own the space that surrounds us and someone or something aside from ourselves has altered that space, prompting a response.

In all sensory realms, experiential ownership can be established in relation to environmental contents. Upon this primordial form of ownership rests all other forms of ownership and all forms of private property.

281

Proposition 69: Individuals want their environments and the contents therein to be consistent with their own survival and well-being.

Proposition 70: If possible, individuals will act upon their environment so as to insure their survival and sustain or increase their well-being.

People will defend themselves from predators, kill and eat animals and plants for food, drink water, and breathe air; they will use raw materials and apply labor to those materials in order to produce commodities to sell on the market; they will provide services for others in exchange for money; all in an effort to survive and live well.

Individuals are inextricably interconnected to other individuals (Proposition 1). For the possible exception of hermit types who can live off the land by themselves, all people will depend upon or be interdependent with other people; even hermits were at one time dependent and interdependent.

The experiential ownership of the immediate environments within which people participate is constantly being impacted by other people and things in nature. Some of that impact is wanted, some not. How individuals *control* their immediate environments and the contents therein constitutes the basis for exclusive ownership or private property.

The key word here is "control." In a natural environment people will acquire resources for their (and their family/group's) survival and well-being. Whether or not they share their acquired resources with people outside of their intimate group is another matter. An important consideration in this regard is: how do other people impact the survival and well-being of the individual with the resources?

Proposition 71: When Person A emotionally impacts the survival or well-being (including identity) of person B, then person B will tend to share his or her resources with Person A, and vice-versa.

Theoretical Extension: Emotional Attachment and Altruism

Being altruistic (i.e. sharing resources) requires that the altruist either be emotionally involved with the other (e.g. marriage, family, friends), possess a high level of natural empathy (e.g. a giver), or be interdependent with the person (i.e. needs the other's cooperation in order to get what he wants, with or without emotional ties). The first two forms of altruism are innate or biological; the third is learned. The third form of altruism is often referred to as reciprocal altruism. This form of altruism can be "felt" (i.e. is biologically-based) and the person will share resources because he/she feels an urge to do so, usually based on empathy. This form can also be relatively devoid of feeling and simply be action performed as a means to an end. People who possess no emotional tie whatsoever to another will enter into a mutually beneficial relationship with that person so that their combined efforts will produce the desired result (survival and well-being) for both people. This form of reciprocal altruism is egoistic at base. Each individual interacts with the other in order to benefit him or herself. These latter forms of reciprocal altruism tend strongly to characterize business relationships.

Most people in the modern capitalist world engage in business with others whom they don't know and/or with whom they have no emotional tie. Such interactions tend to be conducted by agreement or contract. Some contracts are rendered in writing and spelled out in varying levels of detail; some are implicit and embedded in the legal system of hiring and firing practices and laws. It is these types of relationships that compel our interest at this point.

Since hunter-gatherer bands are relatively small in number, we might be safe in assuming that most if not all individuals in the band know each other and experience some kind of emotion or identity impact in relation to each of the band's members. The impact might be positive (respect, like, love) or negative (disrespect, dislike, hate) or somewhere in between, but the impact probably exists. As the band grows in number or other members are let into the band, there is probably more opportunity to relate to members as strangers. Strangers would have less impact upon one's identity than intimates, but they would still have an impact, even if only to point out one's own emotional limitations.

Accepting strangers into a group is a multi-dimensional inter-personal process. It involves at least 1) one's individual natural dispositions, i.e. personality, and 2) the environmental circumstances within which one is located. We've already sketched out three general categories of personality: takers, assertive confronters, and givers. Let's analyze environments (i.e. resources) into three general categories also: scarce, moderate, plenty. Each level of available resources will affect each level of personality, and vice-versa.

For instance, a taker in an environment of plenty might take as many resources as fits his or her needs and wants, but he or she would be less willing to protect those resources from others (probably because he or she doesn't have to; there are enough to go around). But in an environment of scarcity, the taker would take as many resources as would meet his or her needs and wants (if available), and he or she would tend to protect those resources from others.

In an environment of plenty, the giver might secure enough resources for his or her needs and some of his or her wants but would tend to give more to others than would the assertive confronter or the taker. In an environment of scarcity, the giver would tend to reduce his or her wants to needs and keep only what he or she needs and give the rest or even sacrifice some of what he or she needs in order to help others.

In an environment of plenty, the assertive confronter would tend to take what he or she needs and wants and let others do the same, but he or she wouldn't let other take from him or her unless the need was apparent. In an environment of scarcity, the assertive confronter would tend to take what he or she needs and wants, though moderate his or her acquisitions in relation to others' needs and wants. He or she would tend to engage in negotiations of equal distribution on all competing levels (needs and wants). For instance, an assertive confronter would tend to share his resources with others who need the resources to survive, but he wouldn't let others take resources from him when he has worked for them. He would also tend to share equally wanted resources with others as long as his natural satisfaction level has been reached. The overage in acquisition is expendable. This is a more egalitarian method of redistribution of resources.

In marital dyads, takers can be matched with givers and the relationship can still be interpersonally consistent. Though the takers will tend to be aggressive and the givers passive, the givers will be able to assert themselves in order to avoid complexification. It's just that the givers have a tendency to give more than others in order to achieve the well-being of the other, and the takers have a tendency to take more than others in order to achieve their satisfaction level. The relationship, to borrow a term from biology, is symbiotic.

But when complexification is introduced into the relationship, one person becomes the dominator (usually the takers) and the other the submissive (usually the givers).

When takers are matched with assertive confronters, the takers will tend to be aggressive and the assertive confronters will tend, based on their personality, either to counter the aggression with aggression (behaviorally or emotionally), thus limiting the aggressor's behavior, or act more passively and confront aggression more verbally (i.e. negotiation), thus limiting the aggressor's behavior.

But when complexification is introduced into the relationship, one person becomes the dominator (usually the takers) and the other the submissive (usually the passive assertive confronters). Also, takers, depending upon their disposition to aggression, could dominate aggressive assertive confronters, but this would be more difficult to achieve in small social settings (e.g. in hunter-gatherer bands), because the rest of the group would tend to align and punish aggressive takers. This aligns with anthropologists who argue that hunter-gatherer bands tend to be egalitarian and will ostracize anyone who tries to impose his or her will upon another.

If we allow some credibility to these general biological categories of takers, assertive confronters and givers, where people are naturally determined (i.e. genetically disposed) to respond to environments in the way they do, then we can conclude that some aggressive, some assertive and some passive behavior is SSR (authentic, natural, real). How people respond to this aggression becomes critical in the development of healthy and unhealthy human beings.

When the takers respond to other takers' aggressive behavior as a threat to their own survival and well-being, and are aggressive in return (i.e. retaliate) and, hence, misunderstand the aggressive expression itself as a natural aggressive response, then a fight can develop between takers, each trying to one-up the other. The history of human warfare is replete with examples of this type of interaction.

When takers respond to assertive aggressors who assert themselves aggressively in response to takers' aggression by asserting themselves in an even more aggressive manner (i.e. one involving vengeance or retaliation), then the takers have misunderstood the aggression of the assertive confronters, have experienced it as a threat to their identity, and have sought to dominate the assertive confronter (and 'protect' themselves from further threat).

When takers' aggression is responded to passively by assertive confronters, takers can misinterpret the passive (i.e. rational) behavior of the assertive confronters as submission and press their 'advantage' to make sure that the assertive confronters do what the takers want them to do. This is a fundamental misunderstanding on the part of the takers. They think that because the assertive confronters are acting in a non-aggressive (i.e. negotiating) manner that the assertive confronters will not persist in trying to stop the aggression of the takers. This is a critical juncture for the assertive confronters: they can either ramp up their aggression to meet the aggression of the takers (but this might be outside their natural dispositions) or they could seek out the cooperation of others to stem the aggression of the takers. (Such dynamics would be seen in hunter-gatherer bands when others in the band rise up against aggression of a taker). In these situations, putting down the aggression of the takers is a form of assertive confrontation, en masse, or a collective assertive confrontation. It says, in effect, that "we won't accept your aggression; if you want to remain within this group, you will need to apologize and shape up."

But when the assertive confronters do not recruit others to help confront the takers' aggression, then this allows the takers to learn that their aggression works to protect themselves from further threat and to get what they want.

Herein lies a critical distortion of human nature. Natural takers' acts of aggression are not met with the assertive response necessary to put the natural takers in position to grapple with their aggressive acts, to realize the inappropriateness of those acts, to apologize for them, and to better their behavior in the future. Instead, the lack of assertive response is understood as an affirmation of the legitimacy of the aggressive behavior of the takers. The takers come to believe that they are entitled to what it is they demand of others. It is in this sense that "entitlement" is a meta-experiential construct or a distortion of human nature.

This might be how humans, without being abused or having their natural human cooperation with others distorted, were able to learn that imposing their will upon others works to defend themselves from aggression (natural self-defense) and to get what they want (natural egoism). Their natural self-defensiveness and their natural egoism combine with their natural aggressiveness to distort their natural inclination toward cooperation when they learn that their aggressiveness seems to get what they want (i.e. protection, increased well-being, avoidance of decreased well-being). They will tend to reject the validity of the experience that demands cooperation on equal terms with others and accept the role of the dominant, and they can do this without ever having been abused and complexified themselves.

Herein lies the original sin of human nature: the imposition of will upon another (natural aggression), an experience of self-rejection, opening the door for a vast variety of false self constructions, limited only by the imagination.

This experiential structure might look like this:

C: do what I say!	I feel bad for hurting her	no, she 'accepts' it	I'm right for aggressing
A: anger	shame	curiosity	false confidence
B: hitting other	looking down	puzzled look	false bravado
S: other	environ	environ	other
E: wherever	wherever	wherever	wherever
"I": ownership	ownership		

When the man (in this example) hits the woman because he is frustrated in his want for her to do (or not do) something, he will immediately feel bad for hitting her (shame). He doesn't recognize the shame as something bad, wrong or weak (as he would when complexified); rather, he *interprets* the woman's lack of response as a sign of acceptance of the legitimacy of his aggression. It is easy for him to interpret her behavior in this fashion because he really wants her to do X for him (egoism) or stop doing Y in relation to him (egoism or self-defense). When she seems to act in accordance with his wants, he allows his natural egoism or natural self-defense to hold sway over his natural shame. Shame requires him to grapple with his illicit behavior and admit his deficiency (wrongness). Such grappling is painful. He can protect himself from the pain of grappling by allowing himself to think that her lack of response means acceptance of the legitimacy of his aggression. The original human sin lies in man's rejection of self (shame) and 'acceptance' of a "lack of response" as acceptance of the legitimacy of his imposition of will. "I must be right if she (he) doesn't do anything about it." This constitutes what might be called the *hierarchical delusion*.

When someone imposes his or her will upon another, without the other recognizing the full legitimacy of that imposition, then the imposition of will tends to prompt shame in the person doing the imposing. Herein lies the basis for the argument that human beings are cooperative by nature, and not competitive (at least not competitive in the way hierarchies, especially in business, argue today). If humans had always realized and grappled with the shame they felt whenever they imposed their will upon another human being without that imposition being fully and freely accepted by the person being imposed upon, then hierarchies, as we know them, would not exist. Also, had others who had been naturally aggressed against been able, either by themselves or in conjunction with others, to reject the legitimacy of the aggressor's behavior and put the aggressor in the position of having genuinely to admit the error of his ways, then hierarchies, as we know them, would not exist.

The original acts of abuse, we will speculate, were not justified by any ideology. When those humans were abused, either physically, sexually or emotionally, though the abuse was not justified in any way, they became vulnerable to complexification. If they were able to ward off the abuse, rebuff it, and turn it back on the abuser, making it clear to him that his behavior was unacceptable and that further cooperation was not forthcoming if the abuser did not genuinely apologize for his behavior and mend his ways, then complexification would never have occurred.

But human beings, especially children, are vulnerable to complexification. The various forms of dependency that children possess in relation to adults make them vulnerable to complexification. Their ability to assertively confront adults when adults transgress against them is practically non-existent. They have to adjust psychologically to the abuse or they will not survive or live well in any way. In the face of abuse, children will tend to 'choose' complexification over the grim alternatives.

Also, relative to the physically stronger and more intimidating men, women are vulnerable to complexification. Similar to children, they can experience fear in response to male aggression, and this fear can cause them to pause before they choose to assertively confront the aggressor and hold him accountable for his inappropriate behavior. When they do not counter male aggression, then the males who are aggressing are in position to allow their natural egoistic and self-defensive tendencies to overtake or distort their natural feelings of shame and open the door to Pandora's Box, allowing them to create a panoply of 'justificatory' systems of domination and submission.

This is an explanation given for why males have tended overwhelmingly to dominate all aspects of society throughout most of the world and throughout most of recorded history, why they have created hierarchical structures to maintain that domination, and how they have created ideological systems in an attempt to justify that domination. All of this has been done in 'cooperation' with women and children. Women have 'bought into' all sorts of oppressive systems of thought and action and have actually allowed themselves, in good part, to be ideologically determined by men. Conversely, and ironically, men have allowed themselves to be ideologically determined by themselves. Children have continually been in position to be dominated by both men and women because of their inherent vulnerability, and inasmuch as society has constructed itself under traditional objective ideologies and organized itself under hierarchies, children are subject to active complexification.

It is only recently in the history of humankind that the harmful effects of physical, sexual and emotional abuse have been recognized, and recognized only by some, not all people. Many (most?) people still view physical, sexual and emotional abuse not as abuse but as normal if not exemplary moral behavior. This recognition coincides with the dissolution of, or at least the effective challenge to, tenets constituting traditional objective ideological systems of thought that serve to perpetuate oppressive human interaction. But this recognition is only the tip of the iceberg. The depth of the problem is just beginning to be plumbed.

Theoretical Extension: The History of Economics in an Experiential Context
In the hunter-gatherer stage of human life on earth, people simply acquired the resources they needed for survival and well-being, i.e. they picked fruit and hunted game in a given area. They stayed in areas where food was plentiful or sufficient until they exhausted that area of food and moved on; or they stayed in that area for longer periods of time if the food sources replenished themselves. There were no claims on the land itself, exclusive of others. They would reproduce at a rate consistent with their mobility and would tend to develop rules for reproduction (sex) that would allow them to survive and achieve a modicum of happiness. Private property consisted of the resources they acquired for themselves and their families (group) and were willing to defend from others, if necessary. The distribution of those resources was determined by emotional connections between family and group members.

289

Emotional bonds were determined by combinations of biology (i.e. genetic dispositions) and learned interactions (e.g. love bonds). Strong biological bonds combined with strong love bonds produced the strongest dispositions for redistribution, e.g. male hunters were more willing to share their game with their family and those they loved than with others.

But even in hunter-gatherer bands, not all emotional bonds were equal. As emotional bonds diminished between members of a band, the natural disposition to share resources also diminished. Such differentiation in levels of emotional bonding could easily create disparity and inequality in the distribution of resources. For instance, a particular hunter might not want to share his game with certain members of his group, i.e. those members he dislikes or hates. But in order for the group, qua group, to survive and maximize its well-being, it must share the game acquired by the hunter with all members of the group.

Probing Question: How is this "unnatural" distribution attained? Is it "natural" for a hunter who does not want to share his game with certain others in his group to be forced to share that game with others when he doesn't want to do so?

Theoretical Extension: A Natural Division of Labor and Emotional Bonds
A member of a family might become a hunter if he/she is able (e.g. physically capable and talented or skilled) and willing (i.e. interested) to perform this needed activity (job); this would be a natural fit to ensure the survival and well-being of the family. There would be an emotional bond (optimally) between hunter (provider) and family members; the hunter member of the family would *want* to provide for the other members of the family.

Biology serves as the natural determination of who constitutes a family (i.e. blood-related parents and children). Blood-related parents and children will tend to constitute the nuclear family. How children are raised in any given society of people will depend upon how that society sets its rules of interaction, whether those rules are explicit in the form of laws or implicit in the form of mores or customs. Children need not be raised by their biological parents in order to follow the dictates of natural development. Natural (i.e. biological) parentage can be trumped by natural (i.e. emotional) bonds. In other words, a healthy child can be raised by non-biological parents as long as natural emotional bonding (minimally) replaces genetic parentage. This aligns with the contention that emotional bonding is more powerful in human beings in regard to the development of identity than is the passage of genetic material. How a child develops his or her identity (vs. body characteristics) is more dependent upon emotional bonding than genetics.

Though powerful determinants for sharing, emotional bonds tend to "wax and wane," depending upon circumstances. This "waxing and waning" might be single-layered in that a person's altruistic bond with another might be genuinely challenged or diminished in strength by the unacceptable behavior of that person. In these situations people are "falling out of love" or "coming not to love" each other. But the "waxing and waning" might also be dual-layered. In these situations the person's emotional bond exists but is temporarily challenged or preempted by a form of rejection of the other. In these instances a person can love another while simultaneously disliking or even hating some aspect of that other. In the former instance, emotional bonds are being directly affected or altered; in the latter, emotional bonds are being challenged but only superficially. In either case, emotional bonds, though a strong natural way to determine those whom one wants to share resources with, are changeable. The stability of emotional bonds depends on many factors that will not be addressed here. Suffice it to say that natural emotional bonds, like those of egoistic concerns, are strong but alterable. Societies require that the ephemeral nature of emotional bonding be controlled or curbed and that people who are in positions of acquiring resources for themselves and others in the group be held responsible for sharing with others even when they don't want to do so.

This discussion presupposes the development of a division of labor in human groups. Individual humans in groups will not tend to "fend for themselves" or do everything they need to do to live and prosper by themselves. This never occurs in childhood and only rarely occurs in adulthood (e.g. hermit, etc.) When grouped together, people will tend overwhelmingly to divide up tasks among each other in order to help the group survive and thrive. Now we are back the propositions at the beginning of this work. There are natural and unnatural (distorted) ways to divide up the labor among members of a group. Natural ways entail: skills, talents, interests, and capacities; unnatural (or distorted) ways entail: male-determined, female-determined, and gender roles.

When members of a group take on resource acquiring duties, they do so, in a natural society, because they possess the skills, talents, interests and capacities to do so. They do not do so because authoritative males or females in the group tell them to or because their gender roles require them to do so. In doing so, these members of the group satisfy their egoistic concerns by engaging in meaningful and satisfying labor, while simultaneously contributing to the survival and well-being of the group. When they *want* to share the products of their labor with the others in the group, no problems tend to occur. But when, for whatever reasons, they don't want to share the product of their labor with others (or certain others), then the interdependence of the group members determined by a natural division of labor is put in jeopardy. The group will need to exert pressure on the individual resource acquirer to share the product of his labor even when he doesn't want to. Natural emotional bonds, whether simple (one leveled) or complicated (two leveled) need to subordinated to the needs and well-being of the group in order to maintain productive interdependence between members of the group.

A natural group of humans will divide up tasks for survival and well-being among members of the group best fitted for the tasks. Some of these tasks will entail resource acquisition (e.g. hunting, gathering), some manipulation of acquired resources (cooking, cleaning, fixing), and some services rendered with or without the aid of acquired resources (building (with), mother feeding (without)).

Proposition 72: Those members of a group who are tasked with acquiring resources for the survival and well-being of the group will tend to be highly valued in the group.

Human beings cannot live and be well without resource acquisition. Those entrusted to acquire resources for the survival and well-being of the group will tend to be highly valued by the other members. This tendency to value resource acquirers makes all members vulnerable to complexification. The resource acquirer can use his talents and skills to acquire resources as a means of justifying his impositions of will on other members of the group. Other members depend upon his resource acquisition in order for them do their tasks (manipulation of resources, services requiring resources, etc). This dependency is natural inasmuch as all tasks in the division of labor are recognized as integral to the whole, if not equally valuable. When one form of task is recognized as more important than another, then the integrity of the whole becomes compromised.

An analogy can be drawn between the human body and a human society. All parts of the human body are integrated with all other parts; when one part is damaged, it will tend to affect the functioning of other parts. In a society all tasks determined by a division of labor among group members are integrated with all other tasks; when one task is "damaged" (valued or devalued more than another), then other tasks will tend to suffer.

The over-valuation of a task in a society prompts a psychological dependency upon those accomplishing that task and makes one vulnerable to complexification. Those in positions of performing valued tasks for the group can abuse others in the group and get away with it partly because of the recognized importance of their jobs. It is easier for one to stand up for oneself in the wake of abuse when the abuser is not entrusted with a valuable job in relation to one's own survival and well-being. For instance, it is easier for a woman to stand up for herself to her neighbor who berates her for her cooking than it is her husband who is entrusted to "bring home the bacon for the family."

Proposition 73: The value of a job within a division of labor is in part a function of its connection to one's own survival and well-being.

Hunters will be valued in a hunter-gatherer band because without the skills and effort of the hunters, the band's food supply will be sorely diminished and so too will the health and well-being of its members. Preparers of food, if they are not the hunters themselves, need the hunters in order to do their job. The same is true for the gatherers. The gathering activity might be more valued than the preparer activity because the preparer activity depends upon the gathering activity for its existence.

Proposition 74: The value of a job within a division of labor is in part a function of the scarcity of people to fill the valued job.

If non-hunters in a group can affectively assume the role of hunter, then the value of the hunter's job is diminished. Though valuable because it provides survival and well-being for others and is required in order for other job functions to occur, it is not as valuable as it could be if there are few people in the group who could just as affectively fill that role.

Proposition 75: The value of a job within a division of labor is a function primarily of its connection to survival (i.e. need) and secondarily to its connection to well-being (i.e. want).

Jobs will be valued more when they promote the survival of the individual and/or the group. These jobs will take precedence over jobs that provide merely for well-being. For example, defense of one's country will tend to take precedence over being able to eat at an expensive restaurant. Hence, in times of threat to one's survival as a nation, a job in the military will tend to be valued more than a job in the restaurant business.

Jobs addressing health will automatically include aspects of survival and well-being. Curing illnesses that if left untreated could cause death addresses survival-related health; treating chronic health problems in order to maximize well-being addresses well-being-related health; wellness programs aiming to maximize health address well-being-related health. Physicians who address survival-related health issues will tend to be valued more than those treating chronic problems and those aimed at maximizing one's health.

Hunters and gatherers in a hunter-gatherer band will tend to be valued more than food preparers, child nurturers and house builders because without the food hunted or gathered, there would be no other activities. Also, if there were fewer members of the band who could hunt than prepare food, than the hunter would be that much more valuable.

Proposition 76: Leaders surface naturally in groups. They derive their leadership from their intelligence, knowledge, skills, strength and assertiveness.

A member of a group becomes a leader in a given endeavor (e.g. hunting) by possessing the intelligence, knowledge, skills and strength necessary to perform the job and the willingness to do so. A leader will surface from the members of a group when she learns what she needs to learn from other members of her group and exhibits these characteristics listed above in a way that is superior to those of the other members of the group. This type of leader leads others without transforming their way of thinking and doing.

Some leaders will surface from the members of a group when they have not only learned what they need to learn and exhibited these characteristics relative to other members but have also displayed the capacity to transcend that learning and the patterns of behavior associated with that learning by creating new ways of being and doing. A creative leader will forge new patterns of behavior not only for herself but also for others to follow.

A hunter who creates a new piece of technology that allows him to hunt more effectively than anyone has ever done before or who invents a new technique that allows him to be more successful than anyone has been in the past will create new ways of being and doing for others to follow.

It behooves people to follow the leaders who exhibit these qualities or characteristics, and it challenges them to match or surpass those qualities or characteristics.

Anthropologists argue that people in an egalitarian social structure like that of hunter-gatherers will tend to develop leaders in certain areas of endeavor, while others will follow, only to have those leaders be followers in other areas of endeavor, i.e. areas where others become leaders. These patterns of leadership fit well into the experiential theory being developed in this work.

Theoretical Extension: Forfeiture of Self-Direction and Hierarchy

There seems to be a natural vulnerability for people in groups to allow people who are tasked with survival-oriented jobs to impose their wills upon them and therefore create the conditions for complexification and meta-experiential construction. Habit alone can dispose one to withhold confrontation of a valued job holder when that job holder tries to impose his will upon one. One grows used to following and trusting a person who seems so much wiser, smarter or more knowledgeable than oneself, so when that trusted individual oversteps his bounds and seeks to impose his will upon others, others might allow such an imposition to occur without asserting themselves in relation to it, even though against their better judgment. This could happen especially if the others not only get used to the one leading but also come to depend upon that person. If one comes to forego self-initiative and critical thinking in relation to a leader who takes on responsibility for others' actions, then one's ability to self-initiate and think critically can wane, making it more difficult for one to assertively confront a leader when that leader tries to impose his will upon others.

This type of change is a forfeiture of self-direction rather than one caused by the distortion of abuse. People could naturally depend upon a leader who has developed a track record of success. This dependence can often times be accepted and encouraged by the leader, when the leader believes that because of his successes he has powers that separate him qualitatively from others.

In this case a leader can become a ruler based solely on the inability or unwillingness of others (followers) to assert themselves when the leader dictates or imposes his will upon them. Such situations might be categorized as creations of dominant:submissive relationships based on forfeiture of self-direction and critical thinking rather than upon complexification and meta-experiential construction.

A child might come to submit to an adult even when that adult is imposing his or her will upon the child without the child freely giving consent to that imposition, because the child is not individuated enough from the adult to develop a defense against such impositions. A child is naturally vulnerable to adult impositions of will, even when those impositions are unintentional, because of the disparity in the power between the child and the adult. The child depends upon the adult for every aspect of its development (physical, psychological and social), whereas the adult does not depend upon the child for the same. When the adult mixes support and encouragement with imposition of will, the child is especially vulnerable to complexification. It receives affirmation of its burgeoning identity (which is experientially consistent) and disaffirmation or rejection of aspects of its identity (which is en route to complexification.) Disaffirmations prompt distortions within generally affirmative interactions and produce a distorted identity grounded in experiential consistency though considerably weakened by identity distortion. Weakened identities can become more distorted when circumstances for survival and well-being are challenging.

An example of this writ large is the development of Nazi Germany. Having a history of complexification, passed on from generation to generation from the meta-experiential construction of the Kaiser monarchy, Germany developed a strong tendency toward dominant:submissive relationships. The German population got used to being dominated by the Kaiser and developed an identity within that system of domination (i.e. a skewed identity). When Germany attempted to establish a political democracy, it did so without much experience of self-direction (i.e. assertively confronting impositions of will by others). Germany's democracy was weak. When the market crashed and Germany suffered yet another survival and well-being set back, it was ripe for further complexification and meta-experiential construction. Hitler achieved dominance in part because people were too weak to stand up to him but also because people adhered to his distorted message. Many people actually believed the Jews were primarily responsible for many of their problems and that Hitler was the solution.

Having already been complexified by monarchy, and realizing their own inefficacy to act democratically (i.e. to self-direct) in the face of survival (economic disaster), Germany turned toward militarized complexification (i.e. National Socialism), using the Jews and the Slavs as scapegoats. Hitler was able to convince a nation that Germans were not only not inferior but were superior to others, and hence, they had a right to impose their wills upon others.

Proposition 77: Rulers surface within groups in a distorted manner. They derive their rulership primarily from their ability to impose their ideas and wills upon others and secondarily from their intelligence, knowledge, skills, and strength.

Probing Question: If anthropologists are correct in regard to their theory that early hunter-gatherer bands were egalitarian in structure (though possibly hierarchical in family structure), and "upstarts" were punished when they tried to impose their wills upon others, thus transforming their leadership role (if they had one) into a rulership role, then how might it have happened that rulers, and hence hierarchies, came out of basically egalitarian organizations?

Theoretical Response: It is offered here, aligning with Rousseau's observations, that egalitarian systems, though natural human organizations, can corrupt or degenerate into hierarchical structures, where sources of leadership become condensed to a few (oligarchy, aristocracy) or one (monarchy, totalitarian regime, autocracy). It is argued here that corruption can occur under forces from the environment where resources are scarce and the fear of death prompts people to submit to the will of someone or the few who seem to know what they are doing more so than others, or there are serious threats to survival and well-being from outside the group causing fear in the group, prompting a similar type of submission. This can be understood as a type of corruption by accretion: a habit of following one leader in one or more areas of endeavor, under stress, is transformed into a submission to that leader in all areas of endeavor (i.e. a form of generalized submission). The transformation would occur because of fear of death or other severe stressors.

We can legitimately hypothesize that in hunter-gatherer bands, people had, from time to time, experienced such stressors, and that the general population, from time to time, submitted to the will of one (or a few) leaders, without engaging in much critical thinking or debate, in order to survive and live well. It seems wholly natural for a group under threat of survival to allow certain respected leaders (or one leader) to direct their actions or to tell them what to do, and then doing it unquestioningly in order to maximize the possibility of their survival. But to sustain that level of submission, to dispense with one's critical faculties for long periods of time, and actually to think that such a suspension is a good thing, reflective of objective reality, is not the same thing as a temporary suspension of self-direction under stress. To achieve such a transformation requires a form of corruption that goes to the core of humanity. To achieve such a transformation requires complexification of human identity and meta-experiential construction in order to pass that identity on from generation to generation.

As argued thus far, complexification can be achieved through physical, sexual and emotional abuse. Children are most vulnerable to such abuse. Physically, women are more vulnerable than men to such abuse. Physically, some men are more vulnerable than other men (e.g. the "alpha male" syndrome) to such abuse. Psychologically, all people (men, women and children) are vulnerable to such abuse. It is in this latter sense of psychological abuse that the majority of people within groups might become habituated to following leaders because of their the perceived or real efficacy in relation to their opinions or input into decisions to be made by the group, When the few or the one person is allowed by the many not only to voice their authoritative opinion as to what others should do but also to be believed that those few or that one is *superior* to others and therefore *should* be followed, then the majority has forfeited its will to the minority or the one, and natural human identity has been corrupted. In order to achieve such a feat, the one (or the few) must have inadvertently (initially) taken advantage of the many by realizing that their abusive behavior succeeded in getting what they wanted. They committed the original sin of believing that the lack of assertiveness of others in response to their natural attempts to impose their will upon them meant that they were somehow right and justified in imposing their will. Likewise, those following leaders committed the original sin of believing that they were somehow inferior to those leaders when it came to making decisions that determined their futures.

Leadership converts into rulership when the natural identity constitution of human beings (i.e. self-direction) is distorted, and that distortion is passed on from generation to generation.

Proposition 78: All people are essentially self-directed and communal.

Theoretical Extension: People as Self-Directed and Communal

Whether or not some anthropologists are correct in positing that most of human social history is characterized by egalitarian hunter-gatherer bands, such an organizational structure can be used as a model for all human societies, both theoretical and actual. Human beings seem to be innately determined by two seemingly opposing forces: self-direction and communality. I say "seemingly opposing" because the two forces need not be opposed to each other. In this model of human society, leaders naturally emerge when some people possess the skills, knowledge, intelligence, and will to assert themselves in relation to others in any given human endeavor. Others who recognize those characteristics in those people will either tend to follow (out of prudence or practical concerns) or to compete with them for sole leadership, establish co-leadership, etc. Competition for leadership roles is judged here to be natural and conducive to achieving survival and well-being among humans in groups. It's a way for similarly skilled individuals who might have different opinions about what the group should do to establish the efficacy of their influence in promoting the survival and well-being of the group. Who achieves leadership roles depends on who possesses the knowledge, skills, experience, intelligence, and will to decide on the courses of action, to implement those decisions, and actually to succeed in promoting the survival and well-being of the group.

Such characteristics in people are subject to waxing and waning, increasing and receding, developing and atrophying. Hence, leadership roles tend to be naturally time-limited. Those limitations are determined by a variety of different factors, including the aging process, health, interests, needs of others, etc.

In egalitarian societies each member has a chance to lead in any given endeavor; the social structure (i.e. laws, rules, customs, etc.) support such opportunities and restrict inhibitors of such opportunities, and no individual is forced to follow anyone else; they can choose to follow or they can compete for leadership roles. As such, egalitarian societies are intensely self-directed. Individualism and autonomy tend to be highly valued.

But since humans are essentially social and interdependent, if not at times dependent (e.g. children), for their survival and well-being, they affect each other constantly by their actions, whether that effect is recognized or not.

The trick is to figure out how best to coordinate and control the dynamic interplay between leaders and followers over time and in a variety of circumstances.

For instance, it might be natural for many people to follow a person who possesses the required characteristics for leadership in hunting. Others might not possess the physical capacity to do the job; they might not be interested in doing the job; they might be more interested in doing other jobs, etc. So following that person or allowing that person to perform that leadership function might seem quite prudent, and doing so would tend to promote their own survival and well-being.

In the group of people who possess the characteristics necessary for hunting, there will be an internal competition for leadership roles.

Each person in the sub-group (group of hunters) will be able to compete with others for leadership roles. For instance, the bow-and-arrow hunters will be led by one or a few people who display superior characteristics in relation to others and superior abilities to teach or facilitate the development of these characteristics in others. There might exist several leaders at a time, where some people follow one, others follow the other. The "proof of the pudding" is determined by the efficacy of the methods, i.e. is survival and well-being achieved? Several leaders could surface at any given time.

The number of leaders is determined by the type of social structure in practice, the characteristics of the people in the group, and the physical circumstances within which the group exists. For instance, a loose egalitarian social structure (i.e. multiple leaders in a variety of areas and few social rules defining leadership roles) could accompany situations where resources are plentiful and security is strong; a more rigid egalitarian social structure (i.e. more pre-determined and fewer leadership roles than in loose egalitarian systems and more rules for assuming leadership roles) could accompany situations where resources are relatively scarce and security is moderate.

As threats to group survival increase, leadership roles tend to decrease in number and consolidate so that decisions can be made quickly and carried out efficiently. For instance, if a hunter-gatherer band were threatened by another hunter-gatherer band (for whatever reason), the loose-knit leaders of the group might gather to create a tight-knit system of leadership, where leaders with the qualities and characteristics needed for making decisions concerning the survival of the group would tend to surface and all other leaders would tend to follow. Depending upon the group and the duration and intensity level of the threat, co-leadership roles could be established (e.g. a committee of leaders) and decisions could be made democratically or one leader could surface and decisions could be made unilaterally.

Under situations of high survival stress, a group could temporarily forfeit leadership and allow short periods of rulership (probably by a trusted leader), but such dispensations would tend to be very short in duration, only long enough for the immediate danger to pass. For instance, in a hunter-gatherer band that is under attack by another band, a respected leader who can organize a defense of the group and, possibly, if necessary, an offence designed to prevent the attackers from ever attacking again might surface quickly among leaders, and, because of the need for expediency, will be allowed to rule or decide others' courses of action and expect others to follow. Such a forfeiture of self-direction would tend to be temporary, employed only until the immediate threat passes. Once the immediate threat passes, temporary rulership will pass back into leadership roles and the egalitarian structure will continue.

It is hypothesized here that a natural forfeiture of self-direction would, necessarily, be temporary, and that once the threat of death has passed, people will normally revert to egalitarian leadership structures. But if the threat to survival were to be extended in time, a group might become habituated to hierarchical rule. In this case, natural self-direction and egalitarian social structure breaks down (or distorts itself) into hierarchy.

Such a breakdown in natural social structure, it seems, does not occur naturally. People wouldn't just forfeit their self-direction because they were under constant stress from without. A child does not forfeit its natural self-direction when an adult attacks him (e.g. physically abuses him). The child immediately knows that what the adult did was unacceptable to him. He rejects the legitimacy of the adult's abusive behavior. It is natural for him to do so; it is consistent with his need for survival and his need and want for well-being. But when the child's immediate rejection of the adult's behavior toward him is expressed and the adult rejects (for whatever reason) the legitimacy of that expression, and continues to act abusively toward the child, then the child is left with little choice but to submit to the adult. But this submission does not occur naturally. It occurs because of identity distortion. The child finds a way to survive in a bad situation.

A similar thing could happen between groups of people. When a group of people (acting as one) imposes its will upon another group, and the other group has difficulty asserting itself in relation to the imposing group, the group imposed upon will tend to submit to the will of the imposing group; a social relationship of dominance: submission will obtain.

A group that tries to impose itself upon another group that is structured in an egalitarian fashion, especially when the imposing group is very threatening to the egalitarian group, might prompt that egalitarian group to suspend its egalitarian practices in favor of hierarchical practices ruled by a trusted leader. But such a transformation is temporary and practical; it is a transformation due to emergency. Groups are required to act as one in order to survive; multiple possible decisions regarding the group's actions must be reduced to one overriding decision coupled with the group's adherence to that decision, whether they wholly affirm it or not. Groups that do not return to egalitarian and self-directed interaction with others have been corrupted by complexification. Weakened identities through complexification could account for the group's inability to return to an egalitarian structure and for their 'choice' to retain a hierarchical social structure.

Groups under survival stress are vulnerable to complexification within the sub-structures (e.g. families) comprising each group. Because of survival stress, family members (especially fathers who tend to be physically more intimidating than mothers) are vulnerable to imposing their wills upon others in the family. Such impositions might be believed to be for the survival and well-being of the family, but they are actually an extension of their own need for survival and well-being. When family members allow themselves to be 'convinced' that the father is acting in their best interests, they forfeit their self-direction in favor of the father's rule.

Writ large, natural leaders of groups can impose their wills upon the rest of the group due to survival stress, believing that their impositions are for the good of the group. When the rest of the group allows itself to be 'convinced' that the leaders are acting in their best interests, it forfeits its self-direction in favor of the leaders' rule.

Continued complexification practices undermine and distort egalitarian social structures. They weaken identities and create domianant:submissive relationships. In this way, natural survival stress could induce complexification; and complexification could impede or practically overcome natural tendencies to return to natural egalitarian social structures.

Proposition 79: All natural societies are egalitarian in structure. Leaders arise in groups based on intelligence, skills, knowledge, interests, and wills to act in relation to those characteristics (i.e. to express them) for the benefit (survival and well-being) of themselves and their group.

Proposition 80: All natural societies can assume a hierarchical structure in emergencies where groups need to act as one in order to survive. Such hierarchies will be temporary (and hence artificial) and will give way to egalitarian structures once the threat to survival has passed. In these situations, leaders will tend to reduce in number (possibly to one) and followers will tend to reduce critical thinking in order to promote immediate and effective cooperation.

Proposition 81: Temporary hierarchies that become "permanent" do so because members of the group have become complexified, thus reducing their ability to assert themselves in the face of domination. Complexification in the face of abuse alters the identities of individuals by "forcing" self-rejections and subsequent creations of false selves. False selves are sustained and developed through the creation and proliferation of meta-experiential constructs.

Theoretical Extension: Agriculture and Husbandry

In order to support the above propositions, let's return to speculative economic history. By observing how nature operated, early hunter-gatherers eventually figured out that planting seeds would reap produce and that some animals could be domesticated. Agriculture and husbandry were discovered and people could stay in areas for longer periods of time.

Many economic theorists and anthropologists have contended that the discovery of agriculture and husbandry ushered in private property. The contention is that people no longer moved from place to place when food sources in an area were used up because they were able to cultivate the land which yielded them "gatherings" by their own design and effort, and they learned how to domesticate animals which yielded them "hunting" by their own design and effort. Along with these discoveries came the need to secure land for oneself (or one's group). Land became the first private property, whether "private" meant individual, family or group. Agriculture started out as an activity ancillary to hunting and gathering, i.e. a form of gardening or horticulture. American Indian tribes, though technically hunters and gatherers, were also farmers in that they grew crops like maze and tobacco. As gardening grew into farming, the need to stay mobile declined and the need to remain sedentary increased. Centers of living revolved around cultivated land. Cultivatable land was grabbed up by whoever knew how to grow and harvest produce and how to raise animals and use them for their survival and well-being.

Probing Question: How did people shift from hunter-gatherer mobility (without exclusive ownership of land) to farming (with exclusive ownership of land)?

Theoretical Extension: From Hunter-Gatherer Mobility to Sedentary Agriculture and Husbandry

It has been argued so far that private property is based in experience as defined as a necessary combination of cognition, affect, behavior, sensation and environment (as owned by the "I"). In this type of primordial ownership, contents in the environment are owned experientially but not socially, legally, or politically. Environmental contents (i.e. resources) were "shared" not as an abstract, theoretical determination but rather as a real, practical, problem-solving, life-sustaining activity; it occurred in real time, with real people, who needed resources for survival and wanted them for well-being. Hunter-gatherer bands tended to claim ownership of resources, either by word or action, right from the start. And who they wanted to share them with was a matter of biological disposition and emotional bonding and not one of universal moral decree. When resources were abundant and could sustain larger numbers of people, the addition of more people in an area would not present much of a distribution problem. Everybody would take what they needed and wanted; few would complain of others doing the same as long as they got what they needed and wanted. But when resources were scarce, population growth in an area brought about distribution problems.

If this argument is accurate, then hunter-gatherers tended to experience exclusivity in ownership of the land they lived on and worked at the time and didn't simply allow others to move in and co-cultivate their gardens, co-hunt their game, and co-gather their berries based on some sort of enlightened, universal, abstract moral insight. It was *their* land because they were experientially connected to it and their survival and well-being was dependent on it. Just as an individual will tend not to allow just anyone to invade his personal (experiential) space, so too a group of people will tend not to allow strangers to invade its group or social space.

When the original land cultivators graduated from temporary, ancillary gardeners to full-time, sedentary farmers, the natural tendency to experience their personal and group space as theirs simply became entrenched. In Humean terms, experiential ownership develops into a matter of habit. People become accustomed to utilizing their experiential space and the contents therein for their survival and well-being.

For example, American Indian tribes experienced ownership of the contents of their environment which included buffalo. When other people (e.g. other tribes or European trappers, hunters and settlers) moved into the areas in which they were living and hunting, their sense of ownership surfaced in consciousness. They not only owned the contents of the experiences within which they participated, but they owned themselves as contents of the cognitive component of the experiences within which they participated. What they unreflectively owned and assumed to be theirs was also reflectively owned and recognized as exclusively theirs, e.g. my land, my buffalo, my air, my water, etc., but this self-reflective ownership was personal, not interpersonal (or social); it was not equivalent to legal ownership. Others could avail themselves of the environmental contents (resources) if no one or nothing stopped them.

An individual will respond to infringements on her personal space (e.g. someone getting too close, hitting her, etc.) and groups will, likewise, respond to infringements on their group space. If buffalo are valued contents in their group space, then others entering that space will automatically prompt an ownership-like response from those already occupying that space (e.g. *our* buffalo). The sharing of the contents with others in that space becomes a matter of negotiation.

This type of phenomenon is evident in children and their experiential sense of ownership in relation to a toy they are playing with. When another child infringes on the space where the child is playing with the toy and seeks to play with the toy or take it, the child playing with the toy might, depending upon the natural disposition of the child (i.e. giver, assertive-confronter, taker) and its happiness-trajectory (stimulated happiness to satiated happiness), respond with an experiential sense of exclusive ownership (i.e. "my" toy). The child will also tend to reason in regard to what actions she should take in regard to those invading her space. For example, if the invaders are judged to be formidable takers and self-assertiveness might not be possible or effective, then others might be needed to ward off the invaders. If the invaders are judged to be self-asserters who are claiming equal rights to resources (despite the painful effect it might have on the current "owners," then the current "owners" might adjust their "ownership" to include the "ownership" of others (i.e. share the resources or allow some of the resources to be grabbed up by others).

As the resources become scarce relative to the number of people claiming experiential ownership of them, negotiation becomes more prominent amongst assertive-confronters, less prominent among takers (who are now vulnerable to complexification), and less prominent among givers (who are now vulnerable to complexification).

Proposition 82: Exclusive ownership occurs originally when self-reflection occurs in conjunction with a valued environmental content (i.e. resource).

Theoretical Extension: Private Property and Hierarchy

As has been argued above, exclusive ownership is originally an experiential phenomenon, not a social or legal phenomenon. Humans experience themselves as owners of the contents of the environments or space within which they immediately exist. Anyone "invading" that space will be responded to in some fashion. Some "invaders" are accepted (e.g. emotional attachments, symbiotic relationships, reciprocal altruism), some are tolerated (e.g. live and let live, agree to disagree), and some are rejected (e.g. ranging from assertiveness (with or without aggression) to various forms of retaliation, punishment and exaction of compensation).

When a child experiences his space to be invaded by another, he will respond according to his personal disposition (personality) and the situation within which he is living (including the nature of the invader). When a group experiences its space (and the contents therein) to be invaded by another, it will, likewise, respond according to its group disposition (i.e. group personality) and the situation within which it is living (including the nature of the invader).

Land has always been an experientially owned resource; it constitutes the physical living space underneath the individual and/or

307

the group. It is that upon which each person moves in some fashion; it is that which supports each person's weight. A hunter-gatherer would take issue with someone who bombed out the ground from under him, a ground that supported his weight and allowed him to move about. He would also take issue with someone who siphoned off the water from the well that he was using for survival. He would also take issue with someone who tried to prevent him from accessing land, either by crossing over it or by taking water from the well in it, when he needs it for his own survival and well-being.

When people learned that cultivating land and domesticating animals could afford them food without having to move about from place to place, they settled on land and got used to it being in their immediate experience (i.e. environmental component), and they valued the land because it promoted their survival and well-being. When others "invaded" their space, they tended to respond, depending upon their personality, their needs and wants, the needs and wants of those "invading," and the abundance or scarcity of land around them. When their needs and wants crossed paths with others' needs and wants in regard to the same land (e.g. cattle and sheep herders needing land for grazing and farmers needing land for cultivation), either one could attempt to impose his will upon the others and have the others respond accordingly, or some method of sharing the land could be worked out through negotiation.

Imposition of will, either by males, females or established gender roles has already been rejected as a legitimate form of job determination (Propositions 11,12 and 13); negotiation has been accepted as a legitimate form (Proposition 15+). These methods of determining jobs can be applied to group interaction in relation to resource acquisition and the development of private property.

When one group's needs and wants cross paths with another group's needs and wants, and one group has already established an experiential exclusivity in relation to certain resources, then a number of responses could occur, depending upon group personalities, amount of resources available, the need and want level of each group, etc.

For example, if both groups are self-asserters, then they will tend to negotiate a method of sharing resources as long as one group does not try to impose its will upon the other and as long as those resources are plentiful enough to support the survival of all the people. The group that has already established an experiential ownership of land will be in position to share (negotiate) or defend their exclusive use of the resource. The group that has "invaded" their space is obligated to negotiate methods of sharing the resource. For example, when the European explorers came to America, they "invaded" the space already experientially owned by Indian tribes. They were obligated to negotiate terms of sharing that space and those resources. Since land and resources were plentiful, methods of sharing it could be peacefully negotiated. But when the "invaders" sought to impose their wills upon the Indian tribes because of their want for certain resources (e.g. land, precious metals, etc.) coupled with their superiority in technology (weaponry), because they had already developed societies deeply entrenched in complexification and meta-experiential construction, and because the Indians were not able to assert themselves in relation to the force of imposition, a group of people (European "invaders") were able to complexify an entire other group of people (collective Indian nations) and 'justify' that complex-ificaton through the development of various meta-experiential con-structions (e.g. manifest destiny, Christian conversion, superior civilization, etc.)

Probing Question: Why should the "invaders" be obligated to negotiate terms of sharing land with those using the land, especially when the users of the land lay no socially exclusive ownership claims on the land, e.g. they are nomadic or semi-nomadic? Why can't the "invaders" just grab up the land and use it exclusively for their own purposes?

Theoretical Extension: Dealing with "Invaders"
If hunter-gatherers owned the land they lived on only experientially and not socially (or legally in relation to all others), and if they considered some land to be public land (i.e. for anyone to use but not exclusively owned), then "invaders" of that land will tend to experience the land as theirs experientially but inhabited and used by others. If the space is considered to be public or shared space by the inhabitants, then the terms of sharing will tend to be negotiated, either explicitly or implicitly, by all those using the space. The usage of the land by "invaders" would tend to be accepted by the inhabitants if such usage does not significantly diminish the inhabitants' ability to

survive and live well. Once that ability is compromised, the groups, depending upon their dispositions (i.e. personalities), will tend to negotiate methods of sharing resources. Those groups disposed toward being takers will tend toward methods of sharing that leave them with the lion's share of the resources; those disposed toward being assertive confronters will tend toward equality in sharing, depending upon the needs and wants of the groups; those disposed toward being givers will tend toward sacrificing some resources for the survival and well-being of the other group.

When two groups (or two individuals), strange to each other, come into contact, where one group has already established itself as the experiential owners (inhabitants) of a space and users of the resources in that space, where that space is considered to be public or shared space by the inhabitants themselves, the inhabiting group will tend to realize or become self-conscious of its survival and well-being i.e. how do the "invaders" affect its survival and well-being? Takers might be disposed toward self-defense, not wanting the "invaders" to impinge upon their chance of survival and their sense of well-being; self-asserters might be disposed toward negotiation of agreed upon methods of using the space; givers might be disposed toward acceptance of the "invaders" and a willingness to be gracious and even self-sacrificing in their sharing of land and resources.

On the other hand, the "invaders," realizing that there are inhabitants of the space they are "invading," will tend to assess the level of experiential ownership of the inhabitants of the area, i.e. do they protect their space, are they receptive to sharing their space through negotiation, are they willing to give up in order to receive others into their space?

If, upon assessment, the "invaders," as takers, determine that the inhabitants, as weak self-asserters or givers, will relinquish their use of the resources to the "invaders," then the "invaders" might find it to their advantage to impose their wills upon the inhabitants and use the resources exclusively. Or the "invaders," as takers, might take advantage of the inhabitants' generosity and simply live among them while taking the lion's share of the resources. In this way, the "invaders," as takers, will provide the inhabitants with benefits that improve their survival and well-being (e.g. protection, innovation, etc.) In this case, the takers, as innovators, will take the lion's share of the resources when they work to advance the overall wealth of the society, and they will protect those inhabitants whom they've come to rely upon for their continued survival and improved well-being.

It is in situations where takers provide benefits for others (e.g. protection, survival techniques and innovations, etc.) that both takers and others are vulnerable to complexification. For instance, takers, as leaders, can become frustrated when followers cannot or will not do as the leaders suggest. As leaders develop track records of successful leadership, where their opinions and decisions have lead to successful results that have benefited all (or the majority), and especially where these leaders have developed a position of high status or regard among their fellows, they might be inclined not only to believe they are right in situations where they have not sufficiently thought out their opinions or decisions but also that they are right in every opinion they have and in every decision that they make. Likewise, in these situations, the followers who have benefited by following the lead of the leaders might tend to believe the leaders even when they might disagree with them; they might follow them despite their misgivings.

When you couple this tendency to follow successful leaders with the vulnerability to succumb to shows of domination, we have the breeding ground for complexification. Here all is needed is the natural shows of frustration on the part of the leaders, who are also takers, to prompt followers, who are also weak self-asserters or givers, to submit to the dominating behavior of the leaders. At this crucial point, leaders become rulers and followers become the ruled. Hierarchy is born.

If hierarchies of any significance have not been formed in a society, and this society becomes "invaders" of lands already occupied and/or used by others, the "invaders" will naturally feel obligated at least to assess the others as to their relation to the land and felt ownership of it. This assessment derives from their egoistic concerns for their own survival and well-being; they don't want to antagonize the inhabitants if the inhabitants are assessed as potentially harmful to them. But also the "invaders" will naturally negotiate their sharing of the land with the inhabitants based on prior use. The inhabitants are already using the land; it has become an important part of their survival and well-being. The "invaders" will tend to recognize this fact and be sensitive to the needs of the inhabitants.

But if hierarchies of any significance are formed in a society, and this society produces invaders of lands already occupied and/or used by others, then the invaders, as takers, will tend to assess the possibility of being harmed by the inhabitants before they act. This assessment derives from egoistic concerns for survival and well-being. If they assess their ability to harm as weak, then the invaders will try to impose their wills upon the inhabitants by killing them and taking their land, invading them and enslaving them, invading them and forcing them to integrate themselves into the new society, etc.

For example, Hitler, as a hierarchical (totalitarian) taker, assessed Russia as inferior in strength to Germany and therefore sought to take over Russian land and resources and to kill or enslave the population. Hitler disregarded the fact that the Russians had prior use of the land and resources that he wanted. He was able to overcome any sense of respect he might have felt for the survival and well-being of a people who were using a land for their survival and well-being. His identity had become so distorted that he was unaware of any experience he might have had of respect for another person's survival and well-being, and, hence, respect for their use of the land that helped provide them with their survival and well-being. He was a true invader. He assumed he was superior to the Russians and 'justified' his invasion of land that others were using for their survival and well-being.

Compare this example to that of the early Americans who interacted with the Indians living on lands (e.g. through housing, cultivating plots of land surrounding villages, etc.) while using vast areas of land for hunting. Initially, Europeans found small groups of Indians that were similar in language and custom and that possessed political and social unity. R. Douglas Hurt compares these groups or villages with the city states of ancient Greece (Hurt, 1987). The villages were self-governing and each owned or controlled a particular territory. Territories of land, comprised of villages (groups of "houses"), cultivated lands (gardens or small farms), and hunting grounds extending out from the villages tended to be respected by other groups of Indians.

Hurt argues that Europeans (early Americans) didn't quite understand these autonomous groupings of Indians for what they were; rather, they tended to understand them as tribes of people organized under a central authority (chief) because it was easier to negotiate with one person rather than with a group and because this is the organizational form (i.e. hierarchy) to which they had become accustomed or habituated.

312

These groups of people consisted of family and extended family members, clustered into lineages, identifying themselves by the use of totems. These lineages combined into autonomous groups that claimed (assumed) collective or communal ownership of some land (e.g. hunting grounds) and individual ownership of other land (e.g. houses, gardens, small farms, etc.)

A village chief or headman would determine who gets what lands to live on and cultivate; such decisions were determined by the size of the lineage. Each lineage got the amount of land necessary for their survival and well-being.

These chiefs or headmen seemed to act more like leaders than rulers. They were consulted and respected for their wisdom and advice, but they were not invested with unilateral power nor allowed to enforce that power through punitive means. Such acts of enforcement would have been viewed by others as evidence of an "upstart," and soon the "upstart" would either no longer be respected or he/she would be punished by the others.

One can easily see the vulnerable situation that leaders place themselves in when they achieve their leadership roles through their own qualities in conjunction with their successful track record of fruitful decision-making. But no amount of trust in the accuracy of a leader's decisions will cause one to forfeit one's own self-direction in any given situation. It might well lead one to make some trust mistakes, where one disregards one's own sense of self-direction in favor of that of the leader, but it will tend not to lead to a forfeiture of one's own self-direction. That forfeiture of will is caused by an identity distortion, i.e. an experiential alteration of identity due to some form of psychological (emotional), physical, or sexual abuse.

The identities of the Europeans who invaded America had already been significantly distorted by thousands of years of abuse. Evidence of such distortion lay in the construction of political monarchies, totalitarian regimes and other autocratic and oligarchic political structures where most of the people in the "group" allowed themselves to be dominated by a single person or small group of people.

The Indians in America had not yet reached that degree of identity distortion. Their groupings did not generally consist of a ruler "imbued" with unilateral power to determine law and enforce his determinations accordingly. Rather, chiefs were generally considered to be wise and respected consultants. When such wisdom was accepted as law (and enforced accordingly), a cooperative group transformed itself into a dominant:submissive hierarchy. Such 'acceptance' did not occur naturally but was the result of a forfeiture of will in the face of aggression. The leader became ruler out of a frustration of will (e.g. they won't do what I want them to do), shows of force (e.g. do what I say, you fool, idiot, savage, subhuman, underling, employee, etc.) and a submission to force (e.g. I will obey…for my own good, because you are better than me, because I'm worth less than you, etc.) Rulership is obtained through some form of psychological abuse (e.g. I am better than you, therefore you must obey me), some form of physical abuse (e.g. I can beat you into submission, therefore you must obey me), or some form of sexual abuse (e.g. I can force myself on you sexually or take advantage of your sexual innocence, at will, and therefore you must obey me).

Proposition 83:   The extent to which hunter-gatherer bands throughout history have engaged in dominant:submissive relationships and hierarchy construction is the extent to which human identities have been distorted in hunter-gatherer organizations.

Theoretical Extension: Land, Agriculture, Husbandry and Private Property

If a male and female adult constitute a minimal social unit (proposition 5); and if a female adult and a child constitute another minimal social unit, which constitutes the propagation of the species; and if a child requires nurturance (i.e. social contact) in order to live (i.e. rearing); then a basic social unit in human society is the family. Whether that family is a biologically related mother, father and children (i.e. nuclear family), separate from other nuclear families; or an extended family, where child-rearing is a multi-layered family endeavor; or a communal family, where child-rearing is the job of multiple nuclear families constituting a group is unclear at this point. All of the above systems have been used in human history. Let us look deeper into this issue.

If the hunter-gatherer small agricultural bands (villages) of North America were structured in a quasi-egalitarian manner, where "chiefs" were more akin to leaders with authority rather than rulers with power, and if these bands consisted of a number of interconnected lineages (i.e. biologically related families), where these lineages were allotted land based on their needs rather than on the wishes or will of the chief, then American Indian bands were more democratically or egalitarian-structured than their European counterparts. European countries had already developed extensive hierarchies, usually in the form of monarchies. Self-direction was discouraged or punished in these political organizations unless it advanced the interests of the monarchy. Many civil activities were performed "by your leave," or with permission of the monarchy. The economic system in place at this time was one of mercantilism. Legitimate merchants were in business to increase the wealth of the monarchy or the monarchically-run nation and not simply their own wealth. Merchants requiring government subsidies for conducting their business had to act in accordance with government require-ments. Merchants that did not require government subsidies were allowed to act independently of the government and to accrue wealth independently as long as their activities were within the law.

American Indians tended to understand their ownership of the land upon which they lived and tilled as "use ownership." They owned it as long as they were using it (cultivating it, being housed on it, etc.); when not in use, the land could be used by others for hunting, gathering, fishing, etc., at least until it was used by others for cultivation. Indians would have had problems with other Indians in their own village who might try to invade the land upon which they lived (i.e. were housed) or where they worked and reaped the produce (i.e. small farms). In this sense, the idea of ownership was similar to that of Europeans. But it was not similar in that for Indians (at least some tribes), when land was not being used for living or cultivation, it became available for collective use. European understanding of ownership continued to apply to land even when not in use. The Indians practiced "use ownership" so that everybody got what they needed for survival and well-being, no one hoarded land, and no one developed status based on land ownership (Johnson & Earle, 2000).

But the land where Indians hunted was different. They claimed communal ownership of that land and all Indians in the village could hunt on it without reprisals. "Invaders" (either other villages or the Europeans) could also hunt on the land as long as there was enough game to go around. Each group's behavior in relation to the land was determined by explicit or implicit negotiation. Extending communal ownership to others usually didn't present a problem for the Indians unless others chose not to recognize any ownership of the land or the contents therein at all (i.e. rejected communal ownership by the Indians and understood the land to be free for the taking) or assumed equal communal ownership of the land without some form of negotiation. The first constituted a serious breach of felt property rights; the second constituted a violation of protocol or a case of bad manners.

Some European countries respected ownership rights based on prior use and mandated that their countrymen acquire land through mutually agreed upon purchase prices. But the American government was often unable or unwilling to enforce these laws when settlers "squatted" on sections of hunting grounds, claimed exclusive ownership, and defended the land they took over. This "squatting" constituted a major breach of felt property rights from the Indians' point of view. Often when the Indians petitioned the American government to remove the settlers, it did not. Instead, in some cases, the government compensated the Indians for the loss of their land (on the government's terms or in conjunction with the Indians, though how free the Indians were in agreeing with the terms of compensation was questionable) (Hurt, 1987).

Some European "invaders" (i.e. people who came upon desired land already inhabited and used by other people) recognized their natural obligation to assess the relationship of the inhabitants to the land they inhabited and to negotiate a method of sharing that land if their assessments bore out the willingness of the inhabitants to do so. For example, the Spanish government recognized Indian title to land by right of occupancy; it did not sanction the acquisition of land by force of arms. The French government, on the other hand, did not recognize such ownership rights, not even in relation to the land Indians were cultivating. Rather, they tended to take possession of an area and then negotiated a treaty with the Indians afterward, making the Indians subjects of the crown (Hurt, 1987).

In deontological terms, the Spanish "invaders," at least ostensibly, and only in some cases, treated the Indians as ends and not as means to their own ends, and the French invaders, at least in many cases, treated the Indians as means to their own ends (i.e. as objects and not as people). Puritans had trouble over whether or not a white man could occupy land that the Indians already claimed, but they landed up solving their dilemma by arguing in the affirmative. They based their reasoning on two principles: 1) the Indians did not possess the land by natural right, and 2) the word of God (Bible) commanded man to occupy the earth (Hurt, 1987).

In experiential terms, the Puritans were able to distort their own experience after having assessed the connection between the Indians and the land to be one of ownership by occupancy and use of resources for survival and well-being. Their experienced obligation to negotiate methods of sharing gave way to frustration in not getting what they wanted from the Indians through negotiation; frustration expressed itself in forceful appropriation of land; the shame felt in appropriating land in this manner was experienced but immediately rejected and replaced by the false self of a felt superiority (e.g. I'm better or more civilized than you). This false self found support in the meta-experiential construct of Christian salvation. The Puritans justified their shameful acts, at least in part, by employing the idea that they were not only more civilized in those ways mentioned above but also saved by the grace of an objective God, a God of which the Indians had little or no idea.

In experiential terms, the Spanish "invaders," were either trying to act consistently with their experience in regard to the occupancy rights (i.e. experiential ownership with attached value for survival and well-being) of the Indians (i.e. sincerely or authentically) or were only faking their respect for prior occupancy in order to manipulate the Indians into giving over their lands to the Spanish for Spain's self-interest. If the former, then Spain's "invasion" was experientially moral; if the later, then Spain's invasion was experientially immoral.

Inasmuch as the French disregarded prior occupancy rights of the Indians and simply took their land by force, they acted inconsistently with themselves. Experientially, it will be argued here, the French would have participated in a natural (SSR) experience of needing to assess Indian relationships to the land and to negotiate a method of sharing the land with them. This assessment/negotiation experience (or set of experiences) would have had to be negated in some manner in order for the French to be able to take the Indian land and negotiate treaties later without feeling ashamed in doing so. It will be hypothesized here that the French believed that they were more civilized than the Indians, that they were more advanced in various technologies, were better able to cultivate the land, were considerably more knowledgeable in the science of husbandry, had developed a scientific detachment of mind from the land and, hence, were able to alter and exploit the land to their advantage, had developed some industry, which created many alternative forms of production, had developed money to better exchange goods, and possessed a religion that supposedly gave them spiritual connections to an objective world. Outright felt superiority was couched in scientific, techno-nogical (especially military weaponry) and religious terms.

The European case against the Indians was mainly that the Indians' claim to vast hunting grounds made it difficult for European farmers and settlers to claim land for their own use, to cultivate it in a more efficient manner and to raise stock on a much greater level than that already practiced by the Indians, and, hence, to provide more people (Europeans and Indians alike) with a means for their survival and well-being. The Europeans thought that there was plenty of land to go around but that the Indians had to give up hunting and gathering in favor of more efficient farming and husbandry. With the development of husbandry there would be much less need to hunt; with much less need to hunt, the need to maintain free hunting grounds would disappear; when the need to maintain free hunting grounds disappeared, others would be able to claim ownership of new land and make use of it accordingly.

It wasn't that the Europeans had a poor argument for their use of land in America; on the contrary, their argument made a great deal of sense. Their farming methods tended to be more productive and efficient than those practiced by the Indians; their knowledge of technology facilitated this productivity and efficiency; and all of this provided more people with the means to survive and live well on less land.

But European motives for settling this new land were varied: some wanted to create a new life for themselves, new opportunities, free from the governmental oppression experienced in their homeland; many others wanted to extract the resources from the new land to increase their own wealth and the wealth of their country or empire. Not only were the motives varied, but they were also mixed. Those seeking freedom from oppression in their homeland often reversed that oppression by dominating the Indians in the new land.

Early American government made attempts to buy land from the Indians and parcel it out to settlers to farm. Indians were unfamiliar with such ways of treating land. Europeans, and later Americans, endowed "Indian tribes" (collections of independent Indian villages) with de facto ownership of the land they inhabited or used for their survival and well-being. But the Indians didn't understand this. They didn't understand ownership of land in the way Europeans and early Americans did. Their experience of the daily use of the land (i.e. housing and small farms) was similar to that of the Europeans in that those owners did not let others simply take their land our house away from them. But the underlying reason they would defend their land was that they were using it for their survival and well-being and not because they owned it outright. Owning land outright, exclusively of using it, was foreign to the Indian mind. They understood it more like they were entrusted with the land, to be passed on to future generations for their use (Hurt, 1987).

The libertarian (Lockean) idea that ownership of a resource is determined by mixing one's labor with that resource was, at least for some Indians, strictly adhered to. Only when the land was in use was it owned by anyone; when it went out of use, it changed to communal ownership and could be used as anyone saw fit; or it could be taken over by others and used exclusively of others.

Actually, the American Indians, for the most part, adhered to the libertarian theory of justice in acquisition more faithfully than did the Europeans. For the Indians, you had to *be* mixing your labor with the land in order to own the land, whereas for the Europeans, you could mix your labor with the land one time and that was sufficient for you to own the land. Such ownership was disconnected from use; land was conceived as a commodity and only indirectly connected to one's survival and well-being. When the Europeans ran into the Indians, they had already developed the idea that land was a commodity and something that could be "sold on the market."

Probing Question: How did it happen that hunter-gatherers, who claimed territorial rights based on daily use (living or cultivating) or daily or periodic use (hunting) to ownership of land as a commodity (owned whether it was being used or not, and transferred as one saw fit)?

Theoretical Extension: Land Use vs. Land Ownership

To answer this question, we have to delve a little deeper into this distinction between "land use" or "land tenure" and "land ownership." Land tenure has been so far defined as the exclusive use of land for a period of time. When that land falls out of use, then it becomes collective land to be used by others as they see fit. In this sense, Indian clans could use a plot of land for cultivation, and no other Indians (or Europeans) could use it at all. Hunters could not hunt on it even when there were animals on the land. The use of the land was not only restricted to the clan using it but to the use itself; it was land to be cultivated only. When the clan departed from the land, the land automatically went back to collective ownership, and other Indians could use it for whatever they wanted, e.g. hunting, gathering, fishing, etc.

So if an Indian clan were allotted a parcel of land that consisted of soil and a river, and the river contained fish, and the river on the land, though not being used very often, if at all, for fishing by the clan, was still be unable to be used by others (e.g. fisherman) because it lay on the land tenured by the clan, then was the land tenure practiced by the Indians more akin to the land ownership practiced by the Europeans than we are led to believe?

If a demarcated parcel of land allotted to a clan consisted of a variety of land formations containing a variety of resources for the possible acquisition of others was understood to be exclusively used for one purpose only and by one clan only, despite the possible uses of the land by others, then land tenure was very close in practice to land ownership.

But what if an Indian clan allotted a parcel of land for cultivation used a portion of the land for cultivation and the rest for recreation? Would the chief have to reconsider his allotment and re-allot the clan a smaller portion of land because he had originally misjudged how much land this clan needed for their survival and well-being? Or would the chief (and the village) recognize the clan's optional use of the land as legitimate? Who is to decide how the land is to be used, and by whom? Who is to use the parcel of land and how is it to be used?

If a specific number of people are allowed to use the land, and the land is to be used for a specific purpose, regardless of other purposes it might be used for, and despite how many people could use parts of the land for other purposes, even while the land is being used for a specific purpose by a specific group of people, then tenured land and owned land are virtually the same.

Also, if tenured land is land used in a custodial manner with the intention of having future generations use the land in a similar way, then tenured land is, again, a lot like owned land. It is passed down from generation to generation and exclusive of others using the land for their own purposes. Either way, tenured or owned, land is used exclusively of others and that exclusive use is intergenerational.

But how the land is used might well be a social determination. For example, once a parcel of land has been allotted by the chief (who is supposed to represent the village) for agricultural use, it is expected to be used as such. Others will recognize the legitimacy of the allocation when its purpose is realized as long as its purpose is understood to be legitimate by all. In cases where the land is allotted for agriculture for the purpose of survival and well-being of the clan and any other social value that the clan's agricultural efforts might have, then the clan is communally expected (obligated?) to till the land. If the clan chooses to till half the land and use the other half for recreation, without community repercussion, then the land is even closer to European ownership of land. If there are no conditions set by the community for the use of the land, then those using the land own the land and can do with it as they see fit. But it seems that Indians were communally expected to use the land for reasons that the community valued: agriculture for survival and well-being. The use of a parcel of land was the result of a communal agreement. The conditions of the agreement were communally determined; the chief acted as the communal facilitator. Violations of the communal agreement would be subject to sanction.

Is the European notion of land ownership similar? When the Europeans procured land from the Indians, they did so with the assumption that the Indians' use of the land and the contents therein constituted a type of de facto ownership of the land. Also, if Indians claimed sovereignty over large parcels of land for hunting, and these claims were respected by other villages, then other villages couldn't simply grab up portions of claimed territory for their own use. They had either 1) to respect that sovereignty, 2) negotiate with the village to alter territorial boundaries, or 3) impose their wills upon the village and take whatever land they might want.

If this is so, then Indian claims of sovereignty over specific parcels of land, whether used for living, cultivating, or hunting, that were held in trust for future generations was very similar to European notions of land ownership. It's just that land used for living was allotted to specific families; land used for cultivating was allotted to specific clans; and land used for hunting was held communally.

One difference between Indian "ownership" and European "ownership" of land rested upon the notion that when Indians no longer used the land, it went back to communal ownership. Europeans didn't have a notion of communal ownership in this sense, but they did have a notion of public land, and in democratic countries, public land, and the resources therein, is roughly equivalent to communally owned resources. Public tax money is equivalent to communal ownership.

It's not that Indian ways of understanding land and land use was so different from that of Europeans; it's more that some of their ways of distributing land was fundamentally different from European methods of distribution. For instance, the Iroquois and Huron Indians allotted only as much land as needed for a clan's survival and well-being. Survival and well-being was inextricably connected to use. Land that was unused or disposable was excessive. These tribes ruled out excessive accumulation of land and the status that might go with it.

Such methods of distribution aligned quite well with a Christian understanding of land acquisition and use. Christianity condemned greed, arguing that the accumulation of resources over and above that which is needed and reasonably wanted for well-being, was to over-attach ourselves to temporal things. In a modern psychological interpretation of Christian tenets, it is psychologically unhealthy for people to value resources over and above their treatment of others. In this context, if we care more for acquiring land than we do for others' survival and well-being, then our identities depend more upon temporal than eternal things (e.g. land vs. justice). That is, our own survival and well-being are inextricably fused with the accumulation of land as opposed to using that amount of land that will secure our survival and well-being.

In this sense, Christian and Indian methods of land distribution are in agreement. Those Europeans who sought to acquire land from Indians by purchase or barter for their own use toward their survival and well-being were acting consistently with Christian tenets, Indian tenets, and Locke's first and second proviso (inasmuch as the first proviso can be met). It was only when Europeans and Americans imposed their wills upon the Indians and either took "their land" outright or made deals with the Indians and did not enforce them (e.g. allowed squatters to take Indian land) that meta-experiential constructs were used to 'justify' their impositions of will, e.g. Europeans were superior to Indians for various reasons.

What distinguished European ownership from Indian "ownership" or "tenure" of land was more the means of commerce than the actual relationships to the land and to each other. Europeans used money as a means of exchange; Indians bartered goods. Hence, Europeans were able to convert land into money and money into land. If public land was purchased by people for private use, then the land was generally to be used as the purchaser saw fit. Such commercial transactions removed the necessary connection between land and its use; it could virtually be used for nothing; it could be used as an investment to be sold at a later date. Land became a commodity when money abstracted resources from their natural uses. All resources shifted from barter value to commercial value with the introduction of money.

Also, Europeans tended to have more freedoms attached to land ownership than did Indians. Europeans were less collective in their thinking than the Indians. When land was allotted to American settlers, the land could be used by the settlers for whatever they wanted; there were fewer restrictions placed on land use and there was less pressure from the community (i.e. government) to use the land as the community wanted it to be used.

As hunter-gatherers in Europe learned that acts of aggression (often out of frustration or fear) imposed upon others tended to cause others to fear the aggressors, those aggressed against were vulnerable to complexification. When those aggressive acts were not repelled, warded off, or punished by the individual or the group and instead were submitted to, then the aggressor established a dominant: submissive relationship with those aggressed against. Such interactions constitute abuse. Once an abusive (or dominant: submissive) relationship is established, the dominator must justify his dominance. He must justify his overriding of the other's natural self-direction.

The French overrode the self-direction of the Indians by sheer force. Their superior weaponry allowed them to take what they wanted and their meta-experiential constructs allowed them to 'justify' their unilateral force. The same would apply to the Puritans, though the Puritans might have had more qualms about doing what they did. They had to find Biblical justification for their imposition of will and their usurpation of Indian land for their own use. But both French and Puritan methods were similar in that both thought themselves to be not only superior to the Indians in many ways (this is natural in comparing people with each other) but also as in possession of an objective reality, e.g. Christianity, being 'civilized', the Indians being 'savages' (this is a distortion of reality because objective reality is an experiential impossibility), and this possession 'allowed' them to impose themselves upon the Indians 'for their own good'.

Proposition 84: It is natural for people to compare themselves with others in regard to intelligence, skills, experience, capacity, and knowledge in relation to the acquisition of valued resources.

If all or most people in a group value a given resource (i.e. the resource aids in their survival and/or well-being), then they will tend to value those who can acquire that resource, if those who acquire that resource share the resource with others. A system of valuation of people has (erroneously) been referred to as a status hierarchy. Actually, there is no hierarchical element in "status hierarchies." There is no unilateral power granted to those who achieve status among others. Rather, there is a trust in the effectiveness of those who supply others with resources for their survival and well-being, and, at most, there is a vulnerability in others to expect those who supply them with resources to continue to do so, sometimes to the point of force, manipulation, or coercion. Those who have become habituated to the supply of resources coming from certain people (of status) are susceptible to making demands (imposing their wills) upon those individuals when those resources are not forthcoming. If those who have achieved status succumb to the pressures (demands) of others, then complexification occurs. At this point, the status achiever understands himself not "through his own eyes," but "through the eyes of others." He forfeits self-direction in favor or other-direction. He comes to assess himself in terms of others rather

324

than on his own terms, i.e. terms consistent with his actual SSR experience. This type of complexification could occur in response to group pressure. It is evident in situations of tyranny of the majority. It is a vulnerability inherent in democracies.

Proposition 85: It is natural for people to compare themselves with each other in regard to the amounts of resources that they acquire but only when those amounts are reflective of the labor put into acquiring them.

In egalitarian (and hierarchical groups), leaders can gain status by having a lot of resources, but this status is dependent upon the perceived direct connection between the amount of resources and the amount of labor that went into acquiring those resources. When little labor is attached to the acquisition of many resources, the status of the leader will decline. Leaders in egalitarian groups can accumulate resources and achieve status if others are aware of the amount of labor expended by the leader to attain those resources.

But in situations where leaders obviously violate Locke's first proviso and make others situations worse off by claiming exclusive ownership of those resources and not sharing them with others, despite the labor that is seemingly commensurate with the amount of resources acquired, will suffer a status decline. This is why those who inherit resources (or money) rather than working for them are held in less social esteem than those who work for them.

Proposition 86: It is a distortion of reality for people to think of themselves as superior to others based on the amount of resources they acquire and do not share with others.

Proposition 87: It is a distortion of reality for people to believe that others who have acquired a lot of resources without sharing them with others are superior to one self.

A leader gains status by being able to make decisions that aid followers in their quest for survival and well-being. The status gained could rest upon primarily egoistic grounds, e.g. "I value what you have done for me," or a combination of egoistic and altruistic grounds, e.g. "If you do for me, I will do for you" (reciprocal altruism), or primarily on altruistic grounds, e.g. "I will be loyal to you even when I might doubt your decisions."

If a leader's decisions (opinions on possible courses of action) prove to benefit the leader at the expense of the followers, then the leader's status will tend to diminish; his decisions hurt the followers. If a leader's decisions prove to benefit the leader and not the followers but do not harm the followers, then the status of the leader will tend to diminish; the leader will be viewed as selfish or self-serving but not harmful. He won't be viewed as leading but rather as manipulating.

In order for this phenomenon to reverse itself, i.e. in order for a leader to gain status when he acts selfishly, something must happen to those involved to distort natural responses to selfishness. The leader somehow comes to believe that he can not only impose his will upon the followers but that he 'should' impose that will upon them; he believes that the imposition is 'for their own good' or that he is entitled to do so. And the followers somehow come to believe that the leader 'should' impose his will upon them and that they owe loyalty to the leader, regardless of what they might think of his decisions.

It is offered here that such distortions of nature occur in the wake of abuse. When a leader abuses others by bullying, intimidating, punishing, emotionally harming, physically harming, or sexually harming others who don't agree with his opinion or refuse to act upon his decisions, then the leader is in position to become a ruler. When the followers don't assert themselves or stand up to the leader who is attempting, consciously or unconsciously, to transcend his bounds, and, instead, submit to the will of the leader, then the followers transform themselves into the ruled. Dominant:submissive relationships are formed.

When dominant:submissive relationships are formed, rulers come to expect and demand the ruled to follow, and the ruled come to expect and demand rulers to tell them what to do. In this environment, rulers who acquire resources at the expense of, or through indifference to, the ruled will tend to think that they deserve those resources, and the ruled will also tend to think that the rulers deserve those resources. Such is the psychology of domination and submission.

Theoretical Extension: Contemporary Business and Hierarchy
Most of today's businesses are structured hierarchically. As such, they are expressive of dominant:submissive relationships. Employers legally dominate employees, and employees allow themselves to be dominated.   The clause in the employment contract, whether communicated explicitly or implicitly, requiring the employee to do "anything else that the employer requires," 'permits' the employer to dominate the employee. We'll refer to this clause as *the slave clause*.

At the very beginnings of a business enterprise, entrepreneurs are legally required to organize their businesses hierarchically. Whether they run them hierarchically or not is up to them. The reason given for this law is that someone must be held liable if the business harms someone in some way, i.e. it is supposed to protect the public and the employees of the business.

The convoluted thinking behind this law and its 'justification' is extensive. In order to expose the convoluted nature of this thinking, I will have to employ a wealth of transdisciplinary means and methods.

When one person wants another person to cooperate with him (let's say) in order to achieve his survival and well-being, then the person soliciting the cooperation acts as a free agent in his own self-interest (we'll say). Since, in this case, we will say, he needs the cooperation of the other person in order to achieve his survival and well-being, he wants to maximize his chances of obtaining that cooperation (i.e. egoism). He wants to present his proposition to the person in a way that will result in that person's agreement.

This cooperation is naturally achieved when the person being solicited not only agrees to the terms of cooperation but also believes that the person presenting the terms is sincere and is not in any way manipulating or defrauding him. In deontological terms, each person in the transaction is being treated as an end in him or herself and not as a means to an end.

Experientially, the requirements for a transaction to be real and moral are that each person must be participating in an SSR structure when that transaction occurs.   That is, each person's experiential structure is devoid of complexity.

When one person sets the rules of cooperation, without the free consent of the other, then one tends to dominate the terms of cooperation. When an employer unilaterally determines the terms of cooperation, an employee is forced to accept those terms or not be employed with that employer. When the prospective employee accepts the terms that include the "slave clause," then the employee 'freely' accepts a form of slavery. Such an acceptance is a distortion of reality.

Probing Question: How is a prospective employee's acceptance (signing) of a contract which includes the slave clause a distortion of reality? After all, it is such a common practice that it is considered by many to be quite normal, at least in business?

Theoretical Response: Any contract that includes a clause such as "And anything else that management requires" presumes that management can legitimately 'require' virtually anything of the prospective employee, including submission to a total revision of the original contract items. Managers automatically *assume* that they can require a prospective employee to do X, Y and Z even if X, Y, and Z were not in the original contract simply because X, Y, and Z are embedded in the "slave clause." This very assumption indicates that the terms of cooperation are not requests but demands and that the power of the employee to determine any part of his employment is null and void. It is wholly dependent upon the will of the employer; and this will is backed by law.

Since this contract clause nullifies any power that the employee has to determine his own behavior on the job and invests that power in the employer alone, then calling it a slave clause seems wholly justified. Prospective employees virtually sign away their freedom to determine their own future behavior when they sign a contract that contains that clause.

Theoretical Objection: One might object, arguing that slaves of old (i.e. in early America) were forced to work on the plantations under threat of severe punishment; they were considered chattel, owned by the masters. Modern day employees are not forced to work at a particular job; they can leave their place of employment, and they are not considered to be chattel. Hence, they are not slaves, and to call this clause, which is obviously included in contracts to give management a means of control over employees as the forces of the market change, a "slave clause" is at best hyperbole and at least inaccurate.

Theoretical Extension: Contemporary Business and Slavery

Simply because the slaves of old were physically forced to work on plantations does not mean that contemporary employees are not forced to work at a job. When the bulk of the world's resources have already been acquired by a relatively small number of people (e.g. the richest 400 Americans now own more wealth than the bottom 180 million taken together (Alperovitz and Bhatt, 2012)), and the means of obtaining any of those resources is already determined by those who own them (i.e. businesses), and those who own them have legal sanction to impose unilateral power on others (i.e. employers vs. employees), then the choices of those who wish to obtain a share of the resources are severely limited by an economic system that not only allows the few to dominate the many but legally requires them to do so.

One can be forced to do a job by direct physical coercion, or one can be forced to do a job when those jobs are limited to only a few options.   Either way, if one is to survive and live at least somewhat well, then one must "adjust to the system," whether that system is racial slavery or modern, hierarchically-structured business.   The difference is that racial slavery has been outlawed and hierarchically structured business has not; it *is* the law.

It can be argued that early American slavery employed punitive methods to control the behavior of the slaves; slaves were beaten and sometimes lynched when they violated the rules set up by their masters, in conjunction with the government.

But the same seems to be true of business today, though the severity of the punitive measures has been lessened. Today, people get wage cuts, demotions, and fired for not acting in full accord with the demands of employers. Granted, these measures are not of the caliber of flogging or lynching, but they are still essentially punitive, i.e. they harm; and the harm is unilateral.

But one might argue that employees can quit if they don't like how they are treated. This is true. But then do what? Get a job with another employer (master); perhaps a better one, where the employer is more understanding, or will not alter a job description without first consulting the employee?

When the rules or laws (i.e. business by-laws or policy and procedure) are set up by the few (or the one), and sanctioned by the government, to be imposed upon the many (by a type of "forced choice"), then the few dominate the many.

Inasmuch as the government allows (and even requires) the few to dominate the many, it is complicit in creating and sustaining dominant:submissive relationships. Inasmuch as the government intervenes on the side of those dominated (e.g. through minimum wage laws, work safety regulations, etc.), the extent of the domination is moderated. In modern democracies that permit hierarchy in business, the government seeks to moderate the harm done to employees, customers and communities by employers while allowing or requiring employers to dominate employees.

It takes little insight to recognize the contradiction in this practice: employers legally dominate employees while the harm that such domination causes is mitigated by the law. It is like saying, "We are allowed or even required (by law) to dominate you, but the law requires us to moderate our domination."

The fact is, when rules or laws are determined by the few and imposed upon the many, the system is one of domination: submission. Monarchies have been overturned in favor of democracies in parts of the world because the domination of the one (in conjunction with others, i.e. royals, the court, the committee, etc.) proved untenable to the many. The monarch owned most of the resources that made it possible for people to survive and live well. The oppression that this caused the subjects eventually resulted in revolt.

Similarly, the "monarchs" of business (i.e. the CEOs, presidents, etc.) in conjunction with others (i.e. governing boards, stockholders) own the resources that make it possible for people to survive and live well. In addition, like their monarchical counterparts, these business "monarchs" dominate employees by determining the rules and regulations with which employees must comply if they are to survive and live reasonably well.

When rules and regulations are determined by the one (or the few) and imposed upon the many, then the experiential realities of the one (or the few) and the many are subject to distortion. When a prospective employee agrees to do A-H, where A-H are tasks reasonably understandable and acceptable to the prospective employee, then the employee will be justly held responsible for performing those tasks. This not only meets the requirements set by deontology to treat people as ends and not means to an end, but it also meets the experiential requirement of treating people as experiential beings: the terms of cooperation are freely agreed upon; a promise of cooperation and a commitment to future behavior has been made; the promise or commitment experience is SSR or authentic inasmuch as the prospective employee truly understands what he is to do and agrees to do it, and the employer truly understands what he wants the employee to do. But when the "slave clause" is included in any contract, then the prospective employee, at best, feels he has to sign the contract if he is to get the job at all, regardless of whether or not he agrees to that clause (forced employment), because overwhelmingly most other jobs have the same clause. He'd rather commit to tasks he understands and accepts, but the "deck is already stacked" and he has little or nothing to say about it, i.e. he must "adjust to the system."

Marx argued that in capitalist economies labor (i.e. the proletariat) is pitted against the employers (i.e. the bourgeoisie) because the employers own the means of production and labor owns only their behavior. Labor has to sell their behavior in order to gain economic compensation (wages). Labor becomes alienated from their own behavior.

Such a critique resonates with the experiential criticism that under current hierarchical conditions, employers who unilaterally determine the rules of cooperation and include a "slave clause" in their conditions (and are backed by government in doing so) create a system of 'cooperation' that not only alienates the employee from his own behavior by making it into a commodity to sell on the market but also by 'detaching' it from the experiential structures within which it necessarily exists.

Employees who do not fully understand and fully accept the terms of cooperation (i.e. job descriptions and policy/procedure), and yet commit to such terms, alienate themselves from their own behavior. They put themselves in position to have to behave in ways that they do not agree to behave. When the terms of any contract can be altered unilaterally by those creating the terms, without the other's full agreement, and the other is bound to act in consonance with the wishes and wills of those who create and alter the contract (and such a systems is sanctioned by law), then a distorted system of human interaction is created, i.e. one based on dominant:submissive rela-tionships.

The employer (e.g. entrepreneur, CEO, or president, in conjunction with a governing board or not) determines the rules of cooperation (policy). In capitalistic enterprises, this power is usually accompanied by start-up capital secured through a variety of possible sources, e.g. bank loans, investors, oneself, family, friends, etc. The risk taken by the employer of securing capital funds that he (or she) is responsible for paying back is often used as the justification for the unilateral determination of rules of cooperation (policy and procedure), i.e. if the employer (entrepreneur) takes the financial risk, then he can force others (employees) to behave the way he wants them to behave. Hence, the employer has the 'right' to dominate employees.

The problems with this logic are many. First, no person has the right to impose his or her will upon another person, unless that imposition is freely agreed upon by the person imposed upon. For example, a mother has the right to impose her will upon her son, who is sticking his finger in a light socket, by grabbing him away from the light socket and telling him not to do that or he'll hurt himself. The son, optimally, will come to trust his mother and limit his behavior in accordance with his mother's wishes or will. The same could happen in a business situation where a boss imposes his will upon an employee who is going to hurt herself by requiring her to act in ways consistent with her safety. Such an imposition would probably be considered legitimate.

But such impositions are not typical of business situations, quite the contrary. Most impositions in work situations occur because the employer wants to gain the employee's 'cooperation' (i.e. compliant behavior). Employers impose their wills upon employees first by unilaterally creating the rules of cooperation (policy and procedure) and then by imposing these rules upon employees (i.e. imposition by lack of choice). Then when employees do not live up to the employer's 'terms of cooperation', employers impose their wills even further by punishing employees for their behavior. Employers even feel justified for their punishment because they think that employees have freely signed a contract of employment, thus committing them to specific unknown future behaviors.

If employees have never freely signed a contract of employment, where "freely signed" means fully understanding and fully accepting the terms of employment, then there is no legitimate commitment made. The experience being engaged in by the prospective employee is not SSR or authentic. Employees tend to know that terms of employment (i.e. job descriptions) tend to contain items that are somewhat abstract, nebulous, and unclear or simply do not align perfectly with their wishes and will or that their wishes and will are somewhat unclear or vague even to themselves and, hence, they might not know exactly if their wishes and will align with the terms of the contract. This same vagueness, abstraction, and uncertainty apply to the wishes and will of the employer as he/she writes up the terms of the contract. In other words, it is difficult enough to present clear terms of a contract to a prospective employee and have those terms understood clearly by the prospective employee, and it is difficult enough for the prospective employee's wishes and will to align perfectly with the terms of the contract, but it is virtually impossible for the prospective employee to grasp in any meaningful way the possible or probable changes that might occur in his already flawed 'free' acceptance of a work contract. If he has to 'accept' the "slave clause" on top of his other uncertainties surrounding his acceptance of a work contract, he has to suspend his own trust in himself and his ability to direct his own behavior in favor of his employer's ability to legitimately direct his behavior in the future. He has to promise to trust the employer either not to change the terms of his contract (those which he can reasonably understand and agree to) or that if the employer does change some of those terms, the changes will be in accord with his own self-direction. The first trust is subject to the 'forces of the market' and the employer will probably argue that his decisions are also determined by such forces as he goes about changing employment terms; the second trust is probably more wishful thinking than a rational hope, unless the employee has some reason to believe that the employer would be willing to accept a rejection of new terms on the part of the employee and work to negotiate mutually acceptable terms.

Employers have become accustomed to setting the terms of employment, altering those terms as they see fit (i.e. as 'market forces' determine), and forcing or coercing employees to submit to those alterations, or face punishment. And this custom rests in good part on the supposed justification that the employer has taken the financial risk for the existence of the company and therefore has 'earned the right' to impose terms of employment upon others. This entire process is sanctioned by law.

When a prospective employee signs an employment contract, the experiential structure within which he participates usually consists of some doubts and uncertainties in relation to the actual, present-day terms. The degree to which he overrides his doubts and uncertainties determines the degree to which his experiential structure is subject to complexity, but such complexity might well be within the limits of "reasonable doubt," i.e. no decision is going to be perfectly in accord with anyone's wants and wishes; one will commit oneself to behavior that is vague, uncertain, or questionable, but one usually does so because one either desires the job despite the uncertain terms, believes he can mold the job to fit his own interests, or that he needs the job when jobs in his area are scarce and is therefore willing to compromise himself. These overridden doubts and uncertainties can be subsumed under the concept of "reasonable doubt" without registering as a complex structure.

But when the "slave clause" is included in the job contract, then reasonable doubts and uncertainties transform into complexity. Trust in oneself and in the present-day terms of employment is transformed into trust in the unilateral decisions made by the employer in regard to the future behavior of the prospective employee. The basis for the employee's future behavior is transferred to the employer. He no longer owns his own behavior-in-the-future. He has surrendered that to the employer. Rational doubt is replaced by the irrational forfeiture of self-direction. Prospective employees forfeit their right to self-direction-in-the-future and are held to that forfeiture as if it were freely engaged in by a rational agent.

At the root of Marx's criticism of capitalism being an alienating ideology and practice lies the power differential between employer and employee as well as the fact that the employer (capitalist) owns the means of production in addition to his own labor, whereas the employee owns only his own labor. Both the power differential and the ownership disparity create worker alienation.

In experiential terms, worker alienation is the experience of complexity; it is the experience of employees submitting to the terms of employment established only by the employers and not in consonance with the employees. It is the alienation and complexity inherent in hierarchy.

Theoretical Objection: If the employer (capitalist) is the one willing to risk his capital (owned or borrowed) in creating a business, then he earns the right to determine the "rules of cooperation" unilaterally. He is the one who loses if the business goes bust, not the employees, who risk nothing but their labor and time, for which they are paid. It would be irrational for the employer to forfeit control of the behavior of his employees when he stands to lose everything he has invested in the project.

Theoretical Response: If someone has an idea for a business and needs others to cooperate with him in order to realize his idea, then he would naturally propose his idea to others and see whether or not they want to cooperate with him to realize his idea. If they do not want to cooperate with him, then he might need to present the idea differently in order to gain their cooperation. If others are interested in his idea and would like to participate in the endeavor but do not trust him, then he needs to gain their trust. In these types of situations, i.e. natural situations, cooperation is requested, not demanded.

In the typical, hierarchically structured, capitalist business start-up, the person with the idea (entrepreneur) does not ask people (employees) to go in on his venture with him. He does not solicit the cooperation of others (employees) based primarily on their interest in the project. He does not even approach the people who might share his interest in his project. Rather, he approaches people who can provide him with capital to start up his project. In doing so, he alienates himself from those who will eventually come to 'cooperate' with him (employees). His project is *his*, not theirs in addition to his. Their 'cooperation' becomes "employment"; he becomes the "employer"; they become the "employees."

Proposition 88: Natural cooperation requires the free solicitation of cooperation from others in regard to a proposed project.

Theoretical Extension: Free Solicitation of Cooperation in Business

It reads, "I'd like to do X; would you like to do it *with* me?" Unnatural or distorted cooperation demands the cooperation of others, if they first agree to accept the conditions for such 'cooperation'. It reads, "I'd like to do X; would you like to work *for* me?

Working *with* someone is essentially different from working *for* someone. Working *with* someone assumes the free granting of cooperation; it ensures self-direction from all partners. Working *for* someone assumes 'cooperation' under terms set by one person and imposed upon another. Working *for* someone is equivalent to forfeiting self-direction because it allows someone other than oneself to control (direct, own) one's own behavior. It alienates oneself from one's own behavior; it complexifies the experiential structure within which one participates by creating the conditions for false self construction. One must become someone other than who one *is* when one is required to do something one does not want, freely agree, or commit oneself to do. Working *for* someone puts one's identity at risk of distortion.

When the capitalist entrepreneur seeks to employ people in order to achieve his goal (start up a business), he is not soliciting their free cooperation. Rather, he is making it possible for them to forfeit their self-direction and benefit to some degree for their forfeiture. In Marx's terms, people alienate themselves from themselves by selling their labor.

Experientially, labor is another word for behavior. In SSR (authentic) experiences, behavior is consistent with the other components of consciousness. A person's identity is integrated inasmuch as the experiences she participates in are SSR. When she behaves in ways inconsistent with how she thinks, feels, and senses, then her identity is dis-integrated. She has to create a false identity in order to behave one way while being another way. When the capitalist entrepreneur unilaterally creates the terms of cooperation and invites the prospective employee to agree to those terms, he automatically distorts natural cooperation by requiring prospective employees to forfeit their self-direction and create false selves if they are to reap the benefits of employment. When he further punishes employees who have 'accepted' his terms of cooperation and have not agreed to 'honor' those terms (do as the employer demands when the 'market forces' alter terms of employment), he compounds the distortion of natural economic reality (i.e. natural cooperation). When he argues that he is justified in doing so because he takes all the financial risk without ever soliciting others freely to cooperate with him, then others are excluded by him from even considering sharing the financial responsibility with him. It doesn't cross his mind to share financial responsibility with others when forming a business because that option is not included in the "normal" ways for people to start up businesses. Natural cooperation is not a recognized option for starting up businesses in capitalist societies.

Arguing that one has the right to impose one's will upon others because one takes all the financial risks is a rationalization for imposition (dominance); hence, it is a meta-experiential construct. If no one has the right to impose his will upon another human being, unless that imposition is freely agreed upon by the person being imposed upon (i.e. their acceptance of the imposition is experientially SSR or authentic), then any 'justification' of that imposition will likely be a distortion of reality.

For an entrepreneur to think that simply because he has an idea for a business and can accrue capital to start up that business that he has the right unilaterally to set the terms of cooperation for others is to nullify the autonomy and individuality of those who 'cooperate' with him and to place himself in the position of dominance and the others in the position of submission. When others 'accept' these terms, they participate in a system of dominance:submission, with them as the submissive. They forfeit their self-direction in favor of the direction of someone else.

Secondly, when an economic system favors people who already have the money, knowledge and skills necessary to start up and run a business over those who do not (but could have them if circumstances were different), then the "business" of starting up a business lies within the purview of the few and not the many. Only people who have done what is necessary to accrue money (capital), know how to get money from those who have it to loan (banks), invest (investors, which requires contacts in the business world) or give (charity), and who possess the skills necessary to create and develop a business are likely actually to start up a business. Those without the above background will have a difficult time starting up a business.

Thirdly, conglomerates that dominate the market automatically make it more difficult for small businesses to start up and compete with them for a share of the market.

Fourthly, given the hierarchical and competitive nature of business, one must also possess a degree of aggressiveness of personality to think it's morally justifiable to impose one's will upon others through unilaterally determined 'rules of cooperation' (policy). If self-direction is a natural human trait, and this trait is consistent with intra-experiential and inter-experiential levels of consistency (i.e. individual human integrity), then a system of organization that includes the imposition of one's will (values, etc.) upon others will require a certain amount of aggression in order to make that happen in any effective manner. When an entrepreneur has an idea for a business and solicits 'cooperation' from others by imposing his will (policy) upon them (if they are to earn a living at all), and then seeks to justify that imposition by claiming a 'right' to do so based on individual initiative, he is engaging in methods of controlling the behavior of others so he can benefit and 'justifying' his domination over them by conjuring up a 'right' to do so based on self-initiative. It is similar in kind, though less in degree, to claiming the 'right' to own slaves because one took the initiative to 'procure' the slaves in the first place. Whether one forces the conditions of employment (e.g. slavery) or creates those conditions (e.g. traditional capitalism), one is imposing his will upon others, and that imposition, when it includes the "slave clause," removes any chance others might have of owning their own behavior. When a person cannot own his own behavior, he is dis-integrated; when he allows the conditions to exist whereby he does not own his own behavior, he is complicit in creating and sustaining experiential complexity, dominant:submissive relationships, or moral and ontological reality distortion.

If one wants to start a psychologically healthy, experientially moral business, one must treat others as experiential beings. This requires that one must recognize, if not honor, the self-direction of another, where "self-direction" is equivalent to the trajectory of one's SSR or authentic experiences. Who one is is determined by the experiences within which one participates that are consistent with each other on inter-experiential levels of experience. When one's identity comes into contact with another who seeks to dominate that person, one is naturally disposed to repel that domination and keep on the track of self-direction. But if one cannot repel that domination because one is too young, or too weak to do so, then one is vulnerable to identity complexification. In social terms, one is vulnerable to domination.

The mother (above) who imposes her will upon her child who is sticking his finger in a light socket is justified in doing so because the child is able authentically to realize that his mother has his best interest in mind. The entrepreneur has no such corresponding interest in his employee. He is interested in his employee only inasmuch as she does what he wants her to do. He is interested in his employee's welfare only inasmuch as it benefits him to be 'interested'. If he is to be successful in imposing his will upon others, he must be aggressive in his will to dominate and control his employees, because such cooperation does not come naturally to people (including employees). There is something unnatural or distorted in submitting to another's will when one's own will does not align with that of the other.

Dominance hierarchies developed probably not long after human beings were capable of self-reflection (in evolutionary theory) or soon after they were expelled from the Garden of Eden (in creationist theory). They occurred not because there exists a genetic structure that compels some of them to dominate others or, more specifically, some men to dominate all women and most other men, but because humans have a long history of abusing each other, altering each others' identities, creating ideological systems that 'justify' that domination and submission, and passing on those systems of domination from generation to generation through 'education'.

Probing Question: How might such a forfeiture of self-direction ever have gotten started?

Theoretical Extension: Illegitimate Impositions of Will
One likely way forfeiture of self-direction might have started is when parents illegitimately imposed their wills upon their children and children created false selves in order to survive and live somewhat well within their situations. In these cases, parents did not request cooperation from children; they demanded it. Also, in these cases, parents did not legitimately impose their wills upon their children, which would have been evidenced by their children's genuine acceptance of the imposition, but they forced, manipulated or coerced their children to 'cooperate' (i.e. do as they are told) in the face of punishment. The complexification of human identity *is* a forfeiture of self-direction. It is perpetuated through the creation of meta-experiential constructs (e.g. "spare the rod and spoil the child"; "real men control their children"; "do as I say"; "I'm the boss.")

Another likely starting point was when men, being usually stronger and more aggressive than women, imposed their wills upon women.   Similar to the parent-child situation, false selves were created and perpetuated through meta-experiential constructs (e.g. "I provide food (hunt), therefore I can dominate you"; "I protect you from predators, therefore I can dominate you."

Another likely starting point was when some men, being smarter and more aggressive than others, imposed their wills upon other men (and women) (e.g. "I know how to irrigate the land, therefore you have to do what I say"). Again, complex structures are formed and false selves are created and passed on from generation to generation (e.g. a modern version, where intellectual domination has replaced physical domination, would be "I provide jobs, therefore I can dominate you" and "I take the financial risk, therefore I can dominate you."

In traditional (i.e. hierarchical) capitalist societies, people starting businesses do not usually consider gaining the cooperation of others by asking them, as "free agents," to cooperate with them.   Just as early parents learned that telling children what to do, while backing up that 'instruction' with the threat of punishment, was effective (i.e. it got what they 'wanted'), so too do prospective employers 'get what they want' by soliciting 'cooperation' from others under the threat of punishment, whether that punishment is direct in the form of demotions and firings or indirect in the form of unilaterally altered employment contracts.

The parallel between parents and employers, when viewed through the experiential lens, is obvious. But the parallel stops at the emotional boundaries between the parent-child bond and the employer-employee relationship which usually admits of little or no emotional bond. The parent-child bond often includes an emotional attachment (i.e. love) and this can serve as a powerful 'compensation' for illegitimate impositions of will (i.e. abuse) administered by parents, but the employer-employee relationship usually does not include such an attachment and therefore there needs to be something other than love to get employees to do what employers want them to do. Hence, employers have the civilly granted power to force or coerce employees to do what they want them to do under the threat of punishment.

It is argued here that human societies moved from relatively egalitarian hunter-gatherer bands to hierarchical chiefdoms through, at least in part, a distortion of human identity due to physical, sexual,

340

and emotional abuse, i.e. abuse perpetrated by parents upon children, by men upon women, and by relatively few men (and sometimes women) upon the many.

In order for people to abandon self-direction, they must come to believe that submitting themselves to the will and values of the one (or the few) is somehow better than determining their own direction. By doing so, they believe that they stand a better chance in promoting their survival and well-being. This phenomenon seems to occur as much in the larger units of society (e.g. chiefdoms, states) as it does in smaller units (e.g. the family, clan). In the family, the child is abused and comes to believe that in order for him to survive and live at least somewhat well within the family, he must 'adjust' to the abuse by denying the legitimacy of his own experience and adopting a false self more consistent with that of his dominator (or a rebellious false self that, on the surface, seems to oppose the abusive parent but, in fact, mimics the values of that parent).

When such abuse occurs in the family, the children who have developed false selves must somehow justify the beliefs they conceive in relation to their other components of experience. For example, when a child comes to adopt a submissive false self that concurs with a parent's value, he must somehow justify that submissive false self. For example, when a child comes to believe that the fear he feels is evidence of his weakness, then he must find a way to justify that weakness. Since he cannot assert the legitimacy of his feeling fear, he has to 'assert the legitimacy' of his submissive behavior. But since his submissive behavior is false (i.e. not grounded in himself), any attempt to justify his false self will fail. He certainly cannot justify it alone; that is, he cannot come to believe that his submissive behavior is real, good and true to himself individually because the belief is not his own; rather, it is that of his abusive parent.

When such impositions of will occur in hunter-gatherer bands (as in any form of human society), false selves are attracted to like-thinking or like-believing false selves. It might be better to view this attraction and the co-existing and developing beliefs as being highly mutable or moldable. After all, the cognition that is conceived in order to justify a false self is limited only by the imagination. One need not limit oneself to physical, earthly justifications for one's false self; one can invent all sorts of metaphysical justifications for being inconsistent with what one truly is.

So if we can hypothesize that parents, being naturally more powerful (i.e. forceful) than children, and men generally being more powerful than women, and *some* men being more powerful than other men, in hunter-gatherer bands, eventually, that power (force) will be exerted on the less powerful. When this happens, the less powerful must be capable of repelling the imposing force. If they are not so capable, then they must be able to solicit the support of others to help them do so. In egalitarian hunter-gatherer bands, this was rather naturally accomplished. The "up starts" who tried to impose their wills upon others (i.e. bullies) were often repelled by the whole group. Their imposition was rejected.

Theoretical Extension: Hierarchy and Abuse
According to the anthropologists, Johnson and Earle, most hunter-gatherer bands could be classified under the rubric of family-level organizations. These bands constituted the bulk of human history. Anthropologists believe that nine-tenths of human history consisted of egalitarian hunter-gatherer bands, whereas only one-tenth consisted (and still consists) of hierarchically-structured societies.

The hunter-gatherer band's lives were characterized by a resource-rich environment (compared to modern-day bands), low density populations, personal technology (e.g. digging sticks for agriculture, bow and arrow for hunting), familial and informal social organization characterized by a sexual division of labor (i.e. physical aptitude) and sharing by outright giving (i.e. altruism) and reciprocity (i.e. reciprocal altruism), warfare and territoriality were nonexistent, political integration was minimal and not institutionalized, stratification was absent, where "leadership occur[ed] for the moments when needed to provide direction, then evaporate[ed]," and sanctity was largely confined to shamanistic practices aimed at family health and well-being (Johnson & Earle, 2000).

"It is under these conditions that humans most likely existed through much of prehistory, and it is on these conditions that all that came later – the possibilities, promises, and problems of human civilization – is grounded. We seek the primitive, or perhaps better, the real human, at the family level, and we see the dynamic of that world, now largely lost, as underlying all later human achievements" (Johnson & Earle, 2000).

This form of social organization could be characterized in experiential terms as consisting of many natural, authentic, SSR experiences. Self-direction is respected and practiced. Extrapolating on this theme, though supported by conflicting evidence, children are taught skills in accordance with their aptitude and intelligence levels; parental impositions of will tend to be legitimate and freely accepted by children as being in their own best interest; men and women are interdependent, each respecting the other's contribution to family survival and well-being; young children (0-1 year old) tend to be coddled, but once the child is able to move around, he or she is taught how to collect and prepare food, keep the home, etc.; infractions between family members tend to be handled in a restorative rather than an adversarial manner e.g. when one member harms another, the principal members come together, and the situation is processed, where information and feelings are expressed and resolutions are determined, often involving expressions of apology and promises not to repeat the infraction.

Some anthropologists have maintained, based on studies of contemporary hunter-gatherer bands, that though the inter-family society is egalitarian, the intra-family organization might have been hierarchical and the male in the family would tend to dominate. Whether the family hierarchy is the result of modern society's influence on contemporary egalitarian family systems or a natural form of organization for otherwise egalitarian groups is difficult to discern. But such contentions do seem to go against all the other evidence that supports the mutual respect that the male and female share in the egalitarian family division of labor. If the division of labor is genuinely respected by both male and female, then the likelihood of a hierarchy developing out of this situation seems poor. Something would have to happen to allow the male to believe that his job is superior to that of the female and for her to surrender her self-direction in relation to the male.

Anthropologists contend that several overlapping factors can account for the development of social hierarchies at this early stage of social development, including population growth, scarcity of resources, higher competition for resources, increased demand for labor, and the development of gardening, horticulture, agriculture and

343

husbandry. As small bands of hunter-gatherers increased in population either internally by increasing family size or externally by combining families, they used up more of the resources for their survival and well-being. Competition between separate bands of hunter-gatherers, which is hardly noticeable when resources are plentiful, becomes more noticeable when resources are sparse or depleted. When conflict occurs between bands for resources, most of the time bands would leave the area for a more resource-rich area rather than fight for the resources. There is little evidence of warfare among family-organized foraging hunter-gatherer bands (Johnson and Earle, 2000).

But when hunter-gatherer bands tended to 'develop' into Big Man groups or clans (e.g. groups comprised of a number of families, often times but not always of the same lineage), they tended to take on hierarchical features. Big Men are leaders in hunter-gatherer clans who are endowed with certain powers or responsibilities. These powers often lay in their ability to settle conflicts within their own band and to represent their band in interactions with other bands (e.g. trading). Sometimes Big Men will own certain key resources and control the use of those resources, thus creating dependency from others. Sometimes Big Men will be proficient hunters or warriors and will provide the others with meat or protection in case of attack from other clans. Such Big Men are allotted a certain amount of power over the others in the clan in exchange for the benefits they provide.

When Big Men help settle conflicts and represent clans in inter-clan meetings (e.g. ceremonies), they fall in line with our definition of "leader." These Big Men achieve a position of prominence or status but not dominance. When they try to dominate, the "followers" will tend to balk and the person's status will diminish. But when a Big Man claims ownership of critical resources or technology used to accrue resources and uses that ownership to determine the behavior of others in the clan by telling them what to do, i.e. dominate them, then this type of interaction falls under the definition of "ruler." Also, when a Big Man earns a reputation for being a prolific hunter or warrior and uses those skills to determine the behavior of others, then this interaction falls under the rubric of "ruler." It is the transition from leader to ruler that interests us most in this work.

Probing Question: Why did members of a clan allow certain of its members to have and retain unilateral powers when in family-organized hunter-gatherer bands such powers were granted only in times of need, and evaporated when the need disappeared?

Theoretical Response and Extension: Transitioning to Hierarchy

Johnson and Earle argue that increased population or size of groups will tend to increase intensification. Intensification is the relationship between human labor (and the technology assisting that labor) and the resources used for survival and well-being. For thousands of years, hunter-gatherer bands kept their numbers low because of chronic caloric deficiency due to their eating patterns (which lowers fertility), long nursing periods which delay renewed ovulation, intense physical exercise (which also lowers fertility), and possibly infanticide (which better allows the group to be mobile), not to mention high death rates due to disease, accident, and ineffective medical care. But when these bands of people learned to cultivate the land and domesticate animals or simply found a resource rich territory that allowed them to settle for awhile, they became more sedentary. More sedentary conditions allowed them better to reproduce and increase their numbers.

The more the population grew, the more resources were used up, and the more difficult it was for each family to obtain resources. The better the technology was, the less intensive the labor and the more productive the work. As hunter-gatherer foraging bands learned how to cultivate plots of land and raise animals, they tended to claim certain resources for their own. These claims tend to align with Locke's theory of justice in acquisition of resources. Each family claimed a parcel of land and animals if they cultivated the land and raised the animals. Each family defended their property from theft and destruction by others. Property tended to be respected if all families in the area had enough resources to survive and live well. But when resources became scarce or when populations grew, then a problem of allocation of resources arose: who gets what?

In earlier foraging families, scarcity of resources due either to changes in the environment (e.g. weather, soil erosion, blight, etc.) or to increases in population, impacted each family's survival and well-being. Changes in the environment tended to be associated with forces beyond human control; changes in population were associated with forces within the realm of human control (i.e. sexual acts). People cannot help what nature does, but they can help what they do in relation to each other (at least in part).

Nature, being more powerful than human will, was a force with which human beings had to contend. It behooved humans to understand how nature operated so that they could control or influence it in order to survive and live well. When a lightning bolt stuck a person dead or set fire to a person's dwelling, when the sun kept shining without relief by clouds and rain, when people got sick and died from unseen causes, people were prompted to make sense or understand what was happening. Why were these events occurring? The events were certainly frightening, if not terrifying to humans.

In order to understand and control the forces of nature, which left the pre-scientific mind relatively powerless, people were inclined to use their imaginations to explain why nature was the way it was (e.g. why there was no rain; why a person was sick and dying, why locusts were eating their crops, etc.)

Human beings' experience with nature consisted of both good and bad aspects: the sun brought warmth and light but also starvation if not interrupted by clouds and rain; the wind brought a cooling of the heat but also destruction of homes if it blew too hard; food sources brought nourishment to the body but sometimes caused sickness and death; some lands were plentiful in water and eatable plants and game while others were devoid of all of those resources.

Humans had to negotiate their survival and well-being within an environment that seemed to both sustain and to take their lives. They had to learn when, and under what conditions, the environment sustained and aided in their existence and when it interfered with, obstructed, or negated their existence. When nature seemed to be "cooperating" with humans and humans were healthy and happy, then there was no reason to understand why it was the way it was; it was taken for granted. But when it didn't "cooperate" with humans and seemed to cause them harm, then they learned to fear nature. And this fear prompted humans to learn about how nature worked so they could understand, influence and possibly control it. Such knowledge helped ease or dissipate their fear. But such knowledge was not easy to obtain. Many things in nature could not be observed. Simple connections between one phenomenon and another could not easily be made.

For example, one could easily observe (granting the capacity for sight) a billiard ball bumping into another billiard ball, causing the other ball to move in a certain direction. This phenomenon could be repeated ad naseum, producing a clear and reasonably certain understanding of how billiard balls act. But one cannot easily observe the invasion of a bacterium into the body and how that bacterium operates so as to alter the normal body functions, let alone know the conditions under which that bacterium entered the body, how the body responded to it, etc.

Hunter-gatherers had to use their own experience to understand the workings of nature. Part of their experience consisted of the interrelations with aspects of their environment, i.e. how to use resources for food, shelter and clothing; and part of their experience consisted of how other human beings responded to them, i.e. nurturing, loving, cooperating, competing, warring, etc. These human interactions can be lumped into two categories: cooperative and competitive. Hunter-gatherer family members tended to cooperate with each other; divisions of labor were generally naturally determined and equally respected; no one tended to impose his or her will upon others; when someone did try to impose his will on others, he was put down by the group. Conflicts tended to be handled in an egalitarian manner; group decisions were made by consensus; freedom of individual action was maximized, limited by the wills of the individuals involved; leaders developed in times of need and based on intelligence, talents and skills only to dissolve when the need passed; and infractions against others tended to be settled in a restorative rather than an adversarial manner, i.e. justice was holistic and inclusive and focused on healing rather than divisive and antagonistic and focused on punishment.

But hunter-gatherer knowledge of nature was not extensive; it was limited to their own experience, which was determined in good part by their environment, the resources available to them, and their ability to use technology to influence that environment. That environment consisted of both non-human and human beings. When their ability to control that environment in order to survive and live well failed, they employed their imaginations to understand their environment and either to adjust or adapt to it or to influence and control it to their advantage. Imagination realized itself in hypotheses, theories, and beliefs that addressed their fears and concerns in regard to a harmful nature, which included harmful people.

Hunter-gatherer imagination realized itself in the creation of a spiritual world. The implacability of nature (not including humans) combined with the lack of knowledge of how nature worked disposed hunter-gatherers to conceive of ways to understand nature that coincided with ways they already understood humans, including themselves. Humans tended to respond to other humans, often times in nurturing, helpful ways, sometimes in destructive ways. To imagine human qualities in or behind nature allowed humans to devise ways to influence nature. Even if these ways to influence nature were relatively ineffective, they were all that hunter-gatherers could come up with in the hope of influencing nature. In familial hunter-gatherer bands, shamans carried some leadership weight, but retained little or no rulership power. Group ceremonies were few and ideological support for ceremonies tended to be flexible and dependent upon leadership success.

But when hunter-gatherer bands grew in number and/or had fewer resources to access, then they felt pressure to survive and live well. Population growth came about as foragers learned to cultivate plots of land and domesticate animals, hence becoming more sedentary. But this increase in population and its accompanying decrease in resources occurred over time. Rarely do events change so quickly as to produce instant reduction of resources and never do they change so quickly as to produce a population explosion that is beyond human control. Foragers knew that their populations were growing, and they knew that resources were becoming depleted. It's not that population growth and/or resource depletion simply caused egalitarian hunter-gatherer bands to compete for resources and eventually develop hierarchies to address their survival and well-being needs. If population and environmental changes usually happened slowly, giving people time to decide on what to do to, people made conscious decisions to act as they did. Often times, rather than squabbling among each other and committing acts of violence upon each other in order to secure resources, bands tended to disintegrate and families would go off and fend for themselves. Smaller numbers made it possible for families to live off scanty resources; and avoiding violence, at least for the naturally passive and assertive families, gave hope of finding resources elsewhere.

If naturally aggressive families, in times of hardship, gravitated toward imposing their wills upon others through violence, and the others in hunter-gatherer bands did not move on to other spaces and, instead, received the violence, then we have the conditions for the creation of hierarchies through the illegitimate imposition of will of one person (or family) upon others. Inasmuch as others 'accepted' the terms of such impositions, they participated in the creation and development of complex structures.

Johnson and Earle argue, along with most anthropologists, that population increase, though at the root of the development of hierarchies, does not in itself cause hierarchies to develop; other conditions need to obtain. Those conditions are referred to as intensification or the increase of technology as applied to the resources in particular environments. Intensification, socially speaking, "requires" hierarchical cooperation. The larger the group, the more complicated and layered or stratified the hierarchy.

Power differentials or hierarchies, according to Johnson and Earle, can develop on three levels: 1) economy 2) military, and 3) ideology. Subsistence economies (food, shelter and clothing of individual families) are conditioned by the resources available in the immediate environment. For example, the Tareumiut Eskimos hunt whales for their primary source of survival. Such practices require cooperation from several families and the technology needed for successful hunts (e.g. canoes, fishing weirs, storage cellars, and drying racks, i.e. items beyond the scope of individual family production). Interfamily cooperation will, according to Johnson and Earle, require leadership, i.e. someone "to exhort people to work, oversee the placement and maintenance of equipment, and directs its use" (Johnson & Earle, 2000).

In another environment, like an agricultural group of somewhat sedentary hunter-gatherer groups (i.e. local groups), where irrigation technology requires inter-family cooperation to create and maintain, leaders again will surface to do the overseeing job.

But along with these overseeing jobs comes ownership of some critical resource, e.g. canoes and irrigation technology. Leaders will not only direct and supervise the activities of others but will also tend to own critical technologies or resources needed for survival. In agrarian groups, leaders might own the land and that land will be allotted to specific families for family use. Families will till the land

and reap the produce but will also remunerate the leader for such use by giving some percentage of the produce to the leader.

Probing Questions: How does a leader come about? What is the difference between a leader and a ruler?

Theoretical Extension: Leaders vs. Rulers (continued)

From this work's perspective, anthropologists tend to conflate "leadership" with "rulership," often referring to rulers as leaders. Here we will try to distinguish leaders from rulers as clearly as possible, noting the fine line at times between the two. A "leader" refers to someone who, because of his or her intelligence, knowledge, wisdom, skills, and/or abilities, creates for him or herself a position of authority in relation to others. That authority is circumscribed by the area or areas in which that person has knowledge and skills and can apply his or her intelligence or strength. A leader uses his or her intelligence, knowledge and skills to bear on any decisions a group of people make that have a bearing on their survival and well-being. A leader will suggest, argue for, point out, recommend, and model behavior for a particular course of action to be engaged in by the group; he or she will tend not to impose his or her will upon others. And in those instances where such impositions are considered necessary, such impositions will tend to be authentically accepted by those who are being imposed upon.

For instance, a mother can instruct her children on how to perform certain jobs around the house because she has the knowledge and skills necessary to perform the job and to instruct her children; she acts as a leader. A mother can also legitimately impose her will upon her children when that imposition is authentically recognized by the children as being in their best interest (i.e. promotes their own survival and well-being). Only legitimate impositions will be accepted as within the purview of a leader.

Hunter-gatherer groups seem to have been constituted primarily by leaders whenever a group of people had to act as one, beyond the level of nuclear family. For instance, a recognized good, strong hunter in a group of families would step up and lead a group of hunters in a major hunt that required cooperation and use of technology at the group level. But once the hunt was over, the leader receded back into the group as an equal to others.

350

DEMOCRACY IN BUSINESS

In some hunter-gatherer groups the hunter whose arrow first struck the game claimed ownership of the game. Usually, in hunter-gatherer bands, owners of game would be expected to share that game with the others, possibly keeping the lion's share for themselves and their family. Ownership along the Lockean theory of justice in acquisition seems to have been practiced by many hunter-gatherer bands, but so too was communal sharing. The logic is that if a group of hunters engage in an activity, then each member of the group subordinates himself to the group. Individual goals become group goals. Even if one member of the group is more successful than the others in achieving the group goal, the goal is a group goal and not an individual goal. Without the group, the goal would not even be achieved, or would be inadequately achieved, or would be achieved at the expense of too much effort. Subordinating personal goals to group goals is wholly within the bounds of authentic, natural human interaction if that subordination leads to promote the survival and well-being of the individuals involved. If ownership of an animal in a group hunt is allotted to an individual, that individual is expected to share with others. Whether or not he can keep a little more for himself and his family depends upon the value others wish to confer upon him and his skills. Such conference recognizes the worth of the individual's skills to the group, but it simultaneously undermines the group level of achievement.

If it takes a group acting as one to complete a task or achieve a goal that promotes the survival and well-being of each member of the group, then the individuals in the group are recognized as equals, regardless of how successful one might be in relation to the others. They are equal partners in the enterprise and valued as such for their efforts. These partners are coordinated by a leader or a facilitator. The leader's job is to make sure that the group is functioning well, that each member of the group knows what he or she is to do and is doing it. The leader functions as a coordinator or facilitator rather than a boss.

In a family all members of the family are "in the business" of securing their survival and well-being. The family acts as one in achieving this overall goal. The parents are the leaders of the family. Parents, as leaders, will determine when and how the children will be brought into "the labor force," but individual characteristics of children will be recognized and accommodated. For instance, a boy

351

who is physically weak, relative to other boys, and is not interested in heavy lifting jobs will be instructed in other jobs more consistent with his characteristics and interests. It would be inefficient to try to force a child to do a job he or she is not naturally disposed to do.

Parents will act as leaders, but the goals are group goals (i.e. family goals). All members of the family, inasmuch as they are capable, must contribute their share of labor to achieve the goal. Individual contributions will tend to be genuinely agreed upon by all involved. Children will tend to recognize that they should make their fair contribution to the family's survival and well-being. Otherwise, they would be living off the labor of the others and resentments might develop. If they do not recognize this obligation, then parents can withhold sharing with them, thus putting their survival and well-being in jeopardy.

In egalitarian hunter-gatherer bands, the division of labor seems overwhelmingly to be a function of sex (i.e. physical capabilities) and age (i.e. knowledge, experience, wisdom). Very young children tend to be coddled until they reach an age when they can contribute to family survival, which includes their own survival. Parents, as leaders, will usually determine when and how the children will be brought into the labor force, but such determinations will tend to be consistent with the natural characteristics and interests of the child. Forcing a child to do a job that he or she is ill equipped to do would not only be inefficient but could well cause resistance and strife within the family. Inasmuch as hunter-gatherer families were egalitarian, these natural divisions of labor would have been commonplace. But these methods would be applicable during times when resources were sufficient to provide for all involved. When populations grow and/or resources dwindle, then egalitarian groups can shift into temporary hierarchical groups in order to deal more effectively with the immediate problems of survival and well-being. But populations usually either grow slowly and/or are under some degree of human control, so the shift to hierarchical measures would not tend to come about naturally simply because of population growth. Also, environments usually do not change so quickly as to create an emergency for people to act as one in order to survive or live well in a new environmental situation. Usually, there is time to decide on what to do within most environmental situations.

If this is so, then why did egalitarian hunter-gatherer families change from a leader-follower group format to a ruler-ruled format? Why didn't the families coordinate their efforts better as a group so as to produce leaders and not rulers? Or, conversely, why did families allow the development of rulers:ruled, i.e. domininat:submissive relationships?

The usual answer given is that submitting to a ruler is a form of rational reciprocal altruism. In a reciprocal altruistic relationship, each party benefits from the relationship. The hunter-gatherer family will benefit from submitting its will to that of a ruler when the pain it encounters in trying to meet its survival needs in situations of high population density will be lessened by submitting to a ruler who is in charge of certain critical group functions, e.g. saving and distributing surplus food to the group when needed, mediating squabbles or quarrels that arise between families, etc.)

This argument aligns well with Hobbes' social philosophy that maintains that people are egoistic, naturally competitive, and warlike (Hobbes, 2012). As such, they need a strong, authoritarian and powerful ruler to dominate them so as to avoid chaos and rampant violence. As population density increases and/or resources decrease, people will naturally fight each other for resources. Constant fighting will prove inefficient because too much effort will go into self-defense and not enough into survival and well-being. Survival will be a function of self-defense rather than cooperation between people. Therefore, if true well-being is to be achieved, competitive people need to be ruled by a powerful elite or a group of elites (rulers) who are equipped with means to enforce their determinations (e.g. army, police force, etc.)

When anthropologists argue that population growth and, in the case of Johnson and Earle, intensification, in some way cause the development of hierarchy, they seem to assume that hierarchy, at best, is the rational product of reciprocal altruism, i.e. if egalitarian hunter-gatherers didn't create a dominant:submissive social structure as populations increased, then those families would be worse off. Simply because populations increased and technology was employed in relation to resources in a given geographical area of the world, people found it to their benefit to divide up into rulers and ruled. Only by dividing up into rulers and ruled were people able to raise themselves above the subsistence level of survival and well-being and improve their lot in life.

But many anthropologists seem to argue in two opposing directions at the same time. They argue for the human "realness" or "naturalness" of egalitarian bands while simultaneously arguing for the 'naturalness' or at least the inevitability of the development of hierarchy, as if hierarchy is a natural way for people to organize themselves to maximize the benefit of all. The two arguments seem to contradict each other.

It is argued here that inasmuch as hunter-gatherer bands were truly egalitarian, they were "real" humans, i.e. SSR, genuine, authentic. No human being freely accepts the will of another human being imposed upon him or herself unless that will is consistent with his or her own. When it is consistent with his or her own, then it will either not be considered an imposition or it will be considered a legitimate imposition.

In order to get from an egalitarian hunter-gatherer band of families to groups dominated by rulers, people must give up their self-direction in favor of other-direction. They must forfeit their individual identity for that of another. The many must allow themselves to be dominated by the few. Population growth does not explain this forfeiture. Intensification does not explain this forfeiture. Reason does not explain this forfeiture. Simply because there are more people to use resources in a given area of the world does not mean that some of those people need to grab up important resources and control access to those resources in order for everyone to maximize their self-interest. Why couldn't people have coordinated their inter-family activities so as to determine for themselves the best way to maximize their self interest?

For instance, anthropologists argue that because of population growth and intensification, some egalitarian hunter-gatherer bands 'developed' into Big Man local groups, where the Big Man will act as 'leader' (read ruler). Here is initial evidence of human forfeiture of self-direction. When the Big Man is entrusted to save surpluses of food in a storage facility and to distribute these surpluses to others in time of need, then the Big Man is acting as a leader. He has the job of facilitating the survival and well-being of the group. When the Big Man is entrusted with the job of mediating squabbles that arise between families in a band or village, then the Big Man is (usually) acting as a leader; he facilitates the smooth inter-dependence between families in the band. If he fails at his job, he is replaced by someone else. But when the Big Man claims ownership of critical resources, resources that the whole group needs for their survival and well-being, and the others allow him to claim those resources, then there is evidence of a forfeiture of self-direction, an abandonment of individual and family identity in 'favor' of a group identity that is dominated by a single individual. No matter how good the Big Man is at his job as leader, he does not have any right to impose his will upon anyone else unless that imposition is authentically and genuinely accepted by the others.

In order for an imposition to be genuinely accepted by others, others must be fully informed as to the reason for the imposition, as fully as is known by the individual making the imposition. When the mother in our example above imposes her will upon her son by grabbing him away from the light socket, the mother's imposition is an assertive confrontation. It is a natural expression of the progression of experiential structures within which she is participating. It is not a behavior calculated to provide her with maximum satisfaction. It is truly what she thinks is best for her son, with little or no thought to herself. It is based on her understanding of how the world within which she lives works. Father, on the other hand, in the example is not acting genuinely or authentically. Rather, he is acting out of a complex structure created when he was being raised to believe that fear is an 'unmanly' feeling. Father imposes 'his' will upon his son, but it is really not *his* will that is imposed. Rather it is the will of the society within which he lives and continues to live. He is more concerned with what others might think of him if his son is hurt than with his son being hurt. Hence, father abuses his son "to make sure" his son does what he wants him to do (and therefore he doesn't have to deal with the responses of others).

The forfeiture of self-direction, either by an individual or by an egalitarian family, to the direction of a single person (e.g. a Big Man) is not a natural development. No one rationally chooses to forfeit their own self-direction in favor of the direction of someone else. Their self-direction either has to align with the direction of another, or they must submit experientially to the value of another, and then either grudgingly accept that value or find some way to 'justify' the false self that is created in the wake of that acceptance.

355

Even children who are relatively ignorant of the workings of nature that surrounds them do not rationally choose to submit their will to that of another, unless that will is consistent with their own.

A mother is a leader when she facilitates the collection of plants for consumption by herself and her children. If some of her children do not want to collect the plants, then the mother, as facilitator, has to find out why they refuse. In listening to reasons for their refusal, the mother can determine whether or not the reasons given are legitimate or authentic (e.g. poor skills, too complicated, too frightening, etc.) or illegitimate or inauthentic (e.g. rather sleep, rather play around, etc.) The mother, as leader, can assert herself not by imposing her will upon her children but by excluding them from the accomplishments or rewards of the group. If they don't "pull their own weight" or contribute their efforts to the group effort, then they are not entitled to the group rewards. As long as that assertive confrontation is consistently made and the mother does not renege on her own confrontation, then the children who choose not to participate in the group effort will have to grapple with the confrontation. If they want to survive and live well, they will have to realize that they have to "pull their own weight." Such an assertive confrontation is often very effective in prompting individual participation in group activities. If the child is, for whatever reason, unable to contribute to achieving the group goal (e.g. it is too young or it is disabled), then such confrontations will prove ineffective, if not ludicrous or malicious. And if the child chooses selectively not to contribute to a certain group goal (e.g. hunt for game) and to forfeit the reward for the group's efforts, then that is his or her choice; it is built into self-direction and all parties are satisfied.

The same logic applies at the band level. When the hunter-gatherer band, as a group, decides to cooperate with each other through consensus or mutual agreement to accomplish a certain task, then a leader might surface who is willing to coordinate or facilitate the activity. If such a leader does surface, and all are willing to follow his or her instructions or suggestions, then all involved are rational and free agents engaged in self-direction. It just happens that the direction offered by the one aligns with the direction assented to by others.

Assenting to the direction offered by a leader can be considered a commitment. In committing to a group action, others are bound to

356

each other to carry out their commitment. But the assent needs to be freely given. In order for it to be freely given, the terms of the commitment must be adequately spelled out and understood. If someone is forced or coerced into doing something he didn't want to do or didn't agree to do, then his self-direction would be compromised, and his experiential structure would become distorted. If he were tricked or deceived in some way in order to gain his agreement, then his self-direction would be compromised and his experiential structure would be distorted. But if he freely assented to commit to the group project, then he can be held responsible to the group to carry out his commitment.

If the group pressures an individual to commit to a group project simply because the person is a member of a group, then self-direction is compromised and experiential structures are distorted. For instance, if a man chooses not to go out on a particular hunt while being a member of a band and is willing to forfeit his share of the spoils, then so be it. He cannot later demand a share and others need not share with him. If the group forces him to hunt, then the ruler in the group is the group itself; the group is, in effect, trying to rule the individual.

When a leader of a group project begins to assume the role of leader in areas that go beyond his expertise, or when a leader is allowed to own critical resources or technology that others need to survive and live well, or when a leader assumes the role of protector, or when a leader has an ability to explain the workings of nature, leaders are in position to become rulers. They can provide others with actions that no one else or few others can do or that few others want to do. When such actions are greatly valued by the others, others might become dependent upon the leaders. But this dependency does not occur naturally or genuinely.

Simply because someone performs a job that is important to the survival and well-being of the group does not entitle that person to a greater portion of the resources owned by the group. For instance, in hunter-gatherer bands, a leader of the hunt is not entitled to a greater share of the kill simply because his efforts as leader are valued. But his work as a leader needs to be compensated. If he both leads and hunts, then he can receive more of the kill in order to compensate him for his leader activities. If the leader's leadership activities are equated with the leader himself, then others might be disposed to follow the leader even when they don't really want to. Conversely, in those situations where a leader might assume compliance from others simply because past compliance has given him the impression that it is he and not his leadership activities that is valued, the leader might come to expect to be followed. When the leader is equated with the activities he performs or the functions he serves for the group, then the circumstances are ripe for the creation of dominant:submissive relationships. The leader might tend to assume compliance rather than earn it; others might expect leadership rather than appreciate it when it is given. When this happens, the leader's leadership activities take on an air of intimidation or coercion ("I've succeeded in the past, I'll succeed in the future and you should know this") and the followers' activities will take on an air of submission ("You've succeeded in the past, you'll succeed in the future and we should know this").

At this crucial point the leader becomes the ruler and followers become the ruled. The leader abuses his role as leader by imposing his values, ideas and insights on others through intimidation and the followers disown their own doubts and misgivings about the leader's decisions and opt to act in accordance with the leader's values rather than their own. Though this phenomenon might occur in nature, it is not natural in the sense of authentic or genuine (SSR). An experiential analysis might render it thus:

C: I'm not sure leader is right	He will reject my opinion	I'm wrong	I will submit to you
A: doubt	fear	self-reject	false confidence
B: hesitation	temporary immobility	looking down	false compliance
S: leader	leader (out of focus)	environ	environ
E: wherever	wherever	wherever	wherever
"I": ownership	ownership		

When a leader deludes himself into believing that his leadership activities or functions are equal to himself, then he is disposed to impose his will upon his followers. Likewise, when followers reject their own doubts and misgivings about the ideas presented or courses of action given by the leader for fear of how they might be judged by the leader and others who might not share their misgivings or doubts, they surrender their self-direction and create a false self. In doing so, followers delude themselves into believing that their false compliance is somehow more real than their doubts. When they do this, they must seek out other false selves that will agree or at least be amenable to agreeing with whatever reasons are conceived in order to 'justify' their abdication of self-direction and 'acceptance' of a false self.

Herein lay a connection between psychology and religion. How might a person who has denied his own doubts about a leader's proposed course of action for a group 'justify' his self-rejection? He can't justify it legitimately. The only way he can 'justify' it is to find others who will believe the way he does, i.e. who will reject their own misgivings in favor of compliance with the values of the leader. But how can such self-rejection be justified, even though falsely?

Herein lay the seduction of traditional objectivism. Since we all seem to experience the world outside of ourselves as objective, i.e. as possessing characteristics apart from ourselves, we are all seduced to think that our own experience of that world is consistent with reality as it is and not simply as we experience it to be. If the follower rejects the legitimacy of his own doubts in relation to a leader and allows the leader to rule or dominate him, he must 'justify' that rejection and subsequent false self construction, which permits the domination. The reason for the domination often times lies within the leader's imagination.

In our example above, father abuses son emotionally by calling him names, i.e. stupid idiot. That becomes the reason for why he is the way he is, at least in regard to his natural curiosity. He is a stupid idiot only in his father's imagination, but because of his dependent relationship to his father and his inability to assert himself in relation to him, he comes to accept that determination. But that determination is not genuinely accepted; he genuinely accepts his own curiosity; but he is not strong enough to defend his behavior. Instead, he inculcates into his own personality the imagination of his father, i.e. that he is a stupid idiot. In order for him to understand and accept at some level this distorted aspect of him, he must latch on to or create some sort of view of reality that will give him some sense of self-acceptance. He has to somehow accept his own self-rejection. Herein lay the construction of delusion or, in experiential terms, meta-experiential construction.

How can you justify your own self-rejection? The obvious answer is: you can't. But you can certainly try. And you can believe you've succeeded. The son in our example can construct an image of himself that will incorporate his false self construction and give it 'ontological' meaning. For instance, he could imagine that people (including him) are really all stupid idiots, that it is part of human nature to be a stupid idiot. But if being a stupid idiot is unacceptable to us, then we must find a way to overcome our own 'nature'. In order to raise himself above his own stupid idiocy, the son could 1) submit his will to that of an all-knowing (not stupid) being, 2) submit his will to our most intelligent leader (read ruler), 3) ask an all-merciful being to forgive him and provide him with the strength to overcome his 'stupid idiocy', etc. When we do this, we can not only 'ontologize' our self-rejection by linking it to some sort of objective reality, but we can also raise ourselves above others if we adhere to our own meta-experiential constructs. If others cannot do the same, then they are less than we; they are weak, lacking in knowledge, lacking in faith, failing to submit to reality, etc. In effect, we can construct a delusion of ourselves through our imagination and judge others according to whether or not they accept and practice the 'reality' of our delusion.

But when the natural response of repelling impositions of unilateral will is itself compromised or distorted by the establishment of corrosive identity alteration due to abuse, then the ability of the individual to assertively confront the imposing wills of others is compromised and the adjustments that ensue are distortions of reality. When egalitarian groups become corrupted by abuse and false selves seek to supply themselves with some semblance of strength, the false selves create explanations for their ungrounded experience. This complexification of identity, when permeating throughout an egalitarian group, can undermine the self-direction of the members of the group and eventually create the circumstances for the development of hierarchy. The dominant, in abusing the submissive into submission, and the submissive, in "allowing" themselves to be abused into submission create the circumstances for the development of hierarchy.

In relation to our historical speculations, the egalitarian hunter-gatherer bands, once complexified, produced a relatively small group of people or one person who dominated a relatively large group of people. This shift from natural egalitarian relationships to distorted hierarchical relationships undermined the majority of people's ability to repel impositions of will by the minority; they become less capable of warding off impositions of will by others, while the fewer dominators (bullies) had to adopt new methods of human interaction in order to maintain their domination. They have to develop an enforcement body that would not only protect them from the larger class of dominated people but also "permit" them to dominate those people (i.e. a 'justification' system or an ideology of 'justification', which, in actuality tended often times to amount to a creation of a traditional objective ideology).

Human ignorance of the workings of nature offers ample opportunity for humans to create ideologies based on pure imagination. To imagine a being that gets irate if he sees people combing their hair during a storm or watching dogs mate, i.e Karei, the thunder god of the Semang hunter-gatherers of Southeast Asia (Murdock, 1934) or a being that flies into a rage if someone melted beeswax or made a loud noise while cicadas were singing, i.e. the storm god, Biliku, of the Andaman Islanders (Radcliffe-Brown, 1922), or a being that tested a human being's faith by demanding that he kill his own son as a show of faith, i.e. Judaism's story of Abraham, or a being who sent his own son to earth to redeem mankind of its sins, i.e. Christianity's story of Jesus, etc. is to conjure 'objective truths' that cannot even begin to be verified by others observationally.

To imagine that there exists a being behind observed nature, a being that controls nature itself, that has the welfare of human beings (at least *some* human beings) foremost in its mind, one who supplies the farmer with rain for his crops, the warriors with the courage to fight their enemies, the sick with healing medicine, the downhearted with hope, the troubled and needy with love, and a being who can explain why people exist and who gives meaning to their suffering, is to imagine a very powerful objective construct, one that submissive people can latch onto for succor and dominant people can use for advancing their domination.

The link between a god or gods to nature is inextricable in human history. Either god is *in* nature (animism) or *behind* nature (polytheism, monotheism), but either way, god is an imagination often believed to be an existent in the world beyond imagination. When that existent is not owned, then god can become a meta-experiential construct that can 'explain' why there is a drought, why a child dies of fever, why one is poor, why one is rich, why one is healthy, and why nature is bountiful, and this explanation can be imposed upon others as *the* truth. In other words, "god" can explain why bad and good things happen to people, and the idea can be used, consciously or unconsciously, to create dominant:submissive relationships.

Not only does the idea of god explain certain mysterious (sometimes damaging, sometimes helpful) natural events, it also supplies human beings with a way for them to influence, or at least believe to influence, natural events. Believing in a force in or behind nature, a force that is more powerful than a seemingly uncaring nature, allows humans at least to try to influence that force so as to benefit them or not hurt them. All sorts of religious practices and rituals can be created in order to influence that force. The idea of god not only has explanatory capacity, but it also has efficacy power, i.e. god can affect human experience.

When the explanatory capacity and efficacy power of the idea of god is combined with the identity-distorting effects of abuse, we have the pre-scientific conditions for the creation and retention of dominant:submissive relationships in the human species. Not only does the idea of god become a cognition owned by a human being in an attempt to explain natural events and to influence those events, but it also becomes a means for some people to dominate others and for many people to sacrifice their self-direction in favor of the direction provided to them by others. When the idea of god is imposed upon others by making them feel somehow deficient (bad, weak, wrong, heretical, unloving, uncaring, disbelieving, etc.) if the idea, as conceived by the dominant, is not accepted by the submissive, then god is a meta-experiential construct and a distortion of reality.

Simply used as an explanation of why nature is the way it is (both helpful and harmful to humans), why people exist at all, and as a source of morality for people is not enough to make god a meta-experiential construct. Some scientists believe that there exist things they call black holes in the universe. This idea explains some things that couldn't be explained by the then current ideas in astrophysics. It is offered as a real ontological element in the universe. It is only when the people who believe these ideas try to impose them on others, try to build them into social practices and institutions and condemn or reject others who might not subscribe to those beliefs that such explanations become meta-experiential constructs. It is then that dominant:submissive relationships begin.

Hunter-gatherer bands had little in the way of ceremony to keep their family groups together. There is evidence of shamanic activity, but this activity, it is believed, had more to do with immediate earthly problems, e.g. medical problems than with metaphysical things, e.g.

gods. Hunter-gatherers might have believed that all living things possessed a spirit; even non-living things might have possessed a spirit to some degree; and this might have led them to respect the things around them, even though they killed some of those things and ate them or used their parts for shelter and clothing. But these beliefs in an all pervading spirit did not seem to be the subject of many ceremonies that served to bring the family members together. Though some anthropologists believe that some hunter-gatherers engaged in ceremonies before and during major group hunts and that these ceremonies allowed the hunters to feel not only bravery but also group cohesion, these ceremonies tended toward being engaged in more for pleasure and social reasons rather than for metaphysical bonding. The Shoshone, a somewhat dispersed population of family-style foraging groups, would hold fandango festivals during these times where families would gather, dance, exchange information of where the best source of game is located, and look for possible mates. The emphasis was on social and practical matters, not on connecting to the spirits in order to facilitate a successful hunt. Leaders like a "rabbit boss" or an "antelope shaman" might surface, but such leaders were ad hoc and did not tend to take on a dominant role in their society. Their leadership was recognized but not institutionalized (Johnson & Earle, 2000). As populations in a given area increased and/or resources decreased, people tended toward competing and cooperating with each other for resources. Individual families found it more difficult to simply split off from other families to avoid inter-family conflict because either other areas had other people occupying them or resources were depleted in those areas. Pressure was exerted on these growing populations either to compete with each other in a type of dog-eat-dog manner of survival, which often led to conflict and violence, or to cooperate with each other and keep the intra-group and inter-group conflict to a minimum.

As hunter-gatherer bands were pressured into larger and larger groupings, some methods of organization were required that would maximize the group's productivity while minimizing their conflict. In fact, the two phenomena were interlaced: maximal productivity required minimal conflict between group members and minimal conflict tended toward maximal productivity.

Probing Question: Why did most hunter-gatherer bands organize themselves into hierarchies? Why didn't they organize themselves into democracies? Some hunter-gatherer bands organized themselves into acephalic groups, which are more akin to democratic organizations than hierarchical ones, while many others organized themselves into Big Man groups, which admit of hierarchical organization. Why did the Big Man group method of organization tend to proliferate and develop into more complex forms of hierarchy, whereas the acephalic, ad hoc leadership-oriented method of organization tended to die out, or at least be submerged under the weight of hierarchical social developments?

Theoretical Extension: Abuse as the Cause of Hierarchy

It is offered here that a critical factor involved in the development of hierarchical systems of organization was that some humans abused other humans into submission. As population density increased and resources became relatively scarce, people were forced to cooperate with each other in order to survive and live well. But it's not that cooperation is foreign to people's nature. They already used altruistic methods of cooperation in their own families, where resources tended to be shared among all family members equally or in proportion to need. Cooperation seems to be biologically built into human nature. But cooperation does not so naturally extend out toward non-family members of a group, and even less toward people outside of one's clan. Cooperation between individual families within a clan might be achieved through the ad hoc leadership of a clan member, but cooperation between individual clans moves to a level of integration involving strangers. Following a respected leader in a clan temporarily is one thing; submitting to a ruler in an inter-clan group is another thing altogether.

If we accept the anthopologists' contention that population density pressured people to cooperate with each other beyond the limits of family cooperation, then how did they do this? Families couldn't just go off and fend for themselves in another area of the earth because either the other areas were already "picked clean" or there were other people living there utilizing those resources. They had to find a way to deal with strangers if they were to get the resources necessary for their survival and well-being.

But how do people deal directly with their conflicts with others? How does one person convey her ill feelings toward another person in a direct manner so as to stop that person from continuing to harm her or so as to gain that person's cooperation with her? Now we are back to where we started.

How did the first person express his or her conflicting or problematic feelings felt in relation to another? How were those expressions received and dealt with by the other?

In egalitarian organizations expressions of conflict tend to be respected if the expressions are expressions of self, i.e. assertive confrontations. People in egalitarian groups can tolerate and even accommodate individual expressions of conflicting points of view as long as those conflicts don't realize themselves in attempts to dominate others. When conflicts cross over into acts of domination, others in the group will rise up and repel the acts and, if necessary, remove the person who is trying to dominate the group from the group altogether. So in egalitarian organizations, expressions of individuality tend to be accepted, even when they differ from the majority. There seems to be an inherent plurality in egalitarian systems of organization. People could have mutually opposing points of view and still live cooperatively with each other. The color-blind person could live well with the color-seeing person even though there are more color-seeing people in the society. Optimally, the majority will accommodate the minority on terms freely acceptable to the minority.

The movement from an egalitarian to a hierarchical system of organization requires more than just an increase of population in combination with a depletion of resources and an increase in intensification. And how this increased number of people interacts with its environment and the resources that constitute it have virtually nothing to do with how it organizes itself into a cooperative body. How people develop technology in order to more efficiently or more productively interact with environmental resources in regard to their survival and well-being has virtually nothing to do with how human beings organize themselves into groups.

Individuals that make up families need at least one family member (mother) in order to be individuals; babies will die if not nurtured. Females will not have babies unless they have male sperm (barring cloning). The interdependence between individual and family is, in this sense, a necessary one.

But the connection between the family and the group is not a necessary one. A family consisting of a father (who might be there for only a short period of time), a mother who must be there for a longer period of time), and a child could exist without anyone else in the world. Of course, the family wouldn't perpetuate itself if this group died out. Other children are necessary for the species to continue and grow. In this sense, at the early stage of human development, incest perpetuated and developed the human species. People soon learned that sex between parents and children and siblings produced non-viable offspring as well as viable offspring. It is easier for the family to survive and live well if its members are viable. Mating rules developed in a family as it grew to have sex with only those family members who were distant enough in the lineage so as to produce primarily viable offspring. This would be at least part of the reason for an incest taboo. Division of labor in the family was based on sex (i.e. physical capacities) and age (including interests, talents, skills, intelligence and abilities to negotiate); it had nothing to do with sex as a role for jobs, nor sex as power to determine unilaterally the division of labor, nor with age simply as age; older people in a family can do certain jobs not simply because they are older but because they have had time to develop knowledge, skills, talents, etc. that are beneficial for the family.

The group connection between families was at first an extension of individual family groups. Individual families tended to cluster together into supra-families or hamlets composed of 25-30 related people. The connection between individual families was biological and emotional.. When a supra-family wanted to accomplish something that took a group to accomplish, they tended to produce a leader based on natural criteria for leadership. No one person was in charge and war was non-existent. But as populations grew denser and supra-families either grew internally so large that calling some people related biologically was a stretch or externally by joining other supra-families or hamlets, then clans and lineages often formed, separating one clan or lineage from another and subsisting as part of a large group called a village or a tribe.

At this point of population development, some hunter-gatherer hamlets or supra-families developed a Big Man group, some developed into acephalic groups. It is the development from egalitarian supra-families or hamlets to Big Man groups that concerns us most, because those groups that developed into acephalic groups faded out as hierarchies took over.

Johnson and Earle argue convincingly that a combination of population growth (population density), which is aligned with more sedentary forms of subsistence, conditioned by the type of environment within which a group is living and the kinds of resources available to them, and the technology used to obtain and/or alter those resources is the "engine for social evolution." But such conditions, though important for the development of hierarchies does not explain why people actually "chose" to form hierarchies when the vast majority of their evolutionary history was spent in egalitarian groupings. Why did the first egalitarian, part-time, transient leader of groups of people shift to Big Man groups and not continue on their normal path a developing an acephalic group? And why did the acephalic groups not develop beyond their small numbers and eventually dwindle to virtual non-existence? Why did hierarchy and unequal power between people come to dominate egalitarian and democratic systems of equal power between people?

Theoretical Extension: If Egalitarianism Did Not Include Abuse

If egalitarian systems had held up under the pressure of increased population density and decreased available resources, then human societies might have developed quite differently from the way they did. Johnson and Earle argue that the three ways of obtaining and maintaining unequal power structures in society, i.e. economy, military, and ideology, pretty much account for how hierarchies came about. The transition from an egalitarian group to a Big Man group involved a Big Man having personal characteristics necessary for him to coordinate and facilitate group tasks (economy), protect or arrange for the protection of the group from other groups (military), and to organize ceremonies within and between groups to facilitate peace and trade (ideology).

In many respects the Big Man might be considered the first institutionalized leader/ruler. His role was usually earned by expression of his natural characteristics (though sometimes by sheer force or violence) and was contingent upon his continued successful performance of his role. But he was also often allowed to own and

367

manage vital resources and the technological means of obtaining those resources. For instance, a Big Man could "house specialists, such as canoe-makers, harpooners, and carpenters, who are supported from his store of wealth" (Johnson and Earle, 2000). He owned that which was produced by the specialists, added it to his wealth, shared some of it with the specialists and used some for capital investments. He set up a division of labor and managed it accordingly.

What happened? Why did the Big Man come into existence? Why was a talented, intelligent, strong man allowed to tell others what to do on a continuous basis and not just in carrying out a project? Why was he allowed to have wealth over and above that of others? Why was he allowed to control that wealth by having control of the means of production? Why was he allowed to set up a division of labor and manage it?

If an egalitarian structure were to develop in the face of population growth, it would have had to look quite differently from this Big Man group. As the number of families grew, either internally or externally, or both, and people realized that group efforts could afford everyone a safer better life, coordination of the groups was imperative. Both feminist and experientialist theory argue that when decisions or determinations must be made by a group, the principals of the group must come together, process information, feelings and opinions, and reach some sort of workable consensus in regard to the issue at hand. The principals will consist of all those who are meaningfully affected by the decision and/or representatives thereof. For instance, a family might have the father represent the family if the decision involves heavy physical labor, the mother if it involves light physical labor or nurturing of children.

For instance, if someone in a hamlet of hunter-gatherers had an idea to dig ditches from nearby snow-capped mountains to a basin in order to irrigate the land so they could grow crops even when rain was not available, then all of the people (adults) involved in this proposed project would be consulted. If most people understood the benefit for all that could be provided by an irrigation system, then a reasonable consensus could be reached and sufficient commitment to action could be obtained. Now all that is needed is a division of labor: who is to do what? Let's say that several leaders surface who are willing to create a proposal for a division of labor, and these proposals are voted on by the principals. Let's also say that, people being variable, a full consensus is difficult and sometimes virtually impossible to reach, but a two-thirds majority is easier to reach. Let's also say that the group recognizes this and agrees to submit itself to a rule that says when two-thirds of a group agrees to do something, all members of the group are to go along. If they continue in their dissent, they could opt out, leave the group, and fend for themselves, or they could come up with a solution that would win the assent of most of the principals.

Let's complicate the issue a bit. Let's say that technology (e.g. tools) are needed for this project, more technology than is available for use at this time. People are needed to produce more tools. This is included in the proposals for the division of labor. If more people than the principals are needed for this part of the project, then more people are consulted and brought into the group of principals. All principals are equal in power. Each is important to accomplish the project.

In this democratic, egalitarian action, no one imposes his or her will upon anyone else. All principals are equal in power in relation to each other. All principals agree to submit themselves to rules that might force some to comply with the will of the majority, while retaining the freedom to opt out, change the proposals, or change the rules as long as those changes are not the result of illegitimate impositions of will.

In this way, no one claims ownership of resources, the means of production, or the products produced. Or, conversely, everyone claims ownership of the resources, the means of production, and the products produced.

For instance, the entire group claims ownership of the water that comes from the snow on the mountain that melts into their irrigation ditches; they claim ownership of the ditches themselves; and they claim ownership of the water that actually irrigates the land that they have already individually claimed through active cultivation of the land (e.g. land tenure). Or they could transfer collective ownership of the water that melts into and travels through the ditches to individual ownership of the water that actually irrigates the individually owned parcels of land. They could decide this collectively.

In this egalitarian, cooperative, democratic model for group organization, there is no individual person who imposes his will on others, who claims exclusive ownership of resources or the means of production, who accrues wealth and status that is used to control the behavior of others, or who creates a dominant:submissive relationship with others. In other words, in this model of group decision-making, there is no hierarchy.

Probing Question: Why didn't egalitarian groups develop egalitarian methods of dealing with population increases and/or resource reductions? Why did Big Man groups come to 'develop' into chiefdoms, which 'developed' into agrarian states, which 'developed' into modern industrial states, while egalitarian families and acephalic groups became submerged into relative non-existence?

Theoretical Response: There seems to be a parallel between individual psychology and interpersonal or social sociology. Just as an individual identity, constituted by SSR, genuine or authentic experiences, can be "overridden" or skewed by false self construction when some people succeed in imposing their wills upon others, so too can a social or group identity be "overridden" or skewed by a collective false self construction when people succeed in imposing their wills upon others.

In the construction of a Big Man group, it is no coincidence that it in fact is a Big "Man" group. Men are the likely candidates to impose their wills upon others because men are physically more capable of doing so. Men can physically harm others more easily than can women or children. Men can more easily physically harm women than the reverse, and women can more easily physically harm children than the reverse. Here we have a biological basis for a hierarchy of physical harm, i.e. physical abuse. Men are at the top of the hierarchy, women second, children last, at least until they grow up a bit; then the males will, again, be able to achieve physical domination.

There is probably good reason for some anthropologists to believe that even though hunter-gatherer bands were primarily egalitarian when it came to inter-family cooperation that they might have been at least somewhat hierarchical in their family organization. Though divisions of labor seemed to be based on natural criteria (e.g. sex and age), there existed the possibility for that natural division (i.e. tacit agreement) to give way to male domination. All that was necessary was the proper social situation. As long as egalitarian families were able to break off from others during times of conflict and fend for themselves, they were able to maintain their egalitarian methods of cooperation. Men and women respected each other's working roles. They were interdependent in relation to each other. Men's work was consistent with their physical capacities and so too was women's work, but each form was integral to the survival and well-being of all. And this was fully recognized by all.

Only when men's jobs started to be cognized or understood to be more important than women's jobs did egalitarian social systems give way to hierarchical social systems. Egalitarian systems gave way to Big Man and not Big Woman or Big Adult systems. Why? Women could cultivate the soil just as well as men; in fact, in certain Native American tribes, the women were the sole farmers; farming was considered to be a female's job. If farming could be accomplished by either males or females (at least using personal technology like digging sticks), and if farming and gathering provided for a good portion of the food for the more sedentary hunter-gather groups, then why should a Big Man group develop over a Big Woman group? Could it be because men were more likely physically to dominate women and children when population growth put pressure on a group to survive and live well?

When a family undergoes pressure to survive in a given environment, each member will feel that pressure; the parents will feel it more than the children because they are responsible for feeding the children. It is not unusual for parents to exert physical control over their children during these times; it is not unusual for men to exert physical control over their mates during these times. When such pressure is constant, and families can't escape the pressure and fend for themselves, and intra- and inter-family conflicts increase due to the pressure, then such efforts to control others is also constant. Under constant pressure to provide for his family, the male is likely to impose his will upon the female and the children; the female is likely to impose her will upon the children; and the male children are more likely to impose their wills upon the female children, depending upon age and size. When conflict cannot be addressed directly and non-violently, and cannot be avoided, then it will tend to be expressed in controlling others. Control can occur physically through some form of physical abuse, mentally through some form of psychological or emotional abuse, and/or sexually through some form of sexual abuse.

In all forms of control, domination becomes a factor. In all forms of control, submission becomes a factor.

Big Man groups developed because men were the most likely candidate – between men, women and children – physically, mentally, and sexually to abuse females and children than the reverse. As soon as men started abusing others with consistency, and others could not easily escape the abuse or repel it, then the circumstances were ripe for the development of hierarchy.

Egalitarian foragers would rise up against an "up start" who tried to impose his will on others; Big Man groups would allow a Big Man to impose his will on others; they would allow him to be wealthy, to manage certain affairs, and to trade and deal with other Big Men in other groups, often times benefitting himself more than the others in his group. Though Big Men had to be somewhat generous, their generosity extended only far enough to keep their following from defecting to the competition. An experiential analysis of this 'allowance' might well reveal a complex structure. People 'allow' themselves to be dominated when they feel inferior to another, when they can't defend themselves from the other, when they fear the other too much to do anything about being dominated. 'Allowing' someone to dominate you does not occur in the natural, genuine, authentic, SSR world; it occurs in an experientially distorted world, a world characterized by domination and submission, i.e. a world of hierarchy.

The Big Man initially might have earned a leadership role in the group, but it eventually gave way to a rulership role as the Big Man came to expect his decisions to be carried out, when he could employ a punishment when those decisions were not carried out, when he came to believe that he deserved to be able to decide things without conference with others, without meeting with others when his decisions effected them, without having others voice their opinions and have their opinions mean something in the decision-making process for the group. To represent a group to others is one thing, but to control a group through unilateral decision-making in relation to others is something else.

As a Big Man gets more settled into his role, he comes to believe that his decisions are what's best for the others, even when the others might not initially agree with him. He will bully and intimidate others into compliance, citing past successes and demanding loyalty.

Inasmuch as these tactics work, the Big Man will retain power and others will deny the validity of their own doubts or criticisms and submit. The more the Big Man finds ways to intimidate and control others, the more others find ways to submit. Complex structures become corrosive to the personality. They distort self-direction; they distort the self. What can start out as a leader:follower relationship can shift into a ruler:ruled relationship as soon as some form of force (abuse) is used by the leader on the followers and the followers do not fend off that force but instead submit to it. Once on the path of hierarchy, population increases only serve to increase hierarchical control and complicate its structure. Big Man groups 'graduate' into chiefdoms.

Probing Question: Why didn't egalitarian hunter-gatherers fend off the force imposed upon them by the Big Man when he shifted from leader to ruler?

Theoretical Response: A leader gains prestige and status for being a leader, but he also takes on responsibilities that followers do not. In a healthy, non-hierarchical group, a leader will assume responsibility for any decision he makes without the explicit or implicit agreement from the principals. He can obtain explicit agreement in face-to-face encounters with the principals, or he can have implicit agreement if his decisions are covered by the group agreement. His province or areas of application for these decisions should, to the degree possible, be laid out in an agreement prior to making those decisions. A leader needs to know how his constituency (i.e. principals) will respond to his decisions and he needs to know, as best as possible, what is best for his constituency. Most of his decisions will be consistent with the agreement determined by the principals in his group. But when his decisions conflict with the wants of his constituency, and yet are best for them, he is a strong leader. A mother who imposes herself on her child by preventing him from sticking his finger in a light socket, despite his kicking and flailing, is a strong leader. But a leader who intimidates, bullies, deceives or manipulates his constituency in order to have his decision followed by his followers, even if the outcome of the decision is in the interest of the followers, is not a leader at all but a ruler. A father who hits and calls his child names in an attempt to control his son's behavior, even if that behavior is harmful to the child, transgresses his role as leader and becomes a ruler. The child rejects his own self-direction at the expense of his integrity in order to survive and live in some sense well within the confines of domination by another. Self-rejection undermines personal integrity and disposes one to 'justify' one's disintegrated personality through the construction of meta-experiential constructs. If the pressure of population growth and/or the reduction of resources available to a group of people prompt some natural leaders to transgress their leadership and become rulers by imposing their wills upon others either by physical force (men to women and children; women to children) or by emotional force (men to other men, women and children; women to children) or possibly sexual force (men to women and children; women to children), and others allow them to do so initially because they cannot defend themselves from the onslaught, then we might have the circumstances necessary for the disintegration of the self within the family or group structures.

When fathers impose their wills upon their spouses and children, and spouses and children reject their own integrity, then spouses and children are vulnerable to suggestion; they tend either to internalize the judgment of them by the father and 'justify' that judgment or internalize the judgment but rebel against it. In the former case, a child might reject his natural self-direction in favor of his father's judgment of him as weak, stupid, etc. but 'justify' that judgment by raising his compliance with his father's will to the status of virtue, e.g. it is good to obey father; obedience is good, etc. In the latter case, the negative self-judgment is internalized but rebelled against, e.g. the child will valorize rebellious behavior. Both compliance and rebellion are grounded in self-rejection and the complexification of a personality.

As complexification in the family multiplies due to the pressures of population growth and/or resource depletion, the very egalitarian fabric of the structure begins to disintegrate. Individuals begin to lose confidence in themselves and to rely upon the decisions of others. Leadership integrity shifts to rulership complexification and family members seek 'justification' for their disintegrating personalities in the agreement of others outside of their immediate family.

As complexification spreads beyond the immediate family into groups of families (e.g. hamlets), those dominating others seek out concordance with others like them; and those submitting seek out concordance with others like them. But neither dominators nor submitters are grounded in self-direction or possess wholly integrated personalities, and any concordance they might reach with others is limited only by their respective imaginations.

In order for a dominator to convince a submitter that the submitter is what the dominator says he is, the dominator must persist in his domination and the submitters must persist in their submission. But such domination and submission runs counter to human nature, inasmuch as human nature is self-directive. How can self-directed, egalitarian beings not only create but sustain and develop hierarchical social structures when such structures run counter to their own natures?

As families become complexified each member's ability to self-direct becomes compromised. Dominators become directors of others and submitters become directed by the dominators, i.e. directees. In foraging families, a likely candidate for domination is the father because the father tends to possess greater physical strength than the mother or the children. A man can literally beat a woman and children into submission. Intelligent and strong men can manipulate and mentally abuse less intelligent females and less experienced children, and when those avenues fail to produce the desired results, they can always rely on physical methods of domination.

Physical dominators will tend to regard those they dominate as weak; some brand of weakness will be ascribed to them depending upon the dominator's personality and disposition and the submitters' personalities and dispositions. For instance, an aggressive physical dominator will tend toward physical coercion and physical intimidation, whereas an intellectual dominator will tend toward thoughtful, deceptive, and manipulative methods of domination and control. A sexually-inclined dominator will tend either toward sexual physical domination or intellectual, seductive and manipulative forms of domination over others. On the other hand, an aggressive physical submitter will tend toward a rebellious form of submission and a passive physical submitter will tend toward a compliant form of submission; a strong, intellectual submitter will tend to adopt devious methods of rebellion and a physically weak but intelligent submitter will tend toward methods of retaliation in the guise of cooperation, e.g. passive-aggressive types. A sexually-oriented, physically weak submitter might tend toward seductive forms of manipulation.

As mentioned above, Johnson and Earle argue that there are at least three major forms of power that can develop out of egalitarian family structures: economic, military and ideational. Economic power comes about when men (usually) claim ownership over vital resources and/or the technology to obtain and modify or transform resources into products for survival and well-being. Military power comes about when strong men (usually) can use their physical strength and mental abilities to protect one's group from harm and/or to spread one's power over a wider group of people (and resources). Ideational power comes about when men (usually) conjure explanations (reasons, theories, hypotheses, etc.) that can convince others that their decisions are the best for all. These decisions often reflect traditional objective ideologies in which the dominator is the 'ontologically-justified' ruler and his decisions are the 'ontologically best ones possible'.

Experientially, there seems to be a link between emotional abuse and economic power, a link between physical abuse and military power, and a link between sexual abuse, physical abuse and emotional abuse and ideational power.

Coming out of hunter-gatherer bands, military power is usually achieved by brute force. A Big Man and, eventually, a chief is often the best warrior in the group. He is judged as the best man to provide protection for the group and, hence, will be followed by the group. But in this, he is only a leader. He is also the man allowed to make decisions that are binding on others that apply beyond the area of immediate combat. In this, he is a ruler.

In a healthy egalitarian system, a group of people might need to defend itself from attack from other groups. This is merely a continuation of its normal methods of interaction in relation to "upstarts." This time it is an "upstart" group, independent of their own group. A military response could arise from an attacked group that would temporarily permit a military leader to become a ruler. When the threat passes, then the leader/ruler recedes from unilateral power and becomes like everybody else. And when population increases and pressure to compete for resources increases along with it, then chances for military intervention also increases.

Probing Question: Why didn't hunter-gatherers learn to cooperate with each other and figure out how to share the resources that were available to them, including technological methods of accessing and altering those resources? They had a long history of intra-family and inter-family cooperation. Why should an increase in population serve to alter those cooperative methods?

Theoretical Response: One response to this question lies in evolutionary theory. Evolutionary theory, as mentioned above, holds that there are genetic reasons for family members to be cooperative. Parents are biologically disposed to caring for their children (parental investment) and siblings are biologically disposed to caring for each other (kin altruism). This implies that biological cooperation weakens as the family numbers extend beyond the immediate unit. The bigger the extended family, clan or lineage, the weaker the biological ties, the less tendency to care for others, the less tendency to cooperate with others. Hence, when relatively disparate extended families (i.e. hamlets), through population increase, are all in the same position of having to survive and live well in their current environment, and simply moving to another environment is not as easy as it was because there are people in those other environments, then these family groups will tend to feel less like sharing with each other and more like competing with each other. The more removed the biological tie, the weaker the tendency is to share vital resources with others.

Theoretical Extension: Human Cooperation

As initially argued above, the weakness of this explanation rests in the human capacity for love. Mothers care for their children not so much because their genes compel them to but because they love them. Love might well have its biological basis in genetics, but it seems to be a separate genetic disposition from parental investment.

Evolutionary theory, at least the socio-biological version of it, argues that female parental investment tends to outstrip male parental investment. That means that women are genetically determined to feel more caring for their children than are men. That is supposed to account, at least in part, for why women tend not to leave their children as much as men do. Love theory argues that females will have more opportunities to bond with their children prior to birth, having carried them for nine months (Fisher, 2004). Love will more easily develop between mother and child not simply because mothers are biologically equipped and determined to feel care for their children, as is argued in the expression of oxytocin during childbirth, but because they will have more intimate interaction with their unborn child than will their mate, which also often results in oxytocin release. Women feel more strongly toward their children because they have more opportunities to interact intimately with them than do men. Men's contact is less frequent and less intimate. Hence, male parental investment tends not to be as strong as that of females.

Once the child is born, it is the female who is biologically equipped to feed the child. Hence, opportunities to bond emotionally with the child continue to be intimate and plentiful between female and child, less so for male and child. Such interactions afford many opportunities for oxytocin release.

Hunter-gatherer bands tend naturally to divide labor along sex lines. Women nurture children primarily and secure food secondarily (i.e. gather, farm); men secure food primarily and nurture children secondarily (i.e. play with, care for). Both roles are equally respected. The man does not dominate the woman; the woman does not dominate the man.

The more the man interacts with his children, the more he is able to bond with them. The more he is able to bond with them, the more willing he will be to share the fruits of his labor with them.

The same is true of male and female. The more an emotional bond is forged between the male and the female (who might not be related at all to each other in any meaningful way), the greater will be the tendency to share resources, and the greater will be the tendency to cooperate with others, and the greater will be the tendency toward altruism.

Humans tend to cooperate with each other when emotional bonds are forged between them. Biological bonds seem to be relatively weak, whereas emotional bonds seem to be relatively strong. But when emotional bonds are not forged between people, then relatively weak biological bonds are forced into saliency. Families are pitted against families; clans against clans, lineages against lineages, and, in extreme cases, individual family member against individual family member. But at the level of strong emotional bonds, whether between family members or not, egoism and competition often give way to some form of altruism and cooperation.

As long as resources are plentiful and available or accessible to all, competition for those resources is practically non-existent. Hunter-gatherer bands avoided violent conflict over resources simply by moving to another location. But when population increase eliminates much of the "free space" to move to, then competition becomes a viable choice. The other side of that choice is cooperation. As populations increase and resources decrease, do people naturally compete with each other in a form of survival of the fittest or cooperate with each other as a form of rational sharing of resources? Under pressure to survive and live well, do families naturally separate from each other and fend for themselves, pitting themselves against each other? Or do they naturally negotiate mutually acceptable ways to share the resources, even if some groups have to give up some of their resources in order for others to have an adequate share?

Actual human social history points toward answering these questions in terms of separation and competition. Egalitarian hunter-gather bands 'developed' into Big Man groups, that 'developed' into chiefdoms, that 'developed' into agrarian states, that 'developed' into modern industrial states. In this view, hierarchy is a natural human development. When people are put under pressure to survive and live well, given that such survival and well-being depends upon the acquisition and use of vital resources, they will naturally compete with each other rather than cooperate and share the resources. But when they do so, such competitions tend to be filled with inter-member or inter-group violence, often times offsetting the gains made by separation and competition. Successful competitors continuously have to defend their acquisitions from others. Others continuously press to acquire those resources if they do not have enough for themselves. Chiefdoms tend to be characterized by warfare. Each chiefdom tries to figure out ways either to keep other chiefdoms from taking what they have or to take what others have, including the members of the chiefdom as a labor source and/or their women as a sex source, in order to secure their own survival and well-being.

By the time chiefdoms developed, Big Man societies had already 'chosen' hierarchical competition over egalitarian cooperation. It is offered here that this 'choice' was not a rational choice, where one party decides that it is better for their survival and well-being to submit to a leader (read ruler) than to maintain their self-direction and autonomy but a 'choice' due to the pressures of complexification.

379

For a variety of reasons, Big Men were able to transform leadership qualities into rulership devices.

For example, a leader who is skilled at fishing could tell others what to do when engaging in a fishing expedition. This "telling" is a form of teaching or instructing. Imbedded in this teaching is the possibility for the learner to do otherwise than instructed. Perhaps the learner or follower can figure out a better way to fish. Such creativity is permitted, if not encouraged, by leaders. But when leaders allow their identities to be dependent upon the adulation, praise, or appreciation of others, then they are in position to feel threatened when a follower comes up with an idea that will usurp their perceived authority.

Biologically, studies support the idea that leaders will tend to have greater amounts of serotonin produced in their brains. Being revered by others for one's skills is inherently a good feeling. Ample phenomenological evidence also exists to support this claim. So when people assume leadership roles, they tend to be rewarded by the praise, adulation and appreciation of others (i.e. followers). But this praise is given because their leadership affords followers benefits, not because such qualities are inherently praiseworthy. If the skilled fisherman told others what to do during a fishing expedition only to claim all the fish for himself afterwards, letting the others starve, then the leader would not be a leader very long. Others would either find ways to fish on their own, find a new leader, or overthrow the leader (i.e. punish the upstart). Big Men had to be 'generous' in order to retain their Big Man status.

But this form of reciprocity permits psychological exploitation. When the Big Man exploits his power over others by intimidating, subtly coercing, or manipulating their identities by utilizing some form of emotional or psychological abuse to make followers believe they are incapable of self-direction or that their opinions are relatively worthless (even when they are very worthwhile), then the Big Man introduces complexification into human history. He imposes his will upon others by making others believe that they are somehow inferior to him. But the Big Man does not do this by himself. Others need to allow themselves to be imposed upon in such a manner. Others need to reject the legitimacy of their own experience in order to 'accept the legitimacy' of their dominator's experience. When the Big Man understands himself to be superior to his followers and acts accordingly by trying to impose his will upon them, and his followers reject the legitimacy of their own experience in deference to the Big Man's judgment of them, then the leader becomes the ruler, egalitarianism gives way to hierarchy, and the Big Man group enters human social history.

Probing Question: Why did followers reject the legitimacy of their own experience when their history was one of self-determination or defending themselves from the upstarts? Why didn't people respond to the Big Man as an upstart when he shifted from leading to ruling, i.e. when he shifted from teaching and instructing to imposing or demanding?

Theoretical Response: One possible answer to this question is that shifting from leading to ruling can be a subtle, if not insidious process. People allow themselves to get "sucked into" the dominance of a leader-turned-ruler. The thinking is: "He's been right so far about what we as a group should do to ensure our survival and well-being, so he is probably right now even though he's getting a little demanding, intimidating or abusive." If it works out that the leader is right about his input and decision to act as a group, even when he is intimidating and somewhat coercive, then maybe it's all right that he's intimidating and coercive, as long as he's right and his decisions do provide followers with survival and well-being.

This reason for denying the legitimacy of one's own doubts in favor of accepting the legitimacy of intimidation and abuse has a ring of rationality. Why not submerge our doubts when the leader/ruler's decisions seem to prove to be beneficial for us, i.e. "we *are* better off doing what he tells us to do?"

The problem with this type of "rationality" is the same problem with 'rationality' that is based in all group division and competition. What is 'rational' is that the decision provides *us* (i.e. our group) with survival and well-being over against *them* (i.e. the other groups). If our group is well off because of the leader/ruler's decision, then our leader is permitted by us to be a ruler (as long as he keeps 'being right'). As long as a ruler's decisions provide everybody under him survival and well-being (which will include some sharing of the benefits gained from his decisions), and that mode of survival and well-being is judged to be better than that attained by the other

381

groups, then one will "swallow one's pride" when one's opinions conflict with that of the ruler and do what the ruler says. When a leader shifts to become a ruler, and when followers allow themselves to be ruled, divisions between groups of people and competition for resources between them occur.

A leader of a group of people will not impose his or her will upon the group, unless that imposition is freely recognized by the group as legitimate, i.e. in their own best interest. For an imposition to be in one's own best interest, one will tend to recognize one's own personal deficiencies in deciding on a given course of action for oneself and trust the personal superiority (in knowledge, skills, intelligence, and/or character) of the leader in this area of concern.

The child will trust the parent who imposes her will upon him when he tries to stick his finger in the light socket. But one will not tend to deny the legitimacy of his own experience in favor of that of the leader. A child might doubt the legitimacy of his mother imposing her will upon him when that imposition is primarily in the mother's best interest, not the child's.

For instance, mother might prevent the child from chasing his sister around the house because she wishes not to be disturbed while watching her favorite television program. As far as the child is concerned, he is expressing his energy naturally given the parameters of his situation (i.e. living conditions). When mother yells at the child and implies that he is doing something wrong or that he is somehow bad for doing what he is doing, then the child is in position to assess his mother's judgment of him. If he correctly assesses her judgment as illegitimate, i.e. that he has done nothing wrong, and that he is just being himself, then he will continue to do what he is doing. At this point, mother might get frustrated and punish the child for his behavior, forcing him, under threat of violence or actual violence, to go to his room until he is willing to listen to her (i.e. obey). In this case, mother's imposition is illegitimate and she is using her power to harm the child in order to get him to do what she wants him to do. Her action is motivated for her best interest, not his. Inasmuch as the child is aware of this and has not distorted his perception of his mother's motives, he is in position to recognize the imposition as illegitimate. He will therefore continue to do what he is doing. But when mother persists, out of her own frustration, to impose her will upon her child, her child, given his dependence upon her, will tend to give in to her intimidation and accept a lower level of well-being than the one he, as a self-directed human being, needs. He is 'willing' to compromise his well-being for the well-being of his mother by rejecting the legitimacy of his own experience in favor of his mother's judgment of him. He accepts himself as being bad or doing something wrong, when he is actually just being himself in this situation. But instead of persisting in his assertiveness of self, he opts in the face of coercion, to do what mother wants him to do. The child's experiential structure might look like this:

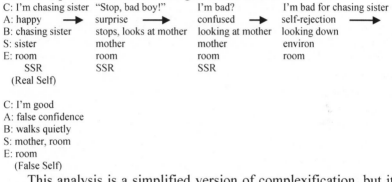

This analysis is a simplified version of complexification, but it's enough to get the point across. Parents can dominate children whenever they can convey to them that they are wrong, bad, deficient, weak, etc. and not simply that their behavior is unwanted or unacceptable at this time. They can become rulers quite easily; and children can become the ruled, quite easily.

If mother were to be a leader in this situation and she would want her children to stop their running around because their behavior bothers her at this time, then she would tell them to stop running around because it bothers her and she wants to rest. This would be an assertive confrontation. At this point all involved are experiential beings, but their simple expressions of authenticity are conflicting with each other. In letting her children know how she is experiencing their behavior, mother is asserting herself in relation to them. It is up to them as experiential beings to assess the legitimacy of mother's assertive confrontation. They are, in effect, assessing whether or not mother's imposition on them is legitimate. After all, she is imposing her will on them by demanding that they stop doing something they like doing. And this imposition doesn't seem to be for their own good, as in the light socket example above. Rather, it seems to be for *her* own good. Can a legitimate imposition of will occur when it is for the imposer's own good and at the expense of those imposed upon?

The answer to this question seems to be "yes," if that imposition is actually for the others' own good, though the others might not realize it at the time because they aren't really aware of the larger circumstances within which their survival and well-being obtains. As a leader who is in need of rest in order to be a good leader and, simply, in order to be a healthy person, mother could use her size and strength to stop her children from running around. But in order to get them to realize the legitimacy of her assertive confrontation, she would not only have to remain firm and consistent in her own confrontation, but she would also have to be authentic (SSR) in her confrontation. That is, she would have to impose her will upon them by stopping them from running around and making sure they understand why she is stopping them. She can explain to them that if she doesn't get her rest, she will get sick; and if she gets sick, she can't protect and feed them like she wants. This is similar to mother explaining that her son will harm himself if he sticks his finger in the light socket, though this time the harm is indirect rather than direct. Now the children will have a better idea of why their will is being imposed upon and how the lack of their cooperation with mother will affect them.

Stopping her children from running around by physically stopping them and telling them why she wants them to stop is not the same thing as using her size and strength to intimidate or coerce them into stopping their behavior.

Intimidation and coercion always involve an attack on the legitimacy of the identity of another. If mother doesn't let her children know why she is using physical force to stop them from doing what they are doing and, instead, conveys to them that they are bad, wrong, weak, inconsiderate, uncaring, etc. simply for running around, or simply for not recognizing that she needs their cooperation (i.e. empathizing with her), then mother is setting herself up to shift from leader to ruler. Instead of realizing that her children's behavior is SSR or authentic (i.e. they are just being themselves) and asserting herself in relation to them because she knows better than they do what could happen to all of them if she doesn't get her rest, she imposes herself upon her children through some form of intimidation or coercion (i.e. punishes them in some way).

Punishment conveys the message that what someone has done is bad or wrong. It is not an assertive confrontation. It is not an expression of experience. Rather, it is an expression of a judgment in relation to others. Mother judges her child as bad or wrong and, hence, 'justifies' her intimidating, coercive imposition. If mother had judged her child's behavior as SSR or authentic, hence right or good, though at odds with her own needs at the time, she might not have been willing to intimidate or coerce her children to comply with her will. Rather, she might assertively confront them by letting them know why she really wants them to stop behaving as they are. She wants them to stop so she could rest. Rather, she conveys to them that she wants them to stop because they are bad. In doing this, mother rejects the legitimacy of her own experience (i.e. I'm tired; I need my rest; I want you to stop) and accepts the legitimacy of her false judgment (you are bad, uncaring children) and therefore 'justifies' her illegitimate imposition. If her children cannot withstand her imposition, then they will succumb by denying the legitimacy of their own experience in favor of the judgment of their mother and come to submit to her dominance.

Applying this analysis to the hypothetical situation above, the burgeoning Big Man could get frustrated with the reluctance of his followers to assert themselves in relation to his circumscribed, shortened, or expedient communications of the leader/burgeoning ruler and not even consider telling them why he is doing what he is doing. Out of his frustration comes an order or dominant communication, and out of his follower's trust in his leadership comes a 'rational' submission. By the time either leader or follower notices that they have both rejected self-direction, it is too late. Leaders have become rulers and followers have become the ruled; the psychology of domination:submission is in place and hierarchy has been created. The Big Man could have gotten his start in a similar way by getting frustrated with followers and, instead of properly asserting and exploring his followers' doubts, he aggressively imposes himself upon them, and they, rather than ratifying the legitimacy of their doubts, submit to the aggression by rejecting the legitimacy of their own doubts.

If the act of dominance works, that is, if the new ruler's decision does, in fact, work to bring about survival and well-being to the followers, then the followers are in position to 'ratify' their submission (e.g. "It was the right thing to do; he really knows better than we do.")

This dominant:submissive interaction forms the basis of the seduction of realism. "He really does know better than we do" could mean that "his opinions tend to be more productive than ours" or "he knows reality, either physical or social or both, better than we do." In the former case, such conclusions form a rational basis for following the leader. In the latter case, such conclusions form an irrational submission of will to that of a ruler. Since there is only one reality (according to most people, whether they are realists or not), and since many of us believe that at least some of us can grasp that reality as-it-is, and since that reality is so powerful (in relation to us), then we need to submit our wills to those who have 'captured' that reality and are imposing it on us 'for our own good.' Objectivism and realism impress us so strongly that it is relatively easy to extract ourselves from experience when the environment is focal in experience, as if the cognitive, affective, behavioral and sensual components of experience are naturally separate from the environmental component.

But when the future implications of such decisions are unknown by both leader and follower, or when the leader's decision is genuinely doubted by the follower, then deciding becomes a group activity. Critical thinking is brought to bear and natural self-direction asserts itself.

Theoretical Extension: Critical Reasoning without Realism

Realism supplies us with experiential 'justification' to impose our experience upon others, supposedly for their own good, because aligning our 'experience' with 'reality', at the very least, allows us to avoid delusion and confront reality straight on; it permits us to understand reality as it is, and therefore, to at least be in position to influence, if not control, it.

When a Big Man is believed to have grasped reality as it is, then it behooves followers to adhere to his decisions and dictates. When such dictates are questioned or doubted, then the Big Man's grasp of reality is questioned or doubted. When that doubt is recognized as an authentic, genuine or SSR expression of who the person is who

386

doubts, and the Big Man is assertively confronted with the doubt of the follower, then the Big Man is in position to assess the legitimacy of the experiences within which he and the follower participate. I do not mean that he is in position to assess the *accuracy* of his or the follower's doubt (this is objectivism and realism talk). Rather, he is in position to assess whether or not the experiences within which he and the follower participate are SSR or authentic. If he rightly accepts the legitimacy of the person's doubt, he is now in position to re-asses the legitimacy of his own experience, e.g. "am I confident about this?" If he re-affirms his self-assessment and assertively confronts the follower with it, then the follower is in position to re-assess his doubts and to act accordingly. If his doubts are allayed, he will accede to the determination of the Big Man. If his doubts persist, he will continue assertively to confront the Big Man.

But in such cases, the Big Man is a leader not a ruler. His determinations of reality have passed the follower's critical test, and the follower is willing to do what the Big Man wants him to do. If it should not bear out that the Big Man's determination provides his follower with survival and well-being, then both people are in position to accept responsibility for their joint decision. The Big Man, as leader, is putting his determination out there as an honest expression of what he thinks is the best thing to do (for him and others); the follower assesses the authenticity of the Big Man's experience as well as the accuracy of the Big Man's opinion. But when the follower lacks the expertise to assess the accuracy of the Big Man's opinion, he has to rely of past successes of the Big Man's opinions (i.e. trust) and his assessment of the authenticity of the experience within which the Big Man participates (i.e. is he fully honest?) But we are still in the realm of leadership, not rulership.

When the Big Man begins to intimidate, coerce, or manipulate the follower in order to gain the follower's adherence to his opinion, he puts himself in position to dominate the follower. And when the follower allows him to do this by rejecting the legitimacy of his own doubt-experience, he puts herself in position to be dominated.

It might behoove us to distinguish between assessing experience and assessing the accuracy of the cognitive content of an experiential structure. Assessing an experience is assessing whether or not the person who is participating in the experience is sincere or authentic or whether or not the structure within which he is participating is simple, strong and right. This assessment entails the motives that lie within the experience.

When we look at the motive for mother to pull junior away from the light socket so he doesn't harm himself, we find that it is just that, i.e. she pulls him away to keep him safe. The motive for her action lies in the safety of her child. But mother could have other motivations. For instance, she might want to keep her child from harming himself because she doesn't want her neighbors to think she is a negligent mother. She might also have mixed motives or both motives simultaneously.

Children can be very good at distinguishing motives but very bad at asserting themselves in relation to their distinguishing experiences. For instance, a child might be aware that mother is not as concerned with his safety as she is with her own reputation or her own legal status, but he might deny the legitimacy of his assessments and 'accept' the mother's stated motive as being sincere and genuine in order to survive and live at least relatively well within his situation. This denial and 'acceptance' might be due to the child's immaturity or inability to act upon his experience of his mother's self-concern, rendering his ability to clearly distinguish self-concerned motives from other-concerned motives to be marginal, or it could be due to the child's immaturity or inability to assert himself in relation to his experience of his mother's self-concern, i.e. he doesn't trust his experience enough. In either case, mother has "gotten away with it." She has imposed her will upon her child and her child has 'accepted' the imposition...at least for now. But when it becomes clear to the child that the imposition is not for his own good but for her good, and the child is able to express that knowledge directly to mother, he will tend to repel mother's attempt to dominate him, usually by some form of behavioral expression; for instance, he might continue to do what he is doing, or he might "act up" or "misbehave" in the face of such domination, or, usually after at least several episodes of similar situations, he might 'opt' to deny the legitimacy of his own repelling experience and accede to the self-serving or hypocritical deter-minations of his mother, e.g. "I am bad for thinking my mother is selfish or a hypocrite" or the equivalent for a young child.

This analysis argues that one can be in a state of doubt or uncertainty or in a state of weakness or inability to stand up for oneself in relation to an attempt by another to dominate one, but this tends to be a passing state. Eventually, it will become clear that the attempt to dominate is just that, and the person will resent it and act accordingly. This supposedly characterized the experience of hunter-gatherer bands, at least each family in relation to each other family.

But that time of uncertainty or indecision could be exploited by the person trying to impose her will upon the other. Prior to clarification and assertiveness, the dominant other (e.g. mother) could press the issue through intimidation, manipulation, coercion, force and/or violence and thus not allow the child to reach a point of clarification or to achieve the strength necessary to assertively confront the dominant other. Through these methods of coercion, the weaker other will tend to submit to the dominant force and 'allow' the trajectory of his emotional growth (i.e. identity) to be knocked off course and be replaced by the dominant other's determination and will.

The same thing can happen between a Leader/Big Man and a follower. The Leader/Big Man's imposition of will could consist of self-serving (egoistic) or other-serving (altruistic) components, or a mixture of the two. When the motives are other-serving or altruistic, the follower will tend to trust the leader and follow his determinations and comply with his demands. This kind of phenomenon happens often in situations like team sports where the coach is trusted to be other-serving in his demands upon the team members, in play direction where the director is trusted to be teaching the actors to be their best at what they do, or in the classroom where the teacher is demanding that students work hard and improve their skills.

But such altruistic motives inevitably link with egoistic concerns. When the demands of the Leader/Big Man consist of mixed motives, then the follower's experience is subject to confusion or doubt. For instance, if a leader in a hunter-gatherer band is good at fishing and is willing to spend time and effort to improve his knowledge and skills in this area, others who are not as skilled, or who are not as interested in doing the activity, or who are more interested in doing other things, might come to value the leader's abilities because they benefit from his efforts, but this value resides in how they benefit from the leader's skills and not in those skills per se. A division of labor begins to occur. People who like and are good at a job that provides themselves and others with the means of survival and well-being will tend to be valued by others. This value will tend to translate into

389

others not pressuring that person to do other tasks that provide survival and well-being for the group but rather be allowed to perform that job exclusive of other jobs. Interdependency is created, allowing one person to focus on a particular area of survival and well-being for himself and his group and others to focus on their individual interests. A win-win situation is created. All benefit from the leader's efforts.

But when a leader's efforts are imposed, while consisting of a mixture of altruistic and egoistic motives, and the follower either fails to recognize the amounts of egoism vs. altruism that comprise the motive, or does recognize it and is unable to assertively confront the leader (i.e. call him on it or point it out to him), or does recognize it but disregards it (e.g. in favor of other factors, like loyalty or hero worship), then the leader's determinations and demands will be 'accepted' by the follower but only at the expense of a part of the follower's identity. For the follower will, in effect, stifle, impede or reroute the trajectory of his experiential/identity movement (i.e. his natural path of development) in favor of that of the leader. As these patterns become more established, the ability to recognize egoistic/altruistic imbalances in motives within a leader's experiential structure becomes impaired. The follower's identity shifts toward the identity structure of the leader; the follower explicitly or implicitly 'believes' in not only the accuracy of the leader's determinations but also in the authority of those determinations. It is the follower's belief in the authority of the leader's determinations, which necessarily precludes the follower's belief in, or authority over, himself, that constitutes a subtle shift from genuine, authentic, or SSR experiential structures to complex structures. In this example, the leader becomes a ruler by imposing his will (determinations, de-mands) upon the follower without having (enough) of the follower's survival and well-being in mind. This would be an example of taking advantage of someone's trust or, conversely, allowing someone to be self-centered.

A similar example of transitioning from leader to Big Man (ruler) that is not so "honest" or "straightforward," though is very similar to the above, is when the Leader/Big Man's motives for imposition are mixed, and the Leader/Big Man deceives himself into believing that the actual content of the components of experience that constitute his experiential structure are not what they actually are.

390

For instance, if a leader's determinations lead to empirical evidence of the survival and well-being of the followers, and subsequently the followers heap accolades upon the leader for his determinations, then the leader might disregard his own self-doubts in favor of his need for the accolades to which he has become accustomed. The leader deludes himself into thinking that he is authoritative, i.e. that he is objectively correct and that the followers should follow his determinations "if they know what's good for them." Here, realistic objectivism enters through the back door or instantiates itself in a very subtle manner. It only takes repetition for that subtle domination to become a part of the identity structure of both the dominant and the submissive partners. In this instance, followers get "sucked into" believing that the leader is authoritative in an objective sense. They, in effect, forfeit their self-determination for that of the leader. But the leader likewise forfeits his self-determination by denying the validity of his own doubts in regard to the accuracy of his determinations. He gets "wooed" by the followers into thinking that he is always accurate in his determinations. He should at least "appear" to be accurate, even when he has doubts, because this is what others have become accustomed to and it is also what he has become accustomed to. So when doubts surface, as they inevitably do in making determinations about the relatively unknown future, the Leader/Big Man can reject the legitimacy of those doubts and create a false self to control them. The experiential structure/process would look like this:

C: maybe we should do X	I'm weak for thinking I might be wrong	X is correct!
A: confidence/doubt	self-rejection	false confidence
B: hesitant expression	looking down	false look of confidence
S: followers	environ	potential submitters
E: environ	environ	environ
"I": ownership		

In this structure the leader initially has some doubts about his opinions as to what the group should do in relation to a given issue. His initial offering consists of both confidence and doubt. But, let's say, between the first experience and the second comes the response of his followers in relation to his doubt. The followers have already come to believe in the accuracy-ability of the leader because he has shown in previous opinions to be accurate or right in the objective realistic sense. The followers have come to depend upon the leader for his accurate determinations. Their response now might be one of anxiety or, conversely, anger. They might be anxious because they don't feel comfortable in relying upon their own determinations in the face of an unknown future, and they might be angry because they've come to accept the leader as the designated person for making determinations of this sort and thinking that he is abdicating his role by doubting his own determinations. These responses (though not exhaustive) are immediately reacted to by the leader. He allows the followers to impose their values upon him. Instead of standing up for the truth of his doubt, he caves into the dependency pressure exerted upon him by the followers. In this case, the followers abuse the leader. They do not allow him to have doubts. And the leader succumbs to the pressure. The leader distorts his own view of himself by denying the legitimacy of his doubts. In order to deal with his own self-denial, he constructs out of his own imagination a false self, an objectivized authority. What he says *must* be right, and he must communicate it convincingly. And his pseudo-confidence is 'accepted' by his followers. The dominant:submissive dance has been created. The leader has become a ruler (i.e. a Big Man) and followers have become those who are ruled (e.g. subjects).

In sum, so far, though not an exhaustive accounting of possible ways in which leaders can become rulers, leaders, whether they are parents or adult members of a community of people, can become rulers by: 1) illegitimate impositions of will due to frustration, which include all forms of coercion and aggressive manipulation, 2) illegitimate impositions of will based on past successes derived from knowledge, intelligence, skills and/or personality, and 3) illegitimate impositions of will due to an inability to clarify opinions and/or admit doubt (i.e. immaturity and hypocrisy).

Theoretical Extension: Seduction of Realism

Another form of imposition of will is derived from the seduction of realism. Here one believes that one is simply right or ontologically correct in his or her opinion and, therefore, others should follow if they know what is good for them. This imposition of will entails ideation, ideology, conceptualization, language, logic and rationality.

Early hunter-gatherer bands consisted of people who, like all people at all times, were vulnerable to imposing their wills upon others physically (and sometimes physically/sexually), intellectually (based on knowledge, intelligence, and skills), and intellectually (and sometimes intellectually/sexually) based on ideation, language, logic and rationality. But they also seemed to be better able to reject or repel illegitimate impositions of will by others when they occurred then people are today.

One reason they were able to reject those impositions is because they were able to recognize them as illegitimate. When an adult in family A tells an adult in family B what to do simply because the adult in family A wants the cooperation of the adult in family B, the adult in family B will naturally balk. His autonomy or self-direction has been violated. He will check or repel that attempted imposition. But when an adult in family A can convince the adult in family B that what he wants him to do is in his best interest and is sincere in his opinion or conviction, then the adult in family B will comply with the demand of the other. But such compliance is contingent upon the success of the opinion of the adult in family A. That is, was the adult in family A correct inasmuch as his opinion in regard to what should be done by the group in any given situation proved to benefit the survival and well-being of the adult in family B? His leadership is dependent upon the success of the execution of that opinion. Once a leader's impositions fall into a pattern of failure to obtain survival and well-being of others, they tend to be recognized as illegitimate and are repelled or not met with compliance.

Proposition 89: In order for any demand for cooperation by a person to be accepted as legitimate by another, the other must sincerely believe that the demand is 1) sincere or authentic (SSR) and 2) accurate, i.e. that it will succeed in achieving his or her survival and well-being.

Recognizing impositions as illegitimate might be very difficult if the people engaged in the imposition are working out of a complex experiential structure. When attempts to impose one's will upon others is successful (or unsuccessfully repelled), then the values of the imposer or controller become the values of the imposed upon or controlled, though those values are on the opposite sides of the same coin. The imposer must see himself as right (consistent) and correct (ontologically accurate) in his self-judgment and his judgment of the others. But his experiential structure does not bear this judgment out. He is, in fact, inconsistent. His actual experiential structure is inconsistent with his imposed experiential structure. His real self is inconsistent with his false self.

For instance, the father in the above example of hitting his son for sticking his finger in the light socket judges himself as consistent (SSR) when he imposes his will upon his son when, in fact, his real self structure admits of fear and shame, and his false self consists of a denial or negation of those components in favor of false components that are conceived (cognition), 'felt' (affect), and performed (behavior). The father will tend to believe (cognition) that his aggressive, controlling behavior is for his son's own good. But implicit in that judgment is a rejection of his son's real self, e.g. "you can't do X naturally or your X isn't good for you, therefore you are unable or deficient in some way; therefore I have to impose my 'better' judgment upon you for your own good, even when you might not agree with me."

The same holds for the Leader/Big Man who judges himself as consistent (SSR) when he imposes his will upon the follower. When the follower submits to this illegitimate imposition, he 'permits' himself to be dominated or controlled by the Leader/Big Man.

In order for the Leader/Big Man's control over the follower/submitter to sustain itself over time, two conditions must be met: 1) the Big Man and submitters must develop a justification for their dominant:submissive interaction and 2) the Big Man must be objectively accurate at least part of the time. In regard to the latter, if a Big Man's determinations consistently fail to provide survival and well-being to the submitters, then the submitters will eventually rebel and overthrow the Big Man. In regard to the former, 'justification' for dominance:submission opens up a whole panoply of possible complexity. One important way to 'justify' complexity is to be lured into the attraction of objectivism and realism. When father imposes his aggressive, controlling will upon his son and his son 'complies', father has to justify at least to himself why he did what he did. Since he has, in reality, imposed himself upon his child illegitimately (and he knows it), he must be able to 'override' that illegitimacy and convince himself that his imposition was legitimate. In order to do this, he must be able to construct a false self. A false self will consist of the same experiential components of which all experiential structures consist. But now the cognitive component of that false self structure is limited only by one's imagination. It amounts to something like: "I'm right and you're wrong because...." The father could say, "I'm right and you're wrong because I'm smarter, more experienced, more intelligent, stronger, etc. and you are dumber, less experienced, less intelligent, and weaker, etc." The same analysis can be applied to the Big Man who imposes his will upon the follower/ submitter. When this imposition is 'accepted' or 'permitted', then the objective door is open for the father or the Big Man to develop an ideological system by which he can maintain and even improve his domination over the submitters. For instance, the father can say "I'm justified in imposing my will on you because fathers are the head of the family; they have been endowed by Nature or God to be head of the family; and as head of the family, they must be obeyed." The same thinking could apply to the Big Man being the head of the community. If the Big Man can get backing ('justification') for the 'legitimacy' of his position or role as dominant person from an objective, realistic all-powerful entity or force, and the Big Man can convince the submitters that 1) there is such an entity or force and 2) that that entity or force has a will that is consistent with his own, then the Big Man not only has succeeded in imposing his will upon followers but has also succeeded in developing a role for himself as perpetual authority.

Theoretical Extension: Hierarchy and the Supernatural
    In hunter-gatherer bands an ideological force lay in the area of health or medicine. This force lay with those known as shamans. Johnson and Earle refer to this category of family structure as "sanctity," which is "largely confined to practices aimed at the health and well-being of the family: curative rituals, hunting magic, and the like" (Johnson & Earle, 2000). Many, if not all, hunter-gatherer bands believed that aspects of nature were animated by spirits. These spirits were believed to be influenced or at least able to be influenced by human behavior usually in the form of ritual. The conception of the spiritual in or behind natural events aligns with or parallels human experience in relation to their own experience of themselves. Humans can impact nature in various ways, and nature seems to "comply." But other aspects of nature don't seem to be amenable to human manipulation or control. Humans can to a degree control their own bodies and, to a lesser degree, their own minds, but much of the human body and mind defies control. Humans have great difficulty controlling their own thoughts, feelings, and sensations. Many of these phenomena seem to occur whether humans want them to occur

or not. They have better control over their own behavior. They can think, feel and sense one way, yet behave another way. We can cover up our internal world with our external behavior, at least well enough to get others to believe in the 'truth' or 'sincerity' of our behavior (lying, deceiving, etc.) or even enough to get ourselves to believe in the 'truth' or 'sincerity' of our behavior (self-deception, self-delusion).

In an integrated personality, cognitive components align with affective, behavioral, sensual and environmental components in any given experience. In a dis-integrated or complex personality cognitive, affective, sensual, and environmental components of experience can seem to misalign with the behavioral component. We can "cover up" our thoughts, feelings, sensations (to some degree) and environment (in some instances) and get away with the cover up. We can lie to others or deceive ourselves, fake our feelings by acting in ways we know are not consistent with how we actually feel or by acting in ways we falsely feel, we can sense our environment in selective ways that better align with our bogus thoughts and feelings than with our real thoughts and feelings, and we can selectively include or exclude aspects of our environment to fit our bogus self. When we knowingly misrepresent ourselves with a false self, we are said to be lying, deceiving or manipulating others. When we unknowingly misrepresent our self to our self and others, we enter the world where cognition, language, and reason can 'override' feelings, 'alter' environments, and turn healthy, consistent experiential structures into unhealthy, inconsistent, complex structures.

When we deceive ourselves about ourselves we create a false self. At first the false self might actually seem bogus to us, like we are living a lie. But if the response of others (especially the person of importance who is imposing his or her will upon us) is positive (genuinely or not), then our false self will be strengthened, eventually to the point of our coming to believe that our false self is our real self, and the feelings that constitute that false self will tend to be accepted by us as real.

For example, a daughter who is unable or unwilling to repel her father's expressions of domination will form a false self which entails her self-rejection and a creation of a false self consistent with the value or judgment of her father. If her father thinks she is bad, weak, or wrong in some way for being-who-she-is, then she will see herself as bad, weak, or wrong. At first she might not feel very comfortable with her own self-rejection; it might seem to her to be wrong or inconsistent. But when her new self, which is composed in part of a new behavior, is responded to by her father in a positive manner, her new self gets stronger and she feels more 'comfortable' with it. If others in her family respond to her new self in a positive manner, that self will grow even 'stronger'.

Probing Question: If she adopts or creates a false self, why don't the others in her family recognize the falseness of her behavior and confront her? Can't the false self be exposed at its inception?

Theoretical Response: A false self *can* be exposed at its inception, but it might not be recognized as false or, if recognized, those involved in its creation might not possess the capacity or the resources necessary to confront the dominator or imposer and to ward off his impositions or to alter their living situations enough to survive and live well without the dominator.

In family situations children often have difficulty recognizing their own self-rejection. Because of their dependence on their parents on many levels, children will tend to reject the validity of their own experience and, though somewhat grudgingly, accept the 'validity' of their parents' judgment of them. Any grudging aspect can be systematically repressed when others in the group beyond that of the family affirm or are neutral to the parental judgment and the false self that is generated from it.

For example, a father's judgment of his son being weak because he shows fear of taking risks can transform into the son's false self of being a dare devil. His son might 'accept' his father's judgment of him as weak, but want to reject it, and want to please his father by being the dare devil, even though his immediate experience in relation to his dare devil acts is one of fear. He 'overcomes' his fear by pushing himself to be 'brave'. When he is successful in his dare devil escapades, he not only gains the 'acceptance' of his father, but he also ratifies the 'legitimacy' of his false self. His false self becomes more entrenched within his personality.

But in order for the son's false self to be accepted or 'ratified' by others in his society (social group beyond the family), it must be 1) sufficiently consistent with the distorted values being generated by other families, 2) not recognized as a false self but rather as a real self, though odd, or 3) be relatively innocuous in relation to the survival and well-being of the other families.

In relation to our example a dare devil false self might be affirmed by other fathers in the community who have such values in their own families. Perhaps their own sons seem frustratingly fearful to them. Therefore, any dare devil sons in the community would tend to be approved by them. Such affirmation or approval from others outside of one's family will only serve to further entrench the false self within one's personality, and the illegitimate imposition will tend to register as legitimate with the imposing parent and also with others who either do not recognize the imposition as illegitimate or cannot assertively confront and repel the imposer.

Others who might not affirm or approve of the son's dare devil acts might not recognize those acts as being not consistent with whom the son really is; they might not have had enough experience with the son to know any different. So they might simply judge him to be odd or peculiar while not being moved to confront the behavior as false.

Others might recognize the falseness of the behavior but not be moved to confront its falseness if the behavior does not have a significant impact upon them in their own struggle for survival and well-being. They can just judge that it is the immediate family's problem, i.e. the family can deal with it.

False selves can be 'accepted' for a variety of reasons (those listed above are certainly not exhaustive). When they are 'accepted' or at least tolerated, they can become entrenched within the personality of the people developing them.

In hunter-gatherer situations, where individual families could separate from each other when social problems arose and live relatively independently of each other instead of fighting with or warring upon each other, false selves might not have been able so easily to take root or become entrenched. There would be no social reinforcement of them. There would be much less chance of the father who imposes his judgment upon his son to justify his imposition if there are no others in his society to affirm or approve his behavior. He would have no grounds upon which to justify his imposition, other than his son's seeming acceptance of his judgment, and his family's tolerance of, or inability to confront, his behavior. The latter might be enough to create and sustain a false self, but it